Indian Urbanization and Economic Growth since 1960

The Johns Hopkins Studies in Development

Vernon W. Ruttan and T. Paul Schultz, Consulting Editors

Also of interest in the series:

Taxation in Developing Countries, 4th edition
edited by Richard M. Bird and Oliver Oldman

*Economic and Demographic Relationships in Development:
Essays Selected and Introduced by T. Paul Schultz*
by Ester Boserup

Agricultural Development in the Third World, 2nd edition
edited by Carl K. Eicher and John M. Staatz

Aid and Development
by Anne O. Krueger, Constantine Michalopoulos, and Vernon W. Ruttan

*The Order of Economic Liberalization: Financial Control in the Transition
to a Market Economy*
by Ronald I. McKinnon

Poverty Theory and Policy: A Study of Panama
by Gian Singh Sahota

Village and Household Economies in India's Semi-arid Tropics
by Thomas S. Walker and James G. Ryan

Indian Urbanization and Economic Growth since 1960

Charles M. Becker,
Jeffrey G. Williamson, and
Edwin S. Mills

The Johns Hopkins University Press

Baltimore and London

© 1992 The Johns Hopkins University Press
Printed in the United States of America

The Johns Hopkins University Press
701 West 40th Street
Baltimore, Maryland 21211-2190
The Johns Hopkins Press Ltd., London

∞

The paper used in this book meets the minimum
requirements of American National Standard
for Information Sciences—Permanence of Paper
for Printed Library Materials, ANSI Z39.48–1984.

Library of Congress Cataloging-in-Publication Data

Becker, Charles M., 1954–
    Indian urbanization and economic growth since
1960 / by Charles M. Becker, Jeffrey G. Williamson,
Edwin S. Mills.
        p.   cm.—(Johns Hopkins studies in
development)
    Includes bibliographical references and index.
    ISBN 0-8018-4179-8
    1. India—Economic conditions—1947–   .
2. Urbanization—India.   3. Rural-urban
migration—India.   4. Cities and towns—India—
Growth.   I. Williamson, Jeffrey G., 1935–   .
II. Mills, Edwin S.   III. Title.   IV. Series.
HC435.2.B383   1992
307.76′0954—dc20   90-28392

Contents

Tables and Figures

Figures

Preface

In the spring of 1982, all three of us were resident consultants at the World Bank, where Becker and Mills were finishing *Studies in Indian Urban Development* and Williamson (in collaboration with Allen Kelley) was finishing *What Drives Third World City Growth?* One conversation led to another, and we eventually returned to our respective universities with an outline of this book in hand. The book took a lot longer to complete than we originally intended, but perhaps the wait was worth it.

We have incurred many intellectual debts over these eight years. Most important, the project has had the good fortune of having some outstanding research assistants along the way: Perry Beider, Prasad Chitamaneni, Koichi Nakajima, Lynne Sherburne-Benz, and Andrew Warner. In addition, we received very helpful support on the modeling and programming side from Jeff Lewis and Robert Schmidt. Sherman Robinson was supportive at all stages, and he also gave us a very useful critical assessment of the manuscript in its final versions. We are grateful to all of these people. Without them, the project might well have taken another eight years.

At various stages in the project, we have had useful advice and criticism from the following: Gary Chamberlain, Hollis Chenery, Devendra Gupta, Allen Kelley, Robert E. B. Lucas, Rakesh Mohan, Samuel Morley, Gian Sahota, Kerry Smith, T. N. Srinivasan, Oded Stark and the Harvard Seminar on Migration, Moishe Syrquin, Anthony Tang, and George Tolley.

And, of course, we must not forget funding. Douglas Keare and Koichi Mera took an early interest in the project and persuaded the World Bank to help finance it. In addition, we have received financial support from Harvard University, the National Science Foundation, and Vanderbilt University.

Earlier versions of parts of this book have been published in journals that we would like to thank for permission to draw on them here: "Dynamics of Rural-Urban Migration in India, 1960–1981," *Indian Journal of Quantitative Economics* 2, no. 1 (1986):1–43, and "Indian Migration and City Growth 1960–2000," *Economic Development and Cultural Change* 35, no. 1 (1986):1–33.

Indian Urbanization
and Economic Growth
since 1960

1 • The City Growth Problem

1.1 Defining the Problem[1]

Have India's cities grown too fast? Has India overurbanized? A reading of the popular press would suggest so, and many specialists seem to agree. Without doubt, India's urban population has grown faster than the cities of today's developed nations did in the past. To add further support for the overurbanization view, manufacturing employment grew more rapidly during industrial revolutions in the past than it has in India over the past two or three decades. To complicate matters, however, Indian cities have not grown as rapidly as those in many other developing countries, nor has Indian city growth accelerated.

Indian experience with city growth is complex, and it raises a host of related questions. What explains the timing and the extent of the transition from a traditional rural to a modern urban society? Why does city growth typically speed up in early development and slow down in later stages? What role does migration play in the process? Do city labor markets absorb urban immigrants quickly? Are rural emigrants driven mainly by "push" conditions in the countryside or by "pull" conditions in the cities? Are there too many migrants rushing to the cities? Do government policies and institutions create a prourban bias?

Speculation on these questions has never been in short supply. Friedrich Engels (1845) thought that Manchester's booming growth in the early nineteenth century—and the urban decay associated with overcrowding—could readily be explained by the rapid development of Britain's manufacturing industries. Ravenstein (1885, 1889) and Redford (1926) thought that rural-urban migration, and thus city growth, was conditioned instead by Malthusian forces in the countryside, agricultural

1. This and the following section are taken from Williamson (1988, pp. 426–30).

1

land scarcity, and enclosure of the open fields. Mayhew (1861) agreed. He documented low-wage, informal-sector labor in London, viewing these urban poor as a reserve army driven to the city for employment of last resort. In short, while Engels favored pull, Mayhew, Ravenstein, and Redford favored push.

Despite a century and a half of debate, we are still uncertain about the sources of urban transition, how it can be influenced by policy, and whether it *should* be influenced by policy. While successful industrialization always fosters urbanization, has it been too fast in the Third World by the standards of the past? What accounts for the explosive growth of cities in the Third World since the 1950s? Two principal hypotheses have been advanced by development analysts, and discussions of them sound very much like the debates over the first industrial revolution in Britain. Rapid city growth can be explained either by unusually rapid rates of population growth pressing on limited farm acreage, pushing landless labor into the cities, or by economic forces pulling migrants into the cities. In the contemporary developing world, the "pull" forces include: policies that distort prices to favor cities (twisting the domestic terms of trade so as to squeeze agriculture); cheap energy (prior to the first OPEC shock), which favors the growth of energy-intensive urban sectors and thus creates urban jobs; the diffusion of technology from early industrializers to latecomers, an event that favors modern, large-scale urban industries; foreign capital flows into urban infrastructure, housing, power, transportation, and large-scale manufacturing, which further augment urban expansion; and the liberalization of world trade since the late 1950s, which has stimulated demand for manufacturing exports produced in Third World cities.

Most demographers favor the first hypothesis. Exploding numbers of people must be employed, and a marginal agriculture with quasi-fixed arable land cannot offer sufficient employment for the Malthusian glut created by the demographic transition. Marginal survival by hawking urban services may be the only way a social system can absorb the population glut, and squalid urban living conditions associated with such gluts have been an attribute of early stages of industrialization since Engels wrote about Manchester in the 1840s, and long before. The demographer, writing in the shadow of Malthus, is likely, therefore, to favor a causal sequence running from population boom, to labor pushed off the land, to city immigration, and thus to rapid urban growth under squalid living conditions. Diminishing returns in agriculture play the key role here. This view has also had a profound influence on economists' thinking about development. It is central to Lewis's (1954) labor surplus model—a model that worked well for the classical economists developing their paradigms of growth during the first industrial revolution in

Britain. It is also central to the Todaro (1969) thesis that rising immigration to the city is associated with high and even rising rates of urban unemployment. On the other hand, most economists now tend to favor the second hypothesis—that is, economic forces that contribute to urban pull.

The literature on Third World migration and city growth is enormous and growing. Development analysts have learned much since we began to worry about such issues in the 1950s. A comprehensive review of that literature is beyond the scope of this chapter and the book, but a brief statement of the demographic dimensions of Third World city growth is essential to place Indian experience in perspective.

1.2 Quantifying the Urban Transition

The sixteen largest Third World cities surveyed by Sinclair (1978, p. 15) had growth rates over the quarter century 1950–75 ranging between 2.4 (Calcutta) and 8.3 (Seoul) percent per annum, a revealing commentary on the slow city growth in India compared with some of its Asian neighbors. The average growth rate was 5.4 percent—a very high rate indeed. Furthermore, by the end of the 1960s, slums and uncontrolled settlements housed a large share of most urban populations. Such rapid growth implies rising density, congestion, and urban land scarcity. Not surprisingly, urban rents have risen, living conditions have often deteriorated, and delivery of public services has been problematic at best. Immigration, of course, played a key role in the process throughout the 1950s and 1960s, accounting for about 58 percent of population growth in the eleven largest cities reported by Sinclair.

Such detailed demographic city accounts are useful, but because 837 cities in the Third World have populations in excess of 100,000, aggregation is necessary to make any progress on the problem possible. Furthermore, given the common alarmist view that the Third World has overurbanized, a brief look at the past might be an effective antidote. The most comprehensive assessment can be found in a United Nations' publication, *Patterns of Urban and Rural Population Growth* (1980), written by Samuel Preston, as well as his own summary of the volume (Preston, 1979).

In the first place, Third World city growth is not a new phenomenon but rather seems to have followed a relatively smooth urban transition since the late nineteenth century. While the urban share of the Third World's population rose sharply between 1925 and 1950 (from 9.3 to 16.7 percent), it had been on the rise since 1850. And while the share rose even more sharply between 1950 and 1975, Third World urbanization over the past century seems to obey the usual laws of motion that characterize the diffusion of new technologies; that is, a logistic curve that first rises slowly from levels of low adoption, then accelerates, and finally slows down as the new technology is everywhere in place. The point of inflection for trends in Third World urban population shares appears to have occurred during the quarter century terminating just after the first OPEC shock. City growth rates trace out a similar pattern, although there is considerable variety in timing by region: Latin America reached a peak rate of city growth in the 1950s, East Asia (excluding China and Japan) in the 1960s, Africa in the late 1970s, and South Asia in the 1980s.

In contrast with the earlier assertions by Hoselitz (1955, 1957), we now know that Third World urbanization rates have been fairly conventional by historical standards. Between 1875 and 1900, currently industrialized countries' urban share rose from 17.2 to 26.1 percent, about the same increase that took place in the Third World between 1950 and 1975—16.7 to 28 percent.

While the rate of urbanization in the Third World has not been exceptional, the rate of city growth has been. Between 1875 and 1900, city populations in the currently industrialized countries rose by about 100 percent; between 1950 and 1975, city populations in the Third World increased by 188 percent, almost double the late nineteenth-century rate. City growth was faster in the Third World in large part simply because population growth nationwide was faster. Furthermore, recent research has shown that manufacturing employment has been a key "engine of city growth" during *both* the nineteenth and twentieth centuries (Preston, 1979; Kelley and Williamson, 1984; Williamson, 1988, 1990).

With that background, how, then, does India's city growth experience since 1960 stack up?

1.3 Has India Overurbanized?[2]

It appears that Indian economic history since 1960 does not fit these stylized facts very well. Until quite recently, and despite an extraordinary investment effort, registered manufacturing output growth has fared poorly compared with the rest of Asia. Indeed, the manufacturing employment growth rate fell short of the national (much less urban) population growth rate between 1965 and 1979. While employment in manufacturing and elsewhere in the organized sector grew slowly, India's urban population grew nearly twice as fast as its rural population. However, those city growth rates were quite a bit below those of most of its Asian neighbors. Furthermore, India has undergone a slowdown in city

2. The following section is taken from Becker, Mills, and Williamson (1986, pp. 1–2).

labor force growth rates since the boom years in the early sixties, from 4.5 percent per annum in the 1960s to 3.9 percent in the 1970s. In short, manufacturing does not appear to have served as an "engine of growth" for India's cities, and thus policymakers, economists, and demographers have all been uneasy about the rising level of urbanization.

India's experience is certainly surprising. After all, economic base theory suggests that city growth ought to be tightly linked to employment growth in industries exhibiting scale economies, advantages of agglomeration, and elastic demands. Elastic demands are important, since they enable such urban-based industries to vent their growing output onto national and world markets, avoiding the constraints of more inelastic, primarily locally based demands. Such industries are concentrated in what are loosely called "modern sector activities," large-scale manufacturing in particular. India appears to offer a counterexample to this "engine of growth" thesis, since significant city growth—although slower than in the Third World as a whole—has coexisted with falling and low rates of manufacturing employment growth. Such trends appear to confirm Hoselitz's overurbanization thesis. They also might suggest that Indian city growth can be explained in large part by rural conditions that are pushing migrants to the cities, rather than by urban conditions that are pulling them there.

This evidence invites analysis: Does recent Indian history *really* support the overurbanization thesis?

1.4 How to Attack the Problem

The overurbanization question is complex, and simple answers are suspect. City growth is a natural correlate of the industrial revolution, to be sure, but the industrial revolution is a complex social event that unfolds in different ways in various countries and epochs. Demographic patterns matter, cultural norms matter, the character of technical progress matters, policy matters, and so do exogenous events such as world market conditions, foreign lending, and arable land scarcity or abundance. City growth, therefore, cannot be analyzed in isolation. In order to assess the sources of Indian city growth and the role of policy, we need an analytical device that identifies the interaction among the city, the countryside, and the world. The device used in this book is general equilibrium analysis, a framework especially suited to the resource allocative issues that bind city with countryside.

What we call the BMW model (developed in chap. 2) is used to account for Indian experience since 1960, first by estimating the economy as it was, and second, by asking how the economy might have behaved had conditions been different. These counterfactual questions include how city growth would have behaved under different population growth rates, world market conditions, prourban biases, sectoral productivity advances and declines, and states of the monsoon. Along the way, we compare Indian experience with those of its Asian neighbors and explore the potential impact of policy alternatives. In addition, the model is used to assess likely future dimensions by projecting to the twenty-first century. But we have run ahead of ourselves. It might be helpful to back up and establish the intellectual ancestry of the model.

BMW is a computable general equilibrium model in the tradition of a growing family of such models used in development, public finance, trade, and economic history. Its immediate ancestor is the eight-sector Third World city growth model used by Allen Kelley and Jeffrey Williamson (1984) to analyze a representative developing country. The child and the parent have much in common that distinguishes them from other computable general equilibrium models. Both contain a rich description of the nontradable service sector, so important for any analysis of urban economies. Both contain a detailed articulation of the housing sector, also important in understanding the behavior of urban economies. And both contain careful attention to rural-urban migration, a phenomenon at the heart of the city growth process. These characteristics are almost always ignored in other models.

On the other hand, the two models are hardly identical. While the Kelley-Williamson (KW) framework serves as a departure for BMW, the latter incorporates much India-specific institutional detail. Capital and labor markets are fragmented, government is omnipresent, and, perhaps most important, the economy is much more closed than is KW's small, open economy. Furthermore, rural-urban migration includes skilled labor in the BMW model. These differences matter, as we shall see.

This book can be distinguished from other general equilibrium applications in another important way. Most applied general equilibrium analysts fail to ask whether their models can adequately account for past economic history. In contrast, we think it is essential to establish the credibility of the model before using it to answer any of the questions raised earlier in this introduction. Indeed, chapter 3 labors long and hard to show that BMW replicates Indian economic history since 1960. It appears to account quite adequately for the trends in overall growth, structural change, relative prices, real wages, urban immigration, employment, and city growth.

This success with our replication of history should not be overdrawn because some dynamic attributes of Indian growth are taken as exogenous in the model. True, overall accumulation and investment distribution are endogenous in BMW. True, employment growth in each sector is also endogenous. However, total factor productivity advance is *not* endogenous in BMW—although it never is in any applied model of economic development. Furthermore, the Indian data are not adequate to estimate independently sectoral rates of total factor productivity advance over the decades following 1960, and we need that information to account fully for India's experience in the long run. Where, then, do we get such evidence? The answer is that we infer it once our model has been estimated for the benchmark year of 1960. Chapter 3 describes that procedure in detail, but the bottom line is that we emerge with estimates of sectoral total factor productivity growth from 1960 to 1981. As far as we know, this is the first comprehensive set of productivity estimates for the entire Indian economy over the full two decades following 1960.

1.5 What Do We Find?

Once we have our model in hand, and once it has been shown to replicate history, we are armed to pursue counterfactual analysis. The term *counterfactual* was first coined by economic historians, for whom it has become a favorite tool of analysis, but it is well established in economics generally, although it carries other names. Demographers assert that city growth is more rapid today in India than it was in the nineteenth century simply because economywide population growth rates are faster. We can test that assertion by using the model to ask how Indian city growth would have taken place had India been blessed with the more modest population growth rates of nineteenth-century Europe. It has been asserted that a prourban policy bias accounts for much of Indian city growth, and we can test that assertion by using the model to ask how the economy would have behaved had those policies not been pursued. This strategy carries most of the analysis for the remainder of the book. What do we find?

Projections

What will the Indian economy be like in the year 2001? Will city immigration and city growth be slower? Will municipal planners, therefore, find it easier to cope with city growth problems? Demographers certainly have supplied answers to these questions, but in so doing they take the migration rate to be exogenous. That is, the demographic projections are made in the absence of any model in which economic forces are allowed to have an impact on city immigration rates. No labor market forces drive their projections. They have nothing to say about the derived demands for labor, which create excess supply in the countryside, excess demand in the city, and the rural-urban migration that accommodates those conditions. In contrast, our model has a great deal to say about those issues. Furthermore, we are in a position to learn a lot more about the future because we are armed with a model that makes it possible to sort out what is likely to be important and what is not. For example, we can explore patterns of migration and city growth in an environment in which world market conditions, productivity advance, aggregate labor force growth, rainfall conditions, land availability, and capital inflow all exhibit stability. Having done so, we can then compare this stable environment with more likely alternatives.

Chapter 8 explores the future in detail, but one finding stands out. Demographers have developed some stylized facts associated with the urban transition. According to this view, city growth rates tend to rise during early industrialization, reaching a peak when the economy reaches newly industrialized country (NIC) status. Migration rates are believed to follow a similar pattern. When India is projected well into the future, this stylized urban transition fails to emerge. Instead, even under the most favorable conditions, India never regains the rapid rates of urban immigration and city growth achieved in the early 1960s. From this perspective, we learn that city growth problems were unusually severe in the 1960s. The 1990s are likely to be very different, if the projected long-run city growth slowdown actually comes to pass. According to the projections, terms like "overurbanization" and "limits to city growth" are likely to disappear from the literature by the year 2001.

The City Growth Slowdown

The dominant feature of the simulated urbanization patterns documented in chapter 3 is a decline in urban labor force growth rates from 6.4 percent per annum during 1960–64 to 3.6 percent thereafter. Why the pronounced slowdown in city growth? Did exogenous conditions less favorable to city growth emerge after the early 1960s, or did endogenous limits to city growth or mistaken policy come into play?

India's economic environment was far from stable between 1960 and 1981. Technological change occurred in all sectors, but the pace was uneven, especially given the often noted retardation in large-scale manufacturing. Relative prices of internationally traded goods also varied over time: the OPEC-induced oil price rise in the 1970s was most dramatic, of course, but the terms of trade between agricultural and manufactured goods also changed sharply, favoring manufacturing in the 1960s and agriculture in the 1970s. Capital inflows declined steeply after the early 1960s and were negative during the Emergency period in the mid-1970s. Typically, the early 1960s were also years of plentiful rainfall, high public savings rates, and large capital inflows from abroad. All of these events define various environmental epochs that mark India's development experience over the past two or three decades, and impressive evidence suggests that the economic environment may have been unusually favorable to city growth in the early 1960s, conditions which disappeared thereafter. What was the impact of these forces on the city growth slowdown? Chapter 6 supplies the answers.

India's slow rate of urbanization reflects both environmental conditions that gave rise to a major growth slowdown after the early 1960s and the gradual emergence of increasing labor scarcity. About 35 percent of the post-1964 slowdown can be attributed to relatively unfavorable environmental conditions. Among these conditions, unfavorable world price trends and slower productivity advance are of roughly equal importance; both are about twice as important as declining capital inflows. The remaining 65 percent reflects rising urban labor costs, largely a result of rising agricultural prices but also of urban labor market policies.

The slowdown was not inevitable, at least not to the extent that poor productivity growth and declining private capital inflows reflected flawed policy. On the other hand, world price trends and reduced aid flows were not of India's making and could not have been avoided. Nor, obviously, did the Indian government have complete control over productivity performance.

Slow City Growth Compared to India's Neighbors

Why was city growth relatively slow in India during the 1960s and 1970s? What would have been India's experience had its economic and demographic environment been similar to that of the typical less developed country (LDC) during these decades? India's cities grew at an annual rate about 0.7 to 1 percent less than that of the rest of the Third World. Chapter 7 shows that demographic trends, world price conditions, and capital inflows were sufficiently different in India to help account for a significant portion of the city growth differential. In contrast, and much to our surprise, slower productivity advance in India does not help explain the differential. When these factors are taken together, it appears that India would have enjoyed city growth rates some 0.3 percent faster had it enjoyed the more favorable environmental conditions that were typical of the rest of the Third World. Yet, the slow city growth differential was between 0.7 and 1 percent. Thus, the relatively unfavorable environmental conditions in recent Indian history account for only about one-third to one-half of the slow city growth differential.

The moral of these historical counterfactuals seems clear. While a significant portion of India's relatively slow city growth can be explained by relatively unfavorable economic and demographic conditions, a much larger portion remains unexplained. These findings suggest that India's relatively slow city growth is due primarily to structural and institutional arrangements that make city growth less responsive to favorable conditions than is true of the rest of the Third World. These arrangements include policies that serve to choke off urban employment.

What Matters Most?

The historical importance of the forces listed above has two sources, the size of the influence itself and the sensitivity of city growth to the influence. Chapter 4 dwells at length on the latter. The short-run impact of seven key influences on urban performance is assessed there: unbalanced productivity advance, drought, world market conditions, capital accumulation, skill formation, demographic change, and land scarcity. It might be useful to summarize some of these here.

We start with unbalanced sectoral productivity advance, since theory suggests it should play a central role, and since an extensive literature notes the poor productivity performance of large-scale urban manufacturing in India after the early 1960s. If urban sectors tend to have relatively high rates of total factor productivity growth—an assumption that economic historians would certainly favor for nineteenth-century industrial revolutions—and if the demand for urban output is price elastic, then final demand shifts toward the dynamic urban sectors, the derived demand for urban employment is augmented, urban jobs are created, migration responds, and city growth takes place. These forces are reinforced, of course, if the income elasticity of demand for urban output is also high, and if the employment multipliers are large (like those associated with urban housing construction). In any case, the higher are price elasticities of demand for urban output, the greater is the city growth impact of unbalanced productivity advance favoring the modern sectors.

Indian agriculture may offer an important counterexample. Although agricultural products are certainly traded internationally, world and domestic agricultural products may be sufficiently imperfect substitutes, and government-imposed barriers to trade sufficiently great (thereby delinking world and domestic prices), that the conventional assumption of agricultural price exogeneity is inappropriate. To the extent that this is true for India, the price elasticity of demand for agricultural commodities may be relatively low there compared, for example, with the small, open economies along the Asian Pacific Rim. Under such conditions, productivity advances in Indian agriculture would be met by a sharp price decline, the marginal value product of farm inputs might fail to rise, and farm employment might fail to expand. Indeed, it is quite possible that productivity advance in agriculture may actually push labor into the cities, rather than pull it back to the countryside. This issue has generated a long debate among development economists: Does productivity advance in agriculture tend to release labor to the city (the inelastic demand case) or the opposite (the elastic demand case)? This is an empirical issue of some importance.

The findings in chapter 4 shed considerable light on these debates. The bottom line seems to be this: Productivity gains in agriculture tended to retard urbanization in India in 1960—attracting rather than releasing labor—but on balance the influence was weak. In contrast, productivity forces that favored urban services clearly fostered urbanization, and the general equilibrium employment elasticities are large. One reason for this result is the excess demand for urban housing created by the city immigration and the additional employment effects induced by the construction response. Furthermore, city growth is *most* responsive to productivity events in the informal service sector, a sobering finding since those activities are given such modest attention by public authorities. The big surprise is that while productivity gains in large-scale Indian manufacturing *did* foster short-run city growth in 1970 and 1980, they did *not* do so in 1960. We offer some explanations for this counterintuitive result and why India should have behaved very differently from the Asian Pacific Rim countries in this regard.

The city growth response to any favorable economic event is constrained in the short run, partly by output absorption problems on the demand side, partly by short-run capacity constraints on the supply side, partly by a rising supply price of urban labor, and partly by a shortage of public urban services. It also turns out that in very poor economies like India's, manufacturing is heavily dependent on raw material inputs produced in the countryside, and these backward linkage effects can serve to curtail sharply the urbanizing impact of productivity gains and accumulation in manufacturing. Chapter 4 explores these short-run "limits to city growth" in detail. They matter.

In sharp contrast with sectoral productivity improvements, chapter 4 shows that the Indian urban economy is fairly insensitive to world market conditions. After all, BMW has been developed to capture India's relative economic autarky in 1960. While world prices do have their influence on domestic prices and output, the link is weak given import-substituting trade regimes and given domestic and world tradables that are only imperfect substitutes. Indian city growth during the 1960s and 1970s was likely, therefore, to have been driven by conditions within the economy rather than by conditions abroad. As we shall see below, however, the Indian economy appears to have become more sensitive to world price shocks by 1981.

Consider one more issue raised in chapter 4: Do high rates of population growth in India account for most of the "urban explosion" taking place there? Certainly most demographers think so, and many economists agree. Indeed, Bert Hoselitz (1955, 1957) had this argument in mind when he drew on experience in South Asia in developing his "overurbanization" thesis. Hoselitz argued that unusually heavy population pressure was forcing labor off the land, thus glutting the cities with an elastic labor supply that could find employment only in the informal service sectors. As is usually the case in such debates, chapter 4 shows that the issues are not so clearcut as Hoselitz made them out to be. Are we talking about city growth (an increase in urban residents)—in which case the demographers are correct—or are we talking about urbanization (an increase in the share living in cities)—in which case the demographers are incorrect? The chapter also documents that increasing arable land scarcity has not been an important ingredient of Indian city growth in recent history.

Chapter 4 goes on to show just how important initial conditions are to these conclusions. As the Indian economy evolved from the early 1960s to the early 1980s, the forces that mattered most to city growth changed. To repeat, the structure of the economy matters. Chapter 4 also offers an assessment of the push and pull forces underlying rural-urban migration experience, an assessment that helps resolve a debate that has been ongoing since the first industrial revolution in England.

1.6 Policy Debates

Many alternative growth strategies employed elsewhere in Asia were never pursued in India, and vice versa. To what extent would radically different policies have mattered, especially those that might have altered the alleged prourban bias? While chapter 5 contains some important preliminaries, the main event appears in chapter 9. Five counterfactual policy regimes are explored in that chapter, each of which is relevant to lively academic and public debates that have sprung up in India over the past quarter century. The first involves a direct intervention in labor markets, the result of which is to restrict sharply the inflow of workers from the countryside. The second considers the consequences of a major sites and services urban housing program. The third explores the implication of a policy that allocates public investment to sectors in which capital's marginal product appears to be highest, that is, an efficient investment strategy. The fourth assesses the impact of International Monetary Fund (IMF)-style liberalization reforms. Finally, the fifth examines the consequence of an augmented Mahalanobis-like regime that extends an era of heavy industry buildup.

Economic policy aimed at protecting the economic interests of the resident urban labor force and restricting migration of newcomers to the cities is hardly new to India. However, we are unaware of any attempt to estimate the quantitative importance of such policies, even if they were politically feasible. We use BMW to explore the consequence of policies designed to lower the rural-urban migration rate of the unskilled by roughly 40 percent, a policy motivated by concern with the urban poor or with city congestion and quality of life. Not surprisingly, the experiment confirms that a regime of cityward migration restriction has little merit. It is inefficient because it exacerbates rural-urban wage gaps, thus generating deadweight losses in the aggregate. It is inequitable since all but the established urban unskilled lose, especially the rural poor who are partially excluded from urban labor markets. The policy is also inconsistent with India's recent push toward an increasingly open economy since it is the export-oriented manufacturing sector that suffers most. Not only does the policy strike hardest at India's most dynamic sectors, but it also discourages capital formation. Furthermore, the impact of all these influences is large.

The point of the previous experiment is that adding more market distortions to an economy already beset with many is not a desirable means to what otherwise might be viewed as a laudable goal. What about an alternative policy regime that is also motivated by a desire to improve the living conditions of the urban poor—namely, heavy public investment in low-quality urban housing? The counterfactual sites and services program involves an approximate doubling of new low-quality housing construction. Urban unskilled real incomes rise substantially, due both to additional employment demands generated by more labor-intensive construction and to a decline in quality-adjusted living costs generated by completed sites and services programs. Urban immigration is, of course, stimulated by those added employment effects. However, since we assume that the benefits of new sites and services programs accrue only to those presently occupying favored sites, only modest gains trickle down to the rural poor, who otherwise might rush into the cities in even greater numbers. While the housing effects are important, so too are some unintentional foreign trade consequences. The housing boom makes workers better off primarily by reducing their living costs, and not by raising their nominal wages. In fact, nominal urban wages decline, thereby raising the profitability of labor-intensive urban activities, including manufacturing, India's main export sector.

Some economies allocate capital more efficiently than others, and some do it better at one time than at another, but no economy has ever been able to allocate capital efficiently. Indeed, the BMW model reflects what Indian observers have claimed all along—namely, that rate of return differentials have been pronounced at various points in the past. This seems to have been the result, at least in part, of public investment allocation decisions motivated by other than conventional rates of return. Suppose these policies were replaced by one that allocated public investment in such a way as to maximize the current rate of return on capital? The analysis focuses on two epochs: 1960–64, when the cities were still starved for capital while the rural sectors had a glut; and 1978–81, when an asymmetric distortion had developed in factor markets—labor's marginal product was far higher in the city, while capital's marginal product was far smaller. What would have happened had an efficient public investment policy been pursued in these two epochs?

Despite the legacy of the Mahalanobis planning era, there was an antiurban bias in Indian public investment policy from 1960 to 1964, *not* a prourban bias. But it is surprising how small the deadweight losses are that the counterfactual policy removes, and how little city growth is fostered. These findings appear to be consistent with the literature, which has shown deadweight losses to be far smaller in developing countries than the stress on factor market failure would have suggested.

For the 1978–81 epoch, the results are even more interesting. First, a counterfactual regime of efficient investment allocation would have caused a shift of capital to the countryside, but the deurbanization effect is trivial. Indian public investment policy in the late 1970s may have had a prourban bias, but it did not play the quantitative role that Michael Lipton or Theodore Schultz might have assigned to it. Second, the deadweight losses are even smaller than those calculated for 1960–64. Part of the reason for this latter result is the presence of asymmetric distortions in factor markets, an issue that we discuss at length in chapter 9.

The chapter concludes with an assessment of two contrasting regimes, one that was popular a quarter century ago—the Mahalanobis strategy—and one that is popular now—the IMF liberalization strategy. The results are far too rich to summarize here, but the reader is in for some surprises.

1.7 The Agenda

This is only a preview of what our analysis of Indian city growth experience since 1960 has uncovered. Some of these findings can be generalized to the rest of the Third World. Some are specific to India. Some are conditional on the assumptions of the applied general equilibrium model invoked. What remains is for us to show the reader how we reached these conclusions.

2 • Modeling Indian City Growth

2.1 An Overview of the BMW Model

BMW is a dynamic computable general equilibrium model (CGE) of the Indian economy. As such, it joins a rapidly growing family of such models applied to developing economies. The framework is a neoclassical one in which households maximize utility and producers maximize profits, both subject to constraints: households have limited endowments, migrants incur costs when they move, firms face capital scarcity, governments have limited revenues, and so on. In addition, labor markets are partially segmented, capital markets are imperfect, and public authorities often act in ways that conflict with optimal resource allocation.

Much of the novelty of BMW, however, lies with the addition of spatial variables likely to influence city growth that have been omitted from all previous models save one.[1] The overriding motivation is to develop a long-run general equilibrium model of city growth in which rural-urban migration is endogenous. Migrants respond to employment prospects, but they also respond to the relative cost of living in the cities. And those employment prospects and living costs are themselves determined endogenously, so that the underlying forces of rural push and urban pull can be identified.

Apart from the addition of these spatial variables, any model of Indian city growth must differ from other CGEs for yet another reason. India is a mixed enterprise economy, and the model must take account of that fact. For example, while most dynamic CGEs minimize government's role by merging public and private investment behavior, BMW does not. Instead, BMW explicitly confronts the independent effects of

---

1. The reference here is to Kelley and Williamson (1984). A more detailed comparison of BMW with the Kelley and Williamson model appears below in section 2.2.

government investment allocation, and such investment is not necessarily allocated to maximize returns. Indeed, government investment allocations in BMW may serve to augment disequilibrium in private capital markets, favoring sectors with low returns. Furthermore, previous models typically have ignored mixed enterprise activity, viewing governments as saving out of tax revenue and foreign aid only. BMW merges central and state governments' investment with that of public enterprises, so that the net income from public enterprises serves to augment the savings pool available for public investment allocation. The model also recognizes the critical role of public services as intermediate inputs and thus their indirect role in private production activities. These public services are often subsidized, and investments in them comprise the majority of India's infrastructure: roads, transport, power, water, and health services. The model assumes that provision of these services is biased in favor of urban industries and households, thus conforming to Lipton's (1976) and Keyfitz's (1982) "urban bias."

Any model of India's urbanization and economic growth also should be consistent with important institutional characteristics in the private sector. These characteristics include partially segmented labor markets. Wages clear each labor market, but the links among them are often weak. Thus, an exogenous "wage gap" separates rural and urban labor markets, a stylized fact of developing economies first stressed by W. Arthur Lewis (1954) and estimated recently to be about 30 percent for India (Mills and Becker, 1986, pp. 173–75). Earnings also differ by skill. Indeed, since laborers of different skill are not close substitutes for one another, and since occupational mobility is limited, skilled and unskilled labor markets are viewed as being segmented in our model. In short, the wage structure is endogenous and skill premiums can rise and fall in response to unbalanced demands for and supplies of labor by different skills. Furthermore, any model designed to analyze Indian rural-urban migration should not ignore the presence of skilled labor in rural India. Thus, skilled and unskilled labor are both employed in rural activities in BMW, in contrast with other models, which employ skilled labor only in urban modern sectors (e.g., Kelley and Williamson, 1984). Finally, the microeconomics of migration in BMW rejects the so-called Todaro model (Todaro, 1969) in favor of an approach that allows labor markets in the urban informal service sectors to obey conventional laws of supply and demand, an approach increasingly supported in the literature (Kannappan, 1985).

Fragmented capital markets are another attribute of BMW. First, government investment allocation is not responsive to rate of return differentials in our model, so that "overinvestment" in public-dominated sectors may well emerge. Second, investment in private sector housing takes place in the absence of mortgage markets, making it likely that housing investment shortfalls will occur in some parts of the economy, especially among the urban poor. Third, a fragmented private capital market ensures that rates of return vary even among nonhousing sectors untouched by public investment, some in capital deficit and some in capital surplus.

The model also incorporates a detailed description of India's fiscal system, making it possible to assess the impact of various taxes and subsidies on city growth. Taxes on factor income, personal income, and property income are included, as are excise taxes, export taxes, and import duties. Similarly, prices of public services can be set to reflect full user cost, or, closer to reality, they can be set at subsidized rates.

The model distinguishes between tradable and nontradable goods, and some consumption is therefore location specific, like traditional services and housing. Since the prices faced by rural and urban households need not be the same, BMW offers the opportunity to assess the impact of cost-of-living differentials on city immigration, in particular urban land scarcity and expensive or inadequate housing.

BMW includes ten sectors. Agriculture and manufacturing absorb most of the labor force, but BMW also contains rural and urban informal service sectors, as well as a capital- and skill-intensive formal service sector that is dominated by education, defense, and public administration. The rural service sector includes (mainly small-scale) rural manufacturing, and this important fact offers the opportunity to assess potential crowding-out effect of urban factories on rural production (Sekhar, 1983). Following Kelley and Williamson (1984), the model has three housing sectors: rural housing produced by the rural service sector and occupied by the rural poor, low-quality urban housing produced by the informal urban service sector and occupied by the urban poor, and higher-quality housing produced by the formal construction sector and occupied by the urban middle and upper classes. Finally, the model distinguishes urban public services (power, utilities, transport) and rural public services (public irrigation, rural public administration) from other services. Although these public services do not employ large numbers in India, they do utilize large portions of the national capital stock and provide essential intermediate inputs to other sectors. The five primary factors of production are capital, skilled labor, unskilled labor, and two types of land (that used in farming and that used as urban housing sites).

Three goods are imported from the rest of the world: agricultural commodities, manufactures, and petroleum products. Our model also allows for the export of agricultural products and manufactures. Following much of the CGE literature,[2] we assume that Indian import-competing goods are imperfect substitutes for imports from abroad, and that Indian exports are also imperfect substitutes for similar world products. World prices thus have a more limited influence on domestic prices than would be true of the "small country" case where the prices of tradables are taken as completely exogenous (as in Kelley and Williamson). We treat India, therefore, as partially shielded from world market conditions, a real-world characterization that has important implications for interpreting the sources of city growth. The prices of all nontradables are endogenous. In addition, like most CGE models, this one has nothing to say about monetary variables and the general price level. Instead, the model deals with relative prices throughout, and the numeraire is the world price of manufactures imported by India.

Urban immigration and city growth are fully endogenous and the focus of the model. They are driven by a variety of forces that have been debated in the literature, and some had manifested an "urban bias." These include capital deepening (favoring capital-intensive urban activities), skill accumulation per worker (favoring skill-intensive urban activities), unbalanced total factor productivity advance favoring urban sectors, demand shifts with an urban bias, changes in world market conditions favoring the prices of urban manufactures, a cheapening in the cost of imported fuel (favoring fuel-intensive city activities), and government policies with an urban bias. Rural forces may offset or reinforce city growth. These forces include any increase in the effective stock of farmland through multiple cropping, productivity change in agriculture, changes in rainfall conditions, and increased population pressure. Urban growth may be limited by various forces, including increasing urban land scarcity, density and congestion in the cities, labor-saving technological progress in urban industries, savings constraints induced by the high capital requirements of city growth, and a diminution of foreign capital inflows. Poor investment choices and a myriad of regulations that hinder productive efficiency (and productivity growth) in the manufacturing sector also may retard urbanization by slowing the engine of growth.

BMW generates labor productivity advance in many ways. Capital accumulation is one endogenous response that raises labor productivity. New capital can be allocated directly to industries producing final goods and services, or it can be used to provide intermediate public services. Inputs per worker increase in either case, and productivity rises. Although the process is not modeled endogenously, each year BMW allows

2. The reference here is to what is known in the literature as the Armington specification. See, for example, Dervis, de Melo, and Robinson (1982).

human capital accumulation to transform a share of the unskilled labor force into skilled workers. The model also assumes exogenous rates of total factor productivity advance, with the rates differing among sectors.

Asset formation is determined by aggregate domestic savings and foreign capital inflows. Household expenditure behavior is described by an extended linear expenditure system in which savings are driven by class-specific savings propensities and the growth and distribution of income. Aggregate household savings join with business and government savings (capital inflows from abroad serve to augment government revenues and thus, indirectly, total savings) to form the investment pool. Some of this pool is retained by households for investment in dwellings and thus is diverted from "directly productive" capital accumulation. Indeed, one of the problems of city growth is to determine the right mix between urban housing, on the one hand, and investment that directly augments urban capacity and city job creation, on the other. If too little is allocated to housing, potential city immigrants may be discouraged by the lack of housing or by high rents. If too much is allocated to housing, the rate of city accumulation slows down, the rate of city job creation declines, and the rate of city immigration slackens. This critical trade-off is embedded in BMW.

This, then, is an outline of the model used in this book. While any model must make concessions to simplicity, this one appears to do limited damage to the realities of the Indian economy. Government receives detailed attention, and there is adequate scope to assess the impact of government policy on resource allocation and city growth. The model distinguishes among modern and informal sectors. Rural nonagricultural employment receives its due, an important reflection of reality given that rural nonagricultural employment was virtually as large as the entire urban labor force in 1960.[3] The public service sector is treated in detail, an approach essential for understanding the nature and extent of the implicit urban bias in government policy. And housing activities receive expanded treatment, which is essential to understanding much about the limits to city growth.

What remains in this chapter are the details. Section 2.2 explores the recent intellectual ancestry of the BMW model to help place it in perspective. The core of the chapter, however, lies with sections 2.3–2.5, where the model is developed and defended. The reader interested in this detail should be alerted to appendix A, which gives a complete mathematical statement of the model. Equation numbering in the text follows that of the appendix. The reader who is willing to take the model on faith should skip ahead to section 2.5.

3. Singh (1979) estimates that 20 to 25 percent of rural employment in India is nonfarm.

2.2 The BMW Model's Ancestry

BMW joins a growing family of computable general equilibrium models used by development economists (Adelman and Robinson, 1978; Dervis, de Melo, and Robinson, 1982; Robinson, 1988), by public finance and trade economists (Shoven and Whalley, 1984), and by economic historians (Williamson and Lindert, 1980; James, 1984; Williamson, 1985). Although BMW differs in significant ways from these earlier CGEs, it has evolved from them. In particular, BMW is an India-specific successor to Kelley and Williamson's (1984) dynamic eight-sector urbanization model of a representative developing country. The two models have much in common that distinguishes them from other CGEs employed by development economists. Both contain a rich description of the tertiary sector. Both contain rural nonagricultural activities. Both share a concern for the provision of housing. All of these sectoral characteristics are almost always ignored in other models.

Given these similarities, one may ask whether a plausible model of India would merely involve making a few minor changes in the KW prototype and adjusting parameter values. Early on, we concluded that such an alternative was inappropriate. Indeed, our unsuccessful efforts to impose some critical features of the Indian economy on the KW framework persuaded us to make several major changes in that model.

One striking difference between the two is BMW's more detailed government sector. BMW distinguishes urban public services from other capital-intensive urban services, and separates rural public services from rural private services and other nonagricultural activities. As a result, BMW has ten productive sectors, compared to eight in KW. Inclusion of public service sectors enables us to assess the impact of the Indian government's efforts to alter directly production conditions in various private industries, since public services are used exclusively as intermediate inputs by the other sectors. Government spending allocation also is more complex in BMW. In addition to allocating part of its budget to current expenditures and capital investments in rural and urban public services, the government funds capital formation by public enterprises. Public service expenditures respond to household demands in BMW, but investment is fixed in the short run by government policy. These and other attributes of the model make it more amenable to government policy analysis than is KW.

A second set of distinctions involves the extent to which factor markets are competitive. Real earnings for skilled and for unskilled worker households do not vary among sectors at any given location in BMW, but they do vary between rural and urban locations. While Indian labor markets appear to be described well by a competitive paradigm within each skill level, capital markets are modeled as being highly segmented. This fragmentation captures one of the essential stylized facts of India's economic structure. BMW does not view private capital markets as integrated. Private and public investment decisions are also independent in BMW, while they are merged in KW. Government savings are combined with private savings in KW, and the combined pool seeks highest returns. This approach is inappropriate for India, and BMW has made an effort to accommodate better the realities of imperfect capital markets.

Perhaps most important, and consistent with most Third World CGEs (Robinson, 1988), BMW treats domestic and foreign agricultural and manufactured tradables as imperfect substitutes, while KW treats them as perfect substitutes. As we pointed out above, this element of realism has important implications: it appears that the "small country" assumption helps account for some (but hardly all) of the key findings in KW.

It is apparent that BMW differs considerably even from its parent model, as well as from its distant cousins. In particular, it differs strikingly from previous models of India. In addition to Mohan's (1977) three-sector model and Kripalani, Tolley, and Payne's (1982) two-sector model, several interindustry and short-run disequilibrium macroeconomic models have been constructed for India.[4] Given our focus on services, on the role of government, on factor and product substitutability in the long run, and on price endogeneity, BMW has little in common with these other models. It is best suited for long-run issues, the focus of this book.

2.3 Comparative Statics in Detail[5]

Production and the Supply Side

Each of the ten sectors produces a single homogenous commodity or service. Each has a specific spatial location, urban or rural, and produces tradables or nontradables. The tradability distinction is central to cost-of-living differentials, and thus is important to both migration and urbanization. While the inclusion of nontradable service activities has become familiar in the literature on CGEs, we feel they are especially important in understanding the urbanization process and deserve far

4. The interindustry (constant coefficient) models include Mohammed (1981), Manne and Rudra (1965), and Sakong and Narasimham (1974). The short-run macroeconomic models include Rattso, Sarkas, and Taylor (1981), and Srivastava (1981).

5. This section leans heavily on the exposition in Kelley and Williamson (1984, pp. 18–73), especially where BMW is roughly comparable with its parent model.

greater attention than they have received to date. They certainly are relevant to specialization choices available to the economy, and thus to international exchange as well.

As table 2.1 indicates, the model has only two main commodity-producing sectors: manufactures (M) and agricultural goods (A). These titles are abbreviations, however, since these two sectors are a composite of more varied outputs: A includes livestock, forestry, and fishing as well, while M includes mining but excludes rural manufacturing.

There are eight service sectors in BMW. The modern or "formal" service sector (KS) has as its empirical counterpart education, defense, public administration, finance, modern commerce, and the formal construction industry producing relatively high-quality residential structures (pucca housing). While the output of KS cannot be traded internationally, it can be traded interregionally. KS is urban based, and is the central activity supplying final demand needs generated by government. Given the demand conditions discussed below, the KS sector has the potential of being one of the leading sectors in our economy, a feature commonly ignored in development models.

Recent qualitative models of migration have focused on the urban traditional or "informal" service sector as a source of (allegedly low-productivity) urban employment, and it has figured prominently in current conventional wisdom regarding the determinants of rural-urban migration in India and elsewhere in the Third World (Todaro, 1969). With the important exception of the KW model, the literature has made little effort to introduce similar activities for the rural sector, ignoring Hymer and Resnick's (1969) useful emphasis on rural "Z" goods and a long tradition in the economic history literature that stresses "proto-industrialization." In our model, the rural labor-intensive service sector RS and the urban labor-intensive service sector US both produce services with empirical counterparts including domestic and personal services, small-scale transport, and commerce. In addition, RS produces rural housing and US produces low-quality (katcha) urban housing, both supplied to poor households and often constructed by the owner. RS activities also include rural manufacturing and cottage industries.

There are three housing sectors in BMW. The rural sector has one (HRS), consisting of low-cost dwellings constructed by the RS sector and supplied (presumably inadequately) by rural public utilities (like piped water and electricity). The model has been developed to permit house rents (including owner-occupied shadow rents) to be lower in rural areas, thereby providing rural areas with another potential cost-of-living advantage. Relatively low rural wages can be expected to yield that result on the house construction side, but high urban site rents attached to relatively scarce urban land are likely to be a more important source of any rent differential.

There are two housing activities in the city: a high-quality housing sector, *HKS*, consisting of (pucca) dwellings constructed by relatively capital-intensive methods supplied by *KS*, and a low-quality housing sector, *HUS*, consisting of (katcha) dwellings and squatter settlements constructed by relatively labor-intensive methods. Inaccessible low-quality housing, a hostile government attitude toward squatter settlements, and thus high urban rents (market *or* owner-occupied shadow rents) may figure prominently in choking off urban immigration in our model. However, the availability of cheap water, electricity, and other services supplied by public utilities to urban housing may have an off-setting influence on the migration decision.

In reality, there is a continuum of dwelling units by quality. The urban dichotomy embedded in BMW reflects important aspects under-lying that continuum—the differing nature of construction technology, the different construction costs implied, the different costs of land on the dwelling sites, and the availability of public utilities. Since housing represents the most important asset in most households' portfolios in our model and accounts for much of their investment activity, we felt it important to elaborate on its nature, especially in cities, where housing may be particularly important to the issues of migration and population growth.

The model is completed by the addition of two public service sectors, *PSR* in rural areas and *PSU* in urban areas. Not only do these sectors include capital-intensive public utilities, but the rural public service sector also includes roads, transport, irrigation projects, and public admin-istration. These sectors supply intermediate inputs to the housing sectors as well as to other producing sectors. Productivity and investment in these two public sectors would, therefore, have an important indirect impact on all those activities for which public sector output is an input. Since so much of the debate over urban bias hinges on the relative performance and size of investments in these two sectors, it is essential to include them explicitly.

Technology, Dualism, and Factor Intensity

Like all models of economic dualism, BMW stresses differences in factor intensity and technology among sectors. Thus, the ten sectors exhibit quite different rates of technical progress, factor requirements, and sub-

Table 2.1. Sector Characteristics of the BMW Model

| Sector | UN Standard (ISIC) Counterpart | Production Inputs | | Production Function Form | Spatial Location | Tradability Characteristics | Market Price Determination |
		Primary	Intermediate				
(A) Agriculture	Agriculture, livestock, forestry, fishing	Capital, skills, land, labor	Public rural services; M, KS; imported fuels and raw materials	Cobb-Douglas, constant returns	Rural	Internationally and interregionally traded	Partially endogenous (linked to world prices by Armington specification)
(RS) Private rural services	Domestics, personal services; rural HRS housing construction; rural manufacturing and commerce	Capital, skills, labor	Public rural services; M, KS, A; imported fuels and raw materials	Nested CES, constant returns	Rural	Nontraded	Endogenous
(PSR) Public rural services	Public roads, transport, irrigation projects; rural public administration and public utilities	Capital, skills, labor	M; imported fuels and raw materials	Nested CES, constant returns	Rural	Nontraded	Endogenous
(HRS) Rural Housing	Rural housing originally constructed by RS sector	Dwellings	Public rural services	Cobb-Douglas, constant returns	Rural	Nontraded	Endogenous (owner-occupied shadow price)
(M) Manufacturing	Urban manufacturing and mining	Capital, skills, labor	Public urban services; KS, A; imported fuels and raw materials	Nested CES, constant returns	Urban	Internationally and interregionally traded	Partially Endogenous (linked to world prices by Armington specification)

Sector	Description	Factors	Intermediate inputs	Production function	Location	Trade	Price
(KS) Capital-intensive services	Education, defense, public administration, finance, modern commerce; construction of urban (pucca) HKS housing	Capital, skills, labor	Public urban services; M, A; imported fuels and raw materials	Nested CES, constant returns	Urban	Interregionally traded	Endogenous
(US) Private urban services	Domestics, personal services; urban HUS housing construction; small-scale commerce and transport	Capital, skills, labor	Public urban services; M, KS, A; imported fuels and raw materials	Nested CES, constant returns	Urban	Nontraded	Endogenous
(PSU) Public urban services	Urban electricity, gas, water, transport and communications	Capital, skills, labor	M; imported fuels and raw materials	Nested CES, constant returns	Urban	Nontraded	Endogenous
(HUS) Low-quality urban housing	Urban (katcha) housing and squatter settlements, originally constructed by US sector	Dwellings, land	Public urban services	Cobb-Douglas, constant returns	Urban	Nontraded	Endogenous (owner-occupied shadow price)
(HKS) High-quality urban housing	Urban (pucca) housing, originally constructed by KS sector	Dwellings, land	Public urban services	Cobb-Douglas, constant returns	Urban	Nontraded	Endogenous (owner-occupied shadow price)

stitution elasticities. Furthermore, technological dualism is not simply an attribute of the well-known rural-urban dichotomy but is an intra-urban attribute as well.

While conventional physical capital, K, is used in each of the non-housing sectors, and while the same is true of skilled labor, S, factor intensity varies sharply among sectors. Specifically, the public sectors and urban manufacturing are the most capital-intensive sectors, while sectors with large public administration components are the most skill intensive. The extreme variation in input intensities is apparent when one looks at the figures. In 1960, and compared with India as a whole, each sector's capital and skill ratio to unskilled labor was:

	Relative Capital–Labor Ratio	Relative Skills–Labor Ratio
A	56	29
RS	66	159
PSR	1782	4665
M	344	380
KS	565	1354
US	152	51
PSU	719	154
All India	100	100

Once in place, capital is specific to that sector and cannot be used in another.

Unskilled labor, L, is also used in all nonhousing sectors, and, like skilled labor, is mobile among them, subject to migration rules discussed below. Land, R, is used as an input in agriculture and in urban housing, but these uses do not compete.

Each of these five factors of production (capital, skills, labor, urban land, and rural land) is homogenous. Production is subject to constant returns to scale and diminishing marginal rates of substitution. Joint products are excluded, and external economies (and diseconomies) do not exist. It is assumed that factor-augmenting technical change applies to capital, skills, and labor, but not to land, although exogenous growth in multiple cropping will play a role in augmenting the effective stock of farmland over time in the model. Each sector can be treated as an aggregate of similar firms, since all production exhibits constant returns to scale; indeed, each sector is analogous to a large firm having a production function and exhibiting optimal behavior. Such behavior implies cost minimization with respect to inputs and profit maximization with respect to outputs.

Development economics has created a long tradition that stresses the role of differing factor intensities and elasticities of factor substitution in contributing to technological dualism. We need to adopt production functions consistent with this tradition and the abundant empirical evidence supporting it (Chenery and Raduchel, 1971; Fallon and Layard, 1975; Yotopoulos and Nugent, 1976). The presence of three or four factors of production makes the conventional constant elasticity of substitution (CES) production function inappropriate. Indeed, we are convinced by several empirical studies that the elasticity of substitution between pairs of inputs is not the same sector by sector. Instead, it appears, for example, that conventional capital and skills are relative complements in urban modern sectors (Grilliches, 1969; Fallon and Layard, 1975; Kesselman, Williamson and Berndt, 1977; Hammermesh and Grant, 1979), and this fact may help to account for the phenomena of rising skilled-wage premiums, wage stretching, and increased earnings inequality in much of the Third World, especially in the 1960s and early 1970s, when capital accumulation was rapid.

All of these considerations lead us to the nested-CES production function for each nonhousing sector, except agriculture:

(1) $\quad Q_i = A_i Q_{i,F}^{\alpha_{i,F}} Z_i^{\alpha_{i,z}} \prod_j Q_{i,j}^{\alpha_{i,j}}$

$\quad Q_{i,F} = \{\xi_i \phi_i^{(\sigma_i - 1)/\sigma_i} + (1 - \xi_i)[z_i L_i]^{(\sigma_i - 1)/\sigma_i}\}^{\sigma_i/(\sigma_i - 1)}$

$\quad \phi_i = \{\xi_i' [x_i K_i]^{(\sigma_i' - 1)/\sigma_i'} + (1 - \xi_i')[y_i S_i]^{(\sigma_i' - 1)/\sigma_i'}\}^{\sigma_i'/(\sigma_i' - 1)};$

$\quad \sum_j \alpha_{ij} + \alpha_{i,F} + \alpha_{i,z} = 1$

$\quad i = M, KS, US, PSU, PSR, RS$

$\quad j = A^*, M^*, KS, k,$

$\quad k = \begin{cases} PSU \text{ when } i = M, KS, US \\ PSR \text{ when } i = RS \end{cases}$

where Q_i is gross output, Z_i is imported raw materials, Q_{ij} are intersectoral inputs (excluding intrasectoral inputs), Q_{iF} is a composite of primary inputs, and ϕ_i is a composite of capital inputs (skills and physical capital). A^* and M^* are composites of imported and domestically produced tradables, to be discussed further below. The parameters are: α_{ij}, the cost shares of each factor in gross sales; ξ_i and ξ_i', the distribution parameters; and σ_i and σ_i', the substitution elasticities. Factor-augmenting technical progress determines the levels of $x_i(t)$, $y_i(t)$, and $z_i(t)$; $x_i K_i$, $y_i S_i$, and $z_i L_i$ are considered "efficiency capital" stocks, "efficiency skilled labor" stocks, and "efficiency unskilled labor" stocks, respectively. The x_i, y_i, and z_i can differ among sectors; the difference reflects the rate of factor saving embodied in the new sector-specific technologies introduced over time. In particular, it should reflect the fact that manufacturing has been labor saving over the past two decades in India, accounting in part for disappointing urban employment growth.

In contrast, agriculture's production function is taken to be Cobb-Douglas (a controversial assumption, but supported by the empirical literature surveyed in Yotopoulos and Nugent, 1976, chap. 4):

$$(2) \qquad Q_A = A_A \cdot [x_A K_A]^{\alpha_{A,K}} \cdot [y_A S_A]^{\alpha_{A,S}} \cdot [z_A L_A]^{\sigma_{A,L}} \cdot R_A^{\alpha_{A,R}} \cdot Z_A^{\sigma_{A,Z}} \cdot \prod_j Q_{A,j}^{\alpha_{A,j}},$$

$$j = M^*, KS, PSR, A^*$$

$$\text{defining } \alpha_{A,F} \equiv \sigma_{A,K} + \sigma_{A,S} + \sigma_{A,L};$$

$$\sum_j \alpha_{A,j} + \alpha_{A,F} + \alpha_{A,R} + \alpha_{A,Z} = 1$$

where Q_A denotes gross agricultural output, Q_{Aj} are intersectoral inputs in agriculture (including fertilizer), Z_A is imported raw materials in agriculture (primarily fuel), and R_A is the effective stock of farmland (augmented to include the impact of multiple cropping). The intercept A_j denotes the component of total factor productivity that is independent of the factor-augmenting sources. In the case of agriculture, A_A includes the important effect of the monsoon on yields, and we will discuss these forces at greater length.

Following Muth (1969, 1971) and others, each housing sector is also taken to employ a Cobb-Douglas production function:

$$(3) \qquad Q_{H,j} = A_{H,j} \cdot H_j^{\alpha_{H,j}} \cdot R_{U,j}^{\alpha_{R,j}} \cdot Q_{k,H,j}^{\alpha_{k,H,j}}$$

$$\sum_{i=H,R,(k,H)} \alpha_{ij} = 1$$

$$\alpha_{R,RS} = 0 \text{ (that is, no land term is present in rural housing)}$$

$$j = KS, US, RS$$

$$k = \begin{cases} PSU \text{ when } j = KS, US \\ PSR \text{ when } j = RS \end{cases}$$

where Q_{Hj} are the "rental units" produced by each of the three housing sectors. Housing differs from other sectors in the economy since it uses neither labor nor conventional capital. It does require land for each of the two urban dwelling sites, R_{Uj}, although we ignore the land site requirements for rural housing on the assumption that rural housing land is a free good. In addition, the flow of housing services is also influenced by the availability of public services supplied by PSR and

PSU, Q_{kHj}. Housing is discussed further below in conjunction with urban land markets.

Price Formation

Two price relationships need elaboration at this point. Consider first the critical relation between world market prices for tradables and their domestic counterparts. As was pointed out above, domestic outputs of A and M are not treated as perfect substitutes for internationally traded A and M. Thus, the domestic prices of these tradables are not simply fixed multiples of world prices for which the multiple is determined by tariffs. Instead, and following standard procedure in the CGE literature (Robinson, 1988), imported and domestic manufactures form a composite of M goods, which has a price, P_{M^*}, that is a weighted average of the two. World market prices of manufactures, $\overline{P}_M^W$, are related to that domestic composite price by tariffs, $\tau_{M,IMP}$, by the elasticity of substitution between domestic and imported M goods, $\sigma_{i,COM}$, as well as by a share distribution parameter in the composite good function, ψ_i^*. Thus, world prices influence composite goods' prices, which in turn determine prices of the domestically produced component:

$$(46) \quad P_i = P_{i^*}(1 - \psi_i^*) \left[\frac{Q_{i^*}}{Q_i - Q_{i,EXP}} \right]^{1/\sigma_{i,COM}}$$

$$i = A, M$$

$$(47) \quad \overline{P}_i^W(1 + \tau_{i,IMP}) = P_{i^*}\psi_i^* \left[\frac{Q_{i^*}}{Q_{i,IMP}} \right]^{1/\sigma_{i,COM}}$$

$$i = A, M$$

where Q_{i^*} is the composite good, $Q_{i,IMP}$ are imports, and $Q_{i,EXP}$ are exports.

Although these issues will be discussed below when we confront foreign trade explicitly, note that the so-called Armington (1969) specification implies exactly how the composite commodities are constructed:

$$(6) \quad Q_{i^*} = \left[\psi_i^* Q_{i,IMP}^{\left(\frac{\sigma_{i,COM} - 1}{\sigma_{i,COM}} \right)} \right.$$

$$\left. + (1 - \psi_i^*)(Q_i - Q_{i,EXP})^{\left(\frac{\sigma_{i,COM} - 1}{\sigma_{i,COM}} \right)} \right]^{\frac{\sigma_{i,COM}}{(\sigma_{i,COM} - 1)}}$$

$$i = A, M$$

Next, we should keep in mind the difference between the value-added price of some domestically produced good, P'_i, and the price paid by all consumers in the market place, P_i:

$$(4) \qquad P'_i = P_i - \sum_j P^{tax}_{ij} \frac{Q_{i,j}}{Q_i} - \frac{\overline{P}_Z Z_i (1 + \tau_{IMP,Z})}{Q_i} \equiv \alpha_{i,F} \cdot P_i$$

$$i = M, A, KS, PSU, PSR, US, RS$$

$$j = A^*, M^*, KS, k$$

$$k = \begin{cases} PSU \text{ when } i = M, KS, US \\ PSR \text{ when } i = RS, A \end{cases}$$

$$(5) \qquad P^{tax}_{i,j} = P_j \text{ for all } (i,j) \text{ except } (i = A \text{ or } RS \text{ and } j = M^*)$$

$$\text{where } P^{tax}_{A,M^*} = P^{tax}_{RS,M^*} = P_{M^*}(1 + \tau_{A,M})$$

where τ_{ij} are tax or tariff rates. P^{tax}_{ij} is the user cost of goods purchased by any using sector, and it may differ from the market price if, in addition, a tax (or subsidy) on intermediate use is imposed.

Labor Markets and Migration

Economywide supplies of skilled and unskilled labor are exogenous at any point in time in the static model. This is not true over time because unskilled labor grows in response to long-run demographic forces and some of these laborers are trained each year, but both trends are driven by exogenous forces. Although total labor supplies are given by previous history in the static model, the distribution of the labor force is not. This section focuses first on labor demand and wage determination in the absence of migration forces and then turns to the migration behavior embedded in the model that determines labor allocation.

Because overt unemployment is not an attribute of our model, wages clear each market. Efficiency factors are assumed to be paid their marginal value products:

$$(7) \qquad \tilde{W}_{i,L} = P'_i \frac{Q_i}{Q_{i,F}} \cdot (1 - \xi_i) \left[\frac{Q_{i,F}}{z_i L_i} \right]^{1/\sigma_i} = \frac{W_{i,L}}{z_i}$$

$$\text{for } i = M, KS, PSU, US, PSR, RS$$

$$(8) \qquad \tilde{W}_{i,S} = P'_i \frac{Q_i}{Q_{i,F}} \xi_i (1 - \xi'_i) \left[\frac{Q_{i,F}}{\phi_i} \right]^{1/\sigma_i} \cdot \left[\frac{\phi_i}{y_i S_i} \right]^{1/\sigma'_i} = \frac{W_{i,S}}{y_i}$$

$$\text{for } i = M, KS, PSU, US, PSR, RS$$

$$(9) \qquad \tilde{W}_{A,j} = P'_A \cdot \alpha_{A,j} \left[\frac{Q_A}{b \cdot J_A} \right] = \frac{W_{A,j}}{b_A}$$

$$\text{for } j, J = L, S$$

$$\text{and } b = \begin{cases} z \text{ for } j = L \\ y \text{ for } j = S \end{cases}$$

where W are annual earnings and $\tilde{W}$ are efficiency wages.

It might be helpful to emphasize two issues at this point: the distinction between wage rates and annual earnings, on the one hand, and the structure of earnings, on the other. Both issues are important to earnings distribution patterns generated by any model. First, wages and earnings can behave quite differently over time in the developing economy, depending on the character of technical progress and labor use rates. (See Kelley, Williamson, and Cheetham, 1972, chaps. 4, 5, and 8.) Labor-saving technological change implies rapid increases in z, an influence which serves to suppress the rise in the real wage among the unskilled, confirming the historical evidence of real wage stability for common labor. Yet that influence also serves to drive a wedge between wage rates and annual earnings, the latter rising even in the face of wage rate stability. Thus, stability in the wage rate of efficiency unskilled labor does not necessarily imply stability in wage earnings or, for that matter, stability in unskilled labor's share in national income.

Second, our choice of migration rules will be crucial in determining the structure of earnings among the unskilled in our model. If we were to assume migration behavior that equated nominal wages everywhere, there would be little room for anything but a fully egalitarian distribution of unskilled wages as well as of skilled wages in BMW: all earnings inequality would take the form of wage differentials between skilled and unskilled labor. If we were to add cost-of-living considerations to the migration decision, so that only real wages were equated, more scope would be added to assess changing size distributions of nominal earnings, but not much more. Migration specifications are relevant, therefore, to distribution patterns generated in any model of the Indian economy. However, with only two types of labor in BMW, the model can hardly be expected to tell detailed stories about the distribution of earnings, even with an elaborate migration specification. BMW was not constructed for that purpose.

Furthermore, since the focus of this book is on the long-run macro-determinants of city immigration, we felt it unnecessary to offer an elaborate migration scheme with distributed lags and expectations. And since overt unemployment has no place in our model either, any Todaro-like specification (Todaro, 1969; Harris and Todaro, 1970; Corden and

Findlay, 1975) would be irrelevant. Indeed, in contrast to other developing countries, urban households have only slightly larger per capita incomes than do rural households in India, and food consumption is roughly the same. The lack of pronounced rural-urban income differentials is yet another reason we do not introduce a variant of the Todaro model into BMW. Instead, BMW adopts migration decision rules that produce the following results:

$$(10) \qquad W_{A,j} = W_{RS,j} = W_{PSR,j}$$

$$j = L, S$$

$$(11) \qquad (1 - \tau_{Y,FS}) \cdot W_{M,S} = (1 - \tau_{Y,FS}) \cdot W_{KS,S} = (1 - \tau_{Y,FS}) W_{PSU,S}$$

$$= (1 - \tau_{Y,US}) \cdot W_{US,S}$$

$$(12) \qquad W_{M,L} = W_{KS,L} = W_{PSU,L} = W_{US,L}$$

$$(13) \qquad \frac{W_{A,L}}{COL_{L_R}} = \frac{W_{M,L}}{COL_{L_U}} - C_{M,L}$$

$$\text{given } COL_{L_U} = COL_{L_{US}}$$

$$(14) \qquad \frac{W_{A,S}(1 - \tau_{Y,A})}{COL_{S_R}} = \frac{W_{M,S} \cdot (1 - \tau_{Y,FS})}{COL_{S_U}} - C_{M,S}$$

$$\text{given } COL_{S_U} = COL_{S_{US}}$$

Migration equates unskilled wages *within* rural areas and *within* urban areas; the same is true of skilled wages, although skilled labor takes account of any possible difference in income tax rates by sector (i.e., the τ_{Yj}). *Between* rural and urban areas, however, migration is influenced by cost-of-living differentials (the COL) and the costs of migration (the C_M)—real wages net of these influences are equated.

Capital Markets and Investment Allocation

Our assumption that efficiency factors are paid their marginal value products applies not only to labor, but to physical capital as well. Thus, the sector rates of return to efficiency capital, $\bar{r}$, are written as

$$(15) \qquad \bar{r}_i = P_i' \frac{Q_i}{Q_{i,F}} \cdot \xi_i' \cdot \xi_i \cdot \left[\frac{Q_{i,F}}{\phi_i} \right]^{1/\sigma_i} \cdot \left[\frac{\phi_i}{x_i K_i} \right]^{1/\sigma_i'} = \frac{r_i}{x_i}$$

$$i = M, KS, PSU, PSR, US, RS$$

$$(16) \quad \tilde{r}_A = P_A \cdot \alpha_{A,K} \left[\frac{Q_A}{x_A K_A} \right] = \frac{r_A}{x_A}$$

We assume capital immobility, so after-tax rates of return need not be equalized among sectors. That is, once investment is allocated to a given sector and used to augment the capital stock there, the new capital stock becomes specific to that production activity. Thus, any economic or demographic event that serves to raise the rate of return in one sector relative to another generates rate-of-return differentials, a disequilibrium attribute typical of most developing countries and often labeled as market failure.

Furthermore, the current pool of productive investment goods is not allocated freely among sectors. Indeed, there are four segmented components of the capital market, each only loosely linked to the others. Housing investment will be discussed at greater length below, but investment in the urban informal sector is constrained by informal sector savings after housing investment requirements are satisfied by households employed there:

$$(19) \quad P_M \cdot I_{M,US} = s_{LU} L_{US} - P_{US} I_{H,US,US}$$
$$- P_{KS} I_{H,KS,US} + \delta_{US} P_M \cdot K_{US}$$

where the value of informal gross investment is given on the lefthand side, s_j is nominal savings per household of type j, $P_j I_{Hjus}$ is the value of gross housing investment made by informal sector income recipients on housing of type j, and $\delta_{US} P_M \cdot K_{US}$ are the funds set aside for depreciation of capital stocks in US.

There are two other private sector capital submarkets, one linking rural services with agriculture and another linking manufacturing with KS. Although these two submarkets are segmented from one another, rate-of-return differentials motivate investment allocation *within* them. The rate-of-return differentials minimized, however, are not simply the net returns on existing capital over and above taxes and depreciation. Rather, private agents in these subsectors form expectations of projected rates of return based on investment plans that will serve to augment capital stocks in the next time period. Thus, the differentials minimized by current investment allocation decisions are ex ante (after-tax) rates of return or quasi rents. Formally, where the $\tau_{\pi j}$ are corporate tax rates, agents

$$(17) \quad \text{MINIMIZE} \{ \text{Return Differentials} = r_M^* \cdot (1 - \tau_{\pi,M}) - \tau_{KS}^*$$
$$\{I_{i,M,FS}\}$$
$$\cdot (1 - \tau_{\pi,KS}) \}$$

such that desired investment in the urban formal sector is completely allocated:

$$I_{M,FS} = \sum_i I_{i,M,FS}; \quad i = M, KS$$

Here r_i^* is the net rental rate expected to prevail in the following year:

$$r_i^* = \left\{ r_i + \frac{\partial r_i}{\partial K_i} \bigg|_{K_i} \cdot [I_{i,M,FS} - \delta_i K_i] \right\} - \delta_i P_{M^*}$$

$$i = M, KS$$

For rural investors, the allocation decision results in

(18)   MINIMIZE {Return Differentials = $r_{RS}^* - r_A^*$}
         $\{I_i, M, R\}$

such that desired investment in rural production is completely allocated:

$$I_{M,R} = \sum_i I_{i,M,R}$$

$$i = RS, A$$

and where

$$r_i^* = \left\{ r_i + \frac{\partial r_i}{\partial K_i} \bigg|_{K_i} \cdot [I_{i,M,R} - \delta_i K_i] \right\} - \delta_i P_{M^*}$$

$$i = RS, A$$

Government investment allocation is exogenous (and quasi-inframarginal in the sense that private investors may respond to government investment decisions, but sufficiently large public investment efforts in a given sector will not permit private responses to equalize the expected rates of return to those in other sectors), and total private and government enterprise investment, I_M, is given by

(23) $I_M = I_{M,US} + I_{M,R} + I_{M,FS}$

Land and Housing Markets

Land can be put to two uses in BMW—farming and urban residential land sites. We shall assume that urban residential sites implicitly include, in fixed proportions, direct site requirements as well as indirect site requirements (roads, schools). The fixed proportion assumption will simplify the analysis considerably, since we can focus exclusively on the residential-site demand component of urban land use. Furthermore, we shall assume that "wasteland" exists in rural areas. This wasteland has no competing use and no inherent site value, but it can be used for rural housing construction. In the real world, of course, wasteland can be and is exploited for both urban and farmland expansion through drainage, filling, and clearing. These activities involve investment, and to confront land accumulation endogenously would require the explicit introduction of urban and rural land-supply functions, which are presumably inelastic to capture investment costs, and competitive with other investments. We ignore such complications and take the expansion of productive land to be exogenous, although not necessarily constant.

The two land markets are segmented: that is, rural and urban land uses are completely noncompetitive. However, all intraurban and intrarural land uses are competitive. The stock of agricultural land is given by R_A, while the urban land stock is

$$R_U = R_{U,US} + R_{U,KS},$$

where urban land sites are used for two types of housing—low-cost katcha dwellings and squatter settlements ($R_{U,US}$) and high-cost pucca dwellings ($R_{U,KS}$).

The urban housing market is central to migration behavior. One of the limits on city growth in India and other Third World countries is the availability and cost of urban housing facing new urban households, whether the housing is of the informal, labor-intensive, owner-occupied type in squatter settlements or substantial dwelling units constructed by capital-intensive techniques in a more formal housing market. Any model of urbanization must admit this possible limit to city growth. The limit may take various forms, but we shall stress two.

First, urban rents may rise in the long run due to the inflation of urban site rents, as in classical urban location theory (Mills, 1972; Henderson, 1977), as well as in fact (Williamson, 1990, chap. 9). In addition, urban rents may rise in the short run if investment in new structure lags behind demands generated by rapid urban population growth (Song and Struyk, 1976; Mills and Song, 1977). Second, to the extent that investment in housing responds to demands generated by in-migration, residual funds available for productive accumulation contract and thus the rate of output expansion suffers economywide (Coale and Hoover, 1958). Since capital is used most intensively in the modern sectors, the rate of urban labor absorption is diminished. In-migration to the cities and urbanization rates should slack off as a result. Our model incorporates these forces, so that overurbanization (Hoselitz, 1955, 1957; Sovani, 1962; Kamerschen, 1969; United Nations, 1980; Kelley and Williamson, 1984) may be forestalled.

As we pointed out above, there are two housing types in BMW: low-cost and high-cost housing. In this we follow the United Nations' *Habitat* (1976, p. 70), which states that "in many less developed countries building is characterized by the existence of two sectors: a) a multitude of very small enterprises . . . which operate in the rural and peri-urban areas, belonging almost entirely to the informal sector of the economy; b) a small number of large firms using modern techniques and organization," and its *Global Review of Human Settlements* (United Nations, 1976, p. 11), where squatter settlements "generally refer to areas where groups of housing units have been constructed on land to which the occupants have no legal claim. In many instances housing units located in squatter settlements are shelters or structures built of waste materials without a predetermined plan. Squatter settlements are usually found . . . at the peripheries of the principal cities."

According to the same source, squatter settlements are by no means a small share of total urban dwellings and may account for the bulk of the growth in cities throughout the Third World (see also Mohan, 1979, chap. 1 and Linn, 1979, table II-7). For 1960, we estimate that Indian informal, low-cost urban housing accounted for about a quarter of the total urban housing stock and for almost half of urban housing services. Thus, it seems to us important to distinguish between two types of urban dwellings and to indicate the different sectors that produce them as well as the different socioeconomic classes that consume the rental services that flow from these residential structures.

What, then, determines rents and land use in BMW? For farmland, the answer is simple enough: land supplies are exogenous, they are assumed to be fully employed, and rents, d_A, are determined by marginal value productivities:

$$(34) \quad d_A = \frac{P_A \alpha_{A,R} Q_A}{R_A}$$

For urban land, the answer is more complex. First, the nominal rent on the jth type of urban housing is

$$(36) \quad P_{H,j} = \frac{r_{H,j} \cdot H_j + P_{k,H,j} \cdot Q_{k,H,j} + d_{U,j} \cdot R_{U,j}}{Q_{H,j}}$$

$$j = US, RS$$

$$k = \begin{cases} PSU \text{ for } j = US \\ PSR \text{ for } j = RS \end{cases}$$

where this rent has three components: the structure rent, $r_{H,j}H_j$, the land site rent, $d_{U,j}R_{U,j}$, and the user cost of public utilities supplied to the housing units, $P_{k,H,j}Q_{k,H,j}$. Second, land site rents are determined by marginal value productivities:

$$(33) \quad d_{U,j} = \frac{P_{H,j}^S \alpha_{R,j} Q_{H,j}}{R_{U,j} \cdot (1 - \alpha_{PSU,H,j})}$$

$$j = KS, US$$

where $P_{H,j}^S$ is the net unit rental cost after property taxes and public utility charges have been subtracted. Finally, equilibrium in the urban land rental market requires that

$$(35) \quad d_{U,KS} = d_{U,US} \cdot \text{GRADIENT}$$

GRADIENT is a parameter that reflects the fact that KS housing is normally built on more valuable urban sites. Otherwise, urban land is allocated between the two types of housing until rents are equated.

Housing Investment and Aggregate Savings

Aggregate savings determines accumulation possibilities in our model, and this savings pool is generated by three sources: retained after-tax corporate and enterprise profits, government savings, and household savings. (Foreign aid and private capital inflows serve to augment government resources and thus indirectly appear as components of government savings. The same is true of retained earnings from public enterprises.) The private sector component of total savings can be written as

$$(82) \quad \text{PRIVATE SAVINGS} = \sum_i (1 - \psi_i)(1 - \tau_{\pi,i})(r_i - \delta_i P_{M^*})K_i$$
$$+ \sum_l \delta_l P_{M^*}K_l + \sum_j s_j J,$$

$$i = M, KS$$

$$l = M, KS, US, RS, A$$

$$j = L_{US}, L_U, L_R, S_{US}, S_U, S_R, C$$

where ψ_i are corporate dividend pay-out rates. Private savings are allocated among informal sector investment, $I_{M,US}$, formal sector investment, $I_{M.FS}$, rural private investment, $I_{M.R}$, and housing. The first three of these add up to total private, nonhousing investment, $P_M \cdot I_M$, and we have already discussed investment allocation among these three competing uses. A critical question remains: what determines the allocation of private sector savings between housing and nonhousing?

Housing investment should be sensitive to both demographic and urbanization forces. We view housing investment in much the same way as subsistence consumption requirements are often treated in the development literature. That is, private households are assumed to attach first priority to housing needs in their investment portfolios. Only after housing investment needs are satisfied do households release their residual savings for nonhousing accumulation purposes through banks, nonbank financial institutions, and informal "curb" markets.

Since the formal mortgage market is poorly developed or nonexistent in much of India, we assume that none of the three housing sectors is able to secure external finance to satisfy investment requirements. Housing investment is, therefore, self-financed by each household type independent of other savings-generating sectors. Although this specification eliminates the possibility of *inter*sectoral housing financial flows, it does not exclude the possibility of *intra*sectoral housing financial flows. Thus, fathers may lend to sons, but middle-class, skilled households never loan to poor, unskilled households. Certain sectors may therefore be starved for housing finance while others have a surplus, which they allocate to the private national savings pool for productive accumulation.

Under conditions of rapid population growth, household savings may be largely exhausted by housing investment requirements. This potential demographic burden is reinforced in BMW by rapid rates of city growth. This follows from the fact that housing is location specific; thus, migration of even a stable aggregate population requires new housing construction in the receiving regions and causes net housing investment economywide. Furthermore, given the cost-of-living adjustment embedded in the model's migration function, rapid in-migration and urbanization may well be forestalled by the urban housing requirements that these population movements imply. An urban housing investment shortfall results in a rise in urban rents and thereby attenuates in-migration. Alternatively, increased urban housing investment inhibits the accumulation of nonhousing capital, and such capital accumulation is a central determinant of the relative expansion of employment in modern urban sectors.

What remains is to convert these qualitative descriptions of investment demand for housing into explicit equations. For given prices and household incomes, we specify the following type of urban housing investment demand:

$$I^*_{Hj} = \min\{s_j L_j P_j^{-1}, I^N_{Hj} + \delta_{Hj} H_j\},$$

$$I_{Hj} = \max\{0, I^*_{Hj}\},$$

where $s_j L_j P_j^{-1}$ is the savings generated by households consuming the jth type of housing (deflated by the construction costs of such housing), $I^N_{H,j}$ is net investment demand for housing (to be discussed below), and $I_{H,j}$ is gross investment in housing. The first expression states that household savings in sector j may be binding on housing investment in that sector, given the absence of mortgage markets. If not, dwelling investment does not exhaust the sector's household savings, and a surplus is available for accumulation in other forms in spite of low per capita incomes. This may also hold for the urban middle and upper classes but is less likely to hold for the urban poor. The second expression given above simply states that gross investment cannot be negative. This expression is unlikely to be binding under conditions of rapid population growth, even with substantial rural out-migration. Depreciation requirements are given by $\delta_{H,j} H_j$.

In discussing net investment demand for housing, it will be helpful to define the following terms. Some of them are new, while others are included to refresh the reader's memory:

P_j per unit construction costs of H_j

$P_{H,j}$ nominal rental cost of the jth type of housing, including site rent and user charges for public utilities

$P^S_{H,j}$ nominal net rental cost of the jth type of housing, after property taxes and user charges for public utilities

$r_{H,j}$ net of tax rate of return on structures of type j or net structure rents

$\hat{r}_{H,j}$ an index of profitability of housing investment in the jth type housing stock, a benefit–cost ratio computed as the ratio of the discounted stream of net rents to current construction costs

r^*_j pretax rates of return on investment in nonhousing capital after accounting for depreciation

Using these definitions, net investment demand for housing in the jth sector is

$$I^N_{Hj} = \theta_{Hj} \{\hat{r}^{\epsilon_H}_{Hj} - 1\}$$

where the index of profitability, $\hat{r}_{H,j}$, is

$$\hat{r}_{Hj} = \{(r_{Hj} - \delta_{Hj} P_j) i_j^{-1}\} P_j^{-1}$$

High values of $\hat{r}_{H,j}$ indicate high profitability with positive gaps between capitalized anticipated net rents and current construction costs. This expression also states that net investment in housing should be zero when the benefit–cost ratio is unity, that is, when the rate of return on nonhousing investment alternatives, i_j, equals the rate of return on sector j's new housing investment. Higher values of $r_{H,j}$ imply more housing investment at the expense of alternative investments elsewhere. The rates of return on nonhousing investment alternatives are weighted averages of expected returns on private capital:

$$(20) \quad i_{FS} = \frac{\sum_{j}(1 - \tau_{\pi,j})K_j r_j^*}{P_{M^*}\sum_{j} K_j},$$

$$j = M, KS,$$

where FS denotes the urban formal sectors

$$(21) \quad i_A = \frac{\sum_{j} K_j r_j^*}{P_{M^*}\sum_{j} K_j},$$

$$j = A, RS$$

$$(22) \quad i_{IFS} = \frac{r_{US}}{P_{M^*}} - \delta_{US},$$

where IFS denotes the urban informal sector.

The housing investment demand equations for all three sectors can now be written formally as (where the subscript FSC denotes high-cost housing demand from capitalists, landlords, and skilled workers receiving incomes from the formal sectors):

$$(70) \quad I_{H,RS}^* = \min\{[s_{L_R}L_R + s_{S_R} S_R]P_{RS}^{-1}, I_{H,RS}^N + \delta_{H,RS}H_{RS}\}$$

$$I_{H,RS} = \max\{0, I_{H,RS}^*\}$$

$$I_{H,RS}^N = \theta_{H,RS}\cdot[\hat{r}_{H,RS}^{\epsilon_H} - 1]$$

$$(71) \quad I_{H,h,j}^* = \min\left\{\frac{s_j J}{P_h} I_{H,h,j}^N + \delta_{H,h}H_{h,j}\right\}$$

$$I_{H,h,j} = \max\{0, I_{H,h,j}^*\}$$

$$I^N_{H,h,j} = \theta_{H,h} \cdot [\hat{r}^{\epsilon_H}_{H,h,j} - 1]$$

$$j, J = L_{US}, L_U, S_{US}$$

$$h = \begin{cases} US \text{ for } j,J = L_{US}, L_U \\ KS \text{ for } j,J = S_{US} \end{cases}$$

(72) $\quad I^*_{H,KS,FSC} = \min\{[s_{S_U} S_U + s_C C] P^{-1}_{KS}, I^N_{H,KS,FSC}$

$$+ \delta_{H,KS} H_{KS,C} + H_{KS,S_U}\}$$

$$I_{H,KS,FSC} = \max\{0, I^*_{H,KS,FSC}\}$$

$$I^N_{H,KS,FSC} = \theta_{H,KS}[\hat{r}^{\epsilon_H}_{H,KS,FSC} - 1]$$

When these housing investment requirements are valued by current construction costs, total gross investment in housing is obtained in value terms:

(81) $\quad$ HOUSING $= P_{RS} I_{H,RS} + P_{US} I_{H,US} + P_{KS} I_{H,KS}$

Private nonhousing investment in value terms is the residual

(91) $\quad P_{M} \cdot I_M = $ PRIVATE SAVINGS $-$ HOUSING

although we should emphasize that housing and nonhousing investment are explicitly competitive in BMW, as we have seen. *Total* investment economywide exceeds private investment, if government savings, G_s, and funds set aside for depreciation in the two public service sectors are positive:

(92) $\quad P_{M} \cdot TI_M = $
PRIVATE SAVINGS $-$ HOUSING $+ G_s + \sum_i \delta_i P_{M} \cdot K_i = \sum_l P_{M} \cdot TI_{M,l},$

$$i = PSU, PSR$$

$$l = R, US, FS, PSU, PSR$$

Government Revenue, Spending, and Savings

The government has three sources of revenue in BMW: endogenous tax revenues, endogenous profits (or losses) in public service sectors, and exogenous net foreign aid and private foreign capital inflows, which are assumed to pass through government channels. These revenues form the total government budget constraint, which is allocated between investment and consumption. The empirical counterparts of these two spending categories are the government's capital and current budgets. All government final demands are produced by the capital-cum-skill–intensive KS service sector (or, in a few cases, PSR), and government demand dominates that sector. These current budget expenditures include defense, education, and administration.

Total taxes, T, come from a wide range of sources. These include:

1. taxes on households' consumption of M^* goods, at the rate τ_M

2. taxes (or subsidies) on agricultural intermediate inputs purchased from manufacturing, at the rate τ_{AM}

3. taxes on high-cost urban housing, at the rate $\tau_{H,KS}$

4. taxes on enterprise and corporate incomes (net of depreciation allowances) in the M and KS sectors, at the rate $\tau_{\pi j}$, which varies by sector

5. taxes on middle-class and rich incomes, at the rate $\tau_{Y,j}$, which varies by sector of employment

6. export and import duties, at the rates τ_{jEXP} and τ_{jIMP}, which vary by commodity.

The tax function (equation 48 in appendix A) derived from these sources exhibits an urban bias, a feature documented in surveys of fiscal finance in India. Only the relatively high-paid urban skilled worker's labor income is taxed. In addition, since urban activities tend to be capital intensive, and since income on capital is subject to relatively heavy taxation, urbanization implies an expanding tax base on that score, too. The urban bias is also evident in our treatment of commodity taxation of manufactured goods, as well as in the (very light) tax on high-cost urban residential property.

Another characteristic of the tax function is its apparent high elasticity with respect to GNP and the attributes of structural change that accompany growth, including an increase in the share of manufactured goods in total household expenditures, a rising share of modern sector output, a shift of the labor force into high-skilled occupations, and perhaps even increasing inequality in the distribution of income in early stages of development. In short, a rising share of taxes and government spending in GNP is a likely outcome from BMW.

Government spending and saving receive a simple treatment in the model. Government saving is taken to be a fixed share of total revenues,

(50) $G_S = \beta_G \text{ GOVREV}$

where, to repeat, total revenues come from taxes, foreign inflows $(\bar{F})$, and net profits generated by the two public service sectors,

$$(49) \quad \text{GOVREV} = T + \bar{F} + \sum_i K_i(r_i - \delta_i P_{M^*})$$

$$i = PSU, PSR$$

Furthermore, current budget general government spending consists entirely of output delivered by the KS sector,[6]

$$(51) \quad \text{GOV}_{KS} = \text{GOVREV} - G_S.$$

Finally, public investment, G_i, is allocated across sectors exogenously

$$(52) \quad G_i = g_i G_s$$

$$i = A, M, KS, US, RS, PSU, PSR.$$

Later, we assess the impact of changes in public investment policy by varying the parameters, g_i.

Household Spending and Saving

To explore the issues surrounding the role of demand in BMW, we have selected the extended linear expenditure system (ELES), initially proposed by Lluch (1973) and investigated on Third World data by Lluch, Powell, and Williams (1977). The ELES framework captures most of the stylized demand facts associated with modern economic growth in the Third World. In particular, it:

captures Engel effects

incorporates dualistic elements in demand behavior across regions and socioeconomic classes

provides an important role for demographic influences

offers explicit empirical content to the concept of "subsistence" in the low-income countries.

Equally important, the framework can be derived from reasonable postulates of household behavior and satisfies the adding-up property common to several modern integrated demand systems. Its only serious

6. General government purchases exclude public utilities and services, which are treated as the independent PSU and PSR sectors. PSR also includes rural administration. Other public enterprises are also treated separately and are regarded as part of the M sector.

competitor is the direct addilog system first developed by Frisch (1959) and extended by Houthakker (1957) and Sato (1972). The ELES has the advantage, however, of having been estimated with data for Third World economies.

In its simplest form, ELES assumes that the household allocates its disposable income (y^*) between various commodities ($q_1, \ldots, q_n$) and savings, where prices ($p_1, \ldots, p_n$) are exogenous to the household and savings is the difference between total income and the sum of all commodity expenditures ($y^* - c$, where $c = \Sigma p_i q_i = \Sigma v_i$). The model further assumes that the household's utility function is such that there is a minimum subsistence demand for each commodity ($\gamma_i \geq 0$), which must be fulfilled before the remaining "supernumerary" income ($y^* - \Sigma p_i \gamma_i$) is allocated at the margin between various commodities and saving. This paradigm of household savings and spending is represented by the expenditure equations

$$v_{ij} = p_{ij} \gamma_{ij} + \beta_{ij} \left\{ y_j^* - \sum_k p_{k_j} \gamma_{k_j} \right\}$$

$$k = A^*, M^*, T, S, H$$

$$c_j = \sum_i v_{ij}$$

$$s_j = y_j^* - c_j$$

where in the empirical application there are five commodity aggregates: food, a composite of domestic production and imports, A^*; clothing and durables, a composite of domestic production and imports, M^*; transportation and communications, T; personal services, S; and housing, H.

A graphic presentation of the ELES for the two-commodity case is provided in figure 2.1. Based on the utility function $u(q_1, q_2)$, and assuming $q_i > \gamma_i$, the household's expenditure and savings allocation follow directly: for q_1, γ_1 represents subsistence needs, $B - \gamma_1$ is supernumerary expenditure on this commodity, and savings is measured by the value of q_1 not consumed, S/p_1. An analogous accounting holds for q_2. Such a representation highlights the role of prices in savings-expenditure allocation decisions, a feature captured in our general equilibrium model, which uses ELES. With rotation of the three parallel lines, alternative prices would prevail; these would elicit quite different allocations between q_1 and S.

The ELES is similar to the more familiar linear expenditure system (LES), with one notable difference: in the extended system, total consumption out of disposable income is endogenous. Thus, the sum of the

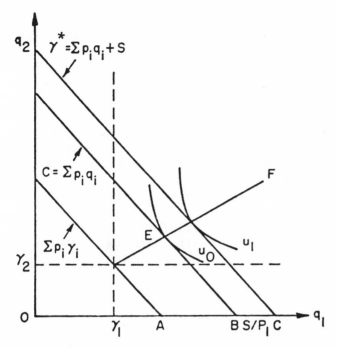

Fig. 2.1. The two-commodity case of the extended linear expenditure system (ELES)

marginal budget shares and savings exhausts disposable income. In the LES, the sum of the marginal budget shares exhausts total expenditure. The ELES thus does not use the strong separability assumption between savings and expenditure embedded in LES but views the household as determining its expenditure allocation simultaneously with its total consumption decision.

The ELES implies a Keynesian savings specification except that supernumerary disposable income rather than total disposable income is the determinant of households savings. The qualification is important because it implies that the ELES predicts a nonlinear relation between average saving rates and income. (See Bhalla, 1980, for an alternative explanation of this nonlinearity in Indian data.) Compositional influences are also captured in our framework to the extent that there may be a shift in the distribution of income to higher-saving households as economic development takes place. That is, in the empirical applications that follow in this book, we recognize seven distinct socioeconomic groups who exhibit different marginal savings rates.

Our marginal specification also permits commodity prices to influence savings. Based on ELES estimates of savings and expenditure allocation for seventeen countries, Lluch, Powell, and Williams (1977) found that for low per capita incomes, a 1 percent rise in the price of food elicited a 1.8 percent decline in the savings rate (p. xxv). If this quantitative result can be extended to India, then omitting prices from the savings decision, as household systems based on the strong separability assumption would imply, may provide misleading results concerning the role of demand in Indian development.

A full statement of the household demand system, as well as statements summarizing their aggregation into final demand categories corresponding to BMW's production structure, is provided in appendix A. Each household's demand statement, irrespective of location or socioeconomic class, possesses the form presented above. In addition, appendix A provides a side equation for the cost-of-living measure relevant to various types of households. This statistic will be important in assessing the impact of government economic policies on various aspects of household welfare, especially policies relating to migration.

Foreign Trade and World Prices

There are no monetary variables in BMW. The numeraire is the world price of manufactures imported by India. This implies that the nominal exchange rate is set equal to unity, a common choice in such models. The balance of payments is exogenous, and the model determines the equilibrium value of the *real* exchange rate. With, in effect, the nominal exchange rate chosen as numeraire, the model solves for the average price of domestically produced goods sold on the domestic market. The external closing equation consistent with these assumptions is

$$(44) \quad \sum_i P_i Q_{i,EXP} (1 + \tau_{i,EXP}) + \bar{F} - \sum_i \bar{P}_i^W Q_{i,IMP} - \bar{P}_Z \sum_j Z_j = 0$$

$$i = A, M$$

$$j = PSU, PSR, KS, US, A, M, RS$$

where the first term is export revenues, the second is foreign capital inflows, the third is "processed" imports, and the fourth is raw materials imports. $\tau_{i,EXP}$ is an export tax. The "bar" denotes a variable's exogeneity.

As we stressed in section 2.2, and in sharp contrast with its parent KW model, BMW treats domestic and foreign agricultural and manufactured goods as imperfect substitutes. We elaborated on this point in discussing price formation in BMW: domestic prices of tradables are not simply fixed multiples of world prices in which the multiple is determined by tariffs. Instead, for example, imported and domestic manufactures form a composite of M goods, and the composite good's price, P_{M^*}, is in turn a weighted average of the two prices. World market prices of manufactures, $\overline{P}_M^W$, are related to that domestic composite price by tariffs, by the elasticity of substitution between domestic and imported goods, and by a distribution parameter in the composite good function. The so-called Armington specification implies exactly how the composite commodities are constructed.

All that remains, therefore, is to specify the demand for Indian exports in world markets. We assume a simple Cobb-Douglas demand function

$$(45) \qquad Q_{i,EXP} = Q_{i,EXP}^O \left[\frac{P_i(1 + \tau_{i,EXP})}{\overline{P}_i^W} \right]^{-\eta_i}$$

$$i = A, M$$

where η_i is the demand elasticity for the ith export, and where exports consist of agricultural and manufactured goods.

Market Clearing

Because prices clear all markets in BMW, supply and demand are everywhere equated. For completeness, we include here the relevant market clearing statements (where D_i denotes aggregate household consumption demand for commodity i and TI_M denotes total gross investment):

$$(93) \qquad Q_{M^*} = D_{M^*} + TI_M + \sum_i Q_{i,M^*}$$

$$i = A, PSU, PSR, KS, RS, US$$

$$(94) \qquad Q_{A^*} = D_{A^*} + \sum_i Q_{i,A^*}$$

$$i = PSU, PSR, KS, RS, US, M$$

$$(94a) \qquad Q_i = Q_{i^*} \left[\frac{P_{i^*}(1 - \psi_i^*)}{P_i} \right]^{\sigma_{i,COM}} + Q_{i,EXP}$$

$$i = A, M$$

$$(95) \qquad Q_{PSU} = \sum_i Q_{i,PSU}$$

$$i = KS, M, US, (H, US)$$

(96) $Q_{PSR} = \sum_i Q_{i,PSR}$

$i = A, RS, (H, RS)$

(97) $Q_{KS} = D_{KS} + \text{GOV}_{KS}/P_{KS} + I_{H,KS} + \sum_i Q_{i,KS}$

$i = PSR, PSR, A, M, US, KS$

(98) $Q_i = D_i + I_{H,i}$

$i = US, RS$

(99) $Q_{H,i} = D_i$

$i = (H, US), (H, RS), (H, KS)$

and a final national income identity,

(100) $\text{GDP} = \sum_i P_i' Q_i + \sum_i P_{H,j}^s Q_{H,j}$

$\qquad + \tau_M P_{M^*} D_m + \tau_{H,KS} V_{H,KS} Q_{H,KS}$

$\qquad + \sum_l \{ P_l \tau_{l,EXP} Q_{l,EXP} + \overline{P}_l^w \tau_{l,IMP} Q_{l,IMP} \};$

$i = M, KS, PSU, PSR, US, RS, A$

$j = US, KS, RS$

$l = A, M$

2.4 Dynamics: Accumulation, Land Expansion, and Technical Progress

Accumulation and Land Expansion

Current net investment equals total gross investment minus depreciation, where depreciation is taken to be proportional to the capital stock. Thus, aggregate nonhousing and housing capital stocks are

(101) $K_i = (1 - \delta_i) K_i(-1) + TI_{M,i}(-1)$

$i = M, KS, A, RS, US, PSU, PSR$

(102) $H_j = (1 - \delta_{H,j}) \cdot H_j(-1) + I_{H,j}(-1)$

$j = US, RS, KS$

where depreciation rates are allowed to vary not only across nonhousing capital (containing equipment of shorter life) and housing (containing structures of longer life only), but also across housing of different quality (pucca housing presumably having longer life than katcha housing).

Urban and farm land are assumed to grow at exogenous rates:

$$(108) \quad R_i = (1 + \rho)R_i(-1),$$

$$i = A, U$$

Training and Skills Investment

Training and skills investment are exogenous in BMW. Define $J(0)$ as the number of households of type j prior to intraperiod equilibrium adjustments and $J(-1)$ as the number of households of type j at the end of the preceding period. Given BR_i as the net rate of labor force entrants in sector i and TR_j as the rate of transfer of workers from unskilled to skilled occupations in sector j, then it follows that

$$(109) \quad S_j(0) = (1 + \hat{BR}_i)S_j(-1) + \hat{TR}_j L_j(-1)$$

$$j = R, US, U$$

$$i = \begin{cases} R \text{ for } j = R \\ U \text{ for } j = U, US \end{cases}$$

Consequently,

$$(110) \quad L_j(0) = (1 + \hat{BR}_i - \hat{TR}_j) \cdot L_j(-1),$$

$$j = R, US, U$$

$$i = \begin{cases} R \text{ for } j = R \\ U \text{ for } j = U, US \end{cases}$$

Exogenous demographic forces are assumed to drive the total labor force, via an economywide BR.

Technical Progress

Factor-augmenting and disembodied technical progress are both present in BMW. The factor-augmenting rates are given exogenously by

$$(103) \quad x_i = x_i(-1) \cdot e^{\lambda_{Ki}}$$

$$i = A, RS, M, KS, US, PSU, PSR$$

$$(104) \quad y_i = y_i(-1) \cdot e^{\lambda_{Si}}$$

$$i = A, RS, M, KS, US, PSU, PSR$$

$$(105) \quad z_i = z_i(-1) \cdot e^{\lambda_{Li}}$$

$$i = A, RS, M, KS, US, PSU, PSR$$

Note that these rates can vary across sectors, a fact which has characterized Indian experience since the early 1960s. In agriculture, the disembodied rates include the impact of the monsoon and rainfall (where RAIN is an index of those rainfall conditions)

$$(106) \quad A_A = A_A(-1) \cdot e^{\lambda_{\lambda_A}} \cdot \text{RAIN}$$

Disembodied rates of technical progress are also allowed to vary across nonagricultural sectors:

$$(108) \quad A_i = A_i(-1) \cdot e^{\lambda_i}$$

$$i = RS, M, KS, US, PSU, PSR, (H, KS), (H, US),$$

$$(H, RS)$$

In short, while technical progress is exogenous in BMW, we *can* assess the impact of its rate and bias on migration and city growth. The sectoral rates can vary, and to the extent that they are high in city production activities, they may serve to augment employment and immigration there. The sectoral factor-saving bias can also vary, and to the extent that labor saving is high in urban manufacturing, then it should help account for disappointing employment growth in India's cities.

2.5 What's Exogenous?

What drives Indian city growth? In the BMW model just discussed, six kinds of exogenous variables help determine the pace and character of city growth.

First, the monsoon and rainfall conditions may matter. Do unfavorable weather conditions and thus low yields serve to push rural labor to the cities? How sensitive is rural emigration to the state of the monsoon?

Second, the addition of new farm acreage may matter. Indeed, it has been argued that land scarcity has pushed rural labor into the cities. If so, how sensitive is rural emigration to land scarcity?

Third, the availability of foreign capital may matter, especially to the extent that cities have heavy capital requirements. What influence did the decline in capital inflows during the 1960s have on city growth?

Fourth, demographic variables should matter. Most development analysts believe that Malthusian forces in the Third World account for most of the rapid city growth there. Has the same been true for India? Would city growth rates have been very different if India had experienced population growth rates more like Africa, or even Europe?

Fifth, world market conditions may matter. What role have trends in world market prices for fuel, raw materials, manufactures, and foodstuffs played in accounting for Indian city growth since 1960? What can we expect in the future?

Sixth, technical progress surely must have had an impact on Indian city growth over the past twenty-five years. This includes the overall rate of total factor productivity growth, the imbalance of that rate among sectors, and the labor-saving attributes of that progress.

Each of these six issues can be explicitly related to the exogenous variables in BMW, and chapters 6, 7, and 8 will explore them in detail.

In addition, key parameters describe government policy, and all of them can be varied to explore the sensitivity of city growth to them. These include government savings behavior, tax subsidy policy, and government investment policy. Chapter 5 will explore these policy issues at length.

Finally, BMW is equipped to assess major policy changes. These include a "liberalization" of segmented capital markets and dramatic changes in housing policy (and public services to housing). While such policy changes may not be politically feasible in the near future, it would be of some use to explore their consequences. Chapter 9 will be devoted largely to such issues.

2.6 The Next Step

Our Indian model of urbanization and economic growth has been developed and defended. Appendices B and C deal with problems of estimation. Chapter 3 attempts to validate BMW on Indian time series from 1960 to the 1981 census. Having convinced ourselves that BMW can replicate recent history fairly well, the remainder of the book is free to raise the questions that motivated our inquiry at the start: What are the sources of Indian city growth? How can policy influence it?

3 · Can We Replicate the Recent Past?

3.1 Fact or Fiction?

How well does BMW account for Indian experience over the past quarter century? Can it account for trends in overall growth and structural change? Does it replicate dimensions of urban in-migration, employment, and city growth?

It is essential to establish the empirical credibility of any model before applying it to the task at hand. Although most CGE analysts try to validate their models, they do so only over the very short run. When dynamic CGE models are applied to developing countries, the typical approach is to "benchmark" the model with data for a base year, then run the model forward over a few years to create what is known as a "dynamic base run." The dynamic base run then becomes the starting point for either counterfactual experiments or policy projections into the future, as illustrated by the work on Turkey by Dervis, de Melo, and Robinson (1982) and the work on Korea by Adelman and Robinson (1978). While such dynamic base run validation has become common in the literature, we know of no examples where such Third World models are tested in detail over long periods of economic history (although economic historians have done so: Williamson, 1985). This chapter will show that when BMW is given empirical content for 1960, it does indeed replicate two subsequent decades of recent Indian economic history. As we point out in the conclusion to the chapter, this is, as far as we are aware, the first attempt to test the empirical plausibility of a Third World CGE model when applied to a long period of economic history.

Section 3.2 discusses the model's estimation. The section is brief because appendices B and C offer far more detail. The discussion covers the model's estimation for 1960—the initial year in the simulations. The section also identifies four key epochs in Indian economic performance between 1960 and 1981. These epochs are identified largely, but not entirely, by sectoral productivity performance. To our knowledge, these are among the first comprehensive estimates of sectoral total factor productivity growth for any Third World economy. Section 3.3 turns to problems raised by the quality of the data base, while the testing procedure is outlined in section 3.4. The core of the chapter lies in section 3.5, where the facts of recent Indian economic history are compared with the model's predictions. The section concludes with detailed attention to India's experience with city growth since 1960. Not only does the model closely replicate that experience from census date to census date, but it also reconstructs Indian city growth experience *between* census dates. The exercise is useful because it uncovers a pronounced city growth slowdown since the early 1960s.

3.2 Estimating the BMW Model

An Overview

Given these models' large size and the poor quality of historical data for countries like India, CGEs are rarely estimated econometrically.[1] An alternative method is used instead. The first step involves estimating the parameters (appendix B). The second step involves estimating the initial conditions for some benchmark year (appendix B). The third step involves estimating the exogenous variables that help drive the model over time (appendix C).

The benchmark year is 1960. To begin with, we insist that the model replicate the national accounts, labor force distribution, and other components of the social accounting matrix for that year. This replicability requirement makes it possible to use all the available evidence to solve for those parameters and initial conditions that are not documented by official Indian statistics or by econometric studies. This step uses what we call the static initial conditions (SIC) program.[2] The SIC program thus solves the model for 1960, but the endogenous solution variables in this case include unknown parameters, which are treated as exogenous in the computable equilibrium model's (CEM) simulations thereafter. The data set containing these "residually determined" parameters and initial conditions guarantees that the CEM solution exactly reproduces

1. There has been some recent discussion on increasing the econometric content of CGE models. See, for example, Jorgenson (1984) and Mansur and Whalley (1984).

2. A detailed description of the methodology and of the values derived from SIC can be found in appendixes B and C.

observed 1960 values. Table 3.1 summarizes the outcome of this step; it reports 1960 inputs, outputs, and investment distribution by sector and region.

Once the parameters have been estimated, simulation of the 1960 Indian economy can be undertaken. To simulate a time series, however, the input data set for 1960 must be updated with each subsequent year. Part of this updating is generated by the static solution for the previous year: an endogenous sectoral investment vector determined last year augments sectoral capital stocks next year. In addition, those exogenous variables that help drive the economy over time must be documented. These include trends in world prices for international tradables, shifts in commercial policy, skilled and unskilled labor force growth economy-wide, productivity advance by sector, and growth in urban and arable land stocks.

Sectoral Productivity Advance and Historical Epochs

Most of the exogenous variables that help drive the Indian economy through time can be documented easily (appendix C), whereas others cannot. One important set of exogenous variables that cannot be adequately documented for India across the 1960s and 1970s is sectoral productivity advance, but it can be inferred once our model has been estimated for 1960. To do so, we first assume that total factor productivity growth was completely absent in each of the ten sectors and sim-

Table 3.1. The 1960 BMW Benchmark Estimates: Inputs, Outputs, and Investment by Sector

	Inputs			Output		
	Capital (Rs. billions)	Skilled Labor (millions)	Unskilled Labor (millions)	Gross Output (Rs. billions)	Value Added (Rs. billions)	Gross Investment (Rs. billions)
Rural activities						
(A) Agriculture	99.663	1.578	132.422	73.641	66.309	5.495
(RS) Private rural services	21.839	1.601	24.440	16.913	14.535	2.672
(PRS) Public rural services	15.000	1.292	0.667	5.775	5.460	1.648
(HRS) Housing	45.390	—	—	5.842	5.769	2.547
Urban activities						
(M) Manufacturing	29.631	1.103	7.043	37.066	18.533	4.079
(KS) Capital-intensive services	17.520	1.336	2.371	20.183	13.152	3.613
(US) Informal urban services	22.847	0.234	10.577	16.461	13.201	1.142
(PUS) Public urban services	28.834	0.201	3.235	6.431	5.881	3.607
(HUS) Low-quality housing	8.805	—	—	2.080	1.988	0.210
(HKS) High-quality housing	24.466	—	—	4.631	4.426	2.215
Total	235.334	7.345	180.755	189.023	149.254	27.228

ulate the economy from 1960 onward. In this simulation, the economy is driven by endogenous accumulation forces, by endogenous labor allocations, and by those exogenous forces that can be documented. Second, we compare the actual historical behavior of sectoral output growth with that predicted by the model when productivity growth is absent. As with standard sources of growth accounting, we treat the gap between actual and simulated output growth as an initial estimate of sectoral productivity advance. Third, these rates of total factor productivity advance are then embedded in the model, and a new simulation is generated from 1960 onward. Since this is a general equilibrium model, nothing ensures that the new output growth predictions will replicate Indian experience, but they should be close. In any case, iteration leads to rapid convergence of simulated and actual values. In short, we emerge with estimates of sectoral total factor productivity growth for the Indian economy from 1960 to 1981 (table 3.2). To our knowledge, this table offers the first comprehensive documentation of Indian sectoral productivity growth, although I. J. Ahluwalia (1983) has recently offered some estimates for industry alone.

Table 3.2. Simulated Real Net Output Trends and Total Factor Productivity Growth by Sector, 1960–1981

	A Agriculture	RS Rural Services and Manufacturing	PSR Rural Public Services	M Urban Manufacturing	KS Urban Modern Services	US Urban Informal Services	PSU Urban Public Services	Total Nonhousing
1960	1.000	1.000	1.000	1.000	1.000	1.000	1.000	1.000
1964	1.095	1.245	1.407	1.467	1.354	1.250	1.322	1.223
1971	1.216	1.417	2.169	1.913	2.066	1.516	1.830	1.507
1977	1.404	1.717	3.076	2.635	2.966	1.884	2.507	1.913
1981	1.444	1.958	4.208	3.094	4.061	2.156	3.076	2.221
Annual Output Growth Rate, %								
1960–64	2.3	5.6	8.9	10.1	7.9	5.7	7.2	5.2
1964–71	1.5	1.9	6.4	3.9	6.2	2.8	4.8	3.0
1971–77	2.4	3.3	6.0	5.5	6.2	3.7	5.4	4.1
1977–81	0.5	3.3	8.1	4.1	8.2	3.4	5.2	3.8
1960–81	1.8	3.3	7.1	5.5	6.9	3.7	5.5	3.9
Estimated Annual Rate of Total Factor Productivity Growth, %								
1960–64	0.18	3.07	3.19	3.56	−0.40	3.23	−0.38	
1965–71	−0.19	−0.25	3.59	−0.76	0.45	1.07	0.13	
1972–77	1.43	0.91	1.17	0.07	3.43	2.34	0.90	
1978–81	−0.85	1.38	5.28	1.00	1.28	1.32	1.45	

Note: The total factor productivity growth rate in agriculture for 1978–81 excludes the impact of drought for those years. In all other years, a rainfall index is available and has been used in the model. The index was unavailable for the later years, thus understating productivity change.

These total factor productivity growth estimates are critical to understanding Indian development and city growth over the past thirty years, and we shall have more to say about them below. But for the moment, note that table 3.2 reveals several distinct productivity epochs. For example, impressive rates were recorded for manufacturing in the early 1960s, but these rates have not been sustained. Since total factor productivity growth is estimated as a residual—absorbing the effects of a long list of forces including shifts in government regulations, short-run macro shocks, as well as true technological events—to assume that the forces affecting it were constant over the two decades would be a mistake. Indeed, government policies toward decentralization and heavy industry have had a strong productivity impact on urban sectors, and these policies have not been promoted uniformly since 1960. In agriculture, the rate of adoption of intensive seed/fertilizer/irrigation packages has had a major impact on productivity advance there, and it too has not proceeded at a steady pace.

Given the variety in productivity advances estimated in table 3.2, we have broken recent Indian history down into four epochs: 1960–64, 1965–71, 1972–77, and 1978–81. While these four epochs in India's recent economic history are guided by what appear to be major shifts in the rate and location of productivity advance, the precise dates marking the beginning and the end of an epoch are dictated in part by data availability. As a result, these epochs may conform only imperfectively to true productivity epochs. Nevertheless, how do these epochs conform to policy regimes, to weather, and to conditions in world markets?

The first breaking point, 1964–65, may be the most contentious. According to Bhagwati and Srinivasan (1975), trade policy regimes coincide only roughly with our first two productivity epochs. Quantitative import restrictions, stagnant exports, abundant foreign aid, and investment shifts toward heavy industry were characteristic of 1960–62, while export subsidies became increasingly important during the following four years. Thus, the first half of the 1960s seems to have been characterized by an import substitution strategy. Marked trade liberalization occurred in 1966, with devaluation of the rupee and reductions in trade subsidies and tariffs. This brief liberalization regime ended with the poor 1968 harvest. Both 1965 and 1966 were years of severe drought, while, in addition, 1965 was a year of war. Although it is clear that changes in government investment policy, trade policy, and agricultural productivity growth all suggest the commencement of a new epoch somewhere in the mid-1960s, exactly where in the mid-1960s is not so clear. We have chosen to begin the second epoch in 1965.[3]

3. The primary drawback of this choice is that it serves to spread the green revolution more evenly across the 1960s, rather than concentrating it in the latter part of the decade.

The second break occurs between 1971 and 1972. It reflects an acceleration in the green revolution. While the green revolution of the 1960s was characterized by large productivity gains largely in irrigated wheat in the northwest (Sanderson and Roy, 1979, p. 5), the second surge in the 1970s saw growth in rice yields and the extension of earlier productivity gains to new parts of India. It also appears that the steep decline in manufacturing productivity growth observed during the latter part of the 1960s continued during this period.

The third epoch ends in 1977[4] because productivity performance was quite different from 1978 to 1981, especially in manufacturing. This shift in sectoral productivity advance is hardly surprising, since Indian economic policy moved away from the Emergency period and began a strong liberalization swing in the late 1970s, and many stagnant industries experienced renewed growth as a result. Such forces are revealed in table 3.2 by the significant rates of productivity growth in manufacturing, although the rate apparently diminished in agriculture.

We shall return to these "epochs" in chapter 6, since it appears that many other differences in the economic environment of these periods, in conjunction with these productivity forces, help account for Indian experience with city growth since 1960.

Assessing the Sectoral Productivity Growth Estimates

Table 3.2 presents value-added growth rates for all nonhousing sectors from 1960 to 1981. During the period as a whole, total (constant 1960 price) value added grew at a rate of 3.9 percent per annum, implying a per capita nonhousing income growth rate of 1.7 percent. Overall, output growth was highest in the modern sectors (*PSR*, *KS*, *M*, and *PSU*). Given the considerable capital accumulation that occurred in manufacturing, however, it is surprising that growth was not considerably more rapid there, especially between 1965 and 1977. The explanation, of course, is to be found in the very disappointing productivity performance.

While the most striking long-run productivity event seems to have been the negative total factor productivity growth registered in manufacturing between 1965 and 1971, as well as the absence of any productivity growth there between 1972 and 1977, other characteristics of Indian productivity performance were notable over the two decades.

4. Comparable rainfall indices end at that point. More critical, 1977 is the last year for which labor force figures have been published offering industry/location/sex cross-tabulations. However, preliminary labor force figures from the 1981 census have become available to us very recently. The text relies on our effort to reconcile the 1977 and the 1981 figures.

One of these was the instability in agricultural productivity advance, which was slow in the 1960s, fast up to 1977, and slow again in the late 1970s. (Actually, estimated total factor productivity growth was negative in agriculture in 1978–81, but this reflects our inability to control for the impact of drought for these recent years.) Another striking attribute was the very slow rate of productivity advance in modern urban services in the 1960s, followed by very fast rates in the 1970s. Yet another was the impressive rate of productivity advance in informal urban services, a sector that conventional wisdom has always characterized as technologically stagnant.

These epochs reflect changes in unbalanced productivity advance that are likely to have had a significant impact on the relative rates of city job creation, city immigration, city growth, and urbanization. For example, the early 1960s seem to conform to the sterotypical pattern of productivity advance, in which manufacturing leads, agriculture lags, and urban services show little gain. This pattern, so typical of industrial revolutions everywhere, is repeated in the late 1970s and early 1980s. In between, however, this stereotypical pattern disappears. Indeed, between 1965 and 1977 agriculture's productivity advance far exceeded that in manufacturing. The point here is not simply the economywide rate of productivity advance that these sectoral rates implied, but the *unbalanced* character of that productivity advance. In the early 1960s, when the rates of total factor productivity growth in manufacturing were very high, 3.56 percent per annum, they exceeded that in agriculture by 3.38 percent ($=3.56 - 0.18$). To the extent that unbalanced productivity advance favoring manufacturing is a key "engine of city growth," the epoch 1960–64 must have been very favorable to city job creation and immigration. The productivity growth gap favoring manufacturing disappeared, however, in the years immediately following. In fact, the gap became *negative* from 1965 to 1971, -0.57 percent, and became even more so between 1972 and 1977, -1.36 percent, before returning to a more conventional difference favoring manufacturing after 1978.

How do these estimates stack up against the scattered studies that appear in the literature? Even under the best of conditions, the studies reported below could not possibly duplicate the estimates reported in table 3.2. After all, those studies have nothing to say about the service sectors, and even in the commodity-producing sectors they cover different time periods, employ different levels of sectoral aggregation, and, for the most part, ignore skilled labor inputs entirely.[5] They do, however,

5. Consequently, most other studies will pick up skill deepening (an important but quite distinct phenomenon) as part of total factor productivity growth.

help confront two stylized facts that emerge from table 3.2: the possibility of negative rates of total factor productivity advance in manufacturing during the middle years of the period, and the stereotypical unbalanced productivity advance with agriculture lagging behind in the early and late years of the period.

The total factor productivity growth estimates for manufacturing generated by BMW seem roughly consistent with those of other studies, the technological regression implied by the negative rates over so much of the period in particular. A. Banerjee (1971, p. 12), for example, estimates annual rates for manufacturing in the early 1960s at -2.9 percent per annum.[6] Although BMW estimated high and positive manufacturing total factor productivity growth for that period, it generates negative rates for the subsequent twelve years. Sakong and Narasimham (1974) found that a major cause of manufacturing's slow productivity advance in the late 1950s was the negative contribution stemming from the relatively rapid expansion of industries with low total factor productivity. While this apparent misallocation of resources probably reflects the second Five-Year Plan's emphasis on heavy industry, it also offers a likely explanation for the negative rates recorded subsequently. I. J. Ahluwalia (1983, table 6.1, p. 212) estimates total factor productivity growth in registered manufacturing to have been -0.3 percent per annum from 1959 to 1965. (Note that 1965 is an unusually unfavorable terminal year, thus explaining much of the difference between Ahluwalia's and our finding for 1960–64.) Moreover, of the twenty two-digit ISIC manufacturing industry groups, eleven recorded negative total factor productivity growth between 1959 and 1965, while ten did so between 1966 and 1978. Mehta (1980, pp. 145–46) finds negative rates at an even more disaggregated level for some important industries between 1963 and 1965, with particularly pronounced declines in iron and steel (-5.9 percent) and woolen textiles (-3.7 percent). Thus, the technological regression in manufacturing implied by our model between 1965 and 1971 is hardly an atypical finding.

On the other hand, Evenson and Jha (1973, pp. 216–17) report much higher rates of total factor productivity advance in agriculture than that generated by BMW. A weighted average of their Indian state estimates implies what we view to be implausibly high rates of total factor productivity growth: 0.66 percent per annum between 1956–61 and 1963–65, and 1.16 percent per annum between 1963–65 and 1969–71. The estimates in table 3.2 imply no productivity advance at all between 1960

6. This extremely negative rate reflects a precipitous drop in 1964 and hence may be unrepresentative of the normal trend during the early 1960s. (Banerjee's series ends in 1964.) Banerjee's implied total factor productivity growth rate estimate from 1960 to 1963 is, however, still -0.5 percent.

and 1971. The disparity may be due to the use of different benchmark dates, but it is more likely to be due to the fact that our measures exclude the influence of monsoon quality, while theirs do not.

This section has dwelt on the productivity growth issue at length since good estimates of sectoral productivity advance are essential to any understanding of Indian urbanization and structural change over the past thirty years, as chapters 4 and 6 will make clear. While there is rough consistency between our new estimates of sectoral total factor productivity advance and older estimates scattered through the literature, ours are sufficiently different to warrant far more future research to resolve the conflict. In the meantime, we believe that the new estimates reported in table 3.2 are superior to the older estimates in the literature. They are certainly more comprehensive across time and consistent across sectors.

3.3 Testing the BMW Model: The Quality of Indian Data

Indian data provide a wealth of information available for very few nations. Indeed, the extent of the labor force and output disaggregation by rural or urban location may be unique, thus permitting an assessment of the predictions of the BMW model in far greater detail than has been possible for previous CGEs. Nevertheless, problems of data comparability across the surveys and censuses for various years are substantial, and they make evaluation of the model's performance difficult. We are often uncertain whether a poor prediction is a fault of the model or of the historical data.

If we had complete confidence in the historical data, a sound testing procedure would involve defining a loss function over the deviations in predicted from observed values of key economic variables. We could then examine both the magnitude of this function (say, the square root of the sum of the squares of predicted less actual values) and compare its performance during the period simulated. We could also examine the sensitivity of the loss function to variations in the parameters for which we have the least confidence.

Our view is that such procedures require far better documentation of recent Indian economic history than is available. The target we are shooting at with the model is, to put it bluntly, blurred. This is particularly true of endogenous variables other than sectoral outputs, and it is these variables against which the model should be judged. These problems are sufficiently important to be dwelt on at length in the next section.

Documenting Recent History

National accounts statistics provide the main source for time series on sectoral output, relative prices, government revenue and expenditures, savings, and sectoral investment.[7] Sectoral labor force allocations are documented in the 1961, 1971, and 1981 national censuses, as well as in the sixteenth, twenty-seventh, and thirty-second rounds of the National Sample Survey.[8] Both sources present problems in generating a consistent data set over time.

A relatively minor problem results from occasional but major revisions in the national accounts by the Central Statistical Office. As a consequence, the figures used to estimate parameters are not completely consistent with the figures used to generate historical time series. While these problems introduce some inconsistencies, there is little reason to believe that they are major.

The more serious problem underlies the construction of the sectoral employment series. The census definitions used in calculating the 1961, 1971, and 1981 labor force estimates are not identical, nor are they consistent with the definitions used in the National Sample Survey (NSS) twenty-seventh (1972) and thirty-second (1977) rounds. Subsequent revisions in the 1971 estimates have attempted to limit the discrepancy between it and the 1961 census definitions, but even these figures clearly omit a large number of workers included in 1961, particularly rural women. The 1981 census divided workers into both "main" and "secondary" categories; the 1971 census definition seems to fall in between the broader and more limited 1981 definitions.

Changing labor force definitions over time introduces substantial uncertainty regarding overall trends. Consider the aggregate rate of labor force growth, taken as exogenous in the model. Census and NSS figures report the following labor force aggregates (in millions):[9]

---

7. The general reference is Central Statistical Office, *National Accounts Statistics* (New Delhi: Government of India, various issues).

8. For the NSS sixteenth round—National Sample Survey (1960); for the twenty-seventh and thirty-second rounds—Seal (1981); for the 1981 census—Padmanabha (1983); for other censuses—Central Statistical Office: *Census of India 1971* and *Census of India 1961*. Results from the censuses and NSS rounds have also appeared in various issues of *Sarvekshana* and *Economic and Political Weekly*.

9. The NSS sixteenth round and the 1961 census figures are consistent. Our most detailed labor force sources follow. For 1961: agricultural laborers and cultivators—*Census of India 1961*, *Census of India 1971* (series-I-India; miscellaneous studies, paper 1 of 1974), *Report on Resurvey on Economic Questions—Some Results* (1974, p. 21); all other workers—*Census of India 1961* (vol. 1, pt. 1-C(i), table B-IV). For 1971: agricultural laborers and cultivators—same as for 1961; all other workers—*Census of India 1971* (pt. II-B(iii),

	1961	1971	1972	1977	1981
Labor force	188.7	180.4	236.3	236.9	221.3
Annual growth rate, based on					
comparisons with 1961 (%)		negative	2.1	1.4	0.8
comparisons with 1971 (%)				4.6	2.1

During the period as a whole, the entire Indian population grew at 2.21 percent per annum, while the prime age male population grew somewhat more rapidly, at about 2.5 percent per annum (Premi, 1982). Consequently, total labor force growth figures of 1.4 percent per annum or less imply implausible declines in labor force participation rates, while the 4.6 percent figure is unbelievably high. World Bank estimates (1983, II, p. 42) suggest growth rates of 1.64 to 1.80 percent per annum. However, because the 1981 and 1971 census figures are most comparable (followed by the NSS twenty-seventh round and the 1961 census), and because comparison of the 1961–72 figures with various versions of the 1971–81 figures suggests a labor force growth rate at roughly the national population growth rate, we have assumed that the aggregate labor force participation rate was stable throughout the period.

Unfortunately, comparability problems are not limited to aggregate labor force growth rates. The sorts of workers included in some estimates and excluded in others were hardly distributed uniformly across the seven sectors that employ labor in BMW. Instead, the workers included in some but excluded in other estimates were overwhelmingly casual laborers, and thus definitional changes influenced disproportionately the employment estimates in informal urban services (US), rural services and small scale manufacturing (RS), and, above all, agriculture (A). Thus, considerable uncertainty surrounds both the true sectoral share breakdown and the true urban/rural distribution of workers.[10] Observed increases in the proportion of the labor force in urban activities may reflect true increases, or they may reflect definitional changes that served to exclude a higher proportion of rural workers, or, most likely, they may reflect both.

Uncertainty about the underlying historical data base on the labor force implies uncertainty about macro aggregates as well. To a large

---

table B-IV). For 1977: *Sarvekshana* (July–October, 1981). For 1981: agricultural laborers and cultivators—Padmanabha (1983), *Census of India 1981* (paper 3 of 1981, pp. 3–4); all other workers—*Census of India 1981* (series 1 India, pt. II, special report and tables based on 5 percent sample data, 1984).

10. The most serious inconsistency occurs between 1961 and 1971. The results of the NSS twenty-seventh round (as reported in Seal, 1981, pp. 70–71) suggest labor force estimates that, at least in the aggregate, appear to be roughly comparable with the 1961 census.

degree, output figures by urban and rural location are available in the official statistics only at high levels of aggregation.[11] Consequently, we converted spatially aggregated national accounts data into the model's spatially distinct sectors by relying on the spatially disaggregated employment figures and assumptions about productivity differentials (appendix B). Moreover, as urban/rural labor force distributions within sectors change over time, sometimes considerably, we have assumed that any such shifts follow a smooth trend. Incorporating these trends is important, as many real shifts have taken place in response to government policies, to changes in technology, and to changes in product mix. Thus, uncertainty regarding the quality of the labor force estimates also implies uncertainty regarding sectoral output estimates.

In addition, since relative prices are derived by comparing current value with constant price output from the national accounts, labor force allocation errors may also spill over into estimates of location-specific relative prices. The same can be said of sectoral investment figures.

The Bottom Line

This somewhat pessimistic recital warns us that the historical data base is imprecise and, hence, that the model's performance can be assessed only in terms of its rough consistency with the historical "facts." Despite this conclusion, however, we should remind the reader that the Indian data are virtually unrivaled by those from other Third World nations. Indeed, the quality of the Indian data makes it possible for us to assess the quality of the model to a far greater degree than has been true for other Third World CGE models.

3.4 Testing the BMW Model: Rules of the Game

The previous section makes clear that the quality of the historical data prevents us from making precise statements about the model's ability to replicate the "facts" of recent Indian economic history. Furthermore, even if these problems were overcome, the nature of the model limits the information to be gained from the use of formal econometric techniques. BMW is, after all, a long-run equilibrium model. While some short-run disturbances are introduced as exogenous variables—like weather conditions and world price shocks, most aspects of short-run disequilibria are omitted. Thus, even for the short-run shocks introduced, the model is designed to capture only their effects on equilibrium

---

11. This should not be taken as criticism of the Indian data. To the contrary, it is remarkable that *any* detailed spatial breakdown exists.

outcomes, not the short-run disequilibria that they tend to generate. As a consequence, we seek only to establish that the model provides a plausible empirical description of India's economic performance over the long run.

Which variables are most important in evaluating the model's performance? To begin with, sectoral outputs are not relevant to the assessment. After all, we have already pointed out that the model has been forced to replicate observed sectoral output growth in order to derive estimates of sectoral productivity advance. Furthermore, since GNP and per capita income growth are derived from sectoral value-added trends, they can hardly be useful in the assessment either.

Other endogenous variables are more appropriate indicators of the model's ability to replicate recent Indian economic history, the pattern of relative prices in particular. If forces prevent product markets from clearing in India, then there is little reason to expect that relative price trends generated by BMW will be similar to those documented in the official statistics. Thus, the behavior of relative prices is critical to an assessment of BMW. In addition, endogenously determined real wages, investment allocations, sources of savings, and government revenues can all be compared with observed series. Finally, and most important, BMW must track Indian urbanization and city growth experience.

In summary, the plausibility of the BMW model is assessed by comparing observed with predicted trends in relative output prices, factor prices, employment distribution, urbanization, investment, sources of savings, and government revenue. It seems likely that any major flaws in the model would be exposed by such comparisons. Indeed, these comparisons can be seen as an unusually severe test of the appropriateness of a modified neoclassical model in a developing country setting, since the ability of models to predict such a wide range of variables is virtually never examined. Instances where BMW tracks poorly also will suggest times and places where market processes in India broke down.

3.5 Testing the BMW Model: Fact or Fiction?

Relative Prices

Table 3.3 documents observed and simulated nonhousing output prices at three-year intervals, with all values expressed relative to the M sector price.[12] As it turns out, BMW does very well in tracking four of the six relative prices, and does badly in only one case.

12. The numeraire in BMW is taken to be the world price of manufactures imported by India. However, looking at prices expressed relative to a domestic good permits us to

Table 3.3. Relative Prices by Sector (Simulated and Actual Values), 1960–1980

Sector:	A	RS	PSR	M	KS	US	PSU
A. Simulated Prices, Relative to the Price of Urban Manufactures							
1960	100.0	100.0	100.0	100.0	100.0	100.0	100.0
1963	119.1	105.7	104.0	100.0	110.2	95.7	102.8
1966	142.5	100.7	96.2	100.0	108.0	86.9	95.0
1969	136.8	112.8	91.6	100.0	104.3	86.2	95.6
1972	141.8	101.0	83.1	100.0	95.1	76.2	87.2
1975	144.4	119.9	92.4	100.0	88.9	77.2	92.5
1978	150.2	117.4	91.0	100.0	83.8	73.6	90.4
1980	150.9	114.3	85.3	100.0	80.4	71.9	87.2
B. Actual Prices, Relative to the Price of Urban Manufacturers							
1960	100.0	100.0	100.0	100.0	100.0	100.0	100.0
1963	109.7	98.8	97.1	100.0	98.7	99.4	99.4
1966	147.2	104.4	99.9	100.0	107.5	118.4	102.0
1969	136.0	105.5	99.4	100.0	107.0	117.3	103.0
1972	135.2	104.4	89.0	100.0	100.3	117.5	95.5
1975	106.5	105.6	79.1	100.0	98.7	117.7	85.4
1978	106.5	108.0	78.6	100.0	97.7	115.2	96.2
1980	103.6	109.3	65.0	100.0	86.9	119.5	81.7

Note: With the exception of 1960 and 1980, A sector prices are based on 3-year moving averages.

The most important relative price is P_A/P_M, since agriculture and manufacturing generate about 60 percent of nonhousing value added. The simulated series tracks the observed relative price closely through 1972, with trivial differences in the latter part of the 1960s. The striking rise in the relative price of food due in large part to the poor 1965 and 1966 crop harvests is recorded (142.5 simulated in 1966 versus 147.2 actual), and the stability in the relative price in the late 1960s and early 1970s is also captured by the model. BMW's predictions diverge from history after 1972, especially between 1972 and 1975. We have no clear explanation for this result, although changing food stock policy and its depressing impact on expectations (not captured in BMW) and hence prices may well have contributed to the divergence. The model does much better thereafter.

The model is quite successful in tracking the relative prices of both urban and rural public services. During the 1960s, P_{PSU}/P_M is stable, hovering between 95 and 103 in the simulation, and between 99 and 103 in reality. The 1970s witnessed a decline in the relative price of urban public services: by 1980 it had fallen to 87 in the simulation (versus an observed value of 82). Since *PSU* provides only intermediates, its price decline reflects a windfall gain to *PSU*-using urban activities. Presum-

concentrate on the model's ability to track internal relative price ratios, the relative prices that matter in the model.

ably, it may also reflect a relative slowdown in the growth of demand for PSU services. In fact, as table 3.2 shows, the 1970s were characterized by rapid KS and slow M growth; because manufacturing is far more PSU intensive than is KS, the pattern of urban output growth was indeed PSU saving.

PSR prices tend to oscillate around a declining trend in the simulation, falling steadily up to 1980. Recorded prices are fairly stable throughout the 1960s, but then they also begin a precipitous decline in the 1970s. By 1980, the recorded P_{PSR}/P_M is only 65 (versus a substantial but smaller decline in the simulated price to 85).

The relative price of modern KS services initially rises, both in history ($P_{KS}/P_M = 107.5$ in 1966) and in the simulation (108 in 1966). After 1966, the model accurately predicts the consistent decline in the relative price of KS.

The model also predicts trends in the relative price of rural services quite well. The RS relative price rises throughout the period, reaching 114.3 in 1980 in the simulation, and 109.3 in reality.

The model does poorly, however, for one sector, informal urban services. The simulated relative price of US declines at a fairly stable rate (to 71.9 in 1980), while the observed price rises erratically (to 119.5 in 1980). In defense of the model, it should be pointed out that this sector is inadequately documented in the official statistics.

Our summary evaluation of the model's ability to replicate relative price trends is that it does extraordinarily well for the 1960s, quite well through the mid-1970s, and credibly even through 1980. The exception to this statement is P_{US}. Otherwise, the simulation consistently tracks trends *and* predicts most turning points.

Fiscal Aggregates, Accumulation, and Investment Allocation

The model replicates aggregate fiscal and savings flows equally well. Table 3.4 presents estimates of real domestic revenue for the state and federal governments. Simulated government income trends parallel observed revenue trends closely, the index undershooting by only 3.3 percent in 1974–76 and by 4.1 percent in 1980–81. The government revenue share in nonhousing GDP rises from 11.4 to 18.7 percent in the simulation and from 12.2 to 21 percent in fact, an increase of 7.3 versus 8.8 percentage points.

Both the simulated and the historical capital formation series in table 3.5 show only modest growth until the late 1970s. During the 1960s, the share of capital formation in GDP was around 18 to 19 percent, save for some "big push" years in the middle 1960s; by 1974–76, the share had risen to 19.7 percent in the simulation, compared with 21.7 percent

Table 3.4. Public Sector Resources from Domestic Sources

			Index: 1960 = 100	
	Actual	Simulated	Actual	Simulated
	Rs. billion (1960 prices)			
1960	17.08	15.66	100.0	100.0
1962–64	22.01	20.48	128.9	130.8
1965–67	25.02	24.19	146.5	154.5
1968–70	29.32	28.22	171.7	180.2
1971–73	34.49	32.59	201.9	208.1
1974–76	43.20	38.29	252.9	244.5
1977–79	54.77	46.63	320.7	297.8
1980–81	59.77	52.57	349.9	335.7

Note: Actual values are deflated by a GDP deflator. Simulated values are deflated by a moving weight deflator. Differences in base year values reflect the use of an improved and revised historical data set.

Table 3.5. Aggregate Capital Formation, 1960–1981

	Gross Domestic Capital Formation		Sources of Investible Funds, %		
	Total	% of GDP	Foreign	Public Sector	Private Sector
(1) Actual Values					
1960	25.44	18.9	18.9	16.7	64.4
1962–64	29.00	18.9	14.9	21.1	64.0
1965–67	35.59	21.9	15.5	14.3	70.2
1968–70	36.77	19.5	5.7	14.6	79.7
1971–73	44.42	22.0	4.3	9.3	86.4
1974–76	48.51	21.7	−4.6	18.2	86.4
1977–79	62.57	24.1	−4.3	14.6	89.7
1980–81	69.38	24.1	6.9	11.0	82.1
(2) Simulated Values					
1960	27.23	18.2	17.8	14.1	68.1
1962–64	33.68	19.7	12.0	15.8	72.2
1965–67	36.12	20.2	12.7	12.2	75.1
1968–70	37.70	18.2	4.2	15.3	80.5
1971–73	43.52	19.2	5.0	17.9	77.1
1974–76	50.85	19.7	−2.7	27.3	75.4
1977–79	58.85	19.5	−0.4	25.0	75.4
1980–81	67.97	20.6	4.5	22.8	72.7

in fact. Both series rise over the remainder of the decade, although the simulation tends to underpredict the increase.[13] Given how complex the determinants of aggregate capital formation are, the model predicts capital formation trends surprisingly well: while gross domestic capital

13. Because the national accounts understate housing's contribution to GDP, the official investment shares may have an upward bias, unless, of course, the official housing in-

formation grew at 4.9 percent per annum 1960–81, the model predicts a growth rate of 4.5 percent per annum. The model does even better in the 1970s, when both series grow at 5.1 percent per annum.

While the model tracks aggregate capital formation closely, it does less well—not surprisingly—in identifying trends in the sources of savings as well as investment allocations across sectors.

A striking feature of Indian development since 1960 has been the rise in the relative importance of private sector savings, while both government and foreign savings shares have fallen. BMW replicates those trends across the 1960s, and it also captures the continued decline in India's relative reliance on foreign capital across the 1970s. However, it fails to predict a continuation of the rise in the private sector's share in the 1970s at the expense of government savings. In other words, while government revenue sources are closely replicated, the model fails to capture the observed rise in debt-financed expenditure across the 1970s. This is precisely what occurred: the ratio of the domestically financed component of the overall deficit to the sum of current and capital expenditures rose from 15.8 percent in 1973 to 22 percent in 1977, peaking at 33.6 percent in 1979.[14]

By far the most difficult task for any multisectoral model is to replicate investment allocation across sectors. As table 3.6 indicates, BMW's performance on this score is fair but hardly outstanding.[15] Consider three examples. First, from the mid-1970s onwards, the model accurately predicts both the continued growth of the urban modern share (M and KS) and the decline in the rural private share (A and RS). But second, while the model picks up the decline in the investment share received by PSU that occurred in the late 1960s, it understates the magnitude of the fall and overstates the magnitude of the rise in the late 1970s. And third, when the rural private and the urban modern sectors are disaggregated, the model's accuracy is further diminished: the model consistently overpredicts the investment shares in A and M, while it underpredicts the investment share in RS.

What accounts for the model's inability to replicate investment allocation? A likely explanation involves increases in intersectoral capital mobility in the 1970s, particularly between rural and urban areas. This

---

vestment figures are also understated, and they are. Indeed, we think the housing investment figures are so poor that we have made no effort here to report the ability of BMW to track the distribution between housing and nonhousing investment.

14. See the World Bank, 1981, table 5.7, p. 254.

15. As we stressed in note 13, housing investment is not reported in table 3.5 or discussed in the text since the official housing investment figures are, we believe, grossly understated. Any comparison of the official figures with the model's predictions would be pointless.

Table 3.6. Sectoral Gross Capital Formation Distribution, 1960–1981

	Rural Private Sector			Urban Modern Sector			Urban Informal Sector	Public Services Sector	
	A	RS	A + RS	KS	M	M + KS	US	PSU	PSR
(1) Actual Values, Share in Total Nonhousing Investment									
1960	15.7%	21.4%	37.1%	21.9%	13.4%	35.3%	8.4%	10.0%	8.9%
1962–64	15.1	18.6	33.7	18.5	13.2	31.7	7.0	16.1	11.2
1965–67	15.8	18.8	34.6	22.3	16.0	38.3	7.1	11.3	8.5
1968–70	18.2	15.9	34.1	24.1	15.8	39.9	8.4	9.6	7.6
1971–73	18.3	16.4	34.7	20.9	16.5	37.4	10.1	9.3	8.5
1974–76	16.4	21.0	37.4	17.7	16.9	34.0	11.3	9.0	7.7
1977–79	19.0	19.7	38.7	17.9	17.4	35.3	8.6	9.4	8.0
1980–81	16.8	18.1	34.9	18.2	18.5	36.7	9.3	10.1	9.0
(2) Simulated Values, Share in Total Nonhousing Investment									
1960	24.7	13.6	38.3	13.2	12.7	25.9	7.6	16.2	11.9
1962–64	25.2	10.7	35.9	10.7	20.1	30.8	6.9	15.6	11.6
1965–67	29.5	7.0	36.5	15.3	20.0	35.3	5.3	14.3	8.6
1968–70	25.9	11.1	37.0	13.6	23.5	37.1	5.6	12.7	7.7
1971–73	25.9	9.4	35.3	12.6	25.8	38.4	5.1	13.9	7.2
1974–76	23.3	9.4	32.7	9.8	30.3	40.1	4.8	15.2	7.1
1977–79	24.9	8.4	33.3	19.0	22.5	41.5	4.2	14.4	6.6
1980–81	22.6	8.9	31.5	14.3	27.6	41.9	3.9	15.6	7.1

increased mobility undoubtedly was enhanced by the dramatic modernization of agriculture in the northwest and much of the southeast, as well as by active government intervention in the capital market. In contrast, the rural/urban capital market segmentation assumed in the model restricted such flows in the simulation.

Our summary evaluation of the model's ability to replicate observed accumulation and investment allocation patterns is mixed. The aggregate accumulation predictions are fairly accurate, but the investment allocation trends are not.

Real Wages and Cost-of-Living Differentials

Observed and simulated urban/rural cost-of-living differentials are presented in table 3.7, and it appears that BMW predicts trends in the urban–rural CPI ratio quite accurately. We were distressed initially to find that the simulations predicted rural prices rising more rapidly than urban prices, since one of the "stylized facts" of economic development is that urban living costs rise at the more rapid pace.[16] However, for

16. This stylized fact is replicated in Kelley and Williamson's (1984, p. 196) simulation of a representative developing country. Historical evidence from other developing economies confirming these stylized facts can be found in Williamson (1986).

Table 3.7. Urban–Rural Cost-of-Living Differential

	Observed Cost of Living Differential			Simulated Differential
	---	---	---	---
	Agricultural Laborers (1)	Industrial Workers (2)	Ratio (2 ÷ 1) (3)	CPI for Urban Formal Sector Unskilled Workers ÷ CPI for Rural Unskilled Labor (4)
1960	100	100	100	100
1961	103	104	101	99
1962	110	108	98	98
1963	118	113	96	98
1964	143	124	87	96
1965	158	132	84	99
1966	190	146	77	98
1967	206	159	77	98
1968	185	161	87	98
1969	193	177	92	98
1970	192	186	97	99
1971	200	192	96	98
1972	225	207	92	101
1973	283	250	88	98
1974	368	317	86	100
1975	317	313	99	97
1976	302	301	100	100
1977	336	324	96	99
1978	329	331	101	100
1979	344	360	105	102
1980				102
1981				103

Note: The observed differentials are constructed from V. K. R. V. Rao (1983), table 3.8, p. 27.

most of the 1960s, India did not conform to those stylized facts. Indeed, the CPI for agricultural laborers relative to that for industrial workers rose even faster up to 1967 than BMW predicts. Why did rural prices rise more rapidly than urban prices in the 1960s? In part, the answer lies with the fact that the very poor harvests of the mid-1960s had a stronger impact on rural than on urban living costs.[17] In the early 1960s, a prourban bias in publicly supplied infrastructure also helped keep the city cost of living down.

17. As M. S. Ahluwalia (1978) has shown, much of the real price and income effects of the poor harvests carried roughly a one-year lag. In BMW, the impact is immediate. There are various subtle reasons why the very poor harvests in the mid-1960s had a stronger impact on rural living costs, but the main reason is simply that their food share in total consumption was larger.

The 1970s were characterized by a rebound in the urban/rural relative cost of living; by 1979 this index had risen to 105, a rise that the simulation captures (102). Presumably, the same factors that caused the index to decline in the 1960s explain its reversal in the following decade. The dismal productivity growth performance of the M and PSU sectors can be contrasted with the high productivity gains in all rural sectors in the early and middle 1970s (table 3.2). Moreover, the high productivity growth experienced by the KS sector had few direct or indirect benefits for unskilled workers' living costs, since KS output is used only minimally as a final good or as an intermediate input into final goods consumed by unskilled urban workers. Thus, urban productivity slowdown combined with large rural productivity gains as the green revolution took hold led to the curtailment of rural relative to urban cost of living.

Consistent time series for real earnings are difficult to obtain, and table 3.8 offers a recorded series only for industrial workers. The comparisons obtained with simulated real earnings of unskilled workers are imperfect, as the coverage in the recorded series includes only a fraction of the urban unskilled labor force, even in the modern sector. Recorded

Table 3.8. Indexes of Real Earnings per Worker (1965 = 100)

	Observed Values for Industrial Workers		Simulated Values for Urban Formal Sector Unskilled Workers	
	Deflated by All-India CPI	Deflated by CPI for Industrial Workers	Deflated by CPI for Unskilled Workers	Deflated by GDP Deflator
1963	101.7	95.8	124.0	113.9
1964	99.7	98.4	123.7	112.9
1965	100.0	100.0	100.0	100.0
1966	96.2	98.2	106.5	104.9
1967	100.8	105.3	115.1	110.1
1968	108.3	113.1	107.9	106.6
1969	111.1	107.5	112.6	109.6
1970	115.1	111.2	114.3	110.9
1971	117.6	114.1	114.0	111.4
1972			95.5	102.1
1973	111.6	107.8	106.9	108.4
1974	109.2	105.5	98.6	104.4
1975	123.2	119.5	111.1	111.6
1976			97.6	105.1
1977			106.1	110.8
1978			106.7	112.2
1979			100.3	110.2
1980			102.1	112.6
1981			99.3	112.4

Note: The observed values are taken from V. K. R. V. Rao (1983, table 8.8, pp. 122–23), whose series starts in 1963.

real industrial wages were stagnant throughout the first half of the 1960s, rose about 15 percent between 1966 and 1971, and then oscillated around this new plateau up to 1975. While simulated wages fall sharply in the mid-1960s, they reveal pretty much the same behavior as actual wages thereafter. Relative stability in real wages both in fact and in the model is hardly surprising given slow growth in per capita output, and given that the growth stemmed largely from capital and skill deepening in capital- and skilled labor–intensive sectors.

Overall, the model does remarkably well in predicting real wage trends and cost-of-living differentials.

Labor Force Distribution

Table 3.9 documents simulated and historical trends for the most critical endogenous variables, those describing labor force distribution. For the period as a whole, the simulated urban share of India's labor force rose from 13.9 to 21.3 percent, with the 1960s recording a slightly larger percentage point rise. Unfortunately, changes in the official definition of the labor force affect the measured urbanization rate and thus restrict our ability to test the model's success in tracking historical trends. As discussed above, the 1971–81 figures are more comparable to each other than to 1961, while the results based on the NSS surveys (1972 and 1977) are implausibly low.

Subject to these qualifications on the quality of the historical data, it is clear from table 3.9 that the simulation tracks history quite well. The model accurately captures both the decline in A and RS labor force

Table 3.9. The Labor Force by Sector (%)

	A	RS	PSR	M	KS	US	PSU	(A + RS)	All Rural (A + RS + PSR)	(M + KS)	All Urban (M + KS + US + PSU)
(1) Simulated Shares											
1960	71.2	13.8	1.0	4.3	2.0	5.7	1.8	85.0	86.0	6.3	13.9
1971	68.0	12.9	1.2	6.4	3.2	5.8	2.5	80.9	82.1	9.6	17.9
1972	69.2	11.1	1.4	6.9	3.3	5.5	2.6	80.2	81.6	10.2	18.4
1977	66.0	12.7	1.4	8.0	3.4	5.6	2.9	78.7	80.1	11.4	19.9
1981	64.9	12.3	1.5	8.5	4.0	5.7	3.1	77.2	78.7	12.5	21.3
(2) Observed Shares											
1960	71.1	13.4	1.5	4.1	2.4	6.4	1.1	84.5	86.0	6.5	14.0
1971	69.7	10.3	2.3	5.1	3.7	7.3	1.5	80.0	82.3	8.8	17.7
1972									83.7		16.3
1977	68.5	12.7	2.1	5.1	3.4	6.9	1.3	81.2	83.3	8.5	16.7
1981	65.7	11.0	2.3	6.4	4.4	8.2	1.8	76.7	79.0	10.8	20.8

Note: Initial differences in observed and simulated shares stem from the use of improved and revised data in generating historical time series. Figures may not add up to 100 due to rounding.

shares and its order of magnitude. The rises in *PSR*, *PSU*, *M*, and *KS* shares are replicated as well, with magnitudes of all but *M* being fairly close to the historical series. The simulated stability of the *US* share and the exaggerated rise in the *M* share are the only significant departures from historical trends.

Migration, Urbanization, and City Growth

With regard to overall city growth, the model seems to perform very well. It generates a rise from 13.9 to 21.3 percent urban between 1960 and 1981, very close to the observed rise to 20.8 percent (table 3.9). Between 1971 and 1981, the simulated rise is 3.4 percent, very close to the 3.2 percent increase recorded between the two censuses. The model does equally well for the 1960s. It predicts a 4 percent rise in the urban share of the labor force during the 1960s; history appears to record a rise of 3.7 percent. Thus, urbanization in the 1970s observed both historically and in the simulation represents a slowdown, but the slowdown is a little greater in the simulation.

Table 3.10 presents a more detailed picture of the simulated urbanization process in India from 1960 to 1981. Annual urban growth figures are, of course, unavailable, but the intercensual rates documented in part C of the table appear to mirror closely the historical series. Both the model and the historical series reported in table 3.10 suggest, once again, that urban labor force growth was slower in the 1970s than in the 1960s.[18]

Part B of table 3.10 documents India's simulated city growth experience in more detail by breaking down recent history into the four epochs discussed earlier in this chapter. The city growth slowdown is much more pronounced when the early 1960s are isolated. Here we see the rate of city growth sharply declining from the impressive 6.44 percent per annum in the early 1960s to 3.60 percent per annum from 1964 to 1971, a decline that is recovered only in part during the 1970s. We see an equally dramatic decline in migration rates over the same period: the city in-migration rate declines from 4.12 to 1.54 percent per annum; the rural out-migration rate declines from 0.73 to 0.28 percent per annum; and neither of these sharp declines across the 1960s is recovered in the 1970s. Finally, we see declines in the contribution of migration to increases in the labor force in rural or urban employment: for ex-

18. Despite the urban labor force growth deceleration, urban population growth rates *accelerated* across the 1970s. Since it hardly seems likely that the urban labor participation rate declined at a significant rate across the 1970s, the divergence in trends must be due to problems in the data. The issue is not resolved here, but surely it should attract high priority in future research.

Table 3.10. Labor Force Migration, Urbanization, and City Growth, 1960–1981

A. *Model's Predictions, Annual*

Year	% Urban	City Growth Rate (%)	Rural-Urban Migration (millions)	Net Rural Out-Migration Rate (%)	Net Urban In-Migration Rate (%)
1960	13.9				
1961	14.3	5.10	0.753	0.47	2.89
1962	15.0	7.65	1.492	0.91	5.44
1963	15.7	6.92	1.391	0.83	4.71
1964	16.3	6.12	1.234	0.73	3.91
1965	16.9	5.68	1.163	0.68	3.47
1966	16.9	2.40	0.067	0.04	0.19
1967	17.4	5.35	1.138	0.64	3.14
1968	17.3	1.55	−0.251	−0.14	−0.66
1969	17.7	4.60	0.929	0.50	2.40
1970	17.8	2.57	0.144	0.08	0.35
1971	17.9	3.12	0.377	0.19	0.91
1972	18.4	4.76	1.096	0.56	2.55
1973	18.6	3.33	0.504	0.25	1.12
1974	18.9	4.15	0.901	0.44	1.94
1975	19.2	3.73	0.734	0.35	1.52
1976	19.5	3.79	0.792	0.37	1.58
1977	19.9	4.18	1.026	0.48	1.97
1978	20.7	6.50	2.330	1.07	4.29
1979	21.1	4.42	1.280	0.58	2.21
1980	21.1	1.96	−0.152	−0.07	−0.25
1981	21.3	3.00	0.488	0.21	0.79

B. *Model's Predictions, Epoch Averages*

Epoch	City Growth Rate (% per annum)	Average Rural Out-Migration Rate (% per annum)	Average Urban In-Migration Rate (% per annum)	Migrants as % of Change in Labor Force Urban	Rural
1960–64	6.44	0.73	4.12	65.78	49.94
1964–71	3.60	0.28	1.54	37.91	14.44
1971–77	3.99	0.38	1.74	44.52	21.43
1977–81	3.96	0.44	1.63	43.29	24.95

C. *Model's Predictions and Indian History, Census Years*

	1960–71	1971–81	1960–81
1. City growth, % per annum (compounded)			
Model	4.62	3.98	4.31
History	4.52	3.87	4.21
2. Total increase in share urban, %			
Model	4.0	3.4	7.4
History	3.7	3.2	6.9
3. Increase in share urban, % per annum			
Model	0.36	0.34	0.35
History	0.34	0.32	0.33

Note: Migration flows and rates are derived assuming identical rates of growth of labor force participation in urban and rural areas.

ample, while immigrants accounted for more than 65 percent of the increase in the urban labor force in the early 1960s, they accounted for a little less than 38 percent of the increase between 1964 and 1971. According to the model, India underwent a profound slowdown in city growth after the spectacular rates of the early 1960s.

It should also be stressed that the rates of city growth in India in the early 1960s were also impressive by the standards of the Third World more generally. In the forty-country sample used by Kelley and Williamson (1984, table 3.13, p. 93), the rate of city growth across the 1960s was considerably lower, 4.60 percent per annum; the city in-migration rate was also considerably lower, 1.81 to 2.26 percent per annum; and the contribution of immigration to urban labor force expansion was also smaller, 39.3 percent versus India's 65.8 percent. Thus, there was nothing sedate about India's city growth performance in the early 1960s. Nor can it be said that India is not capable of realizing the city growth performance that characterizes so much of the Third World.

On the other hand, the rate of Indian urban in-migration and city growth was very modest after 1964. Indeed, at first glance, the spectacular city growth slowdown appears surprising since India's overall urbanization level is far below that at which a city growth slowdown began to occur in more developed countries. Moreover, India's rates of urbanization and city growth across the 1970s are significantly below those recorded for the typical developing country (Kelley and Williamson, 1984, p. 93). The main questions, then, are: Why have Indian cities grown relatively slowly since the mid-1960s? What accounts for the sharp slowdown after the early 1960s? These two questions will occupy much of our attention for the remainder of this book.

3.6 A Final Assessment

To our knowledge, this is the first attempt to assess a CGE model of a developing economy. Given the novelty of the exercise, it is difficult to judge the relative quality of BMW. Our prejudiced view is that the model performs well. Most of the major prediction errors seem to have fairly straightforward explanations, either because of problems with the data or because of the importance of several exogenous events unincorporated in the model. Thus, we are persuaded that BMW is an adequate approximation of the complex events that have driven Indian growth and structural change from the early 1960s to the early 1980s.

Of course, we have no way of knowing whether the structural parameters embedded in the model will remain relatively stable over the next two decades. To the extent that they are stable, we believe we have an empirically relevant paradigm that can be used for three critical purposes: first, to understand better which shocks the Indian urban experience is most sensitive to (chaps. 4 and 5); second, to isolate the key sources of Indian city growth in the recent past (chaps. 6, 7, 9); and third, to explore the likely sources and direction of Indian city growth in the future (chap. 8).

4 • How the Model Works: Impact Multipliers from Demographic and Growth Forces

4.1 Introduction

Which economic and demographic forces, and which policies, have had the greatest impact on Indian city growth? Which are most likely to shape future trends?

The answers to these questions can be decomposed into three parts: first, the quantitative magnitude of the forces and policies themselves; second, the short-run comparative static impact of those forces and policies; and third, the long-run response triggered by the short-run comparative static impact. This chapter focuses on the short-run comparative static impact of various economic and demographic forces, and chapter 5 does the same for policies. The remainder of the book expands the analysis to include a full assessment of the long-run impact of these forces and policies on Indian city growth in the past, the present, and the future. But first, we need to learn more about how the model works.

Section 4.2 explores the impact on urban performance of seven key forces: unbalanced productivity advance, drought, world market conditions, capital accumulation, skill formation, demographic change, and land scarcity. The short-run impact multipliers that guide the analysis are conventional elasticities, but they reflect full general equilibrium influences. These elasticities measure the response of some endogenous variable of interest (e.g., sectoral employment and output, city immigration rates, wages, GDP, the structure of investment, capital market disequilibrium) to some exogenous variable thought to have been important in shaping Indian city growth over the past two decades (e.g., the terms of trade between agriculture and manufacturing in world markets, the relative price of imported fuels, capital accumulation, population pressure, arable land scarcity, drought).

In computing short-run elasticities, labor markets are allowed to adjust through migration, and urban land markets are allowed to find a new equilibrium, but capital markets are severely constrained. Capital accumulated in previous years cannot migrate in response to disequilibrium induced by the shock. Furthermore, new capital goods may be constructed in response to excess demands generated by the shock, but these current investments are not added to sectoral capacity in the short run. As we have learned from Kelley and Williamson (1984, pp. 115–19), inclusion of the investment response is important even in the short run because of significant sectoral employment consequences. Thus, we include investment responses here, but their capacity effects are postponed until later in the book, when full dynamic responses are considered.

Each elasticity is first reported for 1960. Section 4.3 then asks whether these responses were unique to 1960. Has the Indian economy become more or less sensitive to most economic and demographic shocks? Is city immigration less responsive to drought and rural population pressure on the land today than it was in 1960? Is the Indian urban economy more vulnerable to world price shocks today than it will be in 2001? Answers to these questions are important since they make it possible to assess the impact of the evolution of the Indian economy on city growth performance.

4.2 What Drives Indian City Growth?

This section first examines the impact of unbalanced sectoral productivity advance on city growth. Sectoral productivity advance is used as a device to understand how the economy works in general, but it also reveals our judgment that unbalanced productivity advance has been a central supply-side force influencing Indian city growth since 1960. Second, we explore the constraints on city growth that limit the urban economy's response to sectoral productivity advance in the short run. Finally, we offer a comparative assessment of the sensitivity of Indian city growth to the remaining six key forces—drought, world market conditions, capital accumulation, skill formation, demographic change, and land scarcity. While the analysis focuses only on the short run, it should help us better understand what drives Indian city growth in the long run.

Unbalanced Productivity Advance

If demand is relatively price elastic, rapid total factor productivity growth induces a large supply response instead of a sharp price decline. This distinction is important in understanding the impact of unbalanced productivity advance on city growth. In the inelastic demand case, the rise in the marginal physical product of factors used in a technologically dynamic sector is largely offset by price declines, so that the marginal *value* products rise little, and the resource shift to the technologically dynamic sector is small, and this includes employment.

If urban sectors have relatively high rates of total factor productivity growth, and if the demand for urban output is price elastic, then final demand shifts toward the dynamic urban sectors, the derived demand for urban employment is augmented, urban jobs are created, migration responds, and city growth takes place. These forces are reinforced, of course, if the income elasticity of demand for urban output is also high (stemming from the increase in GNP generated by the sectoral productivity gains) and if the employment multipliers are large (like those associated with urban housing construction). In any case, the higher are price elasticities of demand for urban output, the greater is the city growth impact of unbalanced productivity advance favoring the urban sectors.

Indian agriculture may offer an important counterexample. Although agricultural products are traded internationally, world and domestic agricultural products may be sufficiently imperfect substitutes for each other, and government-imposed barriers to free trade sufficiently great (thereby delinking world and domestic prices), that the conventional small country assumption is completely inappropriate—that is, agricultural prices are not exogenous. To the extent that this is true for India, the price elasticity of demand for agricultural commodities may be small. If so, productivity advances in Indian agriculture will be met with sharp price declines, marginal value products may not rise significantly or at all, and employment may fail to expand. Indeed, if demand is price elastic, then productivity advance in agriculture may actually *push* labor into the cities, rather than pull it back to the countryside. This issue has generated a long debate among development economists: Does productivity advance in agriculture tend to release more labor to the city (the inelastic demand case), or is the opposite (the elastic demand case) true? The issue is empirical, and it is made all the more complex by full general equilibrium effects.

The comparative static impact of productivity advance in various sectors on overall city growth is assessed in table 4.1. Consider agriculture first (A_A). The key finding can be seen in panel A of the table: although the magnitudes are small, productivity gains in agriculture tended to *retard* urbanization in India in 1960—attracting rather than releasing labor. A 1 percent improvement in agriculture's total factor productivity tended to reduce Indian city growth by 0.58 percent per annum: that is, the elasticity of city growth to agricultural total factor

Table 4.1. The Comparative Static Impact of Rain and Sectoral Productivity Advance (1960 Elasticities)

Endogenous Variable	RAIN	Tradable Commodities		Nontradable Services and Goods				
		A_A	A_M	A_{RS}	A_{PSR}	A_{KS}	A_{US}	A_{PSU}
A. City growth attributes								
% Urban	−0.02	−0.07	−0.07	−0.36	−0.14	0.29	0.94	0.43
City growth rate	−0.33	−0.58	−0.41	−6.42	−2.49	6.39	18.95	9.42
City in-migration rate	−0.58	−1.03	−0.73	−11.35	−4.39	11.29	33.47	16.63
B. Relative prices								
P_A	−0.34	−0.60	0.54	0.17	0	0.08	0.22	−0.02
P_M	−0.01	−0.02	−0.55	0.07	0.02	0.04	−0.12	0.09
P_{RS}	0.32	0.57	0.27	−0.33	0.11	−0.01	0.09	−0.01
P_{PSR}	0.35	0.62	0.59	0.32	−0.84	0.16	0.25	0.03
P_{KS}	0.11	0.19	0.14	0.04	−0.08	−0.45	0.33	0.02
P_{US}	0.15	0.26	0.36	0.05	−0.14	0.11	−1.74	0
P_{PSU}	0.18	0.31	0.39	−0.01	−0.07	0.03	−0.46	−0.49
C. Sectoral outputs and GNP								
Q_A	0.53	0.93	0.08	−0.12	0.05	0.01	−0.05	−0.05
Q_M	0.12	0.22	1.02	−0.30	0.15	−0.12	0.03	0.69
Q_{RS}	0.24	0.43	−0.46	2.03	0.23	−0.47	−0.38	−0.11
Q_{PSR}	0.18	0.32	0.50	0	1.21	−0.78	−0.05	−0.17
Q_{KS}	−0.02	−0.03	0.25	−0.41	−0.36	2.98	1.40	−0.10
Q_{US}	0.07	0.12	−0.10	−0.19	−0.27	0.13	1.13	0.21
Q_{PSU}	0.02	0.03	0.15	−0.20	−0.05	−0.06	0.33	1.74
Nonhousing GNP	0.31	0.55	0.17	0.05	0.05	0.20	0.20	0.14
D. Unskilled employment								
L_A	−0.06	−0.10	0.12	−0.19	−0.03	0.06	−0.09	−0.07
L_M	−0.06	−0.11	0.07	−0.35	0.26	−0.18	1.18	0.81
L_{RS}	0.31	0.54	−0.64	1.34	0.25	−0.51	−0.51	−0.11
L_{PSR}	0.28	0.49	0.58	0.06	0.27	−0.66	−0.06	−0.13
L_{KS}	−0.08	−0.14	0	−0.48	−0.35	2.37	2.80	−0.07
L_{US}	0.05	0.08	−0.15	−0.25	−0.34	0.16	0.57	0.22
L_{PSU}	0.02	0.03	0.13	−0.30	−0.05	−0.12	0.99	1.21
E. Skilled employment								
S_A	−0.15	−0.27	0.10	−0.12	−0.06	−0.30	−0.13	−0.15
S_M	−0.12	−0.22	0.08	−0.30	0.12	−0.13	−0.40	0.65
S_{RS}	0.20	0.36	−0.59	2.03	0.20	−0.71	−0.48	−0.16
S_{PSR}	0.19	0.33	0.53	−0.01	0.22	−0.95	−0.09	−0.21
S_{KS}	−0.14	−0.24	0.01	−0.41	−0.42	2.22	1.30	−0.11
S_{US}	0.02	−0.04	−0.09	−0.19	−0.34	0.13	−0.73	0.13
S_{PSU}	0.03	−0.05	0.10	−0.20	−0.10	−0.05	−0.30	0.85

productivity growth is −0.58. It is hardly surprising that technological advance tends to attract resources to a dynamic sector, but, as the table shows, that does not happen here with agricultural productivity gains. Why? The answer lies primarily with low price elasticities of demand and thus with the sharp price decline: the elasticity of domestic agricultural prices to total factor productivity advance in Indian agriculture is estimated in table 4.1 to be −0.60. GNP per capita improves, however, and consumption spills over to other rural sectors. Thus, the prices of P_{RS} and P_{PSR} tend to rise, and output accommodates the additional demand there. These nonagricultural rural activities augment their supply by bidding labor away from other sectors. Thus, employment in RS and PSR rises while it falls in A, and, as a result, output expands in RS and PSR, while output in agriculture rises by less than the initial productivity impact (i.e., the elasticity on Q_A is 0.93, less than unity). The net effect, however, is that rural employment expands and urban employment contracts, but only by small amounts. According to our model, Indian agricultural productivity advance did *not* release labor to the cities in 1960, but instead caused weak deurbanization (the urbanization level falls by only 0.07 percent).

Now that we know that agricultural productivity growth causes deurbanization, it follows that drought should have released labor to the cities and fostered industrialization. This should follow inevitably since a 1 percent improvement in rainfall conditions increases yields by 0.57 percent, at least based on time series from 1960–61 to 1977–78 (Sanderson and Roy, 1979, p. 22). Table 4.1 confirms this prediction. There we see that the elasticity of city growth to the rainfall index is −0.33.

What about the impact of productivity advance in other sectors? Each of the internationally nontradable service sectors responds in predictable ways: that is, rapid productivity advance in any of the three urban service sectors tends to foster city growth, while rapid productivity advance in either of the two rural service sectors tends to suppress it. The moral of the story seems clear enough: In 1960, productivity growth forces that favored urban services clearly fostered urbanization, city in-migration, and city growth.

The KS sector offers the cleanest example. A 1 percent productivity gain in KS tends to increase output there by far more. Indeed, the output elasticity is 2.98, the largest output elasticity reported in table 4.1. Symmetrically, the employment elasticities are also large. The explanation has its source in two multiplier effects from the demand side: First, the income elasticity of demand for KS is high (reflecting an "urban bias"), so improvements in GNP spill over into KS demand. Second, city in-migration creates an excess demand for housing, especially pucca housing, since employment in KS tends to be heavily skill intensive. Since KS includes formal housing construction activities supplying dwellings to skilled labor and other high-income families, in the short run employment in KS expands still further. The net effect is a powerful impact of KS productivity advance on city growth.

The impact of productivity gains in the informal service sector, US, is even larger, but the source of that large impact is somewhat different. First of all, the demand for informal services is inelastic. Thus, the productivity gain is offset by an even bigger price decline (an elasticity of -1.74). Once again, however, demand growth due to real income improvements spills over into other urban sectors, especially KS, so that the total impact on urban employment and city growth is large. Finally, the impact of productivity gains in the urban public services sector, PSU, is also quite large, but a significant share of that impact derives from the indirect effect on manufacturing, a heavy user of the outputs of PSU.

The big surprise in table 4.1 is that productivity gains in large-scale Indian manufacturing did *not* foster city growth in 1960, at least in the short run. The deurbanization effect is modest, but nevertheless requires explanation. First note that manufacturing output increases hardly more than the initial productivity advance itself (an elasticity of 1.02), since employment increases so little there (the elasticities are 0.07 for L_M and 0.08 for S_M). The explanation lies in part with the fact that the sector faces output absorption problems, and as a result, the relative price of manufactures declines quite sharply. But the explanation also lies with the fact that the income elasticity of demand for manufactures is relatively low *in the short run*. After all, only about 15 percent of manufacturing output served to satisfy final consumption demand in 1960. The vast majority of the sector's output served instead to satisfy intermediate and investment demand. Furthermore, the M sector is a heavy user of intermediate inputs provided by agriculture (36 percent of gross M output is provided by agriculture; appendix B). Consequently, rural leakages are much greater for M than for other urban sectors. Both intermediate and investment demand tend to have relatively low GNP elasticities in the short run, so manufacturing enjoys only weak additional demand effects generated by the impact of the productivity advance on GNP. Presumably, the impact of productivity gains in manufacturing would have had an unambiguously positive stimulus on city growth if one or both of two conditions had been fulfilled in 1960: if manufacturing had been oriented toward light consumer goods, or if manufacturing had been export oriented and thus faced relatively price-elastic conditions in foreign markets. These conditions were certainly fulfilled by Korea, Taiwan, and other Asian success stories. They were also fulfilled in Kelley and Williamson's account of Third World city growth (Kelley and Williamson, 1984, pp. 102–4). They were *not* fulfilled by India, which, by 1960, had become instead a prisoner of introverted import substitution strategies associated with Mahalanobis and the second Five-Year Plan (Mellor, 1976).

All of these results, we hasten to remind the reader, are for short-run effects only. It is quite possible that the long-run effects of manufacturing productivity advance were far more favorable to city growth, a prediction that we shall see confirmed in the chapters following. It is also possible that conditions had changed by 1981.

Short-Run Constraints on the City Growth Response

The city growth response in the short run is constrained, partly by output absorption problems on the demand side as we have seen, partly by short-run capacity constraints on the supply side, partly by a rising supply price of urban labor, and partly by a shortage of public urban services. Table 4.2 documents these short-run limits in response to the three urban service sectors in which productivity advance fosters city growth.

Urban job creation fosters a city in-migration response, but note the following: Dwelling rents for both pucca and katcha housing almost always rise in the wake of the excess demands generated by the immigrant influx, urban land values always rise in response to greater land scarcity, and city living costs therefore usually rise relative to living costs in the countryside. In the long run, dwelling investment may alleviate the housing scarcity, but in the short run, although housing construction activity creates more urban jobs, housing scarcity also constrains city growth by placing upward pressure on nominal wages. Indeed, although city in-migration tends to augment urban labor supplies even in the short

Table 4.2. Short-Run Constraints on City Growth Response to City-Based Productivity Advance (1960 Elasticities)

Endogeneous Variable	A_{PSU}	A_{KS}	A_{US}
A. City growth attributes			
City growth rate	9.42	6.39	18.95
City in-migration rate	16.63	11.29	33.47
B. Urban "congestion" indicators			
Katcha house rents	0.70	0.89	−0.03
Pucca house rents	0.46	1.57	1.54
Urban land values	0.63	1.27	0.79
COL differential (urban-rural)	0.05	0.13	−0.19
C. City factor market disequilibrium indicators			
Urban unskilled wage (real*)	0.48	0.47	0.58
Urban skilled wage (real*)	0.54	0.44	2.04
Price of public urban services (PSU)**	−0.49	0.03	0.46
Return to capital in M	0.82	−0.93	−0.17
Return to capital in KS	−0.10	3.12	2.10
Return to capital in US	0.21	0.26	−0.75
D. Urban investment response to disequilibrium			
Investment in M	8.46	−33.88	−11.70
Investment in KS	−4.17	12.76	7.76
Investment in US	2.52	0.11	0.07
Katcha housing investment	0.29	0.19	−0.14
Pucca housing investment	−0.57	16.47	10.50

*The real cost of labor reported is the nominal wage relative to the output price in the sector affected by the productivity shock.
**Real price.

run, the real cost of labor rises, choking off part of the employment boom. Furthermore, in the case of productivity gains in KS and US, the relative price of public urban services also rises, at least until additional investment can augment capacity there in the long run. Another constraint on city growth in the short run is plant capacity, and the returns to capital documented in table 4.2 clearly illustrate that capital scarcity constraint. Finally, panel D in table 4.2 shows that current investment responses set in motion precisely the capacity expansion that will release a portion of those constraints in the long run.

World Market Conditions

In sharp contrast with sectoral productivity improvements, our model of the Indian economy is fairly insensitive to world market conditions. After all, the model has been developed to capture India's relative economic autarky in 1960. While world prices do influence domestic prices and output, the link is weak given import substitution policies, low trade shares, and low rates of substitution between domestic and world tradable commodities, the latter due in large part to large differences between the mix of domestic outputs and the mix of traded goods. Thus, a 1 percent rise in the world price of manufactures induces only a 0.24 percent rise in output of domestic manufactures, and a 1 percent rise in the world price of agricultural commodities induces only a 0.01 percent rise in domestic agricultural goods.

These autarkic structural features are reflected in table 4.3. Here we see confirmation of economic intuition on the direction of impact from a price shock in world markets, but the elasticities are small. A rise in the prices of fuels and imported raw materials does indeed choke off urbanization, an expected result since city activities are relatively fuel intensive and manufacturing is raw material intensive, but the elasticity of city growth is only -0.17. A rise in the price of agricultural products certainly favors agriculture at the cities' expense, but once again, the elasticity of city growth is small (-0.84), although it is considerably bigger than for fuels and imported raw materials. The biggest impact is associated with the world price of manufactures. A rise in the world price of manufactures fosters city growth, of course, and the city growth elasticity is 1.59. Yet, even here the elasticity is small compared with most of the urban productivity shocks reported in table 4.1. Nonetheless, it is interesting to note the positive urbanizing effects of favorable *demand* shocks facing manufacturing, in contrast to the deurbanizing consequences of technological shocks in manufacturing that augment *supply*.

In summary, economic autarky ensured that Indian urbanization was

Table 4.3. The Comparative Static Impact of World Market Conditions
(1960 Elasticities)

Endogenous Variable	$\bar{P}_A^W$	$\bar{P}_M^W$	$\bar{P}_Z$
A. City growth attributes			
% Urban	−0.04	0.08	−0.01
City growth rate	−0.84	1.59	−0.17
City in-migration rate	−1.49	2.81	−0.30
Katcha house rents	0.01	0.30	−0.02
Pucca house rents	0.05	0.29	−0.03
Urban land values	0.03	0.29	−0.03
B. Output			
Q_A	0.01	−0.03	0
Q_{RS}	−0.02	0.08	0.01
Q_{PSR}	0.03	−0.07	−0.02
Q_M	−0.06	0.24	−0.01
Q_{KS}	0	−0.12	−0.03
Q_{US}	−0.03	−0.04	−0.01
Q_{PSU}	−0.03	0.05	−0.02
Nonhousing GNP	−0.01	0.01	−0.01
C. Unskilled employment			
L_A	0.02	−0.04	0
L_{RS}	−0.04	0.14	0.01
L_{PRS}	0.01	−0.03	−0.01
L_M	−0.07	0.32	−0.01
L_{KS}	−0.02	−0.04	−0.03
L_{US}	−0.04	−0.04	−0.01
L_{PSU}	−0.05	0.10	−0.01
D. Skilled employment			
S_A	0.04	−0.09	0.01
S_{RS}	−0.02	0.09	0.01
S_{PRS}	0.03	−0.08	0
S_M	−0.05	0.22	0
S_{KS}	−0.01	−0.09	−0.02
S_{US}	−0.02	−0.08	0
S_{PSU}	−0.03	0.04	0

relatively insensitive to world price shocks in 1960. Indian city growth performance during the 1960s and 1970s was likely, therefore, to have been driven by conditions within the economy rather than by conditions abroad. One wonders, however, whether the Indian urban economy had become far more sensitive to world price shocks by 1981.

Accumulation, Capacity, and Job Creation

Table 4.4 summarizes the impact of capital accumulation on urban job creation, employment, in-migration, and city growth in 1960. The results certainly accord with intuition, since accumulation in urban activities

Table 4.4. The Comparative Static Impact of Accumulation (1960 Elasticities)

Endogenous Variable	K_A	K_M	K_{KS}	K_{US}	K_{PSU}
A. City growth attributes					
% Urban	−0.22	0.07	0.07	0.36	0.07
City growth rate	−3.38	2.15	1.98	7.65	2.37
City in-migration rate	−5.96	3.79	3.50	13.51	4.18
Katcha house rents	−0.05	0.51	0.22	0.60	0.14
Pucca house rents	−0.09	0.65	0.54	0.17	0.09
Urban land values	−0.08	0.56	0.40	0.40	0.08
B. Sectoral outputs and GNP					
Q_A	0.06	0	−0.01	−0.03	−0.01
Q_{RS}	0.66	−0.21	−0.09	−0.04	−0.02
Q_{PSR}	−0.16	−0.05	−0.36	−0.03	−0.04
Q_M	−0.41	0.01	−0.05	−0.01	−0.01
Q_{KS}	0.24	0.77	0.89	−0.01	−0.02
Q_{US}	−0.01	0.15	−0.01	0.98	−0.01
Q_{PSU}	−0.07	−0.01	−0.02	−0.01	1.00
Nonhousing GNP	0.06	0.06	0.05	0.07	0.03
C. Unskilled employment					
L_A	−0.13	0.03	0	−0.06	−0.02
L_{RS}	0.87	−0.23	−0.08	−0.07	−0.03
L_{PRS}	−0.12	0.04	−0.34	−0.06	−0.04
L_M	−0.57	−0.28	−0.05	−0.02	−0.01
L_{KS}	0.28	0.89	0.89	−0.02	−0.02
L_{US}	−0.03	0.19	−0.01	0.97	−0.01
L_{PSU}	−0.11	−0.03	−0.02	−0.02	0.99
D. Skilled employment					
S_A	−0.23	−0.11	−0.11	−0.04	−0.03
S_{RS}	0.71	−0.31	−0.16	−0.04	−0.03
S_{PRS}	−0.21	−0.09	−0.43	−0.04	−0.05
S_M	−0.60	−0.19	−0.11	−0.02	−0.02
S_{KS}	0.16	0.76	0.84	−0.01	−0.02
S_{US}	−0.09	0.09	−0.04	0.98	0
S_{PSU}	−0.15	−0.10	−0.05	0	1.00

tends to foster in-migration and city growth. They are also consistent with the conventional wisdom that any investment policy favoring the city at the expense of the countryside fosters urbanization. Furthermore, most of the magnitudes reported in table 4.4 conform with intuition. For example, the finding that accumulation in urban informal services has the biggest impact by far on city growth should strike a responsive chord since this sector is very labor intensive. But the big impact on city growth in *US* is not simply attributable to the capital stock augmentation there: it is also due to the demands that unskilled in-migrants place on the katcha housing stock, the katcha investment housing response, and the strong employment effects associated with that investment activity. For all of these reasons, the impact of accumulation on city growth is less strong in the more skill- and capital-intensive M, KS, and PSU sectors. But in contrast to the deurbanizing impact of disembodied technical progress in urban manufacturing, capital stock growth does raise city growth rates.

Land and Labor

Do the high rates of population growth in India and the rest of the Third World account for most of the "urban explosion" taking place there, at least when compared with nineteenth-century history? Certainly most demographers think so, and many economists agree. Indeed, Hoselitz (1955, 1957) had this argument in mind when he drew on experience from South Asia in developing his overurbanization hypothesis. Hoselitz argued that unusually heavy population pressure was forcing labor off the land, thus glutting the cities with an elastic labor supply that could find employment only in the informal service sectors. As it turns out, however, the facts of the matter are not so clearcut.

Most would agree with Lewis (1978) that, compared to the countryside, cities are highly capital intensive. This was certainly true of India in 1960, since at that time cities had capital–labor ratios about four and a half times that of the countryside (table 3.1). Trade theory has also taught that an increased endowment of any given factor of production should favor the expansion of sectors that use that factor intensively. It follows that rapid labor force growth in India should favor the relative expansion of rural activities since they are, on average, far more labor intensive than are urban activities. The elegant reasoning of simple trade theory leads us to the unambiguous prediction that heavy population pressure should generate *deurbanization*, at least in terms of the urban population share. Table 4.5 confirms the prediction. Whether we focus on all labor or on unskilled labor alone, an increase in the labor force (*ceteris paribus*) reduces the urban labor force (and population) share. Furthermore, the elasticity (-0.50) is rather high. It follows that rapid rates of labor force growth retard the urban transition, and do not stimulate it.

On the other hand, a bigger labor force *does* serve to raise the rate of city growth. This result is, of course, inevitable since an increase in the total labor force expands employment everywhere, including the city. A larger labor force also implies more migrants to clear the wage gap, and thus the rate of city in-migration should increase as well. All of these predictions are confirmed in table 4.5, where the city growth and in-migration rate elasticities are quite large. Note, however, that the employment elasticities are far larger in the three rural sectors, a result consistent with the decline in the urban share discussed above.

Table 4.5. The Comparative Static Impact of Land, Labor, and Skills Growth (1960 Elasticities)

Endogenous Variable	Land in Agriculture	Labor and Skills Unskilled Labor	Skilled Labor	Both
A. City growth attributes				
% Urban	0	−0.58	0	−0.50
City growth rate	0.09	7.42	1.25	10.16
City in-migration rate	0.15	13.11	2.21	17.95
Katcha house rents	0.34	0.31	0.38	0.73
Pucca house rents	0.20	0.29	0.88	1.01
Urban land values	0.24	0.32	0.63	0.87
B. Sectoral outputs and GNP				
Q_A	0.25	0.44	0.08	0.54
Q_{RS}	0.08	0.42	0.70	0.92
Q_{PSR}	0.09	0.33	0.94	1.52
Q_M	0.04	0.07	−0.13	0.34
Q_{KS}	0.10	0.10	0.98	0.51
Q_{US}	0.05	0.32	0.03	0.38
Q_{PSU}	−0.02	0.13	0.10	0.22
Nonhousing GNP	0.15	0.32	0.23	0.56
C. Unskilled employment				
L_A	−0.02	1.08	−0.09	1.02
L_{RS}	0.11	1.05	0.53	1.31
L_{PRS}	0.15	1.41	0.28	1.96
L_M	−0.06	0.35	−0.34	0.46
L_{KS}	0.09	0.46	0.89	0.65
L_{US}	0.05	0.53	−0.03	0.54
L_{PSU}	−0.04	0.36	0.01	0.35
D. Skilled employment				
S_A	−0.08	−0.10	0.97	0.95
S_{RS}	0.05	0.09	1.25	1.12
S_{PRS}	0.09	0.32	1.18	1.81
S_M	−0.09	−0.25	0.28	0.53
S_{KS}	0.04	−0.07	1.35	0.70
S_{US}	0	−0.09	0.43	0.47
S_{PSU}	−0.05	−0.15	0.40	0.35

Finally, table 4.5 rejects the notion that agricultural land scarcity has played an important role in pushing labor into Indian cities. Although an increase in the arable land stock would certainly have served to retain more labor in the countryside, the magnitude of the impact is trivial. The elasticities in table 4.5 suggest, therefore, that increasing arable land scarcity has not been an important ingredient of Indian city growth experience in recent history.

4.3 Looking for the Sources of Indian City Growth: A Comparative Assessment

Table 4.6 summarizes our results thus far, with attention focused on three endogenous attributes of urbanization—the urban share, the city growth rate, and the city in-migration rate—and eighteen exogenous variables.

In 1960, Indian city growth appears to have been most sensitive in the short run to the rate of growth in the unskilled labor force, productivity advance in the three urban service sectors, and capital accumulation in the labor-intensive urban informal service sector. The elasticities of city growth in response to these forces are far higher than for those of the remaining twelve exogenous variables. Second in importance are capital accumulation in the other sectors, skills, and world prices for manufactures. The weakest influences are the arable land stock, rainfall conditions, productivity advance in agriculture, productivity advance in manufacturing, world prices of fuels and imported raw materials, and world prices of agricultural goods.

Table 4.6. The Key Forces Driving Indian City Growth: A Comparative Assessment (1960 Elasticities)

Exogenous Variable	Endogenous Urbanization Variable		
	% Urban	City Growth Rate	In-Migration Rate
A. Land, labor, and skills			
Agricultural land	0	0.09	0.15
Unskilled labor	−0.58	7.42	13.11
Skilled labor	0	1.25	2.21
Both unskilled and skilled labor	−0.50	10.16	17.95
B. Accumulation			
K_A	−0.22	−3.38	−5.96
K_M	0.07	2.15	3.79
K_{KS}	0.07	1.98	3.50
K_{US}	0.36	7.65	13.51
K_{PSU}	0.07	2.37	4.18
C. World prices			
$\bar{P}_Z$	−0.01	−0.17	−0.30
$\bar{P}_M^W$	0.08	1.59	2.81
$\bar{P}_A^W$	−0.04	−0.84	−1.49
D. Productivity advance and drought			
RAIN	−0.02	−0.33	−0.58
A_A	−0.07	−0.58	−1.03
A_M	−0.07	−0.41	−0.73
A_{KS}	0.29	6.39	11.29
A_{US}	0.94	18.95	33.47
A_{PSU}	0.43	9.42	16.63

It is possible that the exogenous variables with the strongest impact on city growth, like accumulation in informal urban services, underwent the least dramatic change in the 1960s and 1970s, thus helping explain the relatively low rates of city growth in India's recent history. It is also possible that the exogenous variables with the weakest impact on city growth, like the rise in the relative price of fuels and raw materials, underwent the most dramatic growth in the 1960s and 1970s, also helping to explain the relatively low rates of city growth in India's recent history. Chapter 6 will, in fact, sort these issues out.

4.4 Do Initial Conditions Matter? Impact Multipliers in 1960, 1981, and 2001

The sensitivity of city growth to economic and demographic shocks is determined by two influences—the parameters describing the economy's behavior, and the economy's initial conditions.

For example, a rise in the scarcity of fuel has a greater deurbanization impact: the more fuel intensive are city production activities relative to those in the countryside, the lower are the elasticities of substitution between energy and nonenergy inputs, and the stronger are the input-output dependencies that link the fuel-intensive sectors to the rest of the urban economy. Thus, production parameters matter. While the elasticities of substitution between energy and nonenergy inputs are assumed to be constant in the model, relative fuel intensities and the input-output links change over time. These have evolved over the past two decades or so in a direction ensuring that city growth would be more sensitive to fuel price shocks in 1981 than in 1960. This prediction is based in part on the knowledge that urban product mix has shifted away from less fuel-intensive, informal urban services and toward more fuel-intensive manufacturing and formal urban services.

Initial conditions matter as well. As we have seen in chapter 3, our model closely replicates India's structural changes after 1960. In the two decades between 1960 and 1981, predicted GNP per capita increased by 38 percent, expenditures on imported fuel consumption as a share of GNP rose from less than 1 percent to almost 3 percent, the share of the labor force classified as skilled increased from 3.9 to 5.4 percent, the share of the labor force in urban manufacturing almost doubled, and agriculture's value-added share in GNP fell from 44 to 29 percent. Furthermore, underlying the projections in chapter 8 is the clear suggestion that these trends are likely to continue up to the year 2001. Clearly, India in 1981 was not the same economy as India in 1960, nor will it be the same as 1960 in 2001. It follows that city growth may respond in different ways to the same economic and demographic shocks at each of these three points in time, and we suspect that the economy has become more sensitive to such shocks over time.

There is another good reason to expect larger impact multipliers on city growth and city in-migration for 1981 and 2001 than for 1960. The actual rates of city growth and in-migration recorded in the early 1960s were unusually high, at least by Indian historical standards. We saw in chapter 3 (table 3.10, panel A) that the rate of city growth fell from more than 5 percent per annum in 1960–61 to about 3 percent in 1980–81, while the rate of in-migration to the city fell from 2.89 to 0.79 percent over the same period. Since the base rates in 1981 were much lower than in 1960, we expect the impact multipliers to be higher on that score alone.

Table 4.7 reports short-run impact multipliers at three dates, 1960, 1981, and 2001. To simplify the comparison, the table presents only two endogenous variables—the city growth rate, and the rate of city in-migration. The short-run impact multipliers are reported for four sets of exogenous variables shown in the previous section to have been important influences on Indian city performance in 1960—capital accumulation, world market conditions, sectoral productivity advance, and labor force growth.

Three important morals emerge from table 4.7. First, in only three cases do these elasticities switch sign. Two of these cases, however, deserve special attention. Although the impact of productivity advance in agriculture tended to cause deurbanization in 1960, it tended to foster urbanization in 1981 and will continue to do so at the end of the century. This is an important finding, for it suggests that the development debate over whether agricultural productivity advance releases labor for city employment is sensitive to the structure of the economy considered. In large part, it reflects the technological consequences of the green revolution: Indian agriculture has grown increasingly dependent on intermediate inputs, and hence leakages to urban areas (as fertilizers and farm equipment are urban-produced goods) have increased. At the same time, the slow but steady rise in per capita income has served to strengthen Engel effects, and thus to weaken multipliers that raise the demand for foodstuffs as incomes rise economywide due to the original productivity advance in agriculture.

Even more surprising is the impact of productivity advance in manufacturing. The previous section showed that manufacturing productivity advance had a perverse, although weak, deurbanization effect. The results in table 4.7 illustrate that by 1981 the structure of the Indian economy had evolved so that productivity advance in manufacturing had a more conventional impact on urbanization; that is, its impact on city growth had become significantly positive. Presumably, much of this shift

Table 4.7. The Evolution of City Growth Forces: Comparative Static Impact Multipliers, 1960–2001

Exogenous Variable		Endogenous Variable		Exogenous Variable		Endogenous Variable	
		City Growth Rate	In-Migration Rate			City Growth Rate	In-Migration Rate
A. Capital accumulation				C. Sectoral productivity advance			
K_A	1960	-3.38	-5.96	A_A	1960	-0.58	-1.03
	1981	1.99	10.04		1981	0.44	2.23
	2001	-1.38	-6.83		2001	7.50	38.13
K_M	1960	2.15	3.79	A_M	1960	-0.41	-0.73
	1981	17.39	87.92		1981	5.18	26.21
	2001	5.10	25.99		2001	11.02	55.91
K_{KS}	1960	1.98	3.50	A_{KS}	1960	6.39	11.29
	1981	12.31	62.23		1981	16.84	85.13
	2001	3.10	15.86		2001	4.29	21.84
K_{US}	1960	7.65	13.51	A_{US}	1960	18.95	33.47
	1981	13.97	70.64		1981	15.65	79.12
	2001	4.35	22.19		2001	23.69	120.11
K_{PSU}	1960	2.37	4.18	A_{PSU}	1960	9.42	16.63
	1981	4.24	21.44		1981	11.55	58.38
	2001	18.68	94.74		2001	14.00	71.03
B. World market conditions				D. Labor and skills			
$\bar{P}_Z$	1960	-0.17	-0.30	L	1960	7.42	13.11
	1981	-0.31	-1.58		1981	24.55	124.11
	2001	-0.04	-0.18		2001	23.93	121.30
$\bar{P}_A^w$	1960	-0.84	-1.49	S	1960	1.25	2.21
	1981	-2.06	-10.40		1981	25.73	130.06
	2001	-1.06	-5.37		2001	11.26	57.18
$\bar{P}_M^w$	1960	1.59	2.81	$L \& S$	1960	10.16	17.95
	1981	1.82	9.19		1981	37.77	190.93
	2001	1.92	9.73		2001	32.88	166.62

reflects the greater maturity of the Indian economy: as its urban and capital-intensive sectors develop, the general equilibrium price elasticity of demand for urban manufactures increases, thus moderating the price decline generated by supply-side productivity gains.

Second, the impact multipliers were far higher for 1981 than they were for 1960. For example, while the impact multiplier of improved world prices of manufactures on city in-migration was only 2.81 in 1960, it is 9.19 in 1981. Consider another example. While the impact of labor force growth on the city growth rate (unskilled and skilled labor combined) was 10.16 in 1960, it was 37.77 in 1981. The sharp increase in these short-run impact multipliers is consistent with the predictions offered above, and they suggest that the Indian urban economy became far more sensitive to exogenous demographic and economic shocks by 1981 than it was two decades earlier. Furthermore, in the case of sectoral capital accumulation, labor force growth, and world market conditions, the Indian urban economy is likely now to be more sensitive to exogenous economic and demographic shocks than it will be in the year 2001 (sectoral productivity advance being the exception to this rule).

Third, the ordering of these exogenous variables in terms of the relative impact on city growth did not change very much between 1960 and 1981. There are two important exceptions to this generalization. When we rank these variables by strong, moderate, and weak effects, it appears that M and KS now join US in capital accumulation among the strong elasticities, and it appears that so does skilled labor growth. By 1981, therefore, Indian city growth was most sensitive to changes in productivity advance in the three urban service sectors, to changes in capital accumulation rates in all the urban sectors except PSU, to changes in the rate of unskilled labor force growth, and to changes in the rate of skilled labor force growth. The effect of manufacturing productivity advance had moved up from "weak" to "moderate" over the two decades.

Initial conditions *do* matter. Indian urban performance is currently more sensitive to exogenous shocks than it was in 1960, when the economy was less developed. This statement is, of course, based on urban attributes only. But although table 4.7 does not display the evidence, aggregate economic indicators—like GDP per capita—also have become more sensitive over time to those shocks to which urban attributes themselves are more sensitive. The explanation is not hard to find: the more economically advanced Indian economy in 1981 was more specialized in urban activities, and thus urban-specific shocks had a larger impact on the economy as a whole than twenty years earlier.

4.5 An Overview and Questions Left Unanswered

Readers should now have a better understanding of how BMW responds in the short run to various economic and demographic shocks, exogenous influences thought to have been important sources of Indian city growth since the early 1960s.

We now know that the structure of the economy matters a great deal in assessing the impact of various economic and demographic events on city growth performance. The Indian urban economy became much more sensitive to these shocks by 1981 than it was in the early 1960s, and it will remain more sensitive to these shocks in the 1990s, and probably beyond.

We also know which of those shocks has the biggest impact on Indian city growth. Accumulation centered on the urban sectors favors city growth, but the most powerful influence seems to have been labor force growth. We have also learned that unbalanced productivity advance favoring urban sectors is a critical determinant of city growth, but productivity advance in the urban service sectors has a much greater influence than does productivity advance in manufacturing. The results also support the conventional view that Indian city growth is fostered by any force that raises the price of manufactures, lowers the price of agricultural goods, or lowers the price of imported fuels and raw materials in world markets. However, while the world price of manufactures has the biggest impact of the three, none of these world market effects are very powerful. Finally, we have learned that arable land scarcity matters very little.

The next step is to extend the analysis to the long run by assessing the impact of the observed historic behavior of these exogenous influences on actual Indian city growth between 1960 and 1981. Chapter 6 will do so, but before we identify the sources of India's city growth in the recent past, chapter 5 will look for important policy influences.

5 • How the Model Works: Impact Multipliers from Policy Action

5.1 Introduction

The previous chapter explored the macro sources of Indian economic growth and urbanization. Demographic change, capital accumulation, technical progress, and changing world market conditions all affect urbanization in complex ways and are clearly among the major determinants of economic growth. Few of these macro forces, however, are under the direct control of the Indian government. The BMW model contains dozens of tax and other parameters that are exogenous to the model but subject to policy manipulation. The present chapter focuses attention on some of those policy parameters by exploring counterfactual simulations.

The next section briefly considers the major policies used in India during recent decades, and section 5.3 provides some general comments on how the counterfactual policy simulations should be interpreted. Section 5.4 then evaluates the short-term impact on Indian urbanization of key fiscal actions. The analysis assesses the importance of these variables and simultaneously uses the counterfactuals to examine how government interacts with the private economy. Section 5.5 then considers the consequences of prorural development policies, food subsidies, and incomes policies. Finally, section 5.6 asks which government policies mattered most.

Like the previous chapter, this one dwells on short-run general equilibrium elasticities. The adjustments assumed permit labor markets to clear in response to relative price changes. Capital, however, is putty-clay with a gestation lag: investment patterns respond to demand shifts, but installed capital does not. The impact of investment responses on installed capacity are analyzed in chapters 6 to 9. Furthermore, in contrast to the previous chapter, this one examines the sensitivity of short-

run elasticities to different characterizations of government budget behavior: the revenue-enhancing aspect of fiscal policy reform is important
but should be distinguished from the effects of these reforms on relative
prices and allocative responses in a fixed budget environment.

5.2 The Impact of Public Policy on Indian Urbanization

Government fiscal policies affect economic development in many ways—
by altering relative prices, by changing the size of government and its
mix between recurrent and capital expenditures, and by altering factor
demands and income distribution. These policies in turn affect patterns
of demand and accumulation. This book captures these effects in general
equilibrium but omits less easily quantified effects, particularly the impact of public policy changes on expectations. The model thus implicitly
assumes that individuals respond myopically to public policies, regarding
tax policy changes as permanent rather than temporary. The model also
does not permit capital flight in response to unpopular policies. Given
these limitations, one should regard the counterfactual experiments reported below as estimating the short-term impact of fiscal policy changes
that the public believes will persist indefinitely.

What have been the major policy changes in recent decades? As table
5.1 suggests, the trends for the post-Independence period from 1950 to
1981 are quite striking. The government's share in GDP rose dramatically over the three decades. In addition, the source of tax revenues
changed. The personal income tax has diminished greatly in importance
since Independence: much but not all of this decline had occurred by

Table 5.1. Sources of Tax Revenue, Combined Union and State Governments

	1950–51	1955–56	1960–61	1965–66	1970–71	1973–74	1976–77	1979–80
Total tax revenue (Rs. bn.)	6.3	7.7	13.5	29.2	47.5	73.9	123.3	172.2
% GDP	7.0	8.0	9.6	13.3	12.9	13.7	17.2	17.7
Share of total tax revenue (%):								
Income tax	21.4	17.2	12.5	9.3	10.0	10.0	9.7	7.7
Corporate tax	6.2	4.8	8.1	10.4	7.8	7.9	8.0	8.0
Customs duties								
Imports	17.7	16.8	11.6	18.4	9.7	12.3	11.6	15.6
Exports	7.5	4.9	1.0	0.0	1.3	1.2	1.0	0.7
Land revenue tax	8.0	10.2	7.2	4.1	2.5	2.2	1.5	0.8
Excise, sales, other taxes	39.2	46.1	59.6	57.8	68.7	66.4	68.2	67.2

Source: World Bank (1981, tables 2.2 and 5.4).

1960. Land taxes also have diminished in importance, largely during the 1960s. Customs duties declined dramatically under the autarckical policies of the 1950s and, although export duties were of minor importance throughout the period 1960–81, the share of import duties has fluctuated considerably according to the trade regime in place. The residual, nearly all of which is sales and excise taxes, enjoyed a secular rise until 1970, and has leveled off since.

Did the rise in government and the shifts in tax structure promote or retard urbanization? Despite all the rhetoric about urban bias, the answers are far from obvious, since most taxes are imposed on urban products and incomes. But the manner in which they are levied varies, so that a switch in tax regimes is unlikely to have had a truly neutral effect on urbanization. In particular, we use the simulations below and in chapter 6 to address the following questions: Would an increase in tax progressivity promote city growth? Do cities gain from more liberal trade policies? Does an expanding government favor city growth?

In addition to purely fiscal policies, India has pursued several other policies that can be captured in our model. It is important to remember, though, that we are reporting elasticities from counterfactual simulations that are similar but hardly identical to the actual policies undertaken. Policies that the government has used include the public savings rate, intervention on behalf of rural manufacturing, food consumption subsidies, and urban incomes policies. This is hardly an exhaustive list, and many other variables are examined in subsequent chapters, but those included here suffice to illustrate the potential impact of these kinds of policies on city growth.

5.3 Interpreting Public Policy Counterfactuals

The strategy pursued here is to present tables showing the effect of various public policy changes on key endogenous variables. To make results comparable, each simulation calculates the effect of a 20 percent increase in each tax parameter on a given set of endogenous variables.[1]

It is important to remember that the model is highly nonlinear. Thus, a 10 percent tax increase would not necessarily have exactly half the impact of a 20 percent tax increase on all endogenous variables. Although the distinction between large and small effects would generally carry over to other changes, simple extrapolation may not always be appropriate. In a linear model, reduced form derivatives of endogenous variables with respect to government fiscal variables would be constant.

1. The only exception is the rural land tax, for which the tables show the consequences of imposing a 2 percent tax on rural land values.

Percentage changes or elasticities would nevertheless depend on base values of all exogenous variables. In our nonlinear model, both derivatives and elasticities depend on exogenous variable values.

Thus, the calculations presented in this chapter are dependent on the characteristics of the Indian economy in 1960. It is our conjecture that approximate magnitudes of the effects discussed below would be similar to those calculated for other years. But as the previous chapter has shown, structural changes *do* matter.

Naturally, a policy change in 1960 matters not only in 1960, but also in subsequent years. These long-run effects are addressed in chapter 9. The impact effects considered here are analyzed in the same general equilibrium model as are the long-run effects. However, some effects of exogenous changes work their way through the economy only gradually. In particular, because of lags in the model, some endogenous variables are unaffected during the year in which exogenous variables change. Changes in government policy parameters affect both housing and nonhousing investment, but these investments are assumed to alter capital stocks only after a one-year gestation period.

In studying the employment effects of the simulations reported here, it must be remembered that *total* employment is unchanged by the tax and expenditure changes analyzed. There is no unemployment in the model, and the total labor force is fixed in the short run. Thus, employment adjusts in each sector so as to equilibrate labor supply and demand, but wages adjust so that all workers are employed both before and after the simulated changes.

The price changes presented are relative price changes induced by the tax parameter changes. Thus, some prices must increase and some must decrease. The sectoral output changes are constrained by the fixed capital stocks in each sector and by the unchanging state of technology. In addition, total supplies of skilled and unskilled labor are fixed economywide. Consequently, not all sectoral outputs can change in the same direction. Likewise, skilled and unskilled employment must each increase in some sectors and decrease in others in response to government policy shifts.

Finally, it must be remembered that all government policy changes analyzed in this chapter take place within a balanced budget framework. The model permits no change in government surpluses or deficits. Thus, tax changes that affect government receipts must similarly affect its spending or transfers. Although the exogenous parameter changes whose effects are analyzed are tax parameters, each tax change is also an expenditure change. We analyze effects of government tax policy changes on expenditures in two ways. First, we assume that changes in government receipts affect government spending according to the constant expenditure share parameters.[2] In these calculations, any additional government revenues resulting from tax increases are distributed among spending programs according to patterns estimated from the historical data. Thus, some of the effects of a tax increase result from the direct effects of taxes and some are caused by the effects of the resulting spending increases.

However, a second calculation is also presented in which government revenue increases are assumed to be returned to households in proportion to their initial income. In this case, real public sector spending is held constant, and only direct tax effects (due to relative price and income distribution changes) have an impact on the new equilibrium. The general income effects of spending changes induced by tax increases are thereby removed in the second calculation. Indeed, by comparing these two experiments, we can assess the impact of an urban bias on the expenditure side of government fiscal action.

The second calculation does not register pure substitution or relative price effects as economists use those terms. The second calculation is simply a device to study the effects of tax changes that are not confounded by changes in government spending. The second calculation assumes that increased revenues are returned to the public in proportion to their initial incomes, not in proportion to the incidence of the tax increase on each group. Thus, the simulation does not completely correct for income effects.[3]

5.4 What Matters Most?
A Comparative Assessment of Tax Policy

Overview

With these caveats in mind, consider the impact of changes in import and export duties, in personal income tax rates, and in sales and land taxes. The results appear in tables 5.2 and 5.3.

The elasticities reported in these tables may appear to be "small," but this reflects in large part the limited impact of any particular tax on macroeconomic variables. Naturally, a concerted policy shift that involved many changes simultaneously would have much greater conse-

2. See appendix A for definitions and appendix B for specific values of these parameters.

3. The initial income shares, in percentages, are:

rural unskilled	41.04	urban informal skilled	1.12
rural skilled	16.99	urban formal skilled	12.62
urban informal unskilled	8.71	capitalists and landlords	9.10
urban formal unskilled	10.42		

Table 5.2. Comparative Static Impact of Customs Duties Shifts (1960 Elasticities)

Endogenous Variables	Import Duty on Agricultural Goods and Raw Materials ($\tau_{IMP,A}$)		Import Duty on Manufactures ($\tau_{IMP,M}$)		Export Duty on Agricultural Goods and Raw Materials ($\tau_{EXP,A}$)		Export Duty on Manufactures ($\tau_{EXP,M}$)	
	(1) Variable Revenue	(2) Constant Revenue	(3) Variable Revenue	(4) Constant Revenue	(5) Variable Revenue	(6) Constant Revenue	(7) Variable Revenue	(8) Constant Revenue
A. City growth attributes								
% Urban	-0.26	-0.15	0.18	0	0.17	0.10	-0.06	-0.14
City growth rate	-4.33	-2.90	3.58	0	3.43	2.00	-1.09	-2.60
City in-migration rate	-7.99	-5.47	5.93	0	5.66	3.14	-2.29	-4.94
Katcha house rents	-0.50	-0.46	0.33	0.23	0.33	0.28	-0.12	-0.16
Pucca house rents	-0.26	-0.22	0.28	0.18	0.21	0.17	-0.03	-0.07
B. Output								
A	0.07	0.08	-0.07	-0.08	-0.05	-0.05	-0.01	-0.01
RS	-0.12	-0.22	0.12	0.38	0.03	0.13	0.03	0.15
PSR	0.16	0.14	-0.14	-0.10	-0.11	-0.09	-0.02	0
M	-0.32	-0.21	0.12	-0.14	0.20	0.09	-0.19	-0.31
KS	-0.05	-0.03	0.32	0.26	0.06	0.04	0.18	0.15
US	-0.12	-0.11	0.11	0.08	0.09	0.07	-0.02	-0.04
PSU	-0.14	-0.09	0.07	-0.07	0.10	0.05	-0.11	-0.08
Nonhousing GDP	-0.04	-0.03	0.04	0.01	0.02	0.01	0	-0.01
C. Unskilled employment								
A	0.08	0.10	-0.07	-0.10	-0.05	-0.06	0	-0.02
RS	-0.22	-0.34	0.07	0.54	0.08	0.21	0.06	0.20
PSR	0.15	0.15	0	0	0	0	0	0
M	-0.34	-0.20	0.11	-0.21	0.24	0.10	-0.21	-0.37

KS	0.25	0.30	0.08	0.13	0.42	0.55	−0.08	−0.13
US	−0.05	−0.02	0.10	0.12	0.09	0.15	−0.15	−0.17
PSU	−0.25	−0.15	0.09	0.19	−0.12	0.12	−0.19	−0.28
D. Skilled employment								
A	−0.06	0	−0.13	−0.13	−0.25	−0.25	0.19	0.19
RS	0.19	0.06	0.12	0.06	0.44	0.12	−0.19	−0.06
PSR	0	−0.08	−0.15	−0.15	−0.36	−0.23	0.15	0.15
M	−0.36	−0.27	0.09	0.18	−0.44	0	−0.09	−0.27
KS	0.15	0.22	0.07	0.07	0.30	0.37	0	−0.07
US	0	0	0	0	0	0	0	0
PSU	0	0	0	0	0	0	0	0
E. Relative Prices, P'_i								
A	0	0	−0.06	−0.07	−0.07	−0.09	0.09	0.09
RS	0.07	0.02	0.05	0	0.16	0.05	0.08	−0.03
PSR	0.02	0.02	0.02	0.01	0.04	0.03	−0.03	−0.04
M	−0.07	−0.03	0.02	0.06	−0.07	−0.01	0	−0.03
KS	0.07	0.10	0.07	0.10	0.17	0.23	−0.08	−0.11
US	−0.03	−0.01	0.04	0.06	−0.06	0.04	−0.05	−0.07
PSU	−0.11	−0.05	−0.07	0.12	−0.07	0.06	−0.11	−0.16
F. Incomes								
Wage rate								
Urban unskilled	−0.01	−0.01	0.01	0.01	0	0	−0.06	−0.06
Urban skilled	0.05	0.03	−0	−0.02	0.08	0.04	−0.03	−0.02
Capital rental rate								
Urban formal	−0.24	−0.16	0.06	0.13	−0.17	0.01	−0.06	−0.18
Rural	0.03	−0.10	−0.18	−0.30	−0.21	−0.48	−0.23	0.35
G. Revenue from tax	0	0.38	0	0.34	0	0.81	0	−0.35

Note: Values reported show the (percentage change) impact of a 20% rise in each duty rate.

Table 5.3. Comparative Static Impact of Tax Revenues (1960 Elasticities)

Endogenous Variables	Personal Income Taxes Raised 20% τA from 2.02% to 2.42% τUS from 4.68% to 5.61% τFS from 8.36% to 10.04%		Sales Tax on Manufactures Raised 20% from 50% to 60%		Rural Land Use Tax Raised from 0 to 2.0%	
	(1) Variable Revenue	(2) Constant Revenue	(3) Variable Revenue	(4) Constant Revenue	(5) Variable Revenue	(6) Constant Revenue
A. City growth attributes						
% Urban	−0.22	−0.89	0.90	−0.36	0.54	0.07
City growth rate	−4.25	−17.43	17.73	−6.96	10.73	1.54
City in-migration rate	−7.86	−31.06	30.85	−12.63	18.52	2.35
Katcha house rents	−1.39	−1.77	0.74	0.01	0.98	0.70
Pucca house rents	−3.43	−3.77	0.54	−0.14	0.42	0.15
B. Output						
A	0.04	0	0.03	−0.04	0.05	0.03
RS	0.77	1.75	−1.30	0.55	−0.89	−0.20
PSR	0.64	0.79	−0.27	0.02	−0.09	0.01
M	1.28	0.27	1.12	−0.80	0.70	0.53
KS	−2.98	−3.25	0.90	0.45	0.26	0.08
US	−1.09	−1.16	0.24	−0.01	0.23	0.13
PSU	0.31	−0.22	0.60	−0.41	0.40	0.03
Nonhousing GDP	−0.07	−0.18	0.15	−0.03	0.09	0.01
C. Unskilled employment						
A	−0.12	−0.22	0.13	−0.06	0.11	0.04
RS	0.70	1.91	−1.56	0.71	−1.12	−0.27
PSR	0.15	0.15	0	0.15	0	0
M	2.16	0.87	1.43	−1.02	0.85	−0.04

KS	-2.83	-3.25	1.27	0.51	0.34	0.04
US	-1.20	-1.43	0.39	-0.05	0.33	0.17
PSU	0.90	0	1.05	-0.68	0.65	0.03
D. Skilled employment						
A	0.82	0.82	-0.06	-0.70	0.06	0.06
RS	1.37	2.50	-1.50	0.62	-1.00	-0.19
PSR	0.85	1.01	-0.31	0	-0.08	0
M	0.63	-0.54	1.18	-1.00	0.82	0
KS	-3.67	-4.12	1.12	0.37	0.37	0.07
US	-1.28	-1.28	0	0	0.43	0
PSU	0	-1.00	0.50	-0.50	0.50	0
E. Relative prices, P						
A	0.09	0.14	-0.10	0	-0.05	-0.01
RS	0.17	0.60	-0.57	0.24	-0.04	-0.11
PSR	-0.42	-0.36	-0.04	0.06	-0.08	-0.04
M	0.64	0.31	0.37	-0.24	0.23	0.01
KS	0.05	-0.21	0.50	0.01	0.20	0.02
US	-0.25	-0.43	0.25	-0.09	0.20	0.07
PSU	0.52	0.02	0.59	-0.34	0.38	0.04
F. Incomes						
Wage rate						
Urban unskilled	-0.06	-0.06	0	-0.01	-0.01	-0.03
Urban skilled	1.72	1.85	-0.07	0.16	-0.16	-0.08
Capital rental rate						
Urban formal	-1.88	-2.55	0.96	-0.34	0.56	0.07
Rural	-0.72	0.32	-1.38	0.63	-0.82	-0.07
G. Revenue from tax	3.14	0	5.92	0	2.20	0

Note: Values reported show the (percentage change) impact of a 20% rise in each tax rate.

quences. Thus, small elasticities do not necessarily mean that tax policies are unimportant: interest should focus instead on *relative* magnitudes.

In general, the share of the population living in urban areas is much less sensitive to changes in tariff rates than to changes in taxes on domestic activities. City growth and immigration rates are naturally far more sensitive to any tax policy than is the urban share: a decline in the urban population of 100,000 people due to an unfavorable shock may have only a modest impact on the urban labor force, but it will have a much larger impact on the rate of change of the urban labor force, or on the rate of rural-urban migration. An additional general point to note is that the effect of a tariff change on output (more precisely, on constant price value added) is virtually identical to the effect on employment. Such a result at the aggregate (skilled plus unskilled) level is inevitable, for the only variable inputs contributing to short-run changes in nonhousing output are skilled and unskilled labor. In a few cases, employment changes in one skill category may differ from the other (and thus from output) if the induced changes in relative wages between skilled and unskilled workers are sufficiently large. But the dominant correlation between output and employment changes is positive. Moreover, since capital inputs are fixed in the short run, and since production functions exhibit constant returns to scale in all sectors, there are decreasing returns to labor inputs. Therefore, employment changes are typically larger in percentage terms than are output changes. The implication is that even modest changes in government tax parameters can have substantial short-run effects on employment in the affected sectors.

Finally, the tables show that the impact of a tax parameter on prices, production, and employment depends very much on induced changes in government expenditures. An increasing tax rate has quite different effects on production and employment depending on whether total government revenues and thus expenditures are allowed to increase.

Import Duties on Agricultural Goods

The agricultural import tariff increase (table 5.2, col. 1) generates classic import substitution effects. Output, relative price, and employment in agriculture rise, and urbanization is choked off.[4] The response elasticities are small, however, reflecting India's virtual self-sufficiency. Tariff rev-

4. The price changes are relative price effects, based on a Laspeyres deflator. The effects of tax changes on nominal prices are also calculated but are not displayed. "Nominal" prices in our model give price changes relative to the world price of manufactured goods, which serves as the model's numeraire. In practice, changes in Laspeyres-deflated and current prices are extremely close.

enue actually declines. Given some substitutability between domestic and imported agricultural goods, such "Laffer effects" are to be expected: producers and consumers shift to untaxed domestic goods (especially lightly taxed rural products), thus shrinking the base by a greater percentage than the tax rate increase.

Greater protection for a rural sector slows urbanization. The story is straightforward: protection builds demand for domestic agricultural goods, bidding up relative wages there and in other rural sectors. Some 59,000 workers leave the cities, modestly reducing the proportion of the population living in urban areas but exerting a considerably greater impact on the rate of growth of the urban labor force or the urban migrant labor force. Since nearly all (55,000) of the migrants are unskilled, one would expect the urban output adjustment to be borne mainly by the more labor-intensive urban sectors: such a pattern is in fact observed.

The importance of tariff-induced government revenue effects can be seen by comparing columns 1 and 2 of table 5.2. In column 1, the decline in revenue forces government spending to contract, causing a considerably greater decline in demand for urban goods and services than if the real size of government were maintained (as in col. 2). In this sense, then, government spending does have a strong urban bias.

Import Duties on Manufactures

An across-the-board tariff increase in imported manufactures has far more complicated effects. After all, Indian manufacturing was highly dependent on imported intermediates in 1960, including capital goods. Although a tariff on imported final goods would protect domestic firms producing the same final manufactures for the local market, a tariff on those firms' intermediates would have the opposite effect. The urbanization impact of the across-the-board tariff increase on manufactures hinges on the behavior of value-added prices. Table 5.2 shows that the net effect of tariffs on those value-added prices (called "relative prices" in the table) is negative: that is, the more expensive intermediates create a cost squeeze, which offsets that protective effect to primary inputs. With that knowledge, the result that larger tariffs on manufactures have little or no effect on urbanization makes sense.

Consider column 3, in which government expenditures are allowed to rise with the augmented tariff revenues. Unskilled manufacturing employment rises, but *KS* sector expansion, fueled by growth in government spending, leads to even bigger employment gains there. Indeed, *KS* output growth is three times that of manufacturing when government expenditures are allowed to rise. Unlike the agricultural tariff, a rise in tariffs on imported manufactures leads to a large revenue increase. In fact, the general equilibrium demand elasticity for M imports is quite low: the 20 percent tariff increase generates nearly a 16 percent increase in tariff revenue.

Column 4 reports instead the case in which the augmented tariff revenues are redistributed back to households. Here it can be seen that there are no net import substitution effects. The value-added price of M declines, output declines, and employment declines as well. However, households spend the redistributed tariff revenues mostly on urban services, so much so that those sectors take up the slack created by manufacturing. The net effect on urbanization and city growth is zero.

Export Duties

The patterns here are largely the reverse of agricultural import tariffs, except that the effects are smaller, primarily because duties on exports are lower. Consequently, an increase in agricultural export duties reduces returns to agriculture, modestly accelerating rural-urban migration. Indeed, the movement out of agriculture is somewhat greater than the urban labor force gain, since roughly one-third of those leaving shift to rural nonagricultural activities. In fact, when one controls for the urban expenditure bias of increased government tax revenues, the major gainer is the RS sector. The losers, of course, are recipients of agricultural land and capital rents, so that real rural incomes decline slightly. Given the sector specificity of these duties, the burden is largely shifted onto fixed factors of production: rental elasticities (including positive ones in sectors receiving an influx of labor) tend to be much greater than wage elasticities.

As one would expect, an export duty on manufactures raises the cost of exports, reducing world demand. The recession in manufacturing generates large reductions in M sector employment, nearly all of which retreats to the countryside. These workers, however, do not return to the farms. In fact, a recession in manufacturing quickly translates into a recession in agriculture: Indian manufacturing is a major user of agricultural intermediate inputs. In addition, unskilled labor receives a large share of factor payments in manufacturing (about one-third of value added), so that manufacturing wage and employment reductions quickly translate into declines in the demand for food. In this case, taxing a modern sector hits unskilled labor much harder than skilled labor (though capital rents are hit hardest).

To summarize, import and export duties do not have large effects on urbanization. Naturally, this conclusion would be quite different if India were a more open economy. To the extent tariffs and duties raise government revenues, demand is shifted toward urban areas. This urbanizing impulse is counteracted to the extent that the tariffs reduce urban competitiveness. Capital and land, which cannot be shifted in the short run, bear the brunt of the deadweight losses imposed; wages are virtually unaffected.

Personal Income Taxes

Unskilled workers in India pay no personal income tax, so the burden falls exclusively on skilled labor, capitalists, and landlords. The effect is striking and is particularly pronounced when not offset by government spending increases. In the variable revenue case, 45,000 skilled and 13,000 unskilled workers leave urban areas. But without rising government demand, the urban decline rises to 233,000. In this latter case, the short-run net urban in-migration rate is cut by nearly one-third.

Although nonhousing GDP falls, the decline is concentrated in the KS and US sectors, the demand for which depends heavily on urban skilled workers' disposable incomes. Real after-tax incomes of skilled workers decline (for urban formal sector skilled, the decline is about 0.90 percent: about half of the tax increase is shifted), while pretax incomes rise. As aggregate demand shifts to rural areas, the losers are those who hold urban assets, as immobile capital assumes virtually all of the shifted burden. With the dramatic skilled labor emigration (in the constant revenue counterfactual, 2.3 percent of skilled urban workers leave for the countryside), pucca housing rents suffer especially, falling 3.8 percent.

The collapse in KS production has both demand- and supply-side causes. On the demand side, disposable incomes of the upper classes (which have high marginal propensities to consume KS and US goods) suffer. On the supply side, rising taxes induce skilled labor flight to rural activities, in which it is easier to avoid taxes. A second round effect that further cripples KS demand works through the contraction of construction for the modern sector housing market, which experiences a short-term investment decline of 41.6 percent!

In short, urbanization is significantly choked off by a rise in personal income taxes, and thus by any effort to make the tax system more progressive. Stated differently, the more progressive personal income tax reduces the urban bias sharply.

Sales Taxes on Urban Manufactures

In BMW, the sales tax on manufactures is a proxy for a variety of taxes levied on sales in India. Naturally, the simplification is great, and our results should not be viewed as a precise calibration of real world policy changes. We model these taxes as affecting consumption of manufactures only (i.e., capital goods are assumed to escape taxation) and as applying to urban manufactures only. This latter assumption is invoked to reflect the ability of small rural manufacturers, with unrecorded transactions, to escape taxation.

Government revenue effects are particularly strong (cf. col. 3 and 4 of table 5.3), as total public sector revenue rises nearly 6 percent. The augmented government revenues translate into a strong increase in the urban labor force (an inflow of 234,000 workers), and all urban sectors, including manufacturing, share in that effect. Government demand, with its strong urban bias, increases manufacturing demand by far more than the decline in private demand stemming from rising prices.[5] In fact, because the tax increase is strongly urbanizing, and urban workers have higher marginal propensities than their rural counterparts to consume manufactured goods, producer prices of domestic manufactures increase, despite the hefty tax rise. The largest price increases, though, are in the skill-intensive *KS* and *PSU* sectors, for skilled labor scarcities induced by skills-using urbanization have the greatest cost-push effects in these sectors.[6]

The results are very different when government revenue is controlled. The urban labor force declines considerably. Rural capitalists and landlords now become gainers, while urban capitalists become losers. Demand for manufactures loses its bouyancy: its output and price now decline. The shift in expenditure patterns favors skilled labor, reflecting consumer substitution and an increase in incomes of groups with large propensities to consume skill-intensive services. Real unskilled wages are virtually constant in the controlled expenditure scenario.

Rural Land Taxes

Because rural land cannot be shifted to untaxed sectors, it makes an almost ideal tax from a collector's viewpoint. Furthermore, as land supply is fixed, demand determines the land rental rate; net rents therefore absorb nearly the entire tax burden, even in general equilibrium.

The imposition of a rural land tax (table 5.3, col. 5 and 6) induces a significant urbanizing effect as labor migrates to the cities, faced as it is

5. The prices reported in tables 5.2 to 5.4 are producers' net prices and thus do not include the first-order effect of the sales tax.

6. When deflated by a GDP deflator, skilled wages rise by 0.20 percent; when deflated by a class-specific CPI (as is the case in tables 5.2 to 5.4), they fall by 0.07 percent, reflecting the added cost of consumer manufactures.

with declining marginal value products on the farm as prices of farm products decline, partly in response to declining rural incomes, and hence declining demands. Urbanization in turn increases demand for urban goods, and hence their prices and outputs increase. Output and employment growth are particularly rapid in urban manufacturing, which absorbs nearly half of the new migrants.

Aggregate demand for agricultural goods is fueled by the urban expansion and by the rise in GDP it generates. Because the urbanizing process causing this rise mostly involves the movement of unskilled workers (with high marginal propensities to consume food) to the cities, where wages are higher, and because taxing an immobile factor does not create cost increases, demand for A goods grows. At the same time, the departure of many workers for the cities depresses the demand for rural-specific services and manufactures. Consequently, there are large flows out of RS, sufficient to cover both migration to the cities and the modest expansion in farm employment.

Even when government spending is fixed, the land tax drives workers to the cities. In essence, the tax strikes at rural workers and landlords; the revenue is then redistributed to all classes, including urban dwellers, leading to a small demand shift toward urban products. However, because land is concentrated heavily in the hands of the rural wealthy (with high propensities to consume RS goods), and because demand for food by peasants near subsistence is extremely inelastic, the brunt of the rural adjustment is borne by the RS sector. Indeed, output expands in every sector in the economy except RS. Because RS is skill intensive relative to A, and because there is little expansion in the urban skill-intensive sectors, real skilled wages fall. Unskilled wages are nearly constant in both simulations, while urban capital benefits from the labor inflow. Rural capital and land rents, of course, fall.

In that they generate large amounts of revenue and are borne almost entirely by the rural elite and the skilled in all areas, land taxes represent a desirable tax. Nor is collection difficult. Their sharply decreasing role in India must therefore be driven by other considerations, of which two seem probable. The first is the continued and probably rising influence of wealthy landowners in the Congress and other parties. Second is the Indian government's desire to promote rural development and stem the tide of migration to the cities. Of course, the two factors may be interrelated: landlords have little desire to see a loose labor market tightened by departures for the city (or to the Punjab, for that matter).

5.5 The Comparative Static Impact of Some Major Social Policies

In addition to altering taxes, the Indian government has pursued many expenditure policies that may have had an important impact on urbanization. This section examines three counterfactuals that are related to explicit or implicit policies followed at various times in recent decades. However, the stylized counterfactuals presented here should not be treated as precise depictions of actual policies: they are not intended to be, but serve only to focus on particular aspects of complex programs. The simulations are reported in table 5.4. Policies amenable to more accurate quantification are analyzed in chapters 6 and 9.

Table 5.4. Comparative Static Impact of Public Policy Shifts (1960 Elasticities)

Endogenous Variables	(1) Rural Manufacturing Subsidy (2% RS production subsidy)	(2) Food Consumption Subsidy (1% food consumption subsidy for all unskilled workers)	(3) Urban Incomes Subsidy (10% curtailment in urban unskilled employment)
A. City growth attributes			
% Urban	−1.11	−0.31	−9.16
City growth rate	−21.64	− 6.31	neg
City in-migration rate	−38.49	−11.17	neg
Katcha house rents	−2.26	−0.19	2.92
Pucca house rents	−1.87	−0.76	−5.60
B. Output			
A	−0.31	−0.08	0.29
RS	2.97	0.82	2.66
PSR	−0.05	0.02	0.05
M	−1.02	−0.16	−2.19
KS	−1.15	−0.87	−5.29
US	−0.74	−0.19	−3.11
PSU	−0.69	−0.16	−4.11
Nonhousing GDP	−0.19	−0.08	−0.85
C. Unskilled employment			
A	−0.53	−0.15	0.99
RS	3.88	1.07	4.23
PSR	0.15	0	1.35
M	−1.14	−0.17	−12.38
KS	−1.31	−0.97	−14.85
US	−0.98	−0.26	−7.51
PSU	−1.05	−0.22	−10.17

Table 5.4. *continued*

Endogenous Variables	(1) Rural Manufacturing Subsidy (2% RS production subsidy)	(2) Food Consumption Subsidy (1% food consumption subsidy for all unskilled workers)	(3) Urban Incomes Subsidy (10% curtailment in urban unskilled employment)
D. Skilled employment			
A	−0.76	−0.13	−0.15
RS	3.37	1.00	2.87
PSR	−0.15	0	0.15
M	−1.36	−0.18	0.27
LS	−1.57	−0.90	−4.27
US	−0.85	0	4.27
PSU	−1.00	0	0.50
E. Relative prices, P_i'			
A	0.06	0	−1.68
RS	1.46	0.38	−0.49
PSR	0.40	0.06	−1.01
M	−0.34	−0.06	1.50
KS	−0.42	−0.17	0.07
US	−0.47	−0.11	7.49
PSU	−0.65	−0.11	4.67
F. Incomes			
Wage rate			
Urban unskilled	0.06	−0.04	11.46
Urban skilled	0.71	0.10	−2.85
Capital rental rate			
Urban formal	−1.56	− 0.83	−5.12
Rural	1.66	0.08	−2.46

Note: All impacts are expressed as percentage change in the base value.

A Rural Manufacturing Subsidy

The first stylized policy simulation addresses the impact of a rural, small-scale manufacturing subsidy. There is no question that the Indian government has promoted rural manufacturing for a long time, although its policies have been far more complex than can be characterized by a simple subsidy.[7] BMW already captures many of these policies; for example, it includes the effects of subsidized rural infrastructure. But to examine the consequences of additional rural manufacturing promotion, we simplify a complex policy regime by focusing solely on the impact of a direct subsidy.

7. For discussions of India's rural manufacturing policies, see Sekhar (1983); Mellor (1976); and Chuta and Sethuraman (1984).

As one would expect, the *RS* sector enjoys a boom in response to a subsidy. A modest 2 percent subsidy raises output in rural manufacturing by almost 3 percent, reflecting both a fairly elastic supply and a supportive demand stimulus. Indeed, demand growth is so great that the manufacturers' price rise exceeds 1 percent. The story is essentially that of a high-multiplier demand spiral in rural areas: *RS* expansion raises rural wages, rural manufacturing profits, and thus rural incomes generally; in addition, return migration ensues; both influences augment demand for rural-specific (*RS*) goods and services. The 289,000 workers who return to the countryside consume few urban products, thus limiting demand leakages for urban goods that would reduce multipliers.

All other sectors contract as they release resources to accommodate the *RS* boom. As it turns out, skilled wages rise at a faster pace than unskilled wages, for two reasons: *RS* uses a fair amount of skilled labor, and a general tightening of the labor market has a greater impact on the less elastic rural skilled labor supply.

Given that this prorural policy benefits rural capitalists and skilled labor (urban capitalists are the big losers), it is not surprising that such subsidies have political appeal. But such programs have been costly: productivity is lower in rural manufacturing than in urban manufacturing (a stylized fact captured in the model), since intermediate services are costlier to deliver, scale economies are rarely realized, and transportation costs are greater. Moreover, not only are the subsidies expensive, but they generate incomes in precisely those regions where marginal tax rates are low, lowering government revenue (by a large amount: 2.3 percent). And as government revenues fall (and the subsidy rises), so do public sector savings.

But there can be no doubt that one of the major objectives of rural manufacturing promotion programs is achieved: urbanization slows down. Indeed, the urban population falls by over 1 percent, thus relieving the pressure on harried urban planners.

A Food Consumption Subsidy

Because domestic agriculture has a lower supply elasticity and must compete, at least in part, with foreign suppliers, policies focusing on agricultural development will not choke off urbanization to the same extent as those focusing on rural manufacturing. This can be seen in table 5.4, column 2, which summarizes the impact of a food consumption subsidy for all unskilled workers. Once again, this counterfactual represents only a simplification of a complex program that includes subsidized "fair price" shops aimed at the poor in both urban and rural areas, rural "food for work" programs, accumulation of public sector grain stocks, and interstate (and at times interdistrict) restrictions on private food grain movements.[8] These policies have sometimes had the unintended consequence of augmenting malnutrition during drought-induced crop failures. Nonetheless, one of the most impressive achievements of the Indian government has been its highly successful control of famine since the mid-1970s, especially by comparison with the early twentieth century (McAlpin, 1983).

Oddly enough, the food subsidy does not augment agricultural production. Since the producer price of food is virtually unaltered (hence, the subsidized price declines by the full amount of the unit subsidy), the demand expansion stemming from the subsidy must be offset by declines elsewhere. Part of this decline comes from the decline in the urban labor force, as aggregate demand is shifted to rural areas: labor productivity, and hence food (and other) consumption, falls in the process. Demand for intermediates used in urban manufacturing also declines, as does demand based on incomes generated by public sector spending, which falls as the untaxed proportion of the economy rises; nonsubsidy spending obviously falls further still.

The balanced budget constraint in the general equilibrium framework is the key to explaining the results. Despite good intentions, the expenditure shift fails to augment total demand for agricultural goods.[9] The shift does shrink demand for urban products, thus reducing city growth, but the main beneficiaries are rural services and manufacturing. Naturally, it would have been possible to devise a subsidy-cum-tax (or a particular expenditure reduction) pattern that does not cause demand for unskilled labor, and hence food, to fall. The important finding is that the policymakers cannot be casual about financing their subsidies: the means of finance may be as important as the subsidy itself.

In reality, it is not likely that a government subsidy program would be financed by proportionate reductions in government capital and recurrent expenditures. A more likely scenario would involve new taxes, a reduction in government savings or (somewhat less likely) borrowing from abroad. Indeed, common Indian government practice appears to have been to diminish public savings during times of need. The historical

8. Nor is this list exhaustive. For discussions of Indian policy, see Oughton (1982), and numerous discussions in the *Economic and Political Weekly*, including George (1984); de Janvry and Subbarao (1984); Dandekar and Sathe (1980); and Ray, Cummings, and Herdt (1979). For a recent discussion and survey, see Arnold (1988).

9. But had demand for agricultural goods risen, government would then have had to confront the problem of a fairly inelastic agricultural supply curve.

consequences of savings rate shifts and capital inflow patterns are addressed in the following chapters.[10]

An Urban Incomes Policy

The issues addressed above reflect highly visible policies at various points since 1960. The remaining simulation addresses a set of policies that are more difficult to quantify, those relating to the incomes of unskilled urban workers. A multitude of policies relating to urban labor have roughly amounted to sporadic intervention in support of organized labor in its confrontation with employers. In particular, recall from chapter 3 that one of the chief events that our neoclassical model did not replicate was the real wage rise (and employment stagnation) in manufacturing during the late 1960s, a period of very slow growth for the economy as a whole. Since neoclassical forces in the model do not generate such an increase, we suspect that much of the wage rise reflects the impact of public policy. To appreciate this point, consider the consequences of government policies that generate a fall in urban unskilled employment by 10 percent. Such a restriction may be accomplished by state promotion (or tolerance) of activities that restrict effective entry into the urban labor force by migrants and other potential unskilled entrants; these activities include unionization, licensing, and requirements of scarce credentials to obtain employment. The net effect is to drive up the cost of obtaining an unskilled job in the city.

The obvious effect of these "incomes" policies is the intended one: unskilled urban wages rise by over 11 percent. Because unskilled labor is now much scarcer, urban output falls precipitously. Rural output, of course, gains, but GDP falls due to economywide allocative losses. Indeed, the cost required to achieve the wage rise is 0.85 percent of nonhousing GDP: some 1.2 billion 1960 rupees. This net efficiency loss is the cost of providing a 1.9 billion rupee income gain to the 20.9 million unskilled urban workers who remain employed. Those returning to the countryside force unskilled wages down there by 1.2 percent, but the big losers (see table 5.4, col. 3) are urban capitalists. This simulation can hardly be regarded as more than suggestive, but it certainly implies that much of India's poor economic performance in the 1960s and 1970s may reflect urban incomes policy failure.

---

10. It turns out that, had the food subsidy been financed by reducing government's capital budget (thereby maintaining the strongly urbanizing expenditures on the bureaucracy), almost no loss in urban population would have occurred. Consequently, total demand for food by unskilled workers would not have declined.

5.6 Short-Term Urbanization Impact: Policy versus Exogenous Forces

Which of the policy changes implemented during the past two decades had the most profound impact on urbanization? How important was government policy relative to the macro shocks analyzed in chapter 4?

Based on the preceding section, government food policies, when likely means of funding are taken into account, probably did not alter the pace of urban growth very much. However, two other policies *are* likely to have played an important role. Intervention in the urban labor market (especially in the late 1960s) was probably important, particularly in view of the considerable real wage increases experienced. Promotion of rural manufacturing probably contributed to India's slow overall pace of urban growth as well. Unfortunately, neither of these two policies can be precisely quantified, and their effects are thus incorporated into the residual estimates of the low and declining sectoral productivity growth rates. Two other forces, foreign borrowing and the public sector savings rate, are also likely to have mattered. These can be quantified, and in the following chapter we consider the role they played in affecting urbanization.

Turning to taxes, it is clear that the urban-specific personal income tax could have played a role in choking off city growth, but it was never given a chance to do so: its share of total tax revenue did not rise, but rather declined modestly, from 12.5 percent in 1960 to 7.7 percent in 1979. Export taxes were already unimportant by 1960 and probably were not a major force either. Trends in import duties were erratic: it is possible that related policy shifts had an important impact on growth in particular urban sectors in certain epochs. For example, the import liberalization in the late 1960s may have spurred city growth. But the impact elasticities are too small to believe that the effect on urbanization was great.

Three additional policy forces remain. First, total tax revenues increased rapidly during the 1960s and 1970s, providing a strongly urbanizing force. Second, taxes related to land, rural goods, and incomes became less important, and this may have been responsible in part for the city growth slowdown. This influence was probably more than offset, however, by the rise in excise and sales taxes, which we have seen to exert a strong urbanizing influence. Our guess is that these last two forces were overshadowed by the first, namely, the overall rise in government intervention and by some of government's nonfiscal policy changes.

6 • The Sources of Indian City Growth since 1960

6.1 The Agenda

This chapter isolates the forces driving Indian city growth since 1960. The dominant feature of the simulated urbanization patterns documented in chapter 3 is a decline in urban labor force growth from 6.4 percent per annum during 1960–64 to 3.6 to 4.0 percent thereafter. Why the slowdown in city growth? Did exogenous conditions unfavorable to city growth emerge after the early 1960s, or were some endogenous "limits" responsible for the slowdown?

India's economic environment was far from stable between 1960 and 1981 (table 6.1). Technological change occurred in all sectors, but the pace was uneven. Relative prices of internationally traded goods also varied over time: the OPEC-induced oil price rise in the 1970s was most dramatic, of course, but the terms of trade between agricultural and manufactured goods also changed sharply, favoring manufacturing in the 1960s and agriculture in the 1970s. Capital inflows declined steeply after the early 1960s and even became outflows during the Emergency period in the mid-1970s. The early 1960s also were years of relatively plentiful rainfall and high public savings rates. In short, some impressive evidence suggests that the economic environment may have been unusually favorable to city growth in the early 1960s—conditions that disappeared thereafter.

The following pages attempt to quantify the impact of these and other forces on India's city growth. Our model is well suited to the task since the simulations permit a precise assessment of the impact of a wide range of exogenous events on the Indian economy. The next section lists the likely sources of Indian urbanization. Section 6.3 focuses on two critical features of India's recent urbanization—questions that serve to organize the remainder of the chapter. Section 6.4 considers the first

Table 6.1. India's Growth Environment, 1960–1981

Exogenous Variable (Dynamic Parameter)	Per Annum Growth (%)			
	1960–64	1965–71	1972–77	1978–81
1. Imported petroleum products' price, relative to price of imported manufactures: P_Z^W/P_M^W	−3.10	−2.15	25.55	44.06
2. Imported agricultural products' price, relative to price of imported manufactures: P_A^W/P_M^W	−0.71	−1.44	3.17	2.44
3. Total labor force: $L + S$	2.21	2.21	2.21	2.21
4. Skilled labor force: S	3.38	3.90	3.90	3.90
5. Land stock (rural and urban growth rates assumed equal)	1.00	1.00	1.00	1.00
6. Total factor productivity:				
A (agriculture)	0.18	−0.19	1.43	−0.85
RS (rural services and manufacturing)	3.07	−0.25	0.91	1.38
PSR (rural public services)	2.80	3.16	1.02	4.54
M (urban manufacturing)	3.56	−0.76	0.07	1.00
KS (urban modern services)	−0.40	0.45	3.43	1.28
US (urban informal services)	3.23	1.07	2.34	1.32
PSU (urban public services)	−0.38	0.13	0.90	1.45
Nonhousing average (weighted by gross outputs)	1.45	0.03	1.40	0.73
	Levels: Epoch Averages			
7. Foreign capital inflows/GDP (%)	2.54	1.54	−0.14	0.68
8. Rainfall index	99.64	96.23	97.42	1.00
9. Government savings rate (%)	38.70	28.13	30.50	33.34

of these, namely, the sources of city growth slowdown. Section 6.5 then explores the second, namely, explanations for India's slow urban transition compared to its Asian neighbors.

6.2 What Do We Mean by "Sources"?

Any exogenous shock can influence city growth, of course, but here we focus only on a limited number of forces that the literature suggests might be critical.

Of special interest are variables that exhibit volatile behavior after 1960, for India's urban transition has been far from smooth. Thus, we may distinguish between sources of urbanization likely to have been stable during the 1960s and 1970s, and others that were not. The former includes endogenous Engel effects, increased capital and skill intensity, and other forces associated with steady per capita income improvement.[1] The latter include key exogenous variables referred to collectively as the "growth environment." These include rates of technological progress in various sectors, world prices, capital inflows, and government policy. This growth environment is documented in table 6.1.

The first item to note is the extraordinary inflation of imported petroleum products' prices *relative* to imported manufactures (which serves as the numeraire in BMW). The 1960s saw P_Z^W/P_M^W decline briskly, while the 1970s, of course, faced an OPEC-induced price explosion. A similar but less dramatic switch in trends is observed in the price of agricultural imports relative to manufactures. World price trends were, therefore, favorable to rapid city growth in the 1960s, as the relative price of two key intermediate inputs into urban production (particularly manufacturing) fell. In contrast, relative price trends in world markets were far more unfavorable to Indian urban growth in the 1970s.

The unfavorable world price trends in the 1970s were joined by dramatic declines in capital inflows and government savings rates. Bountiful aid characterized the early 1960s, but a severe contraction accompanied the 1965 war with Pakistan. Net capital inflows actually became negative with the Emergency in the mid-1970s but then rebounded modestly during the first Janata government toward the end of the decade. Government savings rates (defined as the ratio of public sector savings to total government revenue, both terms including capital inflows from abroad) peaked in the early 1960s but then fell dramatically during 1966–72 before recovering. The higher rates early in the 1960s for the most part reflect large capital inflows, but the unusually low rate in the late 1960s largely reflects a shift in policy.

The economywide rate of technical progress reached a high in the early 1960s (1.4 percent per annum), but it was followed by a dismal period (1965–71), when economywide productivity gains fell virtually to zero. The rate recovered (1.4 percent) during the second green revolution era in the mid-1970s, but in the late 1970s India achieved a rate only about half as great.

With the exception of the *KS* and public service sectors, productivity growth declined everywhere in the late 1960s, and manufacturing led the way. The manufacturing productivity decline reflected in part the impact of the droughts of 1965, 1966, and 1968—through rising input prices—but it also reflected structural rigidities resulting from industrial policy. The early 1960s were therefore years of rapid productivity growth in the "leading" sectors, urban manufacturing in particular. The mid-

1. A discussion of the key forces driving urbanization is given in United Nations (1980, pp. 30–33).

1970s were also years of rapid growth, but in contrast to the early 1960s, agriculture and *KS* were the leading sectors. Urban manufacturing continued to lag behind. Finally, the late 1970s exhibited moderate productivity gains in all sectors other than agriculture and, in that sense, were years of "balanced" growth outside of agriculture.

Other demographic and economic forces were at work as well. BMW captures many of these, such as shifts in the sectoral allocation of public investment and changes in tax rates. Other forces, such as wage policy shifts, cannot be captured as readily, although approximations are possible (see chaps. 5 and 9). There can be little doubt, however, that the economic environment facing India must have played an important role in contributing to the city growth slowdown.

6.3 Two Key Questions

The urbanization of India's labor force is striking in two respects. First, simulation produces a dramatic city growth slowdown (table 6.2), from about 6.4 percent per annum in the early 1960s to just under 4 percent in the 1970s, with even lower rates during the late 1960s. Although it cannot be documented year by year, reality may have differed slightly from the simulation if actual migration adjustments lagged behind current urban employment opportunities. But migration lags could not have altered the true underlying trends by much: the city growth slowdown (captured in both the Benchmark simulation and in the census figures: see table 3.9) must have reflected fundamental urban "pull" and rural "push" forces.

Equally striking is the slow average rate of city growth throughout the period. India's urban population grew at 4.2 percent between 1960 and 1981, well below the 5.3 percent achieved by other low-income countries during this period, or the 4.6 percent achieved by other South Asian countries.[2] Indeed, the comparison is even more striking after 1964: simulated Indian urban labor force growth from 1964 to 1981 was only 3.8 percent.

A second focus of inquiry is, therefore, why India's urban transition has proceeded at such a sedate pace compared with its neighbors and with other nations at comparable levels of development. India's slow city growth may reflect in part the fact that it faced less favorable environmental conditions: this issue is the subject of chapter 7. But it may

2. These figures are taken from the World Bank (1983, table 22, p. 190). The low-income country figure is weighted by population and excludes China; the Southern Asian figure is an unweighted average for Bangladesh, Burma, Nepal, Pakistan, Sri Lanka, and Thailand. India's *urban labor force* grew at 4.2 percent during this period. Its total urban population, however, grew at an annual rate of only 3.5 percent.

Table 6.2. City Growth Response to Productivity, World Price, and Policy Counterfactuals

	Benchmark (1)	Productivity Counterfactual			World Price Counterfactual		Policy Counterfactual		Combined Effects
		(A) (2)	(B) (3)	(C) (4)	(D) (5)	(E) (6)	(F) (7)	(G) (8)	(H) (9)
Epoch I: 1960–1964									
1. % Urban, 1964	16.32	16.32	16.32	16.32	16.32	16.34	16.24	16.36	16.22
2. City growth, per annum	6.44	6.44	6.44	6.44	6.44	6.48	6.31	6.51	6.27
3. Net in-migration rate	4.09	4.09	4.09	4.09	4.09	4.12	3.96	4.15	3.92
4. Net out-migration rate	0.74	0.74	0.74	0.74	0.74	0.74	0.70	0.74	0.70
5. Increase in share urban, % per annum	0.61	0.61	0.61	0.61	0.61	0.62	0.59	0.62	0.59
6. Net in-migration share of urban population increase	65.79	65.79	65.79	65.79	65.79	65.99	65.02	66.18	64.79
7. Share of urban workers skilled	10.71	10.71	10.71	10.71	10.71	10.71	10.71	10.71	10.71
8. Share of migrants skilled	4.35	4.35	4.35	4.35	4.35	4.35	4.08	4.48	4.10
Epoch II: 1965–1971									
1. % Urban, 1971	17.94	18.12	17.97	19.14	17.95	17.88	18.25	17.91	19.39
2. City growth, per annum	3.60	3.75	3.62	4.57	3.61	3.53	3.93	3.54	4.85
3. Net in-migration rate	1.36	1.47	1.36	2.26	1.37	1.28	1.65	1.28	2.55
4. Net out-migration rate	0.28	0.31	0.28	0.49	0.28	0.27	0.34	0.27	0.56
5. Increase in share urban, % per annum	0.23	0.26	0.24	0.40	0.23	0.22	0.29	0.22	0.45
6. Net in-migration share of urban population increase	37.90	40.28	38.44	51.02	38.11	37.15	43.02	37.09	54.19
7. Share of urban workers skilled	11.44	11.51	11.44	10.96	11.44	11.45	11.50	11.36	10.95
8. Share of migrants skilled	10.88	11.91	10.94	6.04	10.87	11.11	11.81	9.58	6.58

Epoch III: 1972–1977

1. % Urban, 1977	19.89	20.50	19.72	21.01	20.10	20.13	20.88	19.85	22.49
2. City growth, per annum	3.99	4.34	3.80	3.81	4.15	4.25	4.53	3.98	4.77
3. Net in-migration rate	1.73	2.08	1.55	1.56	1.89	1.98	2.27	1.72	2.47
4. Net out-migration rate	0.41	0.50	0.36	0.39	0.45	0.47	0.56	0.40	0.66
5. Increase in share urban, % per annum	0.33	0.40	0.29	0.31	0.36	0.38	0.44	0.32	0.52
6. Net in-migration share of urban population increase	44.52	49.16	41.66	41.98	46.67	47.76	51.50	44.37	53.49
7. Share of urban workers skilled	11.99	12.27	12.03	11.18	11.96	11.94	12.24	11.82	11.03
8. Share of migrants skilled	3.56	6.82	3.60	2.09	3.77	3.85	7.48	3.45	4.51

Epoch IV: 1978–1981

1. % Urban, 1981	21.29	22.01	21.23	22.75	21.90	21.86	21.82	21.39	24.64
2. City growth, per annum	3.96	4.04	4.11	4.26	4.43	4.33	3.35	4.14	4.56
3. Net in-migration rate	1.68	1.77	1.83	1.98	2.14	2.04	1.11	1.85	2.29
4. Net out-migration rate	0.44	0.48	0.47	0.56	0.57	0.54	0.30	0.48	0.71
5. Increase in share urban, % per annum	0.35	0.38	0.38	0.43	0.45	0.43	0.24	0.39	0.54
6. Net in-migration share of urban population increase	43.29	44.78	45.42	47.62	49.50	48.31	33.84	45.80	51.41
7. Share of urban workers skilled	12.43	12.70	12.47	11.37	12.27	12.33	12.55	12.34	10.99
8. Share of migrants skilled	8.72	7.78	8.07	4.13	7.46	8.66	2.03	9.39	3.41

A: Maintains 1960–64 $\dot{T}_m$ = 3.56% value through 1981.
B: Maintains 1960–64 $\dot{T}_a$ = 0.18% value through 1981.
C: Maintains all 1960–64 $\dot{T}_i$ rates through 1981.
D: $(P_y^y/P_M^y)^* = -3.10\%$ throughout.
E: $(P_a^y/P_M^y)^* = -0.17\%$ throughout.
F: Foreign aid/GDP maintains 1960–64 average value (2.54%) through 1981.
G: Government savings rate maintains 1960–64 average value (38.70%) through 1981.
H: Combines changes in C, D, E, F, and G.

also reflect structural characteristics of the Indian economy that were inherently unfavorable to rapid urbanization. These structural constraints are the topic of section 6.5, while the next section addresses the sources of the slowdown.

6.4 Sources of the City Growth Slowdown

The Counterfactual

The sources of city growth can be identified by exploiting the counterfactual. The basis for comparison is the Benchmark simulation: this historical simulation calculates a series of annual equilibria, given observed exogenous conditions (including forces driven with a lag by earlier endogenous conditions) like factor productivity gains, world market conditions, rainfall, total and skilled labor force growth, government savings rates, tax and investment allocation policies, and foreign capital inflows. Since the Benchmark simulation seems to replicate fairly closely the historical evidence (chap. 3), counterfactual simulations can then be used to explore systematically the sources of city growth by asking how India would have grown under different exogenous conditions. By comparing these counterfactual simulations with the Benchmark simulation, we ought to be able to identify those forces that best account for the city growth slowdown after 1964. Similarly, we ought to be able to identify those exogenous variables responsible for India's relatively slow urban growth over the period as a whole.

This section focuses on the slowdown. First it examines the impact of productivity change; it then turns to the effects of relative prices, foreign capital inflows, and government savings rates. In each case, we ask how Indian experience would have been altered had the favorable environmental conditions of the early 1960s prevailed for the entire period. Comparison with the Benchmark simulation then permits us to determine the share of the slowdown that can be accounted for by the historical pattern of each environmental variable.

Productivity Slowdown

Tables 6.2 and 6.3 (cols. 2–4) report what would have happened had India maintained its productivity performance of the early 1960s. These counterfactual simulations can then be compared with the Benchmark simulation (col. 1). Table 6.2 focuses on the migration and city growth consequences of differing environmental conditions, while table 6.3 provides information on output, capital formation, and income growth.

Column 2 of tables 6.2 and 6.3 reports the consequences had manufacturing productivity growth ($\overset{*}{T}_M$) maintained the 3.56 percent rate from 1960 through 1981. In contrast, actual productivity growth in manufacturing declined sharply to -0.76 percent in the late 1960s, to 0.07 percent in the early and mid-1970s, and to 1.00 percent at the end of the period. This dramatic retardation should help account for the observed city growth slowdown, and table 6.2 confirms this expectation. But the proportion of the slowdown attributable solely to the evaporation of rapid technological progress in urban manufacturing is small, ranging from 3.2 to 14.3 percent of the total fall in city growth rates from the peak achieved in 1960–64 (table 6.4). Although productivity growth in manufacturing may be an engine of urban growth during most industrial revolutions, it has not been a powerful engine in recent Indian history.

This is not to say that other aspects of the Indian economy would not have departed greatly from their actual path had a manufacturing productivity growth rate of 3.56 percent been maintained for these two decades. In the Benchmark, nonhousing output per worker (in 1960 prices) rises from 729 Rs. in 1960 to 1023 Rs. in 1981, implying an annual growth rate of 1.63 percent. Had the high $\overset{*}{T}_M$ been maintained, however, output per worker would have grown at 3.01 percent per annum. Moreover, as table 6.3 indicates, even the poor would have gained substantially from this additional growth. More striking still is the constant price investment series: while the investment share in GDP oscillates around a very slowly rising trend in the Benchmark simulation, it rises markedly in the high $\overset{*}{T}_M$ counterfactual from 18.2 percent in 1960 to 27.0 percent in 1981.

Part of this improved counterfactual performance is engendered directly by the higher productive efficiency growth rate. The direct gains account for 0.97 percentage points of the increased GNP growth in 1965, and 0.68 points in 1981.[3] In addition, manufacturing productivity growth causes a dramatic fall in the relative price of investment goods, the latter consisting predominately of equipment produced in M (in the Benchmark, P_M falls from an index of 1.00 in 1960 to 0.93 in 1981; in the high $\overset{*}{T}_M$ counterfactual, P_M falls to 0.55 in 1981—by far the largest decline). Consequently, a given nominal savings pool can purchase more investment goods, and the rate of capital deepening is enhanced. Since more than a quarter of this additional capital is reinvested in urban manufacturing, the improved productivity performance has a multiplicative effect on output growth there, but it raises output growth elsewhere, too. In fact, the annual (1960 prices) nonhousing output growth rate

3. Direct gains are calculated as M's gross output share of 26.6 percent, times the 3.56 less 1.00 percent productivity growth rate differential.

Table 6.3. Economic Response to Productivity, World Price, and Policy Counterfactuals

	Benchmark (1)	Productivity Counterfactual			World Price Counterfactual		Policy Counterfactual		Combined Effects
		(A) (2)	(B) (3)	(C) (4)	(D) (5)	(E) (6)	(F) (7)	(G) (8)	(H) (9)
					Epoch I: 1960–1964				
1. Output growth rate (annual average %)									
Agriculture	2.30	2.30	2.30	2.30	2.30	2.30	2.30	2.30	2.30
Rural services and manufacturing	5.64	5.64	5.64	5.64	5.64	5.62	5.89	5.56	5.93
Rural public services	8.91	8.91	8.91	8.91	8.91	8.87	8.87	8.94	8.94
Urban manufacturing	10.05	10.05	10.05	10.05	10.05	10.10	10.03	10.10	10.03
Modern services	7.87	7.87	7.87	7.87	7.87	7.85	7.53	8.01	7.58
Informal urban services	5.74	5.74	5.74	5.74	5.74	5.80	5.59	5.86	5.54
Urban public services	7.23	7.23	7.23	7.23	7.23	7.24	7.17	7.31	7.26
All housing	4.64	4.64	4.64	4.64	4.64	4.65	4.67	4.63	4.67
All nonhousing GDP	5.17	5.17	5.17	5.17	5.17	5.17	5.14	5.20	5.15
2. Capital stock growth rate (annual average %)									
Urban nonhousing	7.16	7.16	7.16	7.16	7.16	7.16	7.19	7.29	7.31
Rural nonhousing	4.05	4.05	4.05	4.05	4.05	4.05	4.08	4.12	4.14
Housing: rural and urban katcha	1.60	1.60	1.60	1.60	1.60	1.60	1.58	1.59	1.59
urban luxury	8.93	8.93	8.93	8.93	8.93	8.93	9.07	8.88	9.06
3. Peasants' real disposable income growth rate, % 1964 (%)	2.16	2.16	2.16	2.16	2.16	2.16	2.17	2.17	2.18
Share of urban labor force in manufacturing, 1964 (%)	34.26	34.26	34.26	34.26	34.26	34.27	34.50	34.15	34.48
Productivity gap Average product/worker in urban manufacturing, divided by average product in agriculture, 1964	0.22	0.22	0.22	0.22	0.22	0.22	0.22	0.22	0.22
Investment/GDP, 1964 (%) (1960 prices)	20.60	20.60	20.60	20.60	20.60	20.59	20.42	20.54	20.38

Epoch II: 1965–1971

1. Output growth rate (annual average %)

Agriculture	2.27	1.58	1.49	1.52	1.52	2.19	1.87	1.89	1.51
Rural services and manufacturing	5.50	2.08	1.58	1.92	1.85	5.48	2.02	2.14	1.86
Rural public services	6.78	6.79	6.22	6.42	6.40	6.51	6.38	6.61	6.38
Urban manufacturing	9.82	4.56	3.70	3.77	3.89	9.19	4.01	8.81	3.87
Modern services	7.64	5.16	7.65	6.22	6.25	7.23	6.25	7.84	6.23
Informal urban services	5.30	2.64	3.25	2.76	2.81	4.90	2.89	3.55	2.79
Urban public services	6.34	5.55	4.87	4.70	4.78	5.28	4.79	5.43	4.76
All housing	5.43	4.78	4.66	4.63	4.63	5.31	4.70	4.26	4.63
All nonhousing GDP	5.33	3.11	3.18	3.01	3.03	5.03	3.22	4.45	3.02

2. Capital stock growth rate (annual average %)

Urban nonhousing	8.77	7.35	6.74	6.49	6.50	7.53	6.53	7.43	6.52
Rural nonhousing	5.12	4.15	3.83	3.75	3.71	4.45	3.73	4.73	3.73
Housing: rural and urban katcha	2.07	1.11	1.02	0.99	1.01	2.06	1.11	0.24	1.01
urban luxury	8.48	8.51	8.17	8.22	8.16	8.18	8.22	8.21	8.18

3. Peasants' real disposable income growth rate, %

Peasants' real disposable income growth rate, %	2.54	0.37	0.26	0.23	0.24	2.35	0.49	1.12	0.23
Share of urban labor force in manufacturing, 1971 (%)	37.41	37.09	34.61	35.73	35.77	37.25	35.72	35.01	35.79
Productivity gap Average product/worker in urban manufacturing, divided by average product in agriculture, 1971 %	0.18	0.21	0.21	0.21	0.21	0.18	0.22	0.16	0.21
Investment/GDP, 1971 (%) (1960 prices)	24.54	20.66	19.64	18.96	18.97	21.68	18.85	21.61	18.97

Epoch III: 1972–1977

1. Output growth rate (annual average %)

Agriculture	2.85	2.46	2.38	2.32	3.06	2.24	1.21	3.16	2.42
Rural services and manufacturing	6.07	3.26	3.14	3.06	3.56	5.76	2.72	4.08	3.25
Rural public services	8.56	6.14	5.43	5.97	6.38	8.52	6.10	5.80	5.99
Urban manufacturing	10.31	5.36	4.73	5.79	6.04	9.10	4.99	9.78	5.48
Modern services	6.67	6.24	9.68	6.23	7.06	4.01	5.97	9.13	6.22

Table 6.3. continued

	Benchmark (1)	Productivity Counterfactual			World Price Counterfactual		Policy Counterfactual		Combined Effects
		(A) (2)	(B) (3)	(C) (4)	(D) (5)	(E) (6)	(F) (7)	(G) (8)	(H) (9)
Informal urban services	3.68	4.93	3.24	4.93	4.11	3.73	4.51	3.68	6.23
Urban public services	5.38	6.35	5.28	4.74	6.09	5.60	5.56	4.01	6.37
All housing	4.10	4.42	3.95	4.89	4.25	4.12	4.26	4.23	5.36
All nonhousing GDP	4.06	6.11	3.40	5.18	4.66	4.08	4.57	4.08	6.27
2. Capital stock growth rate (annual average %)									
Urban nonhousing	5.40	7.70	5.37	7.92	5.54	5.42	6.14	5.70	9.42
Rural nonhousing	2.95	5.24	2.98	5.30	3.07	2.92	3.31	3.18	6.13
Housing: rural and urban katcha	2.42	2.34	2.19	4.25	2.50	2.47	2.43	2.49	4.60
urban luxury	8.24	8.95	8.22	7.25	8.44	8.18	8.53	8.52	7.91
3. Peasants' real disposable income growth rate, %	1.16	2.47	0.24	2.06	1.77	1.12	1.23	1.22	2.91
Share of urban labor force in manufacturing, 1977 (%)	40.10	37.61	40.35	40.40	39.73	40.32	35.96	41.51	39.33
Productivity gap									
Average product/worker in urban manufacturing, divided by average product in agriculture, 1977	0.23	0.14	0.22	0.15	0.23	0.23	0.23	0.23	0.15
Investment/GDP, 1977 (%) (1960 prices)	17.74	22.52	17.88	22.55	17.78	17.65	19.69	19.67	28.10
					Epoch IV: 1978–1981				
1. Output growth rate (annual average %)									
Agriculture	0.71	1.53	1.68	2.41	2.40	0.59	0.91	0.72	4.27
Rural services and manufacturing	3.34	4.97	3.80	6.92	4.32	3.24	3.69	3.38	7.37

Rural public services	8.15	8.37	8.12	6.95	8.40	7.72	9.14	7.90	7.73
Urban manufacturing	4.10	8.26	4.33	8.12	5.78	4.57	5.51	4.22	10.33
Modern services	8.18	8.40	8.56	6.96	9.00	8.29	3.84	8.95	6.86
Informal urban services	3.44	4.38	3.90	5.76	4.65	3.71	2.60	3.75	6.99
Urban public services	5.25	6.48	5.36	4.44	6.49	5.48	5.85	5.32	6.16
All housing	3.94	4.91	3.90	5.49	4.25	3.98	4.24	4.04	6.19
All nonhousing GDP	3.80	5.65	4.35	5.73	5.11	3.88	3.51	3.94	7.21
2. Capital stock growth rate (annual average %)									
Urban nonhousing	5.72	8.69	5.64	8.42	6.03	5.77	6.19	3.74	9.73
Rural nonhousing	3.54	6.63	3.44	6.50	3.80	3.48	3.78	5.93	7.35
Housing: rural and urban katcha	2.80	3.83	2.75	5.46	3.17	2.90	3.09	2.89	6.17
urban luxury	6.75	7.73	6.67	6.46	6.80	6.67	7.32	6.83	7.25
3. Peasants' real disposable income growth rate, %	0.20	1.60	0.94	2.74	1.72	0.21	0.35	0.25	4.30
Share of urban labor force in manufacturing, 1981 (%)	39.88	37.66	39.63	40.58	39.30	40.24	38.41	40.83	39.81
Productivity gap									
Average product/worker in urban manufacturing, divided by average product in agriculture, 1981	0.22	0.12	0.22	0.13	0.23	0.22	0.22	0.22	0.14
Investment/GDP, 1960 (%) (1960 prices)	20.67	27.03	20.70	26.90	20.65	20.63	21.86	21.79	30.39

A: Maintains 1960–64 $\hat{T}_m^* = 3.56\%$ value through 1981.

B: Maintains 1960–64 $\hat{T}_a^* = 0.18\%$ value through 1981.

C: Maintains all 1960–64 $\hat{T}_i^*$ rates through 1981.

D: $(P_i^w/P_i^x)^* = -3.10\%$ throughout.

E: $(P_i^w/P_i^x)^* = -0.17\%$ throughout.

F: Foreign aid/GDP maintains 1960–64 average value (2.54%) through 1981.

G: Government savings rate maintains 1960–64 average value (38.70%) through 1981.

H: Combines changes in C, D, E, F, and G.

Table 6.4. Accounting for India's City Growth Slowdown

	Epoch		
	1965–71	1972–77	1978–81
City growth decline relative to epoch I (1960–64), percentage points per annum	2.84	2.45	2.48
% decline accounted for by changes in:			
1. $\overset{*}{T}_m$	5.3	14.3	3.2
2. $\overset{*}{T}_A$	0.7	−7.8	6.0
3. All $\overset{*}{T}_j$	34.2	−5.2	12.1
4. $(P_Z^W/P_M^W)^*$	0.4	6.5	19.0
5. $(P_A^W/P_M^W)^*$	−2.5	10.6	14.9
6. Capital inflows/GDP	11.6	22.0	−24.6
7. Government savings rate	−2.1	−0.4	7.3
8. 3–7 Combined	44.0	31.8	24.2
9. Residual	56.0	68.2	74.8

gap between the high $\overset{*}{T}_M$ counterfactual and the Benchmark widens between the late 1960s (4.45 versus 3.02 percent) and the mid-1970s (6.11 versus 4.06 percent), this despite a slight narrowing in the high $\overset{*}{T}_M$ counterfactual's productivity advantage in the latter era because manufacturing's relative size increases as well.

The effect of maintained $\overset{*}{T}_A$ on the city growth slowdown is small, in part because the early 1960s did not enjoy a large agricultural productivity growth advantage over other periods. Indeed, both relative and absolute values of $\overset{*}{T}_A$ were considerably higher in the mid-1970s. But in no epoch did changes in agricultural total factor productivity growth account for more than a small portion of the urban slowdown (table 6.4).

The more interesting result concerns the net dynamic impact of increased agricultural productivity, which promotes rather than retards urbanization. This outcome is surprising given that chapter 4 has already established that, *in the short run*, productivity advance in agriculture tends to cause modest deindustrialization and a retention of labor in the countryside. Here, instead, dynamic growth-inducing effects dominate. Agricultural productivity gains raise labor's marginal physical productivity in agriculture. But in a largely closed economy, agricultural productivity gains cause price to fall markedly, offsetting the gains in marginal physical products. This price decline, combined with dynamic Engel effects in the long run, ultimately causes labor shedding in agriculture. The price decline also reduces intermediate input costs in manufacturing—reinforcing the labor-shedding effect in the countryside, although informal services experience most of the urban employment expansion.

The combined effect of maintaining each sector's productivity growth at the early 1960s rates can be seen in column 4 of tables 6.2 and 6.3. In periods when these productivity growth rates represent an improvement over those estimated in the Benchmark, the urban growth slowdown is less pronounced. This is particularly apparent in the late 1960s when India experienced large productivity growth declines in the M, RS, US, and A sectors: maintained productivity growth rates would have raised annual city growth rates from 3.6 to 4.6 percent. The late 1970s was another epoch in which average productivity growth rates were significantly below the 1960–64 average, helping to account for the long-run city growth slowdown.

The combined effect of maintaining all productivity growth rates at 1960–64 levels differs considerably from the effect of maintaining only agriculture and urban manufacturing productivity growth at 1960–64 rates. This pattern reflects the importance of the service sectors and rural manufacturing; it also reflects interaction effects. Rapid manufacturing productivity growth exerts strong pressures on agricultural production, both to supply inputs for processing and to supply food to the growing urban labor force (which consumes more food per worker than does the rural labor force because real incomes are higher). Stagnant agricultural productivity thus serves to brake the urbanizing impulse of manufacturing productivity growth. But even with constant productivity growth in all sectors, urbanization decelerates substantially after the early 1960s.

The city growth record of the constant total factor productivity growth counterfactual in the mid-1970s is of particular interest. Benchmark city growth occurred at an annual rate of 3.99 percent, while urban counterfactual city growth would have been only 3.81 percent. Although the Benchmark did not enjoy a powerful manufacturing productivity boom that pulled in migrants, it offset this disadvantage by experiencing a KS productivity boom, as well as substantial rural labor-shedding productivity gains in agriculture. In consequence, two very different sectoral productivity growth patterns of approximately equal aggregate value serve to generate similar city growth rates. The patterns in the early 1960s tend to mirror closely stereotypical unbalanced productivity growth, in which manufacturing leads and agriculture lags; in contrast, the mid-1970s patterns are quite unorthodox, suggesting that we neglect "secondary" service sectors at our peril.

Maintenance of the early 1960s' productivity growth rates would have had an extraordinary impact on output, incomes, and capital formation.

Even the modest counterfactual rise in $\overset{*}{T}_A$ (from -0.19 to 0.18 percent) and gains in $\overset{*}{T}_{US}$ and $\overset{*}{T}_{RS}$ generate a substantial improvement in real GDP growth in the late 1960s (5.03 percent in col. 4 of table 6.3, versus 4.45 percent in col. 2 when only $\overset{*}{T}_M$ improves, and 3.02 percent in the Benchmark).

The improved productivity performance would have been felt especially by the poor: real peasant income growth rates double from 1.12 to 2.35 percent per annum during 1965–71, when manufacturing retains its early 1960s pace of productivity growth. An almost equally dramatic surge is recorded in the late 1970s. It could be argued, therefore, that the 1960–64 productivity growth patterns had a relatively egalitarian impact. Relative to the Benchmark, three sectors expand dramatically in the counterfactual productivity experiments for the late 1960s and late 1970s: A, RS, and US. These three are the most labor intensive, and, of course, A dominates the budgets of both the rural and urban poor, while RS and US also are important consumption items.

Prolonged rapid manufacturing productivity growth would have generated a large rise in the constant price investment/GDP series because of cheaper capital goods. Although more rapid capital deepening would have been pronounced in the urban sectors (urban capital formation accelerates across epochs in the counterfactuals, table 6.3), rural capital deepening rises at a roughly equal rate in the counterfactual. In fact, the urban/rural capital stock growth rate differential steadily narrows in the counterfactual, as does the luxury/nonluxury housing stock growth differential.

In summary, had India maintained the productivity growth rates of the early 1960s for the entire period, it would have traced out a very different growth path. Sectoral output and capital stock growth rates would have been faster *and* far more balanced. But while technological retardation can account for *all* of the considerable decline in GDP growth, it accounts for only a modest 16 percent of the city growth rate reduction (table 6.5).

The city growth rate still declines by more than 2 percentage points after 1964 even when productivity growth rates are maintained. However, because the more modest slowdown does eliminate nearly half of the difference between Indian and other South Asian city growth rates over the two decades, its influence can hardly be viewed as negligible. The most prominent effect of the stable productivity growth regime is to eliminate completely the large decline in output growth: in the counterfactual case, output per worker growth actually increases over time.

Table 6.5. What If India Had Maintained the Productivity Performance of the Early 1960s?

	Annual Change %				% of Benchmark Decline "Explained"
	A 1960–64	B 1965–81	C 1960–81	D A–B	
Benchmark					
Urban labor force	6.44	3.82	4.31	2.62	
Nonhousing GDP per worker	2.90	1.33	1.63	1.57	
All sectors maintain 1960–64 $\overset{*}{T_j}$ values					
Urban labor force	6.44	4.23	4.65	2.21	15.65
Nonhousing GDP per worker	2.90	2.97	2.96	−0.07	104.46

Relative Price Shifts

World price trends have been volatile since 1960, and they may well have been important in helping account for the city growth slowdown in India. Our model has three exogenous prices, all for imported goods: petroleum products, agricultural commodities, and manufactures, the last serving as the numeraire. India is a large and fairly closed economy, however, so that imported and domestic A and M goods are only imperfect substitutes. Consequently, while world prices influence domestic prices of these key tradables, the link is hardly one for one.[4]

Nonetheless, world price movements were dramatic, and they did favor rapid urbanization in the 1960s and slow urban growth in the 1970s. Imported petroleum products have been used far more intensively in urban than in rural production, especially prior to the rise in fertilizer use and mechanization that accompanied the green revolution. Even by 1981, Z inputs were only 3 percent of gross agricultural output. Consequently, the gentle but sustained fall in the relative price of petroleum products from 1960 through 1969 (P_Z^W/P_M^W fell from 1.00 to 0.62) cut production costs mainly for urban products, thereby favoring urban output expansion. Furthermore, since the model assumes unitary elasticity of substitution between intermediate inputs and value added, falling petroleum costs cause the demand for all primary inputs, including labor, to increase. Consequently, if urban sectors are the main users of

4. Recall from the high $\overset{*}{T_M}$ counterfactual that the price of domestically produced manufactures fell by 45 percent against imported manufactures over the period 1960–81. Even more striking is the 22 percent rise in the price of domestic agricultural products in response to the 1965 drought in the Benchmark simulation—during a period when world agricultural prices were stable.

petroleum products, falling P_Z^W will favor city employment and city growth. In contrast, the extraordinary rise in P_Z^W/P_M^W from 0.62 in 1969 to 12.78 in 1981 should have discouraged city growth.

The counterfactual simulation in column 5 of tables 6.2 and 6.3 reports what would have happened had petroleum products continued to fall at the 1960–64 rate of 3.10 percent per annum. Since the decline during the late 1960s was similar (-2.15 percent), 1965–71 patterns are virtually unaffected by maintaining the initial rate of price decline. The main impact is felt in the 1970s. Had oil price increases in the mid-1970s not taken place but, at the same time, had the relative price decline of the early 1960s continued, the city growth rate would have risen from 3.99 to 4.25 percent.

Only during the late 1970s do world oil price increases have a large impact on Indian urbanization, and even then they account for only 19 percent of the slowdown in city growth relative to the early 1960s (table 6.4). In contrast, rising fuel scarcity accounts for over half of the city growth slowdown in the Kelley-Williamson representative developing country model.[5] The difference reflects India's more closed economy, in which imports play a comparatively minor role.

While fuel scarcity had only a modest impact on urbanization, it had a larger impact on economic performance in general. In the absence of the OPEC-induced price rise, nonhousing GDP would have grown at an annual rate of 5.11 percent in the late 1970s—nearly as high as the 5.17 percent rate recorded in the early 1960s, and far better than the 3.80 percent recorded in the Benchmark simulation. Even during the 1972–77 period the effect of rising oil prices was substantial, causing a fall in output growth from 4.66 percent in the counterfactual to 4.06 percent in Benchmark. Large declines were felt in nearly all sectors, in some cases directly because of soaring input costs and in others because of indirect demand effects stemming from the multiplier.

The relative price trends of other raw material imports mirrored the fuel price patterns but were much weaker. The relative price of agricultural imports declined between 1960 and 1969 and then rose thereafter. This rise in the relative price of agricultural goods choked off urbanization on two counts. First, even though imported and domestic agricultural goods are not perfect substitutes, a rising P_A^W still encourages a strong output (and hence labor demand) response in domestic agriculture. In addition, since urban manufacturing is a major user of agricultural intermediates, it experiences large cost increases and thus an output contraction.

5. See Kelley and Williamson (1984, pp. 133–36). City growth rates decline in their benchmark from 5.41 percent per annum 1970–73 to 4.65 percent per annum in 1973–79; with constant fuel prices, the latter figure would have been 5.09 percent.

Had P_A^W continued to fall at -0.71 percent per annum, as it did in the early 1960s, the city growth slowdown in the 1970s would have been less marked: the relatively moderate price reversals account for 10.6 percent of the city growth slowdown in the mid-1970s and 14.9 percent of the slowdown in the late 1970s (table 6.4).[6] When these are added to the oil price effects, it appears that unfavorable world price trends account for about one-sixth of the city slowdown in the mid-1970s, and about one-third of the slowdown in the late 1970s.

Falling Foreign Capital Inflows and Government Savings Rates

Public intervention plays an important role in the Indian economy, and our model has been developed to account for it. The period 1960–81 was also characterized by many policy changes that might have been responsible for part of the urban growth slowdown. The model can capture changes in tax policy, shifts in spending between current and capital accounts, and changes in the sectoral allocation of government investment. We concentrate here on government savings policy, since it has undergone considerable variability and has received considerable attention.[7]

Government savings as a proportion of revenue were far higher in the early 1960s than subsequently, particularly in the late 1960s. This trend reflects in large part the evaporation of foreign aid, as Bhagwati and Srinivasan (1975, p. 234) have shown. The decline in foreign capital inflow during the late 1960s not only put direct pressure on the government to replace consumption goods provided by foreign aid, but it also occurred during a time of exceptional current expenditure needs, as the nation faced severe drought and war with Pakistan. Pressure to raise public savings to provide for the growing public investment plan was partially successful in the 1970s. But weak economic performance and hence low remittances from public enterprises (also captured in BMW; see chap. 3) have consistently caused projected revenues to exceed realizations. In addition, continued pressure for high current expenditures, in part spurred by growing food grain procurements and inter-

6. The 1960–64 city growth rate in column 6, as well as in columns 7–9, of table 6.2 differs slightly from the annual Benchmark rate. These differences reflect data smoothing over the entire period: P_A^W/P_M^W declines at a constant rate of -0.71 percent in the counterfactual, including the 1960–64, whereas historical values are used in the Benchmark.

7. See, for example, Bhagwati and Srinivasan (1975, pp. 9, 126, 234–35). Like us, they attribute much of the marked decline in public savings rates to decreasing foreign aid. A more detailed discussion of public policy can be found in V. K. R.V. Rao (1983, pp. 146–50).

vention in the Bangladesh war of independence, kept the public savings rate below the very high rates in the early 1960s.

Foreign capital inflows were influenced by many policies. India's reluctance to borrow from abroad during this period was partially responsible for the generally low level of foreign capital inflows,[8] as was a somewhat hostile attitude toward foreign investment. Political differences with major donors led to a suspension of aid in late 1965, while capital flight surrounding the Emergency period had an even more pronounced effect in the 1970s. The ratio of foreign capital inflows to GDP declined from just under 1 percent in 1974 to roughly zero in 1975, and then to about −1.5 percent in 1976 and 1977 before again becoming positive under the Janata government.[9]

In summary, the early 1960s were years of high capital inflows and government savings rates. Capital inflows fell markedly during the late 1960s. Three crop failures and two wars with Pakistan combined with the inflow decline to cause a dramatic reduction in government savings as well. Government savings recovered slightly during the mid-1970s, but foreign capital inflows turned negative during the Emergency period. Finally, the late 1970s were a period of rising inflows and government savings rates, although they did not reach the levels of the early 1960s.

Columns 7 and 8 of tables 6.2 and 6.3 assess the impact of these forces. Column 7 focuses on the decline in capital inflows, and hence in both public sector revenue and foreign exchange availability, but assumes that the government does not alter its savings rate from historical values. Instead, the counterfactual asks how India would have fared if capital inflows had maintained the share in GDP (2.54 percent) enjoyed in the early 1960s. Thus, the simulation permits us to isolate the direct capital inflow effects of government revenue and foreign exchange availability. In column 8, we then focus on the decline in the public savings rate, in part a response to smaller capital inflows.

Foreign capital inflows should favor city growth to the extent that they serve to augment government revenue (all inflows do in the model) and that government expenditure patterns have an urban bias. Since central government purchases consist mainly of employee services (KS) or capital goods (M), they do indeed contain an urban bias. Moreover, government employs skilled labor intensively, and the latter consume

8. India's external public debt as a share of GDP in 1981 was only 10.8 percent; the weighted average for other low-income countries excluding China was 28.3 percent. See the World Bank (1983, p. 178).

9. An erratic decline in foreign exchange reserves continued from 1978 through 1981; it is captured in our model as a foreign capital inflow, as we do not explicitly model monetary stocks. The decline culminated in a precedent-setting and heatedly debated IMF loan. See Datt (1981).

an expenditure bundle that, in turn, has an urban bias. Furthermore, foreign capital inflows generate both per capita GDP growth, hence Engel effects and capital deepening, hence growth in the capital-using (urban) sectors.

A rise in government savings rates also favors city growth rates by augmenting the rate of capital accumulation, GDP growth, and capital deepening. The long-run impact of this shift is to augment urbanization, since a rupee spent on capital goods generates more urban employment than does a rupee spent on bureaucrats' or soldiers' salaries. The short-run effects are less clear, since the rise represents a shift in demand from KS (consumption) to M (investment) goods. Indeed, civil servants' (KS employees) expenditures have much smaller leakages to rural areas than do the expenditures of unskilled industrial workers (M employees), for whom food remains the predominant consumption good. Thus, the short-run impact on city growth of shifts in the public savings rate remains indeterminate a priori.

As it turns out, both the decline in capital inflows and the government savings rate contributed to the city growth slowdown. The impact of the foreign inflow decline is felt mainly during the Emergency period: without the decline, the urban labor force would have grown at 4.53 percent per annum during the mid-1970s rather than 3.99 percent recorded in the Benchmark simulation. But while foreign capital flows account for nearly half (44 percent) of the decline during the Emergency relative to 1960–64, only about 7 percent of the total post-1964 decline in city growth rates can be accounted for by reductions in foreign capital inflows.[10] The effect of diminished foreign capital inflows on real per worker GDP growth is slightly greater: had those inflows remained constant, per worker GDP would have declined from 2.90 percent (1960–64) to 1.50 percent (1965–81), rather than to the historical 1.33 percent rate. In summary, foreign capital inflows mattered, but they were a key force in suppressing city growth rates only during the mid-1970s.

The consequences of falling public savings rates are weaker still. When government savings rates are maintained, the rate of nonhousing capital formation growth is 5.07 percent (1965–81), a considerable in-

10. The negative contribution of foreign inflows during the final epoch (table 6.4) reflects the fact that the inflow has a major impact on the urban labor force *level*. Because negative outflows depressed the Benchmark urban labor force level in 1977, its subsequent growth is large relative to the counterfactual simulation in which levels were not affected. Thus, in the Benchmark, recovery from the Emergency is characterized by a one-time boost in the urban labor force by 6.50 percent between 1977 and 1978; urban population for the rest of the epoch grows at only 3.12 percent, *below* the constant foreign aid share counterfactual rate.

crease over the benchmark rate of 4.66 percent. The net city growth effects are small, however: just under 1 percent of the decline in city growth rates after 1964 can be attributed to the decline in government savings rates. The impact on GDP growth is greater but still modest: about 5 percent of the per worker GDP growth rate decline resulted from falling public savings.

Environmental Impact versus Endogenous Forces

The final columns in tables 6.2 and 6.3 sum up all of these environmental impacts. The counterfactual experiment is to estimate the consequences for Indian economic performance when all major environmental variables are kept at their 1960–64 levels. Thus, rates of technological progress by sector, foreign capital inflows as a share of GDP, government savings rates, and world price trends are all kept at their 1960–64 rates for the entire period following 1960. Any city growth slowdown that still occurs is a residual, attributable either to changes in the growth environment omitted from the select group considered here (but captured in the model) or to endogenous limits on rapid urban growth.[11] The omitted environment factors are difficult to quantify, and some of them—like accelerating skills accumulation—worked to augment city growth rates. In any case, we shall treat the residual as the net effect of endogenous limits to urban growth in what follows.

Comparing the entire period 1965–81 with the early 1960s, we find that unfavorable environmental conditions accounted for just over 35 percent of the reduction in city growth rates. From a rural perspective, the impact is more pronounced, since 71 percent of the reduction in the rural out-migration rate can be explained by the presence of these unfavorable environmental conditions (table 6.6).

The 1960–64 growth environment was indeed conducive to rapid urbanization. The entire difference in 1965–81 city growth rates between India and the rest of South Asia would have been eliminated had the growth environment of the early 1960s continued. But a significant slowdown would have persisted nonetheless.

What were the endogenous forces that caused the city growth slowdown? Much of the answer can be gleaned by noting that out-migration rates from rural areas are nearly as high in the counterfactual constant

11. Since the residual is derived by comparing simulated growth rates from the maintained 1960–64 growth environment with the Benchmark, it follows that the residual is driven only by forces contained in our model. Other factors omitted from the model may also have contributed to the observed slowdown, but since the Benchmark simulation appears to replicate city growth trends fairly accurately, the net effects of such omitted factors should be quite small.

Table 6.6. The Impact of Unfavorable Environmental Conditions on the City Growth Slowdown after the Early 1960s

| | Benchmark Values | | | Constant Economic Environment | Difference Attributable to: | |
	1960–64 (1)	1965–81 (2)	Difference (1 − 2) (3)	1965–81 (4)	Environmental Changes (4 − 2)/3	Endogenous Forces
City growth rate	6.44%	3.82%	2.62%	4.75%	35%	65%
Out-migration rate	0.74	0.36	0.38	0.63	71	29
Nonhousing GDP per worker growth rate	2.90	1.33	1.57	3.81		
Nonhousing capital stock growth rate						
Urban	7.16	5.94	1.22	9.22		
Rural	4.05	3.41	0.64	6.00		

growth environment simulation in the late 1970s (table 6.2 col. 9, 0.71 percent) as in the early 1960 (table 6.2, col. 1, 0.74 percent). That is, the rate of growth in rural excess labor supply would have remained fairly stable. In contrast, capital deepening tended to generate far more rapid growth in urban labor demand in the constant growth environment scenario.

In a sense, then, maintenance of the 1960–64 growth environment would have propelled India along a Lewis-Fei-Ranis development path. In 1960, India might have been characterized as a classic surplus labor economy, but two decades of rapid capital accumulation and productivity growth would have led the economy well into a phase of limited labor and rising food prices. The relative price of agricultural goods accelerates slowly in the constant growth environment counterfactual (the growth in P_A rises from 2.4 percent per annum in 1960–64 to 2.6 percent per annum in 1965–81), while it decelerates in Benchmark (falling from 2.3 percent per annum in 1960–64 to 1.7 percent per annum in 1965–81). At the same time, constant-price peasant incomes undergo accelerating growth in the high-growth environment, rising from 2.18 percent (1960–64) to 2.54 percent (1965–71) to 2.91 percent (1972–78) and to 4.30 percent (1978–81). Apparently, these labor scarcity forces would have swamped the buoyant urban labor demand forces, generating high but declining rates of urban employment growth.

While endogenous forces would have caused a considerable slowdown in the city growth rate even in the absence of unfavorable environmental conditions after 1964, they would not have generated a similar decline in the rate of capital accumulation or in GDP growth. Instead, maintenance of the high rates of total factor productivity growth would have generated the accelerating investment boom described above. By the

1970s, even rural capital stock growth rates would have been impressive. Rapid and accelerating rates of capital formation would have combined with high and rising rates of economy-wide factor productivity growth to yield an acceleration in per worker GDP growth. Thus, nonhousing GDP growth per worker reaches nearly 5 percent per annum by the late 1970s when the high productivity growth environment of the early 1960s is maintained (counterfactual output growth rates per worker are 3.06 percent 1965–71, 3.98 percent for 1972–77, and 4.89 percent for 1978–81, while the Benchmark rates are 0.79, 1.81, and 1.56 percent, respectively).

India did not, of course, enter into an era of prolonged accelerated development. The early 1960s were a uniquely favorable epoch, and it would have been an exceptional piece of good luck for the growth environment of that period to have been sustained. The counterfactual simulations indicate only that endogenous forces would not have prevented India from enjoying rapid development in the presence of favorable environmental conditions.

Characteristics of Rural-Urban Migration

The simulations document many other aspects of the urban transition in addition to city growth. Indeed, some "transition" variables undergo far more dramatic change than does city growth itself—like rural out-migration rates or urban in-migration rates (table 6.2). This fact is of considerable relevance if it is these migration rates that guide policy.

Given constant growth in the indigenous urban labor supply, it is a mathematical certainty that in-migration rates from rural areas exhibit greater variance in response to urban labor demand shocks than does the urban labor force itself. Relatively small changes in urban labor demand imply much larger accommodating changes in immigration rates, emigration rates, and, especially, the migrant share of movements in the urban labor force. These accommodating migrations are the indicators that place greatest pressure on policy reaction. Emigration from densely populated rural areas is a critical indicator of the need to promote land-saving agricultural innovations and nonfarm employment alternatives for a growing rural labor force pressing on the land. New urban migrants are associated with sprawling squatter settlements often completely lacking in basic public services. Failure to expand those public services to a growing indigenous population implies crowding and more intense use of existing infrastructure services; failure to extend those public services to new urban migrants implies the creation of a large group without any basic services at all.

The essential point is simply that changes in migration flows are amplified in city growth performance. Therefore, we would do well to focus at length on rural-urban migration, since it may be government officials' central concern.

Maintenance of the 1960–64 growth environment certainly would have implied a dramatic reduction in the pressure on government to raise the living standards of the rural poor. Sectoral productivity and relative price trends during the early 1960s were, apparently, egalitarian. After all, real peasant incomes growing at rates of 2.2 to 4.3 percent per annum would have made India a model for South Asia, had those conditions persisted. Out-migration rates of 0.56 to 0.71 percent would have limited rural population growth to 1.5 to 1.7 percent per annum. In fact, the urban output and employment growth slowdown in the late 1960s were particularly cruel, since they sharply restricted out-migration during a seven-year period that experienced three severe droughts.

The economic consequences of the counterfactual constant growth environment relative to Benchmark offer a striking contrast for India's urban planners. In the early 1960s, nearly two-thirds of all new urban workers were migrants. This share diminished over time, but new migrants would have remained a majority of the urban population increment under a more favorable growth environment counterfactual. In contrast, India's city growth slowdown must have eased any pressure to accommodate the migrants because the Benchmark simulated share of migrants in urban population growth fell below 45 percent after 1964 and was only 38 percent during the late 1960s. India's policy of discouraging further growth in the largest cities like Calcutta and Bombay, by hindering new investments and redirecting social infrastructural investments, would have been untenable had high immigration rates persisted.

Development specialists hostile to rapid urbanization often focus on the selective aspects of rural-urban immigration: even though their skill level tends to be inferior on average to the nonmigrant urban population, emigrants tend to be among the most productive and skilled rural workers.[12] Urban growth, it is argued, drains the countryside of an important and scarce resource. BMW is faithful to this brain drain view. In the Benchmark simulation, between about 4 and 11 percent of the migrants are skilled. This is below the proportion of all urban workers with skills, which rises from 10.7 to 12.4 percent during the period, but well above the skilled labor share in the rural labor force, which rises from 2.8 percent in 1960 to 3.4 percent in 1981. That emigrants should be more skilled than the average rural worker is an inevitable consequence of urbanization, since urban activities are skill intensive.

12. In fact, Indian migrants may have *better* skills than nonmigrants. See B. Banerjee (1984, esp. p. 249).

6.5 India's Slow Urbanization and Other Issues

Many of the environmental conditions that contributed to India's city growth slowdown after the early 1960s were also present in other developing countries. Yet most developing nations experienced a city growth speedup, not a slowdown (Kelley and Williamson, 1984). What were the forces unique to India that might account for both the slowdown and the relatively modest rate of urbanization throughout the period?

Land Scarcities and Skill Bottlenecks

Based on table 6.7 (col. 2), growing land scarcity is not a very plausible candidate for explaining peculiarities in Indian city growth performance. Here the trivial impact of increasing agricultural land scarcity is clearly illustrated. In contrast with the 1 percent expansion rates assumed in the Benchmark simulation, the counterfactual simulation assumes no land expansion at all. The results are unambiguous: rural land scarcity has virtually no effect on urbanization.

It appears that agricultural land scarcity has had little to do with either the slow pace of India's city growth or its deceleration. Indeed, contrary to common belief, land scarcity in the Indian countryside does not push people into the cities at all. Instead, it tends to reduce incomes everywhere, causing urbanization forces to ebb.[13] Nor, moreover, is *urban* land scarcity of major importance.

If rural land scarcity did not matter, perhaps skilled labor bottlenecks did. Since urban activities are far more skill intensive than rural activities, augmented skilled labor supplies should favor urban output expansion and city growth. Table 6.7 (col. 3) illustrates the impact of a more skills-abundant regime in which the skilled labor force is allowed to grow at 4.92 percent per annum (total labor force growth is held constant). This 4.92 percent figure equals the 1961–81 rate of capital accumulation in the Benchmark simulation, which in turn is very close to the recorded historical capital stock growth rate.[14] The more skills-abundant regime is indeed urbanizing: the average city growth rate rises

13. Even in a small, open economy (such as in Kelley and Williamson, 1984, p. 137) in which rural land scarcity does induce migration to the cities, the net effects are extremely small.

14. The figure is also close to the (endogenous) 5.16 percent annual skilled labor force growth rate from 1973 to 1979 in the Kelley-Williamson (1984, p. 128) representative developing country model. In contrast, their 1960–73 growth rate of 4.06 percent is close to the 3.90 percent skilled labor force growth rate we assume characterized India from 1965 onwards.

from 4.32 percent in the Benchmark to 4.59 percent in the counterfactual.

While the rate of skilled labor force growth matters, its impact is modest. Even with a much more skills-abundant regime, India's cities would still have grown more slowly than those of its neighbors, and much more slowly than the Third World average.

The Monsoon and Droughts

The 1960s experienced severe drought in 1965, 1966, and 1968; poor precipitation was also recorded in 1962, 1972, 1974, and 1976. Since agricultural stagnation appears to retard city growth in the long run, one would expect droughts to curtail urban growth as well, but how important were these effects? Table 6.7 (col. 4) shows the results of a counterfactual in which the state of the monsoon does not vary. It appears that droughts matter little in the medium and long runs. True, city growth rates in the early 1960s would have been lower, and they would have been higher thereafter—thus taking some of the drama out of the city growth slowdown—but the magnitudes are minor. It is also true, however, that short-run effects are often considerable: without droughts, India's urban labor force would have grown at an annual rate of 5.40 percent between 1964 and 1966; in the Benchmark, cities grew at only 4.03 percent over the same two years. But the consequences are temporary, and trends in Benchmark and the counterfactual soon merge.

Suppose, however, India had enjoyed a *prolonged* stretch of favorable weather: would the economy have "taken off" and experienced permanently higher income and urbanization levels, even after a subsequent period of compensating poor rainfall? To address this possibility, rainfall levels are assumed to be 5 percent more bountiful than normal from 1961 to 1971, and 5 percent below average during the following decade (table 6.7, col. 5). Bountiful rains tend to reduce urban labor costs, raising profits and rates of capital accumulation. If enough time goes by, the economy's structure may change sufficiently so that the damage of future droughts will be muted.

As it turns out, prolonged stretches of good or bad weather make little difference to city growth, even though India remains critically dependent on the monsoon. The decade of good weather does release labor to the cities. Consistent with the effects of rising agricultural productivity, per worker income does grow more rapidly, at 1.77 percent per annum (1960–71) instead of the 1.55 percent rate recorded in the Benchmark solution. Peasant real income growth does better still, rising from 0.93 percent in the Benchmark to 1.22 percent in the good monsoon

Table 6.7. City Growth Response to Skilled Labor Availability and Conditions in Agriculture Counterfactuals

	Benchmark (1)	Land Scarcity $\dot{R}_A = 0$ (2)	Skill Scarcity $\dot{S} = 4.92\%$ (3)	Rain		Green Revolution Effects $\dot{T}_A$		
				1.0, 1960–81 (4)	1.05, then 0.95 (5)	0%, 1960–81 (6)	4.55%, 1960–81 (7)	−0.80%, 1960–81 (8)
Epoch I: 1960–1964								
1. % Urban, 1964	16.32	16.31	16.43	16.25	16.41	16.23	16.50	16.28
2. City growth per annum, %	6.44	6.42	6.62	6.33	6.59	6.29	6.77	6.37
3. Net in-migration rate, %	4.09	4.07	4.25	3.97	4.22	3.96	4.40	4.01
4. Net out-migration rate, %	0.74	0.73	0.76	0.71	0.76	0.70	0.79	0.72
5. Increase in share urban, % per annum	0.61	0.61	0.64	0.59	0.63	0.59	0.66	0.60
6. Net in-migration share of urban population increase, %	65.79	65.69	66.71	65.08	66.49	65.12	67.49	65.36
7. Share of urban workers skilled, %	10.71	10.71	10.77	10.73	10.69	10.84	10.60	10.73
8. Share of migrants skilled, %	4.35	4.39	3.77	4.49	4.40	5.74	3.64	4.54
Epoch II: 1965–1971								
1. % Urban, 1971	17.94	17.87	18.41	18.00	18.14	17.63	18.90	17.67
2. City growth, per annum	3.60	3.55	3.89	3.72	3.68	3.42	4.19	3.41
3. Net in-migration rate	1.36	1.29	1.61	1.43	1.44	1.17	1.90	1.22
4. Net out-migration rate	0.28	0.27	0.34	0.30	0.29	0.24	0.41	0.25
5. Increase in share urban, % per annum	0.23	0.22	0.28	0.25	0.25	0.20	0.34	0.20
6. Net in-migration share of urban population increase	37.90	37.10	42.48	39.43	39.00	35.03	46.52	35.76
7. Share of urban workers skilled	11.44	11.46	12.29	11.35	11.28	11.63	11.05	11.52
8. Share of migrants skilled	10.88	11.20	9.19	10.61	10.76	11.00	8.64	11.78

Epoch III: 1972–1977

	(1)	2	3	4	5	6	7	8
1. % Urban, 1977	19.89	19.73	20.78	20.01	19.88	18.36	22.14	18.93
2. City growth per annum	3.99	3.91	4.30	4.03	3.78	2.90	4.94	3.33
3. Net in-migration rate	1.73	1.66	2.03	1.76	1.54	0.69	2.64	1.08
4. Net out-migration rate	0.41	0.39	0.50	0.42	0.36	0.15	0.72	0.24
5. Increase in share urban, % per annum	0.33	0.31	0.40	0.33	0.29	0.12	0.54	0.21
6. Net in-migration share of urban population increase	44.52	43.40	48.52	44.89	41.60	24.22	55.17	33.15
7. Share of urban workers skilled	11.99	12.05	13.54	11.89	12.00	12.85	11.26	12.33
8. Share of migrants skilled	3.56	3.58	4.55	3.06	3.62	8.51	4.03	3.93

Epoch IV: 1978–1981

	(1)	2	3	4	5	6	7	8
1. % Urban, 1981	21.29	21.15	22.50	21.45	21.15	19.33	24.13	20.47
2. City growth per annum	3.96	4.01	4.25	4.00	3.82	3.53	4.44	4.23
3. Net in-migration rate	1.68	1.73	1.97	1.72	1.54	1.27	2.15	1.93
4. Net out-migration rate	0.44	0.44	0.55	0.45	0.40	0.30	0.65	0.47
5. Increase in share urban, % per annum	0.35	0.35	0.43	0.36	0.32	0.24	0.50	0.39
6. Net in-migration share of urban population increase	43.29	43.96	47.44	44.03	41.25	36.77	49.60	46.70
7. Share of urban workers skilled	12.43	12.50	14.54	12.40	12.50	13.53	11.39	12.87
8. Share of migrants skilled	8.72	8.92	8.51	9.06	8.77	11.08	5.19	9.07

2: Benchmark conditions, except $\overset{*}{R}_A = 0$.
3: Benchmark conditions, except skilled labor grows at 4.92% 1960–81 (the Benchmark rate of capital accumulation).
4: Benchmark conditions, except no monsoon variation: RAIN = 1.0, 1960–81.
5: Benchmark conditions, except bountiful rains in early years: RAIN = 1.05 for 1960–71; RAIN = 0.95, 1972–81.
6: Benchmark conditions, except no green revolution: $\overset{*}{T}_A = 0$; no input use shifts, 1960–81.
7: Benchmark conditions, except the Punjab experience generalized: $\overset{*}{T}_A = 4.55\%$, 1960–81.
8: Benchmark conditions, except Maharashtra and Madhya Pradesh generalized: $\overset{*}{T}_A = -0.80\%$, 1960–81.

counterfactual. A decade of bad rains completely offsets these limited gains, however. The effects on city growth are weaker still. Cities grow at a slightly more rapid pace during the 1960s, but slower growth in the 1970s more than offsets the earlier gains. In summary, the effects of rainfall patterns on urbanization tend to be restricted to the short run.

The Green Revolution

More interesting possibilities emerge when agricultural technological change is considered. Not only was the 1960–81 average rate of technological progress slightly positive (0.21 percent), but also the share of intermediate inputs in gross output rose from roughly 10 to 25 percent. Since it is gross output that determines food supply, the labor-releasing consequences of the green revolution were greater than would be suggested solely by value-added trends.

The importance of these green revolution forces can be seen in table 6.7 (col. 6). Here, counterfactual agricultural stagnancy is assumed: neither disembodied technological progress nor changes in intermediate input shares are allowed to occur. The result is a considerable reduction in city growth rates, especially in the mid-1970s. It appears that structural changes associated with the adoption of the HYV seed/fertilizer/irrigation/pesticide package were considerably more important than the rather modest Indiawide technological gains.

A technologically stagnant agriculture would have led to a decline in the 1960–81 city growth rate from 4.32 to 3.84 percent. This fall would roughly double the growth rate difference between India and its neighbors and would increase by nearly 50 percent the gap between India and all poor nations. Furthermore, since the green revolution was most pronounced between 1965 and 1975, it follows that the city growth slowdown would have been even more dramatic under unchanging agricultural conditions. The Benchmark 1965–81 annual city growth rate of 3.82 percent was 2.62 percentage points lower than the 1960–64 rate; in the stagnant agricultural counterfactual, the post-1965 city growth rate of 3.26 percent is 3.03 points lower.

Without the green revolution, considerably fewer workers would have been released from rural activities after 1964, and the city growth slowdown would have been far more pronounced. The technical changes that engendered rapid increases in gross output induced a more dramatic food price decline than would have occurred in its absence, thus releasing labor. In a very broad sense, then, the green revolution has been "rural labor saving."

The rise of intermediate and capital input requirements in agriculture as an influence on urbanization has received scant attention. The simulations presented here indicate that these backward linkages may have been fairly important. Had all of India experienced the same growth in intermediate input use as did the Punjab and other green revolution areas, Indian cities might have grown far more rapidly.

Suppose Indian agriculture everywhere had enjoyed factor productivity growth like that of the northwest? Might a prolonged, well-diffused green revolution have caused India's cities to grow as rapidly as its neighbors' cities? To address this issue, we assume in table 6.7 (col. 7) that all India experienced agricultural factor productivity growth at 4.55 percent per annum for the entire period 1960–81.[15] The response is large: city growth rates over the two decades rise from 4.32 to 4.94 percent, thus eliminating about 60 percent of the difference between India and the Third World average and the entire difference between India and its neighbors. Extraordinary agricultural productivity gains do release large numbers of workers. These gains also would have generated extraordinary income growth: nonhousing output would have grown at 4.17 percent instead of 1.63 percent. But agricultural productivity growth differences can account for only a limited share of the slow pace of Indian urbanization relative to its neighbors, as these countries did not record productivity growth rates in agriculture around 4.55 percent.

While India's green revolution has been concentrated in the northwest and parts of the south (especially Tamil Nadu), in huge portions of the country total factor productivity appears to have been declining. Much of this decline appears attributable to a fall in the share of land devoted to high productivity food grains.[16] Particularly poor performances have been realized in the populous heartland of Maharashtra and Madhya Pradesh. Evenson (1976, pp. 332–33) estimates agricultural productivity growth for Maharashtra and Madhya Pradesh to have been -2.13 and -1.52 percent for the period 1963–65, respectively; Andhra Pradesh, Bihar, and Kerala also experienced declining total factor productivity during this period.

To assess the impact of extreme agricultural retardation, and to contrast this situation with the positive scenario from northwest India, table 6.7 (column 8) considers the impact of setting $\overset{*}{T}_A$ equal to -0.80 percent for all India for the entire period 1960–81. Even this negative value understates central Indian reality, but the impoverishing effect of

15. This figure, 4.55 percent, seems to be close to an upper bound; indeed, it is probably unrealistic for any country for a two-decade period. The value is roughly equal to Evenson's (1976) residual productivity growth estimates (4.7 percent) for Punjab, Haryana, and Uttar Pradesh for 1964–65 through 1969–71, weighted by population. It is also roughly equal to Evenson's estimate (weighted by number of districts) for 1960–71.

16. See Vyas (1983, pp. A151–156).

a persistent productivity decline is so great—the urban poor exhaust virtually all of their incomes on required expenditures in drought years— that the model will not accept greater rates.

Deterioration in agricultural productivity causes output per worker growth to decline (the 1960–81 average nonhousing growth rate falls to 1.10 from 1.63 percent in the Benchmark) and the relative price of agricultural products to rise (the relative price of A rises from 1.00 in 1960 to 1.66 in 1981 in the counterfactual, and to 1.45 in the Benchmark). Food scarcity and slower growth cause real incomes of urban and rural unskilled workers to decline. While declining productivity in agriculture is certainly harmful to peasants, it is much more severe for the urban poor, particularly when a drought year compounds the shortfall. As Sen (1982) has stressed, shrinking entitlements due to adverse terms of trade make famine shortfalls more critical for some groups of poor than for others, while smallholders remain (relatively) secure. In any case, the generalized Maharashtra/Madhya Pradesh counterfactual yields slower city growth rates than the Benchmark: 4.12 versus 4.32 percent (1960– 81).

Getting It All Together

Had the most favorable environmental conditions for rapid city growth persisted throughout the period, how rapidly would India have urban- ized? Conditions for rapid city growth did exist since, after all, extremely high rates are recorded for the early 1960s. It is not obvious, however, that the early 1960s represented the maximum attainable growth rate. In fact, city growth in the early 1960s was below the rate that would have occurred if all of the most favorable environmental conditions had persisted together for two decades (table 6.8). Under these most fa- vorable environmental conditions, Indian cities would have grown at 5.90 percent across the two decades, rather than at 5.07 percent under maintained 1960–64 (favorable) conditions or 4.32 percent in the (less favorable) Benchmark.

The "most favorable" counterfactual is likely to set an upper bound on what Indian city growth might have been. While the counterfactual might appear extreme, it is nonetheless revealing. For example, while city growth does slow down after 1964 in the most favorable counter- factual, the decline is far smaller than in the Benchmark. In fact, the urban labor force growth rate accelerates in the late 1970s. Moreover, while the high city growth rates of the early 1960s are not repeated, rural out-migration rates are considerably higher in the 1970s than even in the early 1960s. Two decades of ideal urban growth conditions would have caused the urban share of India's labor force to more than double.

Table 6.8. India's City Growth Potential: A "Most Favorable" Counterfactual

	Epoch			
	1960–64 (1)	1965–71 (2)	1972–77 (3)	1978–81 (4)
1. % Urban, end of epoch	16.66	21.01	25.41	29.23
2. City growth, % per annum	6.99	5.66	5.50	5.86
3. Net in-migration rate, %	4.59	3.31	3.17	3.52
4. Net out-migration rate, %	0.83	0.78	0.97	1.33
5. Increase in share urban, % per annum	0.70	0.62	0.73	0.95
6. Net in-migration share of urban population increase, %	68.43	60.87	59.73	62.07
7. Skilled share of in-migration, %	9.57	8.91	6.16	5.22
8. Urban nonhousing output growth, % per annum	9.90	10.33	10.73	11.27
9. Rural nonhousing output growth, % per annum	3.90	3.68	4.63	5.69

The counterfactual assumes the following environmental conditions most favorable to city growth:
Technological progress: A 1.43% (1972–77)
$\quad\quad\quad\quad\quad\quad RS$ −0.25 (1965–71)
$\quad\quad\quad\quad\quad\quad PSR$ 4.54 (1978–81)
$\quad\quad\quad\quad\quad\quad M$ 3.56 (1960–64)
$\quad\quad\quad\quad\quad\quad KS$ 3.43 (1972–77)
$\quad\quad\quad\quad\quad\quad US$ 3.23 (1960–65)
$\quad\quad\quad\quad\quad\quad PSU$ 1.45 (1978–81)

World price: $(P_A^W/P_M^W$ grows at −1.44% (1965–71)
$\quad\quad\quad\quad\quad (P_Z^W/P_M^W)$ grows at −3.10% (1960–64)
Foreign capital inflow: F/GDP = 2.54% (1960–64)
Government savings rate: 38.7% (1960–64)

An economic transformation would have occurred as well: a 7.52 percent annual growth rate would have caused per worker output to nearly triple; agriculture's share in nonhousing value added would have fallen from 48 to 25 percent (versus 31 percent in the 1981 Benchmark simulation). Thus the conditions for extraordinarily rapid urbanization and economic growth were present in India, as the environmental conditions in the "most favorable" counterfactual were all drawn from the set of observed values. Slow growth persisted instead because environmental conditions were not consistently favorable; rather, they tended to be unfavorable most of the time.

6.6 Summary

India's slow rate of urbanization reflects both environmental conditions that gave rise to a major growth slowdown after the early 1960s and the gradual emergence of increasing labor scarcity. About a third of the post-1964 slowdown can be attributed to relatively unfavorable environmental conditions. Among these environmental conditions, unfavorable world price trends and slower productivity advance are of roughly equal importance; both are about twice as important as declining capital inflows. The remaining two-thirds reflect rising labor costs, largely a result of rising agricultural prices.

The slow urban transition was not inevitable, at least not to the extent that poor productivity growth performance and declining private capital inflows reflect flawed policy. On the other hand, world price trends and generally reduced aid flows for the most part were not of India's making and could not have been avoided. Nor, obviously, did the Indian government have complete control over productivity growth rates. All of this leaves one question unanswered: what would have been India's experience had its growth environment been similar to the typical LDC during these decades? The answer to this question might suggest the extent to which the structure of the Indian economy inhibits city growth. It might also suggest the extent to which India's growth environment was particularly unfavorable. These issues are the topic of the next chapter.

7 • Why Have India's Cities Grown Slowly?

7.1 Slow City Growth in India? A Comparative Assessment

Three recent publications have offered detailed comparative evidence showing that Indian urbanization experience seems to conform closely with Third World patterns as a whole (Mohan, 1985; Mills and Becker, 1986, chap. 3). Thus, Mohan concludes that "over 75 percent of the variance between levels of urbanization observed for 110 to 120 countries for which data are available can be explained by per capita income differences between these countries. India lies close to the regression line: hence the level of urbanization in India is consistent with the experience of other countries throughout the world" (p. 620). On the other hand, Indian city growth over the past two decades or so has been relatively slow. To quote Mohan again, "India is not faced with 'urban explosion' as compared with trends in many other parts of the world. . . . The rate of growth of urban population in India is . . . among the slower rates in the world" (p. 620).

Table 7.1 documents the relatively slow city growth in India for 1960–81. Based on population figures, India's cities grew much slower than cities did in the Third World as a whole ("average," 97 countries), 3.5 versus 5.3 percent per annum. Nor does Indian city growth look any better when the comparison is limited to low-income countries, or even to nineteenth-century America. The difference is still large when India is compared with the Kelley/Williamson forty-country sample, 3.5 versus 4.5 percent per annum. The KW sample is restricted to countries that have a good historical data base, enjoyed per capita income growth of at least 1 percent per annum, were not major mineral exporters (including oil), and were not heavily dependent on foreign capital (Kelley and Williamson, 1984, pp. 76–77), conditions which India satisfies as well. The comparison with the KW forty-country sample is, therefore,

Table 7.1. Comparative City Growth Performance, 1960–1981

Countries	Rate per Annum (%)	Source
India, based on		
Population, actual	3.5	WDR 1983, table 22
Labor force, actual	4.2	Table 3.10, panel C
Labor force, model	4.3	Table 3.10, panel C
Low-income economies		
34 Countries	4.3	WDR 1983, table 22
Those in 40-country sample	5.1	WDR 1983, table 22
Middle-income economies		
63 Countries	4.2	WDR 1983, table 22
Those in 40-country sample	4.3	WDR 1983, table 22
Average Third World		
97 Countries	5.3	WDR 1983, table 22
40-Country sample	4.5	WDR 1983, table 22
Industrial market economies	1.6	WDR 1983, table 22
Addendum: 19th-century America	4.8	KW 1984, p. 135

Unweighted averages are used throughout, and except for the two labor force entries for India, all are based on population. WDR refers to the *World Development Report,* and KW to Kelley and Williamson (1984, pp. 76–77). The 40-country sample refers to those countries analyzed by Kelley and Williamson. The sample was restricted to those that had a good data base, enjoyed per capita income growth of at least 1% per annum, were not major mineral exporters (including oil), and were not heavily dependent on foreign capital imports.

especially relevant, and the remainder of this chapter will find it useful to use that sample as a yardstick in searching for the causes of slow Indian city growth.

The key puzzle revealed by these city population growth figures is that Indian cities grew at least 1 percentage point per annum slower than the typical Third World country between 1960 and 1981. But Indian city growth looks much faster when labor force figures are exploited. This finding implies rising labor participation rates in the city relative to the countryside. Since these alternative city growth estimates are much closer to Third World averages, the reader might be encouraged to conclude that the relatively low city growth in India would disappear if growth were measured properly. Such inferences are, however, unwarranted: city growth rates may be understated by the same amount in other Third World countries where labor participation rates in the city relative to the countryside are likely to exhibit the same trends, given that urban immigrants always tend to be young adults (Williamson, 1989). While we shall be dealing with Indian labor force figures in what follows, we still have that slow city growth differential of 1 percentage point (and possibly more) to explain.

7.2 Why Did India's Cities Grow Slowly?

There are three possible explanations for slow city growth in India. First, indigenous demographic, accumulation, and productivity forces may account for the slow growth. That is, whatever explanations we may offer for the relatively modest rate of economic growth in India should help account for the slow city growth as well. Second, India may have faced external conditions in world commodity and capital markets that were less favorable to city growth. Third, the structure of and the institutional arrangements in the Indian economy may be such that city growth is less responsive to favorable forces than is true of other Third World countries. These would include structural imperfections in labor and capital markets, and they might also include the deleterious impact of policies that reduce labor intensity in manufacturing and deflect investment from private urban services, all of which would tend to choke off urban employment and thus city growth.

This chapter offers a brief assessment of these issues. Section 7.3 explores the impact of demographic forces, section 7.4 estimates the role of world commodity and capital markets, and section 7.5 isolates the influence of sectoral productivity performance. Each section exploits counterfactual analysis in which we ask questions like, What would city growth have been like if India had faced the conditions that prevailed in the rest of the Third World? The chapter concludes with section 7.6, in which all of these forces are combined, thus making it possible to see how much of the 1 percentage point slow city growth differential can be explained by these environmental factors and how much is left as a residual.

7.3 What if India Had Faced Different Demographic Conditions?

Can the slower rates of population and labor force growth in India account for most of the slow city growth differential? Certainly the conventional literature would suggest so. More than a decade ago, a World Bank team told us that "the increase in population growth of the twentieth century is *the single most important factor* distinguishing present and past urbanization" (Beier et al., 1976, p. 365, italics added). Preston (1979, p. 204) agreed, telling us that "the rate of population growth in the nation in which a city is located has a powerful effect on a city's growth rate." Similar comments can be found elsewhere in the literature. If it can be shown that India had significantly lower rates of population and labor force growth, then the argument certainly sounds plausible. And population growth rates *were* lower in India: while the rate of growth was 2.2 percent per annum in India between 1960 and 1981, it rose from 2.5 to 2.7 percent per annum in the KW forty-country sample over the same period, and it averaged 2.6 percent per annum in nineteenth-century America, a country that also registered higher rates of city growth.

Table 7.2 asks: How would city growth rates have behaved had India faced different rates of population and labor force growth? The counterfactuals are implemented by changing the aggregate labor force (and population) growth parameter, while holding all other conditions in Benchmark constant. The results, at least in part, confirm the stress that Beier et al., Preston, and others have placed on overall population growth. Had India been burdened with nineteenth-century America's higher rates of population growth, it would have had city labor force growth rates averaging almost 4.7 percent per annum, remarkably close to the 4.8 percent city growth rate that America in fact achieved (U.S. Bureau of the Census, 1975, pp. 11–12). More to the point, had India been burdened with the higher labor force growth typical of the rest of the Third World, it would have achieved city labor force growth rates averaging 4.68 percent per annum. Compared with Benchmark, this implies that Indian urban labor force growth rates would have been 0.36 percentage point higher, a large share of the 1 percentage point slow city growth differential to be explained. However, there is an even larger share left unexplained. While the slower population growth in India

Table 7.2. What If India Had Faced Different Demographic Conditions? Counterfactual City Growth, 1960–1981 (% per annum)

| | | Under Counterfactual Labor Force Growth: | | |
	Benchmark (1)	US 19th Century (2)	Average Third World (3)	Post–World War II Europe (4)
1960–66	5.63	5.93	5.88	4.63
1966–71	3.43	3.75	3.69	2.37
1971–76	3.95	4.35	4.36	2.66
1976–81	4.00	4.47	4.55	2.85
1960–81	4.32	4.68	4.68	3.20

See text for counterfactual experiments' motivation. $\overset{*}{S}$ adjusted so that skill-deepening rates are all like Benchmark, and aggregate labor force growth rates per annum are:

Period	Benchmark	Average Third World	US 19th Century	Post–World War II Europe
1960–64	2.21	2.54	2.61	0.9
1965–71	2.21	2.54	2.61	0.9
1972–77	2.21	2.68	2.61	0.9
1978–81	2.21	2.68	2.61	0.9

certainly helps account for the slower city growth, it does not account for all or even most of the slow city growth differential. Population growth is *not* "the single most important factor" accounting for India's relatively slow city growth. Other forces played a more important role.

The same point can be made in another way: compared with the industrialized countries, rapid population growth is *not* "the single most important factor" accounting for the unusual city growth problems that characterize India and the rest of the Third World. Had India enjoyed the much lower rates of population growth that prevailed in post–World War II Europe, 0.9 percent per annum, it still would have registered unusually rapid city growth rates by twentieth-century European standards, around 3.2 percent per annum. Economic factors have played a far more important role in accounting for the "urban explosion" in the Third World, even in India where city growth has been less spectacular.

7.4 What If India Had Faced Different Conditions in World Commodity and Capital Markets?

Since India's import and export mix differed from that of other Third World countries, it may have faced somewhat different trends in the relative prices of tradable primary products and manufactures. Moreover, these different trends in the terms of trade between agriculture and manufactured goods, as well as in the relative prices of imported fuels and raw materials, may have implied a less favorable city growth environment. Finally, India may, relative to its GNP, have absorbed smaller capital inflows from abroad. How much of the slow city growth differential can be explained by such forces?

Table 7.3 supplies some answers. Here we report four counterfactuals. Two involve world commodity markets: column 2 reports a counterfactual in which India experiences the slightly more favorable relative price trends that faced the KW forty-country Third World sample, while column 3 reports a counterfactual in which relative world prices are taken to be constant over the two decades. The second of these suggests that Indian city growth would have been a bit faster had world relative prices remained stable over the two decades. However, the influence of world price shocks was uneven across the period. While world price trends offered a modest stimulus to Indian city growth in the 1960s (the Benchmark figures for 1960–71 are somewhat larger than than those for the counterfactual "constant price" regime), they generated a more powerful negative influence on city growth in the 1970s, especially late in the decade. The first counterfactual indicates that only a trivial part of the slow city growth differential can be explained by less favorable world price shocks facing India across the two decades. Once again,

Table 7.3. What If India Had Faced Different Conditions in World Commodity and Capital Markets? Counterfactual City Growth 1960–1981 (% per annum)

		Under Counterfactual World Price Conditions		Under Counterfactual Capital Inflow Conditions:	
	Benchmark (1)	Average Third World (2)	Constant Prices (3)	Average Third World (4)	No Inflow (5)
1960–66	5.63	5.37	5.44	5.76	5.11
1966–71	3.43	3.36	3.39	3.72	3.71
1971–76	3.95	4.17	4.22	4.53	4.50
1976–81	4.00	4.38	4.69	3.65	3.62
1960–81	4.32	4.37	4.48	4.48	4.27

See text for counterfactual experiments' motivation. The experiments assume the following about world prices and net foreign capital inflows (as a share in GNP):

	Prices (% per annum)						F/GNP (%)		
	Benchmark		Average Third World		Constant Prices			Average Third	No
	P_z	P_A	P_z	P_a	P_z	P_A	Benchmark	World	Inflow
1960–64	−3.15	−.71	0	0.7	0	0	2.54	3.0	0
1965–71	−2.17	−1.45	0	0.7	0	0	1.54	3.0	0
1972–77	22.75	3.12	6.8	1.6	0	0	−.14	3.0	0
1978–81	36.51	2.41	6.8	1.6	0	0	.68	3.0	0

however, the influence is uneven. Although in the early 1960s India enjoyed world price shocks more favorable to city growth than the rest of the Third World (the Benchmark figure for 1960–66 is larger than that for the counterfactual "average Third World" regime), it suffered by comparison in the 1970s. For the two decades as a whole, however, world price trends cannot account for much of the slow city growth differential (4.37 − 4.32 = 0.05 of the 1 percent differential).

The remaining two counterfactuals in table 7.3 involve capital inflows: column 4 reports a counterfactual in which India faces the more favorable capital inflow conditions that were typical of the KW forty-country sample, while column 5 reports a saving self-sufficiency counterfactual in which there are no foreign capital inflows at all. These counterfactuals suggest that a significant part of the slow city growth differential can be explained by the smaller capital inflows (as a share of GNP) into India between 1960 and 1981. The second counterfactual illustrates how modest were capital inflows to India across the two decades as a whole since without any foreign capital at all city growth would not have been much slower (the Benchmark figure for 1960–81 is 4.32, while in the "no inflow" counterfactual regime it would have been 4.27). Once again, however, the impact was uneven. Indian city growth was powerfully stimulated by capital inflows in the early 1960s and the late 1970s, but it was seriously constrained during the Emergency period of capital flight. Overall, the rest of the Third World was favored by heavier capital inflows, which helped to finance the extensive capital requirements of city building and thus of city growth. Indeed, had India been favored with those more generous capital inflows, it would have achieved significantly, but not dramatically, higher city growth (the counterfactual "average Third World" capital inflow regime records a city growth figure of 4.48 for 1960–81, significantly larger than the Benchmark figure of 4.32). In short, a small portion of the slow city growth differential *can* be explained by the more modest capital inflows into India across the two decades.

In summary, India faced unfavorable world commodity and capital market conditions compared with the rest of the Third World, and that fact helps explain a portion of the slow city growth differential. These influences were modest, however, when compared with the demographic differences discussed in section 7.3 and the productivity differences discussed below.

7.5 What If India Had Achieved Faster Rates of Productivity Growth?

Compared with the rest of the Third World, India underwent slower per capita income growth over the period 1960–81; one would therefore expect that it also achieved lower rates of total factor productivity growth. While that was especially true of agriculture and manufacturing, it is not necessarily the case that the sectoral total factor productivity growth *differentials* were any lower in India. To illustrate this point, consider a portion of the evidence presented in the note to table 7.4, say the rates of total factor productivity growth in agriculture (A) and manufacturing (M) for India (Benchmark) compared with the Third World average underlying the KW forty-country sample:

Total Factor Productivity Growth Estimate 1960–81 (%)

	Agriculture	Manufacturing	Difference
India (Benchmark)	0.18	0.62	0.44
Third World average	1.54	2.03	0.49

Productivity advance in these two sectors was far slower in India than in the rest of the Third World. Surprisingly, however, the difference between the two sectors was roughly the same, and this differential—

Table 7.4. What If India Had Achieved Different Rates of Sectoral Total Factor Productivity Growth? Counterfactual City Growth, 1960–1981 (% per annum)

Period	Benchmark (1)	Under Counterfactual Sectoral Total Factor Productivity Growth Conditions		
		Average Third World (2)	Average Asia (3)	Taiwan (4)
1960–66	5.63	4.97	5.68	5.75
1966–71	3.43	3.75	4.45	4.44
1971–76	3.95	3.50	3.95	4.09
1976–81	4.00	4.26	4.76	4.73
1960–81	4.32	4.16	4.76	4.80

See text for counterfactual experiment's motivation. The experiments assume (% per annum):

$\dot{T}_j$:	A	Rs	PSR	M	KS	US	PSU
1960–64							
Benchmark	0.18	3.07	3.19	3.56	−0.40	3.23	−0.38
Average Third World	1.54	1.12	1.12	2.03	1.12	1.12	1.12
Average Asia	2.23	1.81	2.99	1.81	1.81	1.81	1.81
Taiwan	2.10	1.86	1.86	3.59	1.86	1.86	1.86
1965–71							
Benchmark	−0.19	−0.25	3.59	−0.76	0.45	1.07	0.13
Average Third World	1.54	1.12	1.12	2.03	1.12	1.12	1.12
Average Asia	2.23	1.81	1.81	2.99	1.81	1.81	1.81
Taiwan	2.10	1.86	1.86	3.59	1.86	1.86	1.86
1972–77							
Benchmark	1.43	0.91	1.17	0.07	3.43	2.34	0.90
Average Third World	1.54	1.12	1.12	2.03	1.12	1.12	1.12
Average Asia	2.23	1.81	1.81	2.99	1.81	1.81	1.81
Taiwan	2.10	1.86	1.86	3.59	1.86	1.86	1.86
1978–81							
Benchmark	−0.85	1.38	5.28	1.00	1.28	1.32	1.45
Average Third World	1.54	1.12	1.12	2.03	1.12	1.12	1.12
Average Asia	2.23	1.81	1.81	2.99	1.81	1.81	1.81
Taiwan	2.10	1.86	1.86	3.59	1.86	1.86	1.86

The sectoral total factor productivity growth estimates are taken from: "average Third World," Kelley and Williamson (1984, table C.8, p. 236), underlying their 40-country sample; "average Asia," Kelley and Williamson (1984, table C.8, p. 232), an aggregation of Hong Kong, Singapore, South Korea, Taiwan, the Philippines, and India; and "Taiwan," Kelley and Williamson (1984, table C.2, p. 231).

unbalanced productivity advance—has been shown to be central to city growth performance. In any case, let us turn directly to the counterfactual experiments.

Table 7.4 assesses the role of sectoral productivity advance in accounting for the slow city growth differential by posing the following question: How much of the slow city growth differential would disappear if India had enjoyed the sectoral total factor productivity growth typical of the rest of Asia and the Third World in general? Three counterfactuals are reported in table 7.4: column 2 allows India to face the productivity experience that was typical of the KW forty-country sample; column 3 allows India to enjoy the even more rapid productivity experience of "successful" Asia; and column 4 allows India to enjoy the especially rapid productivity experience of Taiwan.

Much to our surprise, India's slower overall productivity performance did not contribute to its slower city growth, since the degree of imbalance was no less dramatic than in the rest of the Third World. That is, India's poor productivity growth performance was not limited to urban sectors but was an economywide phenomenon. Consequently, experiencing average Third World patterns would have raised productivity and incomes in both rural and urban areas but would not have greatly favored more rapid urbanization. Thus, none of the slow city growth differential can be explained by differences in productivity growth experience.

Had India achieved the rates of productivity growth typical of "successful" Asia or even of Taiwan, however, it would have undergone much faster rates of city growth, perhaps almost 0.5 percentage point faster, a magnitude comparable in importance to the demographic effects. These increases in city growth are particularly pronounced in the low productivity growth periods before and after the first OPEC price shock, 1966–71 and 1976–81. The stronger urbanizing effects (relative to the average Third World productivity counterfactual) appear for two reasons. First, the Asian and Taiwanese productivity growth experiences were on average far higher than the Third World mean. Incomes rise more rapidly in the Taiwan and Asian counterfactuals, and Engel effects are therefore stronger. Second, because the Taiwan-Asian differences from the Third World mean are particularly pronounced in urban sectors (especially manufacturing), the urban bias in factor productivity growth patterns is stronger. The second of these forces is the more important, confirming once again the key role of *unbalanced* sectoral productivity advance on the supply side in accounting for rapid city growth. To repeat the moral once more: it is not so much rapid productivity advance that contributes to city growth during industrial revolutions, but rather the fact that the most spectacular productivity advances are typically urban based.

7.6 The Bottom Line

Why was city growth relatively slow in India during the 1960s and 1970s? India's cities grew at an annual rate at least 1 percentage point less than that of the rest of the Third World. We have seen that demographic trends, world price trends, and capital inflows were sufficiently different in India to help account for a significant portion of the slow city growth differential when each was assessed separately. In contrast, slower pro-

Table 7.5. What If India Had Faced the Demographic, World Commodity Market, World Capital Market, and Productivity Conditions of the Rest of the Third World? Counterfactuals, 1960–1981

	Benchmark			Average Third World		
Year	City Growth (% per annum) (1)	City In-Migration Rate (% per annum) (2)	Share Urban (%) (3)	City Growth (% per annum) (4)	City In-Migration Rate (% per annum) (5)	Share Urban (%) (6)
1960	—	—	13.9	—	—	13.9
1966	5.63	3.47	16.9	5.12	2.65	16.1
1971	3.43	1.25	17.9	4.14	1.64	17.4
1977	3.95	1.78	19.5	4.69	2.06	19.2
1981	4.00	1.83	21.3	4.63	1.99	21.1
1960–81	4.32	1.97	—	4.66	1.90	—

See text for counterfactual experiment's motivation. The counterfactual combines the P^*_j, T^*_j, F/GNP, and labor force growth assumptions under "average Third World" reported for each group of exogenous variables reported separately in tables 7.2–7.4.

ductivity advance in India vis-à-vis the entire Third World does not help explain the differential (although it does when the comparison is with its more successful Asian neighbors). What about the combined influence of all of these forces?

Table 7.5 reports a final counterfactual in which India takes on all the environmental attributes of the KW forty-country Third World sample. To summarize, these include experience with the share of foreign capital inflows in GNP, with the terms of trade between agricultural and manufacturing products in world markets, with the relative price of imported fuels and raw materials, with overall rates of labor force and population growth, and with sectoral rates of productivity advance. The combined influence of these environmental forces is certainly significant: city growth rates in India would have been 0.34 percentage point higher had the country enjoyed the environmental conditions that were typical of the Third World. Thus, the relatively unfavorable environmental conditions in recent Indian history account for at most one-third of the slow city growth differential.

The moral of these historical counterfactuals seems clear. While a significant portion of India's relatively slow city growth in the 1960s and 1970s can be explained by relatively unfavorable economic and demographic conditions, a larger portion remains unexplained. These findings are tentative, of course, but they suggest that India's relatively slow city growth results primarily from structural and institutional arrangements that make city growth less responsive to favorable conditions than is true of successful developers in the rest of the Third World. These arrangements include all those policies that serve to choke off urban employment, policies that will attract our attention at length in chapter 9.

8 · Projections to 2001

8.1 Predictions, Projections, and Counterfactuals

What will the Indian economy be like in 2001? What share of the Indian work force will be in its cities? Will city immigration and city growth be much less dynamic? Will municipal planners therefore find it easier to cope with city growth problems?

Demographers and statisticians certainly have supplied answers to these questions. Under various assumptions about migration rates and urban–rural birth and mortality differentials, the United Nations (1980, 1987), Rogers (1984, chap. 11), Mohan (1985), and the Indian Planning Commission, the registrar general, Raghavachari, Ambannavar, and Chandrasekhara (all five cited in Bose, 1978) have offered a number of city growth and urbanization projections over the next two decades. Some of these projections assume a constant migration rate and some allow the rate to vary, but all take the migration rate to be exogenous. That is, the demographic projections are made in the absence of any model in which economic forces are allowed to have an impact on city immigration rates. No labor market forces drive these projections. The projections are quiet when it comes to the derived demands for labor that create excess supply in the countryside, excess demand in the city, and the city immigration that accommodates these conditions. Since demographic projections typically contain no endogenous forces driving rural emigration or urban immigration, city growth responses to altered demographic and economic conditions must be viewed as exogenous in these projections.

Although our predictions for 2001 may not be more accurate than those of the demographers, we are in a position to learn a lot more about the future because city immigration flows are endogenous in BMW. First, we can explore long-run patterns of migration and city growth in a stable environment in which world price patterns, productivity advance, aggregate labor force growth, rainfall conditions, land availability, and foreign capital inflows all exhibit smooth trends, shielded from the disturbances of demographic transition, OPEC price shocks, rising protectionism in the advanced economies, productivity speedup and slowdown, changing foreign capital austerity, and drought. By isolating these influences, which have been important in the past, we will, in effect, be able to explore a counterfactual world of city growth where the endogenous forces of development are allowed to have their unfettered impact on the spatial distribution of population. How would Indian city growth behave over the century 1960–2061 under such conditions? This counterfactual is called our Stable projection. Second, we can explore long-run patterns of migration and city growth in the economic/demographic environment that is most likely to prevail over the next two decades if the years between 1978 and 1981 are any guide. This counterfactual is called our Benchmark projection. Third, we can explore some scenarios that will serve to set likely upper and lower bounds on city growth in the future. To do so, we look to epochs in India's recent past to identify conditions that have been most favorable and unfavorable to city growth (although not necessarily to overall per capita income improvement). We then imagine two decades of future Indian development in which all of these conditions are either favorable or unfavorable at the same time. This exercise serves to set an optimistic upper bound, Favorable, and a pessimistic lower bound, Unfavorable, to future city growth. Finally, we can assess the impact of Malthusian population pressure and demographic transition on the future of Indian city growth by exploring the impact of alternative demographic scenarios suggested by the ILO.

Section 8.2 defines the economic and demographic conditions underlying Stable and Benchmark. It then examines the attributes of these projections into the distant future and compares them with the demographers' projections. The comparison complete, sections 8.3 and 8.4 turn to the sources of future Indian city growth.

8.2 Projecting Future Indian City Growth

Defining Stable and Benchmark

Table 8.1 reports the values of the dynamic parameters underlying Stable and Benchmark. They can be quickly summarized.

Stable is used to explore city growth and the urban transition in the very long run, the century from 1960 to 2061. Our purpose here is to isolate the long-run characteristics of Indian city growth under conditions

Table 8.1. Dynamic Parameters Assumed in Stable and Benchmark

Variable	Stable 1960–2061 (1)	Benchmark 1982–2001 (2)
per annum growth		
$\overset{*}{P}_Z$, Imported fuel and raw material prices relative to manufactures	−0.0310	0
$\overset{*}{P}_A$, Traded agricultural products prices relative to manufactures	−0.0071	0.0244
Total labor force, skilled plus unskilled	0.0221	0.0221
$\overset{*}{S}$, Skilled labor force	0.0338	0.0390
$\overset{*}{T}_i$, Sectoral total factor productivity growth in:		
A, agriculture	0.0018	0
RS, private rural services and manufacturing	0.0307	0.0138
PSR, public rural services	0.0280	0.0454
M, urban manufacturing	0.0356	0.0100
KS, capital-intensive urban services	−0.0040	0.0128
US, private urban services	0.0323	0.0132
PSU, public urban services	−0.0038	0.0145
$\overset{*}{R}_A = \overset{*}{R}_U$, Farmland and urban land stock growth	0.0100	0.0100
indices and ratios		
RAIN (rainfall index)	0.9964	1.0000
Government savings rate	0.3870	0.3334
F/GNP, foreign capital inflow share in GNP	0.0254	0.0068

Stable simply assumes that the average conditions for 1960–64 prevail 1960–2061. Benchmark assumes the actual conditions up to 1981 (repeating chapter 6), while the projection 1982–2001 assumes that the average conditions for 1978–81 prevail in the future, with the exceptions that $\overset{*}{P}_Z = 0$ and that $\overset{*}{T}_A = 0$. See text.

in which the size of exogenous economic and demographic shocks remain unchanged. To do so, we could, of course, set the dynamic parameters in BMW at any levels desired, but it seemed most sensible to select some period from the past in defining Stable's economic and demographic environment. Averages for the period 1960–64 have been selected for this purpose. For example, the average 1960–64 ratio of foreign capital inflows to GDP is assumed to remain unchanged at the 2.54 percent level throughout the following century, the relative price of imported fuels and raw materials is allowed to fall at the rate of 3.10 percent per annum as it did in the early 1960s, the skilled labor force is forced to grow at 3.38 percent per annum as it did during those four years, and so on.

Benchmark contains more likely assumptions for projections over the next two decades, making it more useful for comparisons with the demographers' projections and as a benchmark for counterfactual analysis.

Here we assume that the conditions prevailing between 1978 and 1981—the last years that can be well documented—will continue to characterize the future, with two exceptions. The enormous boom in the relative price of fuel (which dominates P_Z) after the second OPEC shock is unlikely to persist to the year 2001, as the events of the past few years have clearly revealed. We thought it wiser simply to assume no change in the relative price P_Z over the next two decades. The second exception relates to total factor productivity growth in agriculture. In chapter 3 we estimated the rate of total factor productivity growth in agriculture to have been -0.85 percent per annum between 1978 and 1981. Technological regression of this magnitude is certainly inconsistent with a green revolution, and it could hardly be expected to continue over two decades. In fact, we suspect that all of that "regression" is attributable to our inability to control for unfavorable rainfall conditions over these years.[1] As a result, Benchmark assumes no significant total factor productivity improvement in agriculture over the next two decades, a pessimistic assumption, but less so than that implied by the 1978–81 experience.

City Growth in the Very Long Run, 1960–2061

Figure 8.1 summarizes Indian city growth over a century in the absence of any changes in the macroeconomic/demographic environmental conditions underlying Stable. While these conditions are hardly realistic, they do serve the useful purpose of illustrating that India is *not* likely to conform to the stylized patterns normally associated with the "urban transition."

Following Zelinsky's (1971, p. 233) hypothesis of mobility transition (see also Ledent, 1980, 1982; Rogers, 1977, pp. 164–67; United Nations, 1980, p. 29; and Kelley and Williamson, 1984, pp. 148–52), demographers and economists have come to believe that urbanization passes through a logistic curve, while city growth passes through a derivative bell-shaped curve: that is, city growth tends to accelerate during early stages of the industrial revolution, reaching a peak somewhere in the NIC range of development, before undergoing a retardation as the economy completes the urban transition in late development stages. Stable fails to conform to that pattern. Instead, India never recovers the dramatic rates of city growth achieved in the early 1960s, but instead undergoes retardation up to the end of the twentieth century, after which it exhibits stability in both the rate of city growth (at about 3 percent per

1. As far as we know, a consistent rainfall index extends only through 1977 (Sanderson and Roy, 1979).

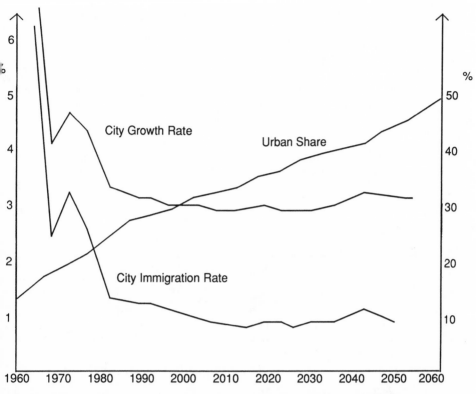

Fig. 8.1. A century of migration, urbanization, and city growth in India: 1960–2061, STABLE

annum) and the rate of city immigration (at about 1 percent per annum). Indeed, figure 8.1 looks very much like a standard neoclassical growth path after a sharp technological or savings rate shock: the economy undergoes retardation from the high city growth rates generated by the favorable initial shocks and reaches what appears to be an equilibrium steady-state growth path thereafter; in 2061, about half the labor force is urban.

Economic Development to 2001

Table 8.2 summarizes the Benchmark's growth performance over the four decades, 1960–2001. Since our primary interest is in urbanization and city growth, we shall not dwell on this projected development performance, but some attributes reported in table 8.2 are worth noting.

The growth rate in constant price GDP per capita generated by the

Table 8.2. Growth, Accumulation, and Structural Change: Benchmark, 1960–2001

Panel A. Growth and Accumulation

			Per Annum Growth (%)			
Year	GDP per Capita (constant price)	Investment Share in GDP (%)	GDP per Capita (constant price)	Capital Stock per Worker	Housing Stock per Worker	Skilled Labo Force per Worker
1960	100.0	18.2	—	—	—	—
1966	103.9	19.5	0.64	3.50	1.64	1.26
1971	119.4	19.0	2.82	2.31	2.07	1.69
1976	125.0	18.7	0.91	2.17	3.06	1.69
1981	141.6	20.7	2.53	2.21	3.19	1.69
1986	159.1	21.1	2.36	2.54	3.35	1.69
1991	180.2	21.3	2.53	2.59	3.45	1.69
1996	205.0	21.5	2.62	2.64	3.47	1.69
2001	234.4	21.6	2.71	2.67	3.47	1.69

Panel B. Structural Change

	Sectoral Output Shares in GDP (%)					
Year	A	M	KS	RS + US	PSR + PSU	Housin
1960	44.4	12.4	8.8	18.6	7.6	8.2
1966	34.4	15.7	12.1	18.9	9.9	9.0
1971	35.6	15.7	12.0	17.9	10.0	8.9
1976	31.1	17.0	13.4	17.8	11.4	9.2
1981	28.6	17.2	16.0	17.0	12.3	8.9
1986	26.3	17.4	17.1	16.6	13.8	8.8
1991	24.2	17.5	18.0	16.3	15.3	8.7
1996	22.1	17.6	18.9	15.9	16.9	8.6
2001	20.2	17.5	19.6	15.6	18.5	8.6

	Labor Force Distribution (%)				
Year	A	M	KS	RS + US	PSR + PSU
1960	71.2	4.3	2.0	19.6	2.9
1966	70.5	5.8	3.0	17.3	3.5
1971	68.0	6.4	3.2	18.7	3.7
1976	66.5	7.9	3.3	18.0	4.3
1981	64.9	8.5	4.0	18.0	4.6
1986	64.3	8.8	4.3	17.8	4.8
1991	63.6	9.1	4.5	17.8	5.0
1996	62.8	9.3	4.8	17.9	5.1
2001	62.0	9.6	5.2	17.9	5.3

Table 8.2. *continued*

Panel C. Distribution

	Index of		
Year	GDP per Worker ÷ Farm Wage	Urban Skilled Wage Premium	Productivity per Worker (M ÷ A)
1960	100.0	100.0	100.0
1966	107.1	146.4	119.6
1971	104.4	142.6	100.9
1976	109.6	175.6	98.9
1981	113.9	178.4	98.7
1986	116.7	180.0	103.9
1991	118.8	177.2	108.7
1996	120.5	171.1	115.7
2001	122.0	162.0	120.2

model is 1.67 percent per annum between 1960 and 1981. The most notable finding in the Benchmark projection is that per capita GDP growth rates rise over the 1980s and 1990s and reach about 2.7 percent per annum by the end of the century. The explanation for this significant acceleration does not lie with sectoral productivity performance, since, of course, Benchmark assumes stable rates of sectoral total factor productivity growth throughout the two-decade projection beyond 1981. *Aggregate* total factor productivity growth does rise, however, since the more dynamic sectors increase their shares in GDP. Additionally, the rate of capital deepening quickens modestly over time. The rate of growth in capital stock per worker generated by the model is 2.54 percent per annum between 1960 and 1981, after which the rate drifts upwards to 2.67 percent per annum at the end of the century. The modest increase in the rate of capital deepening can be explained, at least in part, by the modest upward drift in the investment share in GDP, from 20.7 percent in 1981 to 21.6 percent in 2001. By assumption, the rate of skill deepening plays no role in accounting for the acceleration in GDP per capita growth rates, as the skilled labor force per worker index in table 8.2 confirms.

Meanwhile, industrialization and structural change trace out the stylized "patterns of development." Panel B in table 8.2 shows that the urban manufacturing labor force increases its share from 4.3 percent in 1960 to 9.6 percent in 2001, while agriculture undergoes a decline from 71.2 to 62.0 percent. The sectoral output shares also conform with the stylized patterns of development: the agricultural value-added share declines from 44.4 to 20.2 percent over the four decades as a whole, the manufacturing share rises from 12.4 to 17.5 percent, the housing share is relatively stable, and the service sectors (including rural manufacturing) combined rise dramatically from 35.0 to 53.7 percent (most of which is attributable to *KS*'s growth from 8.8 to 19.6 percent). A somewhat curious phenomenon is the urban manufacturing share's near stagnancy after 1976. Were such stagnation actually to occur for a prolonged period, pressure for public policies favoring manufacturing would surely develop. Indeed, it may not be unfair to view the liberalizing trends of the late 1970s and early 1980s as a response to such pressures.

Finally, table 8.2, panel C, offers evidence on likely future inequality trends in India. First, the farm wage lags modestly behind GDP per worker improvements since the ratio of the latter to the former rises from a base of 100 in 1961 to 122 in 2001. Second, the premium on urban skills rises sharply over the period, from a base of 100 to 162. Apparently, the derived demand for skills will outstrip the growth in supplies if the Benchmark assumptions come to pass. And third, product per worker in manufacturing rises relative to agriculture, from a base of 100 to 120.2 in 2001, a trend driven by the relatively pronounced capital and skills deepening in *M*. Based on these indicators, rising income inequality is likely to be an attribute of Indian development over the next two decades.

Migration, City Growth, and Urbanization to 2001

Table 8.3 documents six key aspects of the urban transition in India over the remainder of this century: the share of the labor force in urban areas; per annum city growth rates; the per annum rural out-migration rate; the per annum urban in-migration rate; net urban immigrants as a share of increases in the urban labor force; and the ratio of the labor employed in manufacturing to the total urban labor force.

Figure 8.2 plots the time series for three of these variables, and in both cases Stable and Benchmark are offered together for comparison. A city growth slowdown takes place in both cases, but the growth rates are far more rapid in the Stable counterfactual, in which the favorable 1960–64 environmental conditions are assumed to prevail throughout the four subsequent decades. This result confirms the findings of chapter 6, where we found that a good portion of the city growth slowdown in the 1960s and 1970s was due to the disappearance of conditions in the early 1960s that were especially favorable to city growth in India.

If Benchmark conditions come to pass, table 8.3 and figure 8.2 both show that urban problems in India are likely to be far less severe by the end of the present century. The annual rate of city growth will have

Table 8.3. Migration, Urbanization, and City Growth: Benchmark and Stable, 1960–2001

Panel A. Benchmark

Year	% Urban	% Labor Force in M ÷ % Urban	City Growth (% per annum)	Net Rural Out-Migration Rate (% per annum)	Net Urban In-Migration Rate (% per annum)	Net In-Migrant Share of Urban Labor Force Increase (%)
1960	13.9	0.312	—	—	—	—
1966	16.9	0.342	5.63	0.64	3.47	64.0
1971	17.9	0.359	3.43	0.26	1.25	37.3
1976	19.5	0.407	3.95	0.41	1.79	46.2
1981	21.3	0.399	4.00	0.36	1.39	35.4
1986	22.0	0.399	2.85	0.18	0.67	23.7
1991	22.7	0.400	2.87	0.19	0.68	23.9
1996	23.4	0.400	2.85	0.20	0.66	23.6
2001	24.1	0.399	2.84	0.20	0.65	23.2

Panel B. Stable

Year	% Urban	% Labor Force in M ÷ % Urban	City Growth (% per annum)	Net Rural Out-Migration Rate (% per annum)	Net Urban In-Migration Rate (% per annum)	Net In-Migrant Share of Urban Labor Force Increase (%)
1960	13.9	0.312	—	—	—	—
1966	17.4	0.364	6.17	0.75	4.00	67.6
1971	19.3	0.377	4.35	0.49	2.18	51.3
1976	22.0	0.396	4.91	0.72	2.74	57.4
1981	24.5	0.402	4.38	0.67	2.20	51.7
1986	26.0	0.405	3.45	0.43	1.27	37.5
1991	27.5	0.406	3.35	0.43	1.17	35.6
1996	29.0	0.408	3.33	0.45	1.15	35.2
2001	30.4	0.405	3.19	0.42	1.00	32.0

declined to 2.84 percent, considerably lower than the 4 percent recorded in the late 1970s, and far lower than the 5.63 percent of the early 1960s. Rural out-migration and urban in-migration rates will have declined sharply as well. Based on Benchmark, urban planners will find it easier to cope with the far lower city growth rates in 2001, and issues of overurbanization may disappear from development debates. Furthermore, note that this slowdown is not in any way driven by aggregate demographic forces because Benchmark assumes stable rates of population and labor force growth at 2.21 percent per annum. *It is economics, not demography, that accounts for the long-run decline in city growth.*

Table 8.3 offers more information of interest to the urban analyst. For example, recall the overurbanization debate that was introduced by Hoselitz in the 1950s. His thesis was that urbanization was outpacing industrialization in the Third World in the sense that urban population shares were large in comparison with industrial employment shares, at

Fig. 8.2. Migration, urbanization, and city growth in India: BENCHMARK (-------) and STABLE (——), 1960–2001

least when Third World performance is compared with the historical performance of currently developed countries. The implication, of course, was that the service sector was absorbing the immigrant inflow and that immigrants were pushed there by poor employment conditions elsewhere. While this view was confirmed by Hoselitz (1955, 1957) on the basis of Asian evidence from the 1950s, the United Nations (1980) has rejected it on more recent evidence. The thesis was tested by examining trends in such statistics as the percentage of the labor force in industry relative to the percentage of the population in urban areas. This statistic is reproduced in the second column of table 8.3, although "industry" is confined to manufacturing alone, and "percent urban" refers to the labor force. Comparing 1970 with 1950, the United Nations (1980, p. 17) concluded that "urban growth is no longer outpacing industrial growth: if anything, a slight reversal of the overurbanization tendency has appeared." Benchmark's predictions are consistent with the UN finding since the statistic rises sharply in recent Indian history from 0.312 in 1960 to 0.407 in 1976. Benchmark predicts that the statistic will, however, remain remarkably stable over the next two decades, and the same is true of Stable. Thus, manufacturing *was* an engine of past city growth in India, although the engine was not running very fast. In the future, India's cities will reflect a more balanced employment growth, since, according to both Benchmark and Stable, the manufacturing labor force will grow at almost exactly the same rate as the total urban labor force.

Consider another issue. Keyfitz (1980) asked, "Do cities grow by natural increase or by migration?" While Keyfitz stressed natural increase in his answer, Todaro (1984) disagreed. While this question has attracted considerable attention from demographers (see Rogers, 1984, chap. 11), it is of interest to an economist only because the in-migration rate is endogenous in any model of development. For the early 1960s, the figure is 64 percent in Benchmark—that is, almost two-thirds of the labor force increase between 1960 and 1966 was satisfied by urban immigration from the countryside. The figure had dropped to a third by 1981, and stabilizes at about a quarter over the next two decades. While the early 1960s were exceptional years, the immigrant shares from 1976 to 1981 seem to conform to Third World norms. That is, the range 35.4 to 46.2 percent in panel A of table 8.3 brackets the United Nations (1980, table 11, p. 25) estimate of 39.3 percent and is close to Keyfitz's (1980, p. 151) estimate of 49 percent. More to the point, Benchmark predicts a long-run decline in the relative importance of in-migration as a source of urban population growth. These predictions are consistent with the work of others. For example, using a purely demographic model with migration rates exogenous, Rogers (1984, table 5, p. 290) predicts that Indian city migrants will account for 22.7 percent of city population increase by 2000; the Benchmark prediction in table 8.3 is remarkably close, 23.2 percent in 2001.

Table 8.4. Projected Indian City Growth Rates (% per annum)

| | Labor Force | | Population | | | | | | | | |
| | | | Mohan | | Registrar General | Raghavachari | Chandrasekhara | | Rogers | United Nations | |
Period	Benchmark	Mohan	Variant I	Variant II			Model A	Model B		1980	1987
1981–86	2.85	3.94	3.84	3.73	2.30	3.17	3.35	4.85	3.24	4.32	3.64
1986–91	2.87	4.22	3.49	3.50	2.30	3.17	3.35	4.85	3.12	4.32	3.58
1991–96	2.85	3.68	3.10	3.28	—	3.09	3.32	5.32	2.99	4.34	3.59
1996–2001	2.84	3.27	2.75	3.08	—	3.09	3.32	5.32	2.87	4.34	3.49

Sources: Mohan (1985, table 8, p. 631 and table 11, p. 635); Rogers (1984, table 5, p. 290); United Nations (1980, table 48, p. 140); United Nations (1987, table A-10, p. 197). The remainder are taken from Bose (1978, tables 10 and 13–15, pp. 161–63).

Comparisons with Purely Demographic Projections

The advantage of BMW lies with its endogenous treatment of labor markets and city immigration. This is not true of purely demographic models, which have been used extensively for Indian urbanization projections. The accuracy of these competing projections is not at issue since all of them, including our own, must guess about the environment of future Indian development. However, even the most elaborate demographic model suffers the debilitating weakness of being incapable of counterfactual economic analysis. Sections 8.3 and 8.4 will illustrate the point by showing how Indian urban experience over the next two decades might behave under alternative demographic conditions, world market conditions, technological progress, policy regimes, and the like. But before we turn to such experiments, how does the Benchmark projection of 2001 compare with the purely demographic projections?

Table 8.4 summarizes the results of nine demographic projections, four by independent scholars (Mohan and Rogers), one by the UN, and the rest by official Indian statistical agencies (the registrar general, Raghavachari, and Chandrasekhara). With the exception of the UN, Chandrasekhara's model B, and the registrar general (whose projection stops with 1991), all of these demographic projections imply a slowdown in city growth up to 2001. In that sense, these demographic projections agree with Benchmark. Furthermore, with the exception of the UN and Chandrasekhara projections, the range of predicted rates of city growth by the end of the present century conforms closely with Benchmark: while we predict a city growth rate of 2.84 percent per annum 1996–2001, the others (excluding UN and Chandrasekhara model B) range between 2.75 and 3.32 percent. Such comparisons serve to increase the credibility of Benchmark's projections, but one significant difference should be stressed. While each of these demographic projections exhibits a gradual slowdown in city growth throughout the two decades, Benchmark's city growth slowdown is much more dramatic and centered earlier in the period. That is, all of the decline in city growth in Benchmark takes place between the late 1970s and the early 1980s.

8.3 What Will Matter Most in the Future?

Migration is at the heart of the urban transition, and a purely demographic model is inadequately equipped to explore the impact of endogenous economic events associated with long-run development on the relative attractiveness of the city and thus on changing migration rates. BMW, however, is fully equipped for the task. Furthermore, it is also able to assess the impact of *exogenous* economic shocks on Indian urban

Table 8.5. Dynamic Parameters Assumed in Benchmark, Favorable, and Unfavorable, 1982–2001

Variable	Benchmark Parameter	Favorable		Unfavorable	
		Parameter	Epoch	Parameter	Epoch
per annum growth					
$\overset{*}{P}_Z$, Imported fuels and raw materials prices relative to manufactures	0	−0.0310	1960–64	0.3651	1978–81
$\overset{*}{P}_A$, Traded agricultural products prices relative to manufactures	0.0244	−0.0144	1965–71	0.0312	1972–77
Total labor force, skilled plus unskilled	0.0221	0.0221	—	0.0221	—
$\overset{*}{S}$, Skilled labor force	0.0390	0.0390	—	0.0390	—
$\overset{*}{T}_i$, Sectoral total factor productivity growth in:					
A, agriculture	0	0.0143		−0.0019	
RS, private rural services and manufacturing	0.0138	0.0091		−0.0025	
PSR, public rural services	0.0454	0.0102		0.0316	
M, urban manufacturing	0.0100	0.0007	1972–77	−0.0076	1965–71
KS, capital-intensive urban services	0.0128	0.0343		0.0045	
US, private urban services	0.0132	0.0234		0.0107	
PSU, public urban services	0.0145	0.0090		0.0013	
$\overset{*}{R}_A = \overset{*}{R}_U$, Farmland and urban land stock growth	0.0100	0.0100	—	0.0100	—
indices and ratios					
RAIN (rainfall index)	1.0000	1.0000	—	1.0000	—
Government savings rate	0.3334	0.3870	1960–64	0.2813	1965–71
F/GNP, foreign capital inflow share in GNP	0.0068	0.0254	1960–64	−0.0014	1972–77

All three projections assume the actual conditions up to 1981 (repeating chapter 6), while the projections 1982–2001 assume the conditions stated above. See text. "Epoch" denotes that period from which an estimated parameter was taken.

experience. Thus, we are ready to explore Indian urban experience to 2001 under alternative scenarios and policy regimes.

Which scenarios and policy regimes? Based on past sources of Indian city growth analyzed in chapter 6, our examination of the sources of future urbanization and city growth is motivated by five key issues: (1) alternative views of fuel and natural resource scarcity over the next two decades; (2) alternative views of the likely trends in the terms of trade induced by world market conditions between agriculture and manufacturing; (3) alternative views of the likely austerity of world capital markets; (4) alternative views of the future pace of Indian productivity advance over the remainder of the century; and (5) alternative views of Indian policy toward saving out of government revenues. These issues may be illustrated best by the most favorable and the most unfavorable conditions that have characterized India's recent past.

Defining Favorable and Unfavorable Scenarios

Table 8.5 summarizes the dynamic parameters embedded in two projections, Favorable and Unfavorable, that supply an optimistic upper and a pessimistic lower bound on Indian city growth experience up to 2001. While it is impossible to determine precise bounds on dynamic parameter values, recent experience offers a plausible if conservative range of alternatives. Each of these projections will be compared with the middle ground, Benchmark, and in both alternatives all of the parameters of Benchmark are retained except trends in the relative price of imported fuels and raw materials, in the relative price of agricultural goods prevailing in world markets, in sectoral total factor productivity, in the government savings rate, and in the share of foreign capital inflows in GNP. Table 8.5 reports the historical epochs in which these parameters were most unfavorable or most favorable to city growth in India. Consistent with the findings of chapter 6 and the sources of the city growth slowdown, the epoch 1960–64 appears most frequently in the Favorable column, while the epochs of 1972–77 and 1978–81 appear most frequently in the Unfavorable column. Yet the correspondence is hardly perfect. That is, India never experienced all of the favorable or unfavorable conditions at the same time. Suppose, however, it was able to do so over the next two decades. Table 8.5 and the projections that follow assume as much. Favorable assumes that the next two decades will be favored by the impressive decline in the relative price P_Z that characterized 1960–64, by the strong decline in the relative price P_A that characterized 1965–1971, by the unbalanced sectoral total factor productivity growth rates that characterized 1972–77, by the high government savings rate that characterized 1960–64, and by the large foreign capital inflow that characterized 1960–64. In contrast, Unfavorable selects the parameters in those epochs that were least favorable to city growth. The experiments are reported in tables 8.6 through 8.8: the first two report each influence separately, while the last, table 8.8, reports their influence in combination.

Before we look at the results, an important qualification should be added. Favorable and Unfavorable refer to city growth conditions, not to aggregate GDP per capita growth conditions. They need not be the same. For example, while a rapid rate of total factor productivity growth in agriculture obviously contributes to GDP growth, chapters 4 and 6 have shown that it does *not* significantly affect city growth. The reader should keep the distinction in mind.

World Markets and the Terms of Trade

The impact of world market conditions on future Indian city growth is revealed by the P_A and P_Z counterfactuals displayed in table 8.6. It might be helpful to dwell on the assumptions underlying one of them, say the P_A counterfactuals. If a world price shock causes domestic agriculture's terms of trade to deteriorate, real incomes of farm laborers will suffer, and they will be encouraged to seek employment elsewhere. The same price shock favors manufacturing (the terms of trade being the ratio of agricultural to manufacturing prices) by tending to create more urban jobs and thus helping absorb the new immigrants. In short, city growth is fostered by a deterioration in agriculture's terms of trade, even though aggregate national income may suffer. Which epoch in recent Indian history faced the most dramatic deterioration in P_A? Table

Table 8.6. Indian City Growth (% per annum), 1960–2001: Projections under Various Assumptions about World Commodity Markets, Availability of Foreign Capital, and Government Savings Rates

Year	Benchmark (1)	$\overset{\bullet}{P}_A$ Counterfactual Favorable (2)	$\overset{\bullet}{P}_A$ Counterfactual Unfavorable (3)	$\overset{\bullet}{P}_Z$ Counterfactual Favorable (4)	$\overset{\bullet}{P}_Z$ Counterfactual Unfavorable (5)	F/GNP and GSR Counterfactual Favorable (6)	F/GNP and GSR Counterfactual Unfavorable (7)
1960	—	—	—	—	—	—	—
1966	5.63	5.63	5.63	5.63	5.63	5.63	5.63
1971	3.43	3.43	3.43	3.43	3.43	3.43	3.43
1976	3.95	3.95	3.95	3.95	3.95	3.95	3.95
1981	4.00	4.00	4.00	4.00	4.00	4.00	4.00
1986	2.85	3.14	2.80	2.88	2.61	3.22	2.67
1991	2.87	3.11	2.82	2.90	2.64	2.93	2.83
1996	2.85	3.07	2.81	2.88	2.58	2.90	2.81
2001	2.84	3.04	2.80	2.87	2.58	2.88	2.81

The Favorable, Unfavorable, and Benchmark projections are described in table 8.5 and the text.

8.5 confirms that 1960–64 wins that dubious honor, while in contrast 1978–81 registered the most dramatic improvements in P_A. Table 8.6 projects that experience over the two decades 1981–2001, while in all other respects the Favorable and the Unfavorable projections are exactly like Benchmark. The two projections isolate the influence of world-market–induced changes in P_A on city growth in the future.

The experiment illustrates how future trends in the world relative price of P_A matter in city growth projections. Under favorable conditions, city growth at the end of the century would be considerably higher, 3.04 percent per annum, than under unfavorable conditions, 2.80 percent. As we shall see, the terms of trade could be one of the more important forces influencing Indian city growth up to 2001.

Natural Resource and Fuel Scarcity

The relative price of imported natural resources and fuels, P_Z, could also significantly affect future Indian city growth. Under favorable P_Z trends, city growth rates at the end of the century would be 2.87 percent per annum, while under unfavorable conditions, the figure would be much less, 2.58 percent per annum. This range in city growth performance is, in fact, the biggest reported in table 8.6. In contrast with the importance of future trends in P_A, however, the large variance between the favorable and unfavorable city growth projections in the P_Z counterfactuals is due to the enormous variance in world prices of imported natural resources and fuels in India's recent past, rather than to the sensitivity of the Indian economy to such price shocks.

Foreign Capital Conditions and the Government Savings Rate

To our surprise, table 8.6 suggests that the availability of foreign capital and the government rate of saving out of public revenues are unlikely to influence future city growth much. By the end of the century, the Favorable and Unfavorable city growth projections are almost exactly the same, 2.88 versus 2.81 percent per annum. These figures tightly straddle the Benchmark estimate, 2.84 percent per annum. This result is somewhat different from that obtained for the 1960s and 1970s (see sec. 6.4); to a large extent it reflects India's continued capital deepening and diminished capital scarcity—especially in those sectors that are the main recipients of public investment and foreign capital inflows.

Sectoral Productivity Performance

Based on table 8.7, sectoral productivity performance will have a far more important impact on future city growth in India than world capital and commodity market conditions. While it is true that India will undergo city growth slowdown over the next two decades even under the most favorable productivity growth conditions, city growth performance at the end of the present century would be far greater under Favorable technological progress conditions, 3.28 percent per annum, than under Unfavorable conditions, 2.73 per annum.

Getting It All Together

Table 8.8 combines all of these influences so that we can see how much they matter to future growth projections. Under Favorable conditions, city growth rates at the end of the century (3.55 percent) would be almost half again greater than those under Unfavorable conditions (2.44 percent). The experiments in table 8.8 also suggest the exaggerated optimism that underlies some of the projections reported in table 8.4. Those by the UN (4.34 percent per annum 1996–2001) and by Chandrasekhara's model B (5.32 percent per annum) imply a favorable city growth environment that far exceeds even the most favorable conditions in any epoch between 1960 and 1981. Even the more modest projections in table 8.4 (Mohan labor force and variant II: 3.27 and 3.08 percent per annum 1996–2001, respectively; Raghavachari, 3.09 percent per annum; Chandrasekhara model A, 3.32 percent per annum) tend to make optimistic assumptions about the economic environment for future city growth. Of course it is possible that India may undergo some structural break with past performance over the next two decades, but the

Table 8.7. Indian City Growth (% per annum), 1960–2001: Projections under Various Assumptions about Sectoral Productivity Performance

Year	Benchmark	Favorable	Unfavorable
1960	—	—	—
1966	5.63	5.63	5.63
1971	3.43	3.43	3.43
1976	3.95	3.95	3.95
1981	4.00	4.00	4.00
1986	2.85	3.54	2.83
1991	2.87	3.50	2.81
1996	2.85	3.26	2.80
2001	2.84	3.28	2.73

The Favorable, Unfavorable, and Benchmark projections are described in table 8.5 and the text.

Table 8.8. Indian City Growth (% per annum), 1960–2001: Getting All the Favorable and Unfavorable Forces Together

Year	Benchmark	Favorable	Unfavorable
1960	—	—	—
1966	5.63	5.63	5.63
1971	3.43	3.43	3.43
1976	3.95	3.95	3.95
1981	4.00	4.00	4.00
1986	2.85	4.23	2.32
1991	2.87	3.71	2.44
1996	2.85	3.63	2.36
2001	2.84	3.55	2.44

The Favorable, Unfavorable, and Benchmark projections are discussed in table 8.5 and the text. Favorable and Unfavorable explore simultaneously all the forces listed separately in tables 8.6 and 8.7.

recent past does not offer conclusive evidence to justify such optimism. Moreover, even under the most favorable conditions, India's city growth rates would not rival those of the more rapidly urbanizing LDCs.

8.4 Malthusian Pressure and Demographic Transitions

Demographers are uncertain about future trends in birth rates, death rates, and activity rates—sufficiently uncertain that the ILO (1977, vol. 1, table 6, p. 119) has offered high and low projections of the Indian labor force to 2001. Does this uncertainty matter in projections of city growth performance over the next two decades? Apparently not.

Table 8.9 reports the impact of the ILO high and low aggregate labor force projections. They hardly matter at all. The urban share in 2001 is almost exactly the same, and the city in-migration rate at the end of the present century differs between them only trivially. City growth rates, in contrast, *do* differ—2.99 versus 2.58 percent per annum in 1996–2001—but given the differences in the underlying labor force growth rates assumed in the high and low projections—2.37 versus 1.93 percent per annum in 1996–2001—the variance in the city growth rate differentials is predictable.

We conclude from this experiment that unpredictable world commodity market conditions, capital market conditions, and sectoral productivity advance are far more likely to influence future Indian city growth performance than are unforseen departures from predicted paths by demographically driven labor force growth rates.

Table 8.9. Indian Migration, Urbanization, and City Growth, 1960–2001: Projections under Various Assumptions about Future Labor Force Growth

Year	Benchmark			High Labor Force Growth			Low Labor Force Growth		
	% Urban	City Growth (% per annum)	Net Urban In-Migration Rate (% per annum)	% Urban	City Growth (% per annum)	Net Urban In-Migration Rate (% per annum)	% Urban	City Growth (% per annum)	Net Urban In-Migration Rate (% per annum)
1960	13.9	—	—	13.9	—	—	13.9	—	—
1966	16.9	5.63	3.47	16.9	5.63	3.47	16.9	5.63	3.47
1971	17.9	3.43	1.25	17.9	3.43	1.25	17.9	3.43	1.25
1976	19.5	3.95	1.79	19.5	3.95	1.79	19.5	3.95	1.79
1981	21.3	4.00	1.39	21.3	4.00	1.39	21.3	4.00	1.39
1986	22.0	2.85	0.67	23.0	2.82	0.67	22.0	2.75	0.68
1991	22.7	2.87	0.68	22.7	2.84	0.68	22.7	2.70	0.70
1996	23.4	2.85	0.66	23.4	2.98	0.64	23.5	2.71	0.67
2001	24.1	2.84	0.65	24.1	2.99	0.63	24.2	2.58	0.67

	High		Low	
	Total Labor Force	Skilled	Total Labor Force	Skilled
1981–86	2.17	3.86	2.09	3.78
1986–91	2.18	3.87	2.02	3.71
1991–96	2.35	4.04	2.06	3.75
1996–2001	2.37	4.06	1.93	3.62

The Benchmark projection is described in table 8.5 and the text, where the total labor force growth is 2.21% per annum, where the total labor force growth is 2.21% per annum and skilled labor force growth is 3.90% per annum. The high and low projections are based on the ILO percentages per annum (1977, vol. 1, table 6, p. 119): and the skilled labor force growth rate is adjusted so that the rate of skills deepening is the same as Benchmark in both cases.

8.5 Summary

Predictions about the future are always hazardous, and they are certainly limited by the quality of the model that makes them. Our confidence in BMW's predictions is reinforced by the close correspondence reported in this chapter between these predictions and those of demographic projections. But what else do we learn from the exercise?

Demographers have developed some stylized facts associated with the urban transition. City growth rates, according to this view, tend to rise through early stages and to reach a peak in the middle stages of industrialization. The key demographic component of this stylized urban transition is city migration, and these migration rates are also alleged to follow a similar pattern. When Indian experience of the recent past is projected into the future, the resulting urban transition fails to conform to these stylized facts. Instead, India exhibits very high rates of urbanization, in-migration, and city growth early in the 1960s and never regains those levels thereafter.

From this perspective we can now see that city growth problems in the 1960s, and perhaps even the 1970s, *were* unusually severe in India. The 1990s are likely to be different, since city growth rates will continue a long-run slowdown. The extent of the future slowdown will be conditioned by the economic environment surrounding the urban transition, but even the most favorable city growth environment is unlikely to reverse the slowdown.

9 · Assessing Major Policy Changes and the Urban Bias

9.1 What If Policy Had Been Different?

Indian economic policy has varied considerably since 1960. But many alternative growth strategies employed elsewhere in Asia were never pursued in India. In view of the modest economic expansion and slow city growth experienced in India during these decades, it is of some relevance to ask to what extent different policies would have mattered, especially those in which the alleged urban bias might have been moderated or augmented. It is also important to examine the degree to which implicit but unacknowledged policies may have mattered and how nascent ones currently becoming popular might affect growth and urbanization. To help provide answers, BMW is used to generate counterfactual simulations of alternative policy regimes over the long run.

This chapter examines five such regimes. The first has its source in a tendency that has appeared from time to time in the recent past—to protect urban workers, either directly, by intervening in the labor market on their behalf, or indirectly, by restricting the inflow of competing workers from the countryside. The second counterfactual considers the consequences of a major public sites and services urban housing program—an extreme example of those that have become commonplace in India during the recent past. We then consider a more radical option: what would have happened had the Indian government pursued policies that served to allocate its investment to those sectors in which capital's marginal product was highest, that is, had it pursued an efficient investment strategy? Finally, we contrast IMF-style liberalization reforms with an augmented Mahalanobis-like regime.

The results in many cases are surprising and often do not support prevailing doctrine. IMF reforms or efficient investment strategies do not necessarily generate big GNP gains and a quickening in city growth;

import-substituting industrialization is not *always* undesirable. The success or failure of policies depends instead on the conditions under which they are implemented and whether or not an entire package is adopted. No doubt the impact of such policies also hinges on total factor productivity responses at the sectoral level, but such responses are not captured in our experiments. Finally, the counterfactuals also confirm how aggregate GDP masks complex distributional influences; GDP is especially misleading as an index of welfare for the rural poor.

9.2 Economic Regression: Restricting Migration to the Cities

Despite India's modest urban population growth rate, there has been considerable pressure from policymakers and even from some demographers (who should know better) to put the brakes on rural-urban migration. Nor is this pressure unique to India. A 1978 UN report concluded that "among the developing countries, the predominant perception is that the present distribution of the population within the national territory is very unsatisfactory from the point of view of optimum utilization of the nation's . . . resources. Fifteen of the thirty Asian nations thought it was 'highly unacceptable.' "[1] Moreover, as chapter 3 has shown, it is difficult to explain the urban unskilled wage rise in the late 1960s without positing an incomes policy aimed at favoring those already with urban jobs, and, implicitly, reducing opportunities for potential migrants.

Thus, economic policy aimed at protecting the current urban labor force and restricting migration is hardly new to India. The goal could be achieved through many policies, including parastatal and public sector wage and hiring policies, government intervention on behalf of labor in union-management disputes, legal restrictions on private sector wage and hiring activities, public policy restricting squatter settlements, a scarcity of employment identification cards for urban workers, and, more generally, limiting public services provided to new urban residents. Each of these policies may deter migration from the countryside—or equivalently, tighten the unskilled urban labor market.

As these policies become increasingly unfavorable to potential migrants, willingness to migrate to the cities should diminish. Put differently, urban wages must rise to compensate potential migrants for poorer services and quality of life, and for greater job search costs induced by government action. As the opportunity cost of leaving rural areas rises

---

1. United Nations (1979, p. 27). The report also finds that of 116 developing countries, 76 desired to slow down migration from rural areas and 14 sought to reverse it; only 3 sought an acceleration (p. 29). Similar results appeared in a 1984 report.

for potential migrants, the wages of those already in urban areas are bid up.

In the present simulation, we examine the consequences of policies designed to lower the rural-urban migration rate of unskilled labor by roughly 40 percent, and the migration rate of all labor by one-third, during the period 1978–83. A summary of the findings appears in table 9.1, in which elasticities for the first and final year of the policy regime are presented (relative to the historical Benchmark simulation).

The most notable result is that city growth diminishes considerably. The policy package reduces unskilled immigration from 3.87 million in the Benchmark to only 2.35 million, a decline of 39 percent; the total migration rate falls 33 percent. Since natural increase is estimated to be about 57 percent of urban population growth during the period 1977–83, the implied fall in the city growth rate is just over 13 percent. The proportion of the population living in urban areas rises from 19.9 to 21.6 percent in the Benchmark, but increases only to 21 percent in the counterfactual, implying a city growth rate of only 3.15 percent. In short, the urban slowdown is considerable.

The city growth consequences are strongest at first, before offsetting

Table 9.1. Rural–Urban Migration Restriction, 1978–1983

Endogenous Variables	1978	1983
A. City Growth Attributes		
% Urban	−1.78	−2.51
City growth rate (1977–78, 1977–83)	−29.19	−13.16
City in-migration rate (1977–78, 1977–83)	−44.21	−32.56
Pucca house rents	0.07	0.35
Katcha house rents	3.58	3.45
B. Output		
A	0.16	0.19
RS	0.37	−0.39
PSR	0.02	0.26
M	−0.65	−0.87
KS	−0.33	−0.30
US	−0.18	0.17
PSU	−0.94	−1.35
Nonhousing GDP	−0.15	−0.24
C. Unskilled employment		
A	0.44	0.81
RS	0.68	0.17
PSR	0.48	1.06
M	−2.74	−4.14
KS	−2.18	−3.15
US	−0.92	−0.86
PSU	−2.26	−3.25

Table 9.1. *continued*

Endogenous Variables	1978	1983
D. Skilled employment		
A	0.04	0.07
RS	0.30	−0.46
PSR	0.08	0.37
M	−0.25	−0.35
KS	−0.12	0.07
US	1.33	2.09
PSU	0.00	−0.17
E. Relative prices		
A	−0.38	−0.71
RS	−0.27	−0.65
PSR	−0.22	−0.48
M	0.13	0.49
KS	0.08	0.44
US	1.38	2.61
PSU	0.65	1.50
F. Incomes		
Capital rental rate		
Urban formal	−0.64	−0.41
Urban informal	2.01	3.90
Rural	−0.18	−0.89
Disposable incomes, 1960 prices		
Rural unskilled	−0.40	−0.84
Rural skilled	−0.03	−0.10
Urban unskilled	2.60	5.27
Urban skilled	−0.56	−0.98
Capitalists and landlords	−0.74	−1.68
G. Real government revenue	−0.21	−0.07
H. Exports		
A	−1.14	0.41
M	−1.90	−1.38
Total	−1.68	−0.84
I. Capital formation		
Rural nonhousing	−0.57	−0.79
Urban formal nonhousing	−0.21	−0.66
Urban informal nonhousing	0.00	0.00
Urban informal housing	5.14	13.01
Urban formal housing	−1.45	−0.38
Rural housing	1.67	−0.47
Total nonhousing	−0.34	−0.68
Total	−0.24	−0.49

Simulation involves lowering the long-run rural-urban migration rate by one-third. All values shown are elasticities.

dynamic effects come into play. The most important of these is that the proportionate reduction in capital formation is greatest in rural sectors, ultimately stemming rural labor demand. On the other hand, income effects tend to be compounded over time. The policies provide a windfall to the urban unskilled, whose incomes jump initially by 2.6 percent. As their numbers decline only by 2.0 percent, total income of the urban working class rises. This rise in spending power of the urban unskilled puts upward pressure on the prices of urban goods and services, eroding a bit the net real income gains to the urban unskilled.[2] Ultimately, however, the real incomes of the urban unskilled rise by more than 5 percent, while peasant real incomes, depressed by reduced emigration opportunities, fall by nearly 1 percent.

Except for the urban unskilled, all classes lose from migration restriction. This fact perhaps explains why these policies have never really been tried (Williamson, 1988). Rising labor costs squeeze returns to urban formal sector capital and skilled labor; falling urban skilled incomes also depress rural skilled wages. The consequences for fixed rural factors of production are, in principle, ambiguous. Given the terms of trade, cheaper rural labor raises the return to land and capital, but in fact the terms of trade deteriorate, and for two reasons: first, agricultural supply is augmented; and second, as GDP and rural incomes fall, demand for farm products declines. These latter effects turn out to dominate, especially in the long run. Rising costs of capital goods also inhibit asset formation: the savings pool purchases fewer capital goods. Capital formation therefore declines in the nonhousing sectors, except for *US*, where replacement investment is maintained.

This policy regime imposes deadweight losses on the economy, as workers are kept out of the more productive urban sectors. The loss is not large (in 1983 it amounted to only 0.24 percent of nonhousing GDP), but it is an expensive way to subsidize urban labor. Real incomes of the 56.6 million urban unskilled workers in the 1983 counterfactual are about 2 billion Rs. (in 1960 prices) greater than they would have been; the deadweight loss of 800 million Rs. implies a loss–transfer ratio of about 40 percent.

The rise in unskilled urban incomes generates a boom in sectors that cater mainly to that class—informal housing and services. Rates of return to capital and output prices rise in these sectors. Rising labor costs push up the relative price of all urban goods, but the effect is most pronounced for the informal sector.

---

2. BMW's rural-urban migration equilibrium requires equality between gap-adjusted wages with living cost differentials lagged one year. Thus, the full effect of the migration restriction measures will only be felt in the long run.

Finally, a regime of migration restriction would serve to further insulate India from the rest of the world. Export values decline 1.68 percent initially, and 0.84 percent in 1983, as rising costs of processed goods and other manufactures make India less competitive in world markets. Not surprisingly, trade and urban migration policies are not independent: a buoyant external sector is hindered by policies that raise costs in the traded goods' sectors.

In summary, a regime of city immigration restriction has little merit. It is inefficient because it exacerbates rural-urban wage gaps, thus generating deadweight losses in the aggregate and income losses for all classes except the established urban unskilled. It also discourages capital formation and strikes hardest at India's most dynamic sectors. Finally, the policy is inconsistent with India's push toward an increasingly open economy, which has characterized the 1980s.

9.3 Economic Reform: Housing Investment in Urban Slums

The preceding section does not imply, however, that the Indian government should take no steps to help the urban poor. Rather, the point is simply that adding more market distortions to an economy already beset with many is not a desirable means to what may be a laudable end.

This section asks if an alternative regime—heavy public investment in low-quality urban housing—might be a more effective means of improving the economic position of India's urban poor. As table 9.2 indicates, the answer is a qualified yes.

The public sector has long been involved in India's urban housing market, both directly, as a supplier of housing services, and indirectly, as a regulator. Both national and local governments have sought to provide housing for what is euphemistically termed the "economically weaker sections" of society, and to control urban housing prices.[3] The focus in this section is on the first goal, assisting the urban poor by raising the quality of the housing they consume.

That Indian housing standards are poor is hardly a contentious claim; it can be supported by surveys of the National Buildings Organisation and the National Sample Survey.[4] For example, the 1971 census reported that 77 percent of Bombay households and 67 percent of Calcutta house-

3. Much has been written on Indian housing; the most recent, extraordinarily comprehensive survey and analysis is by D. B. Gupta (1985). The numbers and descriptions of policies provided in this section, unless otherwise noted, are based on Gupta's work.

4. The basic figures are provided in D. B. Gupta (1985). For greater detail, see National Buildings Organisation (1981); for National Sample Survey findings, see various issues of its journal, *Sarvekshana*.

holds lived in one-room dwellings; even in relatively low-density Bangalore, the figure was 45 percent. However, the trends in housing standards are even more surprising: despite modest growth in per capita income, urban housing conditions appear to have deteriorated. For example, in urban India as a whole, the number of persons per room rose

Table 9.2. Impact of International Grants for Urban Sites and Services Housing Schemes

Endogenous Variables	1978	1980	1983
A. City Growth Attributes			
% Urban	0.32	0.39	-0.09
City growth rate (1978, 1977–80, 1978–83)	5.19	3.36	-0.40
City in-migration rate (1978, 1978–80, 1978–83)	7.86	6.75	-1.16
Pucca house rents	2.42	0.96	-3.87
Katcha house rents	5.52	-18.66	-39.44
B. Output			
A	0.04	-0.03	0.04
RS	-0.12	0.02	0.13
PSR	-0.06	0.52	0.64
M	-0.52	-0.25	0.07
KS	0.56	-0.07	-2.07
US	2.19	2.11	1.14
PSU	-0.09	-0.06	0.05
Nonhousing GDP	0.19	0.17	-0.18
C. Unskilled employment			
A	-0.06	-0.13	0.01
RS	-0.20	-0.06	-0.09
PSR	-0.08	0.64	0.33
M	-1.16	-0.57	-0.24
KS	0.09	-0.49	-2.43
US	2.72	2.67	1.45
PSU	-0.44	-0.33	0.03
D. Skilled employment			
A	-0.09	-0.16	0.67
RS	-0.22	-0.04	0.39
PSR	-0.12	0.55	0.90
M	-0.53	-0.27	0.47
KS	0.52	-0.21	-1.87
US	2.33	1.92	1.49
PSU	0.00	0.00	0.34
E. Relative prices			
A	-0.07	0.18	0.46
RS	-0.06	0.18	0.21
PSR	-0.03	0.41	0.13
M	-0.05	0.23	0.22
KS	0.05	0.07	0.04
US	0.99	1.01	0.74
PSU	0.18	0.26	0.45

Table 9.2. *continued*

Endogenous Variables	1978	1980	1983
F. Incomes			
Capital rental rates			
Urban formal	0.16	−0.25	−1.68
Urban informal	5.42	4.68	2.12
Rural	0.33	0.09	0.04
Disposable incomes, 1960 prices			
Rural unskilled	0.14	0.12	0.10
Rural skilled	0.15	0.09	−0.52
Urban unskilled	0.59	1.09	1.52
Urban skilled	−0.31	−0.12	−0.30
Capitalists and landlords	−0.46	−0.30	0.11
G. Real government revenue	4.25	3.47	0.14
H. Exports			
A	−5.17	−3.42	5.10
M	−5.19	−3.49	5.50
Total	−5.19	−3.46	5.38
I. Capital formation			
Rural nonhousing	0.65	0.03	−1.04
Urban formal nonhousing	0.46	0.28	−1.60
Urban informal nonhousing	0.42	0.30	−0.43
Urban informal housing	102.50	108.64	102.64
Urban formal housing	0.39	−1.51	−2.75
Rural housing	−1.12	1.41	1.38
Total nonhousing	0.53	0.19	−1.34
Total	1.55	1.09	−0.42

All values shown are elasticities in response to an annual grant from 1978–1983 of 700 million 1960 Rs.

from 2.62 in 1960 to 2.77 in 1970—and in densely populated urban areas, such as in West Bengal, the rise was from 3.05 to 3.63 persons per room.

Other indicators of housing quality also suggest extremely low standards. In the mid-1970s, only 67 percent of urban Indian households had access to a water tap, only 53 percent enjoyed electricity, and 33 percent had no latrine arrangement. Furthermore, access to a water tap could still mean a significant walk to the site.

Not only do urban Indians have quite modest housing, the majority live in rental units. While census estimates indicate that the proportion living in owner-occupied units rose from 46.2 percent in 1960 to 47.1 percent in 1970, according to table 9.3 the proportions in major cities are very low (and in many cases are declining over time). Indian public authorities have at times sought to increase owner occupancy, especially of the poor; at other times they appear to have followed policies that

Table 9.3. The Proportion of Households in Owner-Occupied Units (1961, 1971) and Slums (1980)

City	1961	1971	1980
Ahmedabad	17.62%	3.67	24.69
Bangalore	29.96	25.84	10.42
Bombay	10.00	14.85	34.63
Calcutta	17.29	18.63	35.05
Delhi (metro)	33.52	16.67	27.75
Hyderabad	32.99	21.69	19.65
Kanpur	12.87	8.67	38.92
Madras	26.06	26.77	25.42

Source: Gupta (1985, pp. 53, 92).

virtually ignored the issue; and at still other times have sought to tax landlords.

Indian federal and local governments do not, at least in principle, accept the status quo. Nearly one-fifth of the entire urban population, and 30 percent of those in the largest cities, live in areas legally defined as "slums."[5] There have been ongoing efforts to combat poor urban living conditions, beginning with the Slum Clearance/Improvement Scheme of 1956, which involved compulsory land acquisition and redevelopment. By 1972 it has become apparent that redevelopment schemes would never have adequate funds to eliminate slums; moreover, as D. B. Gupta (1985, p. 100) notes in somewhat understated fashion, "There was . . . widespread resentment against the wholesale demolition of established communities that redevelopment often entailed."

The result has been greater emphasis on local environmental improvements by providing water, latrines, drainage, pavement, lighting, electricity, and the like. This "minimum amenities" approach has dovetailed nicely with the World Bank's "sites and services" focus, which includes programs for the provision of minimum amenities, often accompanied by cleared sites and building materials that enable families to build their own housing. Not only are these programs less disruptive, but they also involve far less expense per household. Furthermore, they tend to encourage substantial investments by affected households.

The simulation we examine here explores the impact of an interna-

5. The definition of slums is not constant across India, and the designation of an area as a slum undoubtedly involves much local interpretation. The federal government defines a slum as an area with buildings "unfit for human habitation" (as determined by repair, stability, freedom from damp, natural light and air, water supply, drainage and sanitation, and food preparation, storage, and waste disposal conditions) or "detrimental to safety, health or morals . . . by reason of dilapidation, overcrowding, . . . lack of ventilation, light or sanitation facilities." See D. B. Gupta (1985, p. 221).

tional development agency loan for low-quality katcha housing improvement or slum upgrading. Since both Indian and World Bank programs have involved investment in low-quality housing stock rather than low-interest loans or construction subsidies, we assume that the loan is used exclusively for direct investment. The simulation further assumes a five-year (1978–82) international grant of 700 million Rs. (1960 value) annually (or about 2.1 billion Rs. in late 1970s prices), which obligates the government to continue the program afterward as well. Thus, table 9.2 reports elasticities for an initial impact year (1978), a grant year that captures dynamic effects (1980), and a nongrant year in which the program continues but without international support (1983).

How does this counterfactual regime compare with actual recent investment experience? Simply put, it is far larger. Present World Bank housing projects in Madras, Bombay, Kanpur, and Madhya Pradesh involve the construction of at most 15,000 units per year and external infrastructure costs of at most 2,000 Rs. (1960 value) per unit: the simulation reported in table 9.2 examines the impact of a loan at least twenty times as great.[6]

The simulated sites and services program involves an approximate doubling of new low-quality housing construction, raising the 1977–83 annual rate of growth of the low-quality housing stock from 2.05 to 7.03 percent. As this rate of expansion is far greater than the addition to the city population growth rate induced by the new construction, housing consumption per urban household jumps markedly, by nearly 24 percent by 1983.[7] As a result, urban unskilled real incomes rise substantially, and this expansion continues to increase as the investment program is maintained.

No other income class exhibits welfare gains comparable to the urban unskilled. Although the housing of the rural poor is not directly affected by the urban housing program, why don't greater gains trickle down to the rural poor? The answer lies in the implications of the model's labor market equilibrium statement: intersectoral migration equates expected real wages, not average nominal incomes. The benefits of new public services accrue to those presently occupying favored sites. Consequently, there is no incentive for peasants to migrate, unless they believe that they will be able to occupy new land without paying for it (i.e.,

6. We gratefully acknowledge the assistance of Mr. Evan Rotner of the World Bank in deriving these estimates. Although a twentyfold increase in Indian housing development is not imminent, it is important to recognize that the local effects of such schemes approximate the national impact of a much larger scheme.

7. The 1983 per household rise in the consumption of housing services over the historical counterfactual, in 1960 rupees, is from 96 to 119 Rs.

live in squatter settlements) and that the new land will also receive public services. As current programs focus primarily on older settlements, sites and services schemes are unlikely to raise such expectations.

The rural poor do benefit indirectly and modestly by an expansion of the urban housing stock, which, after all, drives down rental rates per "housing unit" (or raises the quality of housing at given rents). This decline raises the purchasing power of a nominal wage, induces some migration, and therefore creates modest labor scarcity in rural areas. More important, the real income increase experienced by urban households induces a modest substitution away from housing toward other items, including food, so that value added in agriculture rises once the new construction comes on stream.

The initial impact of the program is somewhat different from the long-run impact, mainly because construction is assumed to involve a one-year gestation lag. The program generates a boom in US, the sector that provides construction services for low-quality housing. This boom accounts for the real income rise experienced by unskilled urban workers early in the regime. After this initial employment effect and after the urban investment is added to capacity, katcha and semipucca rents fall dramatically, and these "expenditure" side effects dominate the real income gains in the longer run.

While the housing effects are important, so are the foreign exchange consequences. Foreign exchange enables the Indian government to purchase local construction labor, which it pays in rupees; the foreign exchange is then available for additional imports, which rise 1.5 percent in 1980. To some extent, these added imports displace domestic production, notably urban manufactures. When the capital inflow ends, however, imports fall by 1.5 percent, while exports surge by 5.4 percent. What accounts for the net export growth? The answer is that the sites and services scheme unintentionally promotes development of sectors in which India has an international comparative advantage. The housing boom makes workers better off by reducing their living costs, not by raising their nominal wages. In fact, urban nominal wages decline, thus raising the profitability of labor-intensive urban activities, including manufacturing, India's main export sector. When the rupee declines following the cessation of the large loan, labor-intensive sectors are then in a position to respond.

This mini-export boom is important, for it suggests that India would have little trouble repaying urban housing loans directed toward the poor. It is less clear, however, that such loans would be cost effective. As can be seen from table 9.4, total GDP is higher in the 1983 counterfactual than in the Benchmark. But with accumulated interest charges (assuming a 10 percent discount rate), the Indian economy would be

Table 9.4. Housing Loan Counterfactual less Benchmark GDP (in millions of 1960 Rs.)

Year	Counterfactual GDP	Benchmark GDP	Difference	Loan
1978	306497	305961	536	700
1979	312012	311440	572	700
1980	326174	325342	831	700
1981	335593	334295	1298	700
1982	349237	348718	519	700
1983	365163	364993	170	0

saddled with a 3.633 billion Rs. debt at the end of 1983. Net (of loan) gains in GDP are only 170 million Rs., generating a social return of only 4.7 percent—not a figure high enough to encourage an unsubsidized increase in international debt.

Yet even if the program does not generate dramatic GDP gains that make the loan meritorious in its own right, the egalitarian consequences may well make it desirable. By pushing demand away from modern, capital-intensive sectors toward labor-intensive sectors, GDP gains may be limited. The moral of the story is that GDP alone is not a good measure of welfare among the groups targeted by the policy.

9.4 Economic Reform: Efficient Public Investment Policy

No economy has ever been able to distribute capital efficiently, but some do it more efficiently than others, and some do it better at some times than at others. In principle, close approximations to static efficiency may be generated either by laissez-faire market economies or by those highly planned capitalist or socialist economies in which policy is geared to maximize GNP at world prices. In practice, countries with massive government intervention in a relatively small slice of the economy, but limited government control over the economy as a whole, are unlikely to approximate this ideal. This is especially true in countries such as India, where capital markets are fragmented and where public policy employs economic tools to pursue many noneconomic goals.

Indeed, BMW reflects what observers of the Indian economy have claimed all along: namely, that rate of return differentials *are* pronounced in some periods.[8] As the simulation in chapter 3 indicates: investment in the public service and infrastructure sectors had relatively low rates of return throughout the period 1960–81; the informal *US* service sector and the katcha housing sector were capital starved throughout the entire period; and returns to modern sector investment

8. Wolf (1978) in particular focuses on the extraordinarily high incremental capital–output ratios in India's public service sector investments.

exceeded returns to rural investment in the early years, but by the late 1960s this pattern had reversed. This switch reflected rapid modern sector capital deepening combined with small or negative total factor productivity gains.

Given these patterns, this section considers the impact of an "efficient" policy in which public investment is allocated across sectors so as to maximize the current rate of return on capital—that is, public investment is allocated only to those sectors offering the highest return. The analysis focuses on two epochs: epoch I (1960–64), a period of rapid early development with lagging agriculture and leading industry; and epoch IV (1978–81), a period of more balanced growth characterized by high oil prices and modest liberalization. In epoch I, the cities were starved for capital, while the rural sectors had, at least relatively, a glut. Note that rate of return differentials were of the same sign as wage gaps, replicating the stylized facts of development. By epoch IV, things had changed. Accumulation in urban activities had driven down r_M and r_{KS}, while, in contrast, the green revolution and limited rural access to public and private capital caused net returns to capital in A and RS to rise from 7.7 percent in 1960 to 8.6 percent in 1981. By the early 1980s, therefore, an asymmetric distortion had developed in factor markets; while labor's marginal product was higher in the city, capital's marginal product was not.

It may seem inevitable that GNP will rise as investment is shifted to sectors offering the highest return to capital. In fact, the matter is somewhat more complicated when asymmetric distortions are present. Consider a two-sector economy with an urban production function, $U = U(K_u, L_u)$, a rural production function, $R = R(K_r, L_r)$, and where P is the terms of trade between rural and urban goods. GNP in this economy can be written as

$$(9.1) \quad GNP = U(K_u, L_u) + P \cdot R(K_r, L_r)$$

Consequently, transferring resources from rural to urban activities will raise GNP if and only if

$$(9.2) \quad (U_K - P \cdot R_K)dK_u + (U_L - P \cdot R_L) \cdot \left(\frac{\partial L_u}{\partial K_u}\right)dK_u > 0$$

The first term is the standard one: GNP will increase when investment is diverted to urban activities (dK_u) if capital's marginal product (U_K) is higher there than in the countryside (PR_K). The second term is less obvious. In BMW, moving, job search costs, and other distortions lead to a wage gap favoring city (U_L) over countryside (PR_L). When urban investment takes place, migrants are pulled into the city and

$$\left(\frac{\partial L_u}{\partial K_u}\right) dK_u$$

is positive. This secondary effect raises productivity if urban labor has a higher value of marginal product than rural labor, which is in fact assumed. On the other hand, when investment is withdrawn from urban areas because the marginal product of capital is higher in rural activities, the implied loss of labor reduces efficiency gains—and may even render net gains negative in a labor-intensive economy. That is, when factor market distortions are asymmetric, the standard deadweight loss effects may be overturned.

It can also be shown that an efficient investment allocation can be dynamically inefficient to the extent that sectoral reallocation reduces domestic savings rates, and the economy is not well integrated into world capital markets. Furthermore, the planner who wishes to maximize GNP must also consider the consequences of his investment decisions on the terms of trade.[9]

In summary, the standard textbook diagram dealing with the allocation of one input—in this case, capital—is often deceptive. High rates of return in capital-starved areas warrant investment, especially if labor chases after capital into areas where labor's marginal productivity is also higher. This general equilibrium phenomenon is especially important given the labor-intensive production that characterizes developing economies. It should have prevailed in India in epoch I, where cities had the higher labor productivity *and* were starved for capital. Epoch IV is another matter entirely since asymmetric factor market distortions held. Even in epoch I, however, deadweight losses may be overstated in the standard diagram to the extent that investment reallocation toward urban activities causes the terms of trade to shift in the favor of rural goods.

Let us now examine the results of rate of return–equating public investment policy (table 9.5), focusing first on epoch I. The investment distribution in the efficient investment allocation counterfactual is very different from the Benchmark, although the drift from 1960 to 1964 in the Benchmark (and in history) was in the right direction. That is, Indian

9. These results are derived in a more formal dynamic model of capital allocation in Becker (1987). The seminal analysis of optimal investment in a two-sector model that considers price variability (and the need to feed urban workers) can be found in Dixit (1969).

policy was pushing investment in the right direction, but it was not pushing hard enough. Investment in urban manufacturing was sufficiently large to raise that sector's capital stock by 46 percent by 1965 in the Benchmark. But, according to table 9.6, the counterfactual urban investment spurt is even greater (especially if the public service sectors

Table 9.5. Impact of Efficient Sectoral Investment Policies

Endogenous Variables	1964	1981
A. City Growth Attributes		
% Urban	3.63	0.66
City growth rate (1960–64, 1977–81)	14.80	4.34
City in-migration rate	22.62	10.14
Pucca house rents	−6.83	0.27
Katcha house rents	0.70	−6.95
B. Output		
A	−1.58	0.18
RS	−8.34	5.74
PSR	−12.02	−5.16
M	6.82	0.07
KS	16.56	0.39
US	4.59	1.19
PSU	−11.90	−8.90
Nonhousing GDP	0.63	−0.13
C. Unskilled employment		
A	0.59	−1.06
RS	−6.46	4.67
PSR	−2.11	−1.11
M	−0.30	2.17
KS	11.60	3.57
US	4.32	−2.32
PSU	0.25	0.87
D. Skilled employment		
A	−3.00	−1.20
RS	−9.26	5.12
PSR	−6.99	−2.19
M	6.52	−0.41
KS	13.67	0.45
US	7.33	1.58
PSU	−7.76	−7.48
E. Relative prices		
A	1.75	−0.70
RS	2.14	−0.81
PSR	12.27	5.41
M	−6.75	−0.18
KS	−6.38	1.19
US	−1.88	−5.09
PSU	12.92	9.19

Table 9.5. *continued*

Endogenous Variables	1964	1981
F. Incomes		
Capital rental rate		
Urban formal	−33.43	−1.19
Urban informal	−5.07	−30.75
Rural	17.11	−11.72
Disposable incomes, 1960 prices		
Rural unskilled	−1.02	1.07
Rural skilled	3.91	1.07
Urban unskilled	−3.45	−1.44
Urban skilled	−0.14	2.54
Capitalists and landlords	2.21	0.98
G. Real government revenue	0.43	1.82
H. Exports		
A	−7.14	1.44
M	5.83	0.66
Total	2.33	0.88
I. Capital formation		
Rural nonhousing	−54.53	18.98
Urban formal nonhousing	43.94	−23.32
Urban informal nonhousing	64.23	111.02
Urban informal housing	−3.15	−6.79
Urban formal housing	103.23	1.24
Rural housing	−30.05	35.37
Total nonhousing	1.00	−1.89
Total	4.92	1.74

Counterfactual simulation involves government policy to minimize rate of return differentials across nonhousing sections. All values shown are elasticities.

Table 9.6. 1964 Sectoral Investment: Efficient Allocation versus Benchmark (Rs. billion, 1960 prices)

Sector	Efficient Counterfactual	Benchmark	EC/B Ratio
A	2.905	5.803	0.50
RS	3.160	4.452	0.71
PSR	0.306	3.576	0.09
M	13.048	7.616	1.71
KS	7.698	2.397	3.21
US	3.232	1.968	1.64
PSU	0.556	4.786	0.12
HR	2.691	3.847	0.70
HUS	0.461	0.476	0.97
HKS	5.335	2.625	2.03

are excluded). Urban investment is roughly 50 percent greater in the efficient investment counterfactual.

Despite this dramatic investment reallocation, the deadweight losses removed by the efficient investment policy are modest. In the 1964 efficient counterfactual, nonhousing GDP is only 0.63 percent higher than that of the Benchmark. Annual GDP per capita growth over the period 1960–64 rises from the Benchmark 2.89 to 3.06 percent—not a trivial rise, but hardly dramatic. One reason for the modest impact on GDP is that it takes large changes in investment allocation to have even a modest impact on capital stocks. In any case, the finding is consistent with the literature from Leibenstein (1957) to Williamson (1987), all of which shows that Harberger triangles and deadweight losses tend to be far smaller in developing countries than the stress on factor market failure would have suggested.[10]

The impact on the *structure* of the economy is, however, far more significant. Manufacturing output is 6.8 percent higher by 1964, *KS* output is 16.6 percent greater, and *US* output is 4.6 percent larger. The rural sectors, of course, lose: agriculture declines by 1.6 percent, while *RS* declines by 8.3 percent. Clearly, these are dramatic structural changes for an economy whose nonhousing GDP rose only 22 percent between 1960 and 1964. How, then, can the total efficiency gains be so small? It is certainly not that initial gaps are small; nor it is because city production activities are weakly affected. Rather, the reason is simply that India's rural sectors were so big and the economy so labor intensive in the 1960s that even large capital market distortions did not matter much.

The important policy moral that follows is that the first aim of policy reform in backward economies, apart from raising labor productivity through technological advance, is the elimination of labor market distortions, not capital market distortions. However, it is important to recognize that small, short-run efficiency gains may portend much greater dynamic gains in the long run. Massive urban investment drives down prices there, the price of capital goods (P_M) in particular. Consequently, a given savings pool can purchase more capital assets. Furthermore, since urban saving rates are higher, the savings pool is *not* given, but grows. Thus, real capital formation is nearly 5 percent greater in the 1964 efficiency counterfactual.

The impact on urbanization is, in theory, ambiguous. The epoch I efficient investment policy reform involves a large increase in urban capital formation: this can either pull in migrant labor as its marginal

10. See the summary in Williamson (1987) for additional citations to this extensive literature.

productivity is augmented in urban employment, or it can crowd out labor as falling urban output prices decrease the *value* of marginal products. As we have seen in chapter 4, price elasticities for urban goods tend to be somewhat large, so that the productivity term dominates. Consequently, the urban in-migration rate rises by nearly one quarter this period, and the city growth rate rises from 6.4 to 7.4 percent per annum—a substantial increase.

Since the efficient investment counterfactual raises total output, aggregate personal incomes rise, but not for all classes. Indeed, the effects of the efficient investment reform are highly inegalitarian. Unskilled workers are hurt because the gains in labor demand due to increasing urban capital formation are less than the losses in rural labor demand as capital formation is reduced there. That is, the shift in capital formation is from relatively labor-intensive to relatively capital-cum-skill–intensive sectors; the net effect is unskilled labor saving. Thus, efficiency gains are hardly Pareto improving since the losses suffered by the poor are quite significant.

Although the consequences are inegalitarian, they do lead to a surge in trade, which accompanies the rise in city growth. Manufactured exports rise nearly 6 percent, and agricultural imports grow almost 8 percent; total trade volume rises 2.3 percent. These patterns reflect the movement in capital formation and production toward manufacturing and away from agriculture.

Consider now epoch IV. Here, efficient investment allocation implies a shift from urban to rural activities, as table 9.7 shows. The urban losers are not the leading urban *M* and *KS* sectors. Instead, it is public services that loses capital to all other sectors, especially *US*. On net, however, capital moves from urban to rural areas, with agriculture a big gainer.

The economywide efficiency gains realized by transferring investment

Table 9.7. 1981 Investment: Efficient Counterfactual versus Benchmark (1960 Rs. billion)

Sector	Efficient Counterfactual	Benchmark	EC/B Ratio
A	19.030	12.051	1.58
RS	4.451	4.153	1.07
PSR	0.188	3.690	0.05
M	14.809	14.543	1.02
KS	7.754	7.327	1.06
US	4.271	2.034	2.10
PSU	0.468	8.165	0.06
HR	8.026	5.929	1.35
HUS	0.574	0.615	0.93
HKS	10.733	10.602	1.01

from infrastructure to more productive uses are trivial: total GDP is augmented (over the Benchmark) by only 0.09 percent. In part, the smaller gain in epoch IV reflects the fact that few workers are pulled from low-productivity rural jobs to higher-productivity urban employment. But while aggregate GDP gains are tiny, investment reallocation now takes capital away from where it is used intensively and, for the most part, places it in labor-intensive sectors. Peasant incomes rise sharply, although a concomitant increase in living costs prevents the urban working class from benefiting immediately. Because both export sectors receive more capital, a modest trade boom occurs once again, with total exports rising almost 1 percent.

In general, the urbanization impact of capital misallocation was nowhere near as great in epoch IV as in epoch I. In 1977–81 urban inmigration rate rises by only 10 percent, city growth rates rise from 3.96 to only 4.13 percent, and the 1983 proportion of the labor force living in urban areas rises from 21.3 to only 21.4 percent. In short, the city growth and urbanization consequences of capital market distortions hardly seem worth mentioning in epoch IV.

This exercise makes it apparent that real GDP growth is an inadequate indicator of welfare gains among the poor. The epoch IV counterfactual investment reallocation, largely to agriculture, generated an increase in the overall labor intensity of the urban economy while simultaneously inducing a marked fall in food prices. While these forces eliminated tiny deadweight losses economywide, they led to substantial real income gains (over 1 percent) by the rural poor, who in 1981 still comprised 76 percent of the Indian labor force. In terms of welfare gains for the poor, these forces were even more important than the larger GDP gains from the efficient investment allocation counterfactual applied to epoch I.

9.5 Contrasting Reforms: IMF Liberalization Packages versus Continued "Mahalanobis" Investment Patterns

There are many possible development strategies, of which seeking short-run capital market efficiency is but one. Two others have had a special impact on Indian policymakers, and this section examines the consequences of implementing these alternative strategies.

The first stems from what is known as the closed two-sector Feldman-Mahalanobis-Domar (FMD) model.[11] In their framework, the economy is closed to trade (and thus to capital goods imports), and it is divided into capital and consumer goods sectors. When growth paths under

11. For a brief exposition, see Taylor (1976); for more detailed presentations, see Domar (1957) and Mahalanobis (1953, 1955). See also Bhagwati and Chakravarty (1969).

different investment allocation regimes are examined, the following important result emerges: planners with a low discount rate seeking to maximize consumption over time will at the outset reinvest heavily in the capital goods sector and restrict the production of consumer goods. This model formed the basis for early Soviet plans, and was also essentially responsible for India's extremely rapid capital formation rate achieved between the mid-1950s and the mid-1960s, especially in large-scale manufacturing.

In contrast, the received wisdom currently popular in most international organizations, in developed countries' governments, and, increasingly, in developing countries' ministries emphasizes economic liberalization. Economic liberalization has many dimensions: it includes the removal of distortions, the shrinkage of the public sector, and the promotion of exports. As the previous section examined the consequences of removing distortions, the focus here is on export promotion and the diminution in the size of the public sector.

A Prolonged Mahalanobis Strategy

We start with the Mahalanobis strategy. It was first embodied in the second Five-Year Plan (1955–60) for which P. C. Mahalanobis, as head of the Indian Planning Commission, was responsible. The plan led to a set of sophisticated intertemporal, multisector planning models emphasizing capital formation. The principles continued, but with increasing opposition, through the 1960s. The official abandonment occurred in 1971 in response to Indira Gandhi's populist electoral appeals, to the new emphasis on employment creation stressed by international development organizations and the academy,[12] and, perhaps, to the poor economic performance during the preceding seven years (epoch II). Actually, the dismal modern sector employment growth experienced during this period (especially in manufacturing) came as something of a surprise to the planners. In any case, severe droughts highlighted the importance of food output growth, especially given the combination of a poor export performance and diminished foreign aid, both of which restricted import capabilities.

But if the Mahalanobis strategy had its shortcomings, it also provided the basis for further development, especially in building a modern industrial sector. The important questions, then, are: What would Indian history have been like had the strong emphasis on modern sector industrialization been reaffirmed rather than abandoned? Were the mid- and late 1960s especially unfavorable periods for this strategy, and might

12. Mellor (1976, chap. 1); Bhagwati and Srinivasan (1975, chap. 1).

it have done better in other economic environments? Would continued consumption sacrifices eventually have brought accelerated growth?

Our counterfactual experiment poses a dramatic reaffirmation of the weakness of the Mahalanobis strategy. We assume that 75 percent of government investment is ploughed back into urban manufacturing, while each public service sector receives 5 percent and agriculture receives 15 percent:

Government Investment Sectoral Allocation

	Mahalanobis	Historical Benchmarks	
Sector	Counterfactual (%)	1960–64	1978–81
A	15.0	0.0	0.0
RS	0.0	11.7	12.5
PSR	5.0	27.0	14.2
M	75.0	10.0	14.0
KS	0.0	10.0	23.6
US	0.0	6.3	6.3
PSU	5.0	35.0	29.4

Thus, the counterfactual simulation reduces the rural share of public investment from about 39 percent in the early 1960s, and about 27 percent in the late 1970s, to only 20 percent; similarly, it involves a sharp cutback in urban public nonmanufacturing investment to 5 percent. Since the allocation of private investments tends to offset partially these shifting public sector patterns, the impact on total investment allocation is likely to be somewhat less dramatic.

In the short run, the impact on output of this counterfactual policy should be positive. Rates of return to capital were higher in the cities through the early 1960s, especially in manufacturing, so there would have been an efficiency gain from building up capacity there. This gain would have been reinforced by increased migration to the cities, since labor productivities were higher there, too. GDP gains would have been further reinforced to the extent that capital moved away from the low-productivity public service sectors in the counterfactual regime.

In fact, GDP does enjoy a modest initial boost from following an accelerated Mahalanobis strategy (table 9.8), and city growth quickens, a result that confirms the findings of chapter 4. However, by 1964 rates of return to capital are already higher in the countryside and the initial GDP gains quickly dissipate. As the accelerated capital deepening takes place in the modern urban sectors, the terms of trade there deteriorate sharply, and by 1965 employment in the cities begins to fall off. Indeed, returns in the formal sectors begin to fall off as well. The losses in manufacturing and PSU employment exceed the gains in the other urban sectors, so that city growth is retarded in the medium term and long run. In short, after a few years, a Mahalanobis policy favoring industrial investment actually causes a city growth slowdown, not a speedup. These results are naturally sensitive to the precise nature of the in-

Table 9.8. Maintaining the Mahalanobis Era over Several Decades: Economic Consequences of Maintaining Very High Levels of Public Investment in Modern Manufacturing

Endogenous Variables	1960	1964	1965	1971	1977	1981
A. City Growth Attributes						
% Urban	0.12	−1.42	−1.60	−1.64	−1.70	−2.08
City growth rate	3.77	−6.40	−6.93	−0.92	−0.27	−2.53
City in-migration rate	4.54	10.04	−11.35	−2.35	−0.60	−5.73
Pucca house rents	0.00	−6.22	−20.91	−21.86	−16.46	−23.68
Katcha house rents	0.00	10.53	19.19	10.12	6.89	7.65
B. Output						
A	0.00	−0.30	−0.14	−0.38	−0.73	−1.23
RS	0.00	−1.08	−1.90	−3.73	−3.59	−3.71
PSR	0.00	−8.72	−9.72	−13.44	−15.56	−16.68
M	0.00	1.66	3.77	2.14	0.53	0.10
KS	0.00	9.78	4.89	8.67	10.53	8.29
US	0.00	−0.20	−0.32	−1.05	−2.25	−3.06
PSU	0.00	−12.18	−14.04	−22.41	−29.05	−32.94
Nonhousing GDP	0.00	0.08	−0.30	−1.05	−1.78	−2.76
C. Unskilled employment						
A	0.00	0.47	0.56	0.95	0.90	1.03
RS	0.00	−0.08	−0.31	−2.09	−1.17	−0.99
PSR	0.00	−0.99	−0.84	−0.98	−1.13	−0.28
M	0.00	−8.31	−6.50	−7.42	−7.66	−7.63
KS	0.00	4.00	−4.33	−1.21	1.62	−0.72
US	0.00	2.62	3.19	3.61	4.48	4.82
PSU	0.00	−5.27	−4.56	−6.08	−6.59	−7.46
D. Skilled employment						
A	0.00	−2.15	−1.19	−1.30	−1.26	−1.16
RS	0.00	−2.05	−2.02	−3.94	−3.23	−3.09
PSR	0.00	−4.66	−4.32	−5.72	−6.32	−5.98
M	0.00	0.97	4.73	4.03	2.95	3.70
KS	0.00	8.54	2.99	6.62	8.62	6.95
US	0.00	3.02	−4.20	4.51	3.78	3.80
PSU	0.00	−8.16	−7.89	−14.54	−20.22	−22.99
E. Relative prices						
A	0.00	−0.47	−0.59	1.13	−1.74	−2.12
RS	0.00	0.00	0.71	−0.45	−0.39	−1.06
PSR	0.00	8.29	9.58	13.45	15.26	17.01
M	0.00	−4.98	−3.44	−3.08	−3.25	−2.81
KS	0.00	−2.23	−4.68	−5.32	−5.62	−5.93
US	0.00	6.17	8.68	9.60	10.06	12.26
PSU	0.00	12.41	18.02	29.23	39.41	46.63

Table 9.8. *continued*

Endogenous Variables	1960	1964	1965	1971	1977	1981
F. Incomes						
Capital rental rate						
Urban formal	0.00	−23.05	−30.86	−36.12	−41.57	−42.54
Urban informal	0.00	32.42	41.74	38.29	43.95	47.25
Rural	0.00	4.31	2.83	−0.12	−1.34	−2.14
Disposable incomes, 1960 prices						
Rural unskilled	0.00	−0.37	−0.69	−1.02	−1.46	−2.19
Rural skilled	0.00	2.70	1.48	1.99	1.37	0.75
Urban unskilled	0.00	2.59	3.78	3.10	2.28	2.86
Urban skilled	0.00	−1.65	−2.10	−2.24	−2.97	−3.19
Capitalists and landlords	0.00	−2.55	−2.84	−4.06	−5.32	−5.54
G. Real government revenue	0.00	−0.43	0.93	1.78	2.85	1.80
H. Exports						
A	0.00	−9.24	−1.13	−3.44	−4.40	−3.20
M	0.00	−2.71	3.31	−0.50	−2.16	−2.17
Total	0.00	−4.47	2.39	−1.10	−2.78	−2.47
I. Capital formation						
Rural nonhousing	−14.56	−19.09	−9.48	−10.69	−9.05	−11.76
Urban formal nonhousing	23.21	15.49	15.10	9.67	4.02	6.07
Urban informal nonhousing	−32.43	−32.22	−5.99	−16.71	−17.62	−24.76
Urban informal housing	0.00	3.30	*	4.78	4.08	6.58
Urban formal housing	0.00	78.12	−2.43	23.82	31.59	21.10
Rural housing	0.00	−3.70	8.80	−10.39	−6.85	−4.36
Total nonhousing	0.00	−3.21	2.70	−0.50	−2.47	−1.96
Total	0.00	2.51	1.81	1.61	2.40	1.45

*No informal urban housing investment in the 1965 Benchmark simulation; 131,200,000 Rs. (1960) in the Mahalanobis counterfactual.
Counterfactual simulation involves reducing the share of public investment devoted to rural areas from 39% in the early 1960s and 27% in the late 1960s to only 20%. Fixed sectoral public investment allocation shares are: agriculture—15%; urban manufacturing—75%; rural public services—5%; urban public services—5%; all other sectors—0%. All values reported are elasticities.

vestment counterfactual posed, but the patterns for the early 1960s reported in table 9.8 certainly look unhappily familiar. It is most certainly a capital accumulation–oriented strategy (1964 investment is 2.5 percent greater in the Mahalanobis counterfactual than in the historical benchmark), but it is *not* an employment-oriented strategy. Rural wages are depressed, and rural inequality grows. The strategy furthers import substitution as a by-product: trade volumes fall.

The flaws of the Mahalanobis strategy do not really become apparent until the economy is confronted with an agricultural disaster, the drought of 1965. The drought was severe, causing value added in agriculture to fall by nearly 24 percent from 1964 levels, a bountiful year. Problems were compounded by the war with Pakistan, which was responsible as well for the decline in foreign aid. But per capita income declines more in the Mahalanobis counterfactual than in the historical Benchmark. The disaster is magnified mainly because rural capital formation is smaller in the Mahalanobis counterfactual. When a drought occurs, there are fewer irrigation canals to offset the blow. Redirecting investment works reasonably well when rural sectors are growing rapidly; it does poorly when a rural catastrophe strikes. Furthermore, because incomes are more severely depressed by the drought, demand for food falls even more sharply in the counterfactual than in the historical Benchmark. Food prices therefore rise slightly less in the Mahalanobis counterfactual—but this "success" reflects greater impoverishment, not wise policy.

Nevertheless, the Mahalanobis policy *does* increase manufacturing capacity relative to the historical Benchmark. As capacity expands, P_M falls and a given savings pool purchases more capital goods; aggregate capital formation therefore increases. Accelerated capital accumulation was, of course, the target set by Mahalanobis and his Soviet predecessors. As we have seen, however, the negative effects on output and productivity dominate the positive impact on aggregate accumulation. Worse yet, the gap grows over time: by 1981, GDP is almost 3 percent lower in the Mahalanobis counterfactual. Capital formation does rise as intended, but its declining productivity offsets the impact. Constant capital productivity FMD models with fixed coefficients missed this effect, which stems both from diminishing returns and falling product prices in rapidly expanding sectors.

The consequences of a prolonged Mahalanobis strategy would have been even worse had private investment patterns not to some degree compensated for the policy. Extensive capital market segmentation in BMW ensures that such private investment reallocation is limited to the switch of household savings from M to KS investments by formal sector firms' modern sector nonhousing investments to high-quality housing by the wealthy, and from low-quality housing to US sector asset formation by the urban poor. Nonetheless, the moral is clear: the greater the degree of capital market integration, the smaller is the cost of public investment policy errors. Policy mistakes are most catastrophic in extremely underdeveloped economies characterized by poorly organized factor markets; equally incompetent policymakers can do less harm in the developed world.

Finally, consider the income distribution consequences of a prolonged Mahalanobis era. While income as a whole declines, it can be seen from table 9.8 that the distributional consequences are far from neutral. In fact, three groups are major gainers: urban unskilled, rural skilled, and landlords. All other groups lose. Urban capitalists are flooded with public sector capital, and the combined effects of diminishing returns and deteriorating terms of trade reduce profits. Urban skilled laborers, employed intensively in M and KS, lose for much the same reasons. The rural unskilled suffer, too. It is ironic that urban capital formation is in effect funded by poor peasants and urban skilled rather than by well-to-do farmers and landlords, since it contrasts sharply with the Preobrazhenski notion of "primitive socialist accumulation".

While the Mahalanobis model may have been appropriate for its time, it was an inappropriate development strategy after the mid-1960s. The model's obsolescence reflected in part increasingly inappropriate assumptions, and in part the successful capital deepening engendered by the policy. In any case, this "old" paradigm was replaced by several new ones over the two decades that followed; the dominant ones appear to have been a set of increasingly market-oriented policies of economic liberalization that we call "IMF" strategies.

An IMF Liberalization Strategy

Historically, India has been reluctant to borrow from the IMF and, more generally, to accumulate large international debts. The break with tradition first occurred in 1980–81, when India drew 8.15 billion Rs. from the IMF Trust Fund and the Compensatory Financing Facility. A still sharper break occurred in November 1981, when India accepted a SDR 5 billion Extended Fund Facility from the IMF.[13] Other foreign borrowing also increased during this period, and by 1985 India's external debt–GDP ratio had risen to 17 percent—still very small by LDC standards.

The IMF loan of November 1981 was one of the fund's early medium-term loans and was granted in response to balance of payments difficulties stemming from the second OPEC shock. In obtaining the loan, the Indian government committed itself to energy development, export promotion, reduced public enterprise subsidies, diminished agricultural imports, encouragement of the private sector, further liberalization of raw material, intermediate and capital good imports, disinflation, maintained investment rates, and encouragement of foreign direct investment.[14] While a reduction in the growth of government was not mentioned explicitly, the guidelines for monetary and fiscal policies clearly combined to serve as a restraint. While the agreement was hardly as

13. See Joshi and Little (1987, p. 374). The extended facility arrangement was terminated in May 1984 after 3.9 billion Rs. of the loan was used. Concessional loans and World Bank funding also began to rise considerably in the early 1980s; so did commercial loans.

14. The agreement is summarized in Datt (1981, pp. 11–23).

precise and imposing as some have been, it represented nonetheless an unprecedented international intrusion into Indian policy formation. It also, of course, committed India to the IMF paradigm, touching off debate in the Indian press.

The question to which we turn here is: How appropriate were the IMF conditions? More generally, is the IMF model good for countries such as India? To address these issues, we abstract from the capital inflows, and focus solely on the policies embodied in the IMF paradigm. Two counterfactuals are simulated over the period 1977–83 and then contrasted with the historical Benchmark. The first is a "bare bones" IMF program, committing India to export promotion (the manufactured exports' tax rate is reduced to zero from 12 percent) and import liberalization.[15] A more elaborate package includes these reforms plus agricultural promotion through a redirection of public investment.[16] Because of the decline in tax revenues and the balanced budget restriction in the model, the policy shift also implies a decline in public sector expenditures. The consequences of these two counterfactual packages are summarized in table 9.9.[17]

Perhaps surprisingly, the "bare bones" IMF strategy does not increase India's growth rate in the long run. The story centers around the manufacturing sector, which is hit simultaneously with heavy doses of competing imports and export promotion. The import liberalization suddenly transforms modern manufacturing from a protected sector to one forced to compete at world prices. Whether on net this increased openness will be beneficial depends on the relative strength of the growth in world demand for Indian manufactured exports and of the cost of Indian manufactures relative to world manufactures—that is, India's comparative advantage in manufacturing. During the period under consideration, 1977–83, the world price of manufactures fell relative to other goods because of the second OPEC shock, but this decline was even

15. Import liberalization essentially involves the removal of nontariff restrictions to permit greater competition between imported and domestic manufactures. To capture this, we raise the Armington composite manufactured good substitution elasticity between domestic goods and imports from 2.25 to 18.0.

16. This promotion comes either through an expansion in agricultural credit provided by the public sector or a decrease in debt finance obtained by the government from rural savers. The simulation assumes a reduction by 5 percent of the total public investment pool available to the *PSU* and *KS* sectors, and hence an increase of 10 percent of the total pool available to agriculture.

17. Because the government investment shifts in the second policy counterfactual have minimal initial impact (reflecting the gestation period before new projects come on stream), the short-run impacts are virtually identical. Therefore, only the long-term elasticities for the second IMF counterfactual are reported.

Table 9.9. IMF Liberalization Strategies: Potential Impact, 1977–1983

	(a) Export Promotion and Import Liberalization		(b) Export Promotion, Liberalization, Public Sector Deemphasis and Agricultural Promotion
	1977	1983	1983
A. City Growth Attributes			
% Urban	0.13	−0.14	−0.46
City growth rate (1977–78, 1977–83)	3.31	−0.55	−1.86
City in-migration rate	7.02	−1.38	−4.68
Pucca house rents	4.88	−3.05	−1.45
Katcha house rents	5.46	−2.29	−1.67
B. Output			
A	0.19	−0.04	0.30
RS	−0.40	0.19	1.95
PSR	0.93	−0.37	−0.28
M	0.86	−0.11	−0.62
KS	−1.15	−0.31	−0.99
US	−0.41	−0.18	−0.45
PSU	0.08	0.08	−1.66
Nonhousing GDP	0.09	−0.11	−0.19
C. Unskilled employment			
A	0.05	0.01	−0.16
RS	−0.60	0.22	1.66
PSR	1.05	−0.66	−0.66
M	1.03	−0.08	−0.39
KS	−1.62	−0.32	−0.64
US	−0.55	−0.25	−0.44
PSU	0.96	0.00	−0.40
D. Skilled employment			
A	0.09	0.26	0.26
RS	−0.52	0.35	2.04
PSR	0.97	0.40	−0.28
M	0.96	0.09	−0.44
KS	−1.45	−0.16	−0.66
US	−0.34	0.00	−0.30
PSU	0.88	0.17	−1.20
E. Relative prices			
A	−0.01	0.05	−0.45
RS	−0.11	0.04	−0.35
PSR	0.21	−0.36	−0.47
M	0.08	0.03	0.33
KS	−0.55	−0.04	0.51
US	−0.17	−0.06	0.15
PSU	0.20	−0.10	1.51

Table 9.9. continued

	(a) Export Promotion and Import Liberalization		(b) Export Promotion, Liberalization, Public Sector Deemphasis and Agricultural Promotion
	1977	1983	1983
F. Incomes			
Capital rental rate			
Urban formal	0.83	−0.63	1.43
Urban informal	−0.12	−0.80	−1.31
Rural	0.71	−0.23	−4.86
Disposable incomes, 1960 prices			
Rural unskilled	0.28	−0.07	0.35
Rural skilled	0.20	−0.07	−0.17
Urban unskilled	0.06	−0.18	0.58
Urban skilled	0.12	−0.11	−0.18
Capitalists and landlords	0.31	0.07	−0.61
G. Real government revenue	−2.45	0.38	0.78
H. Exports			
A	−11.58	6.11	13.81
M (constant domestic prices)	16.65	40.23	40.35
M (world prices)	4.36	25.45	25.56
Total (domestic prices)	8.95	29.89	30.38
Total (world prices)	0.00	19.59	20.08
I. Capital formation			
Rural nonhousing	0.44	−0.03	8.45
Urban formal nonhousing	0.07	0.04	−6.13
Urban informal nonhousing	−0.12	−0.04	−0.06
Urban informal housing	0.43	−0.73	0.98
Urban formal housing	−2.23	−1.08	−4.51
Rural housing	0.21	−0.29	7.54
Total nonhousing	0.22	0.01	−0.30
Total	−0.06	−0.20	−0.33

Export promotion counterfactual involves reducing duties on manufactured exports to zero, import liberalization involves raising the composite manufactured good substitution elasticity between imports and domestic production to 18.0, and agricultural promotion consists of raising the share of government investment devoted to agriculture by 10% drawn evenly from modern services (including public administration) and urban public services. All values shown are elasticities.

greater for the relative price of domestic manufactures.

Because India remained cost competitive, exports should have risen greatly with a removal of export tariffs. This is exactly what happens in the model: relative to the Benchmark, 1983 manufactured exports increase by 25 percent in value and 40 percent in volume in both counterfactuals. This boom in manufactured exports causes the rupee to appreciate, agricultural exports to fall, and imports of all goods to rise. So far, the liberalization model is executed flawlessly.

In the short run, domestic manufacturing output registers a net expansion, and as capital is fixed, employment expands. Multiplier effects then come into play, and urban employment grows overall. Movement of labor to higher productivity urban sectors in turn causes real GDP to increase. As urban labor-intensive sectors share in the expansion, the income distribution consequences of the policy are about neutral. As a by-product of the growth in unskilled workers' income and in raw material requirements by the manufacturing sector, demand for agricultural output increases and the agricultural sector grows, thereby neutralizing the urbanizing impact.

Under happier circumstances, these short-run effects could have been converted into even stronger long-term effects, for the liberalization also generated an increase in capital formation. But 1978–79 ushered in the second OPEC shock: the relative price of oil soared (driving up domestic production costs) and the relative cost of imported manufactures plunged (driven by world market conditions and by the rupee appreciation). An IMF liberalization package would have made India more vulnerable to these world market events: 1979 manufacturing output in the first liberalization counterfactual falls by more than 2.5 percent relative to the historical Benchmark. Put differently, the counterfactual IMF reforms make India a more open economy just as an international recession strikes, and the price shocks consequently hit the economy far harder than they do when it is more closed. Rising oil costs push up domestic manufactures' prices relative to imported manufactures' costs, causing production to decline. With the fall in output comes return migration to rural areas; the ensuing productivity decline causes further real GDP losses.

As it turned out, the OPEC price increase was quickly translated into an increase in the costs of imported manufactured goods (through world cost push forces), so that by 1983 the counterfactual reduction in manufacturing value added and GDP was minimal. The moral of table 9.9 is not that trade liberalization cannot work; instead, the moral is that it need not be advantageous under all circumstances. Trade liberalization has its most pronounced positive impact when world demand for one's exports is buoyant, when relative price distortions are great, when imports are of noncompeting goods (so that revaluation of the equilibrium exchange rate benefits domestic industry rather than undercutting it), and especially when capital goods are mostly imported. These traits represent an apt characterization of many developing economies, especially in Africa. But in India, with its large manufacturing sector and fairly developed capital goods industry, and with policy interventions so ubiquitous that true price distortions are not always obvious, the gains from liberalization are likely to be more modest.

Consider now the more broadly defined package that includes agricultural promotion and a central government deemphasis. It looks superficially even worse, since GDP falls even more. Yet, the package is at least highly egalitarian in that it generates substantial benefits for the poor while reducing real incomes of skilled labor and the property-owning classes. The shift in resources to rural areas causes the agricultural sector to expand—leading to, inter alia, an agricultural boom that almost matches that in manufacturing. The growth in agricultural output induced by capital accumulation leads to a decline in agricultural prices, however, and this causes the value of agricultural labor's marginal product to decline. But this decline is more than compensated for by expansion in rural service employment, so that the rural labor force grows as a whole. With that growth comes productivity losses that lower GDP, but these are not nearly great enough to offset the net benefit to the poor from increased demand for unskilled labor and falling food prices.

9.6 Concluding Remarks

Several morals emerge from the preceding sections. The first is that standard illiberal policies focusing on boosting urban incomes or increasing rates of capital accumulation have severe weaknesses and are inegalitarian. But liberal policies that center on efficient capital allocation or freer trade regimes are flawed as well and hardly produce unambiguously desirable outcomes. A second moral is that what is desirable for a small, open economy may not be so beneficial for India. A third moral is that GDP is a poor measure of welfare for those with egalitarian instincts: unskilled real incomes and GDP trends may diverge sharply, as is illustrated most clearly in table 9.9.

Fourth, intersectoral investment efficiency promotes urban growth, but rapid modern sector capital deepening actually retards urbanization. This feature may be one of the attractions of the Mahalanobis strategy to planners. The urbanization impact of IMF strategies is mixed: when urban manufactures expand in consequence, so does the urban labor force. On the other hand, when the manufacturing sector contracts, return migration occurs. Return migration is still more pronounced when the IMF package includes a slimmer government and increasingly proagricultural policies.

Most important, for those concerned with raising the welfare of India's poor, there is a viable development strategy. As John Mellor and others have stressed, this strategy centers on promotion of agriculture (the driving force behind the gains in the second IMF liberalization simulation) and on labor-intensive employment creation (which drives much of the gains in the housing counterfactuals). Getting prices right, promoting exports, liberalizing the economy, shrinking government, and increasing the rate of capital accumulation all have merit. But focusing on them to the neglect of agriculture, employment opportunities, and expanded supply of foodstuffs consumed by the poor is misguided policy.

10 · What Have We Learned?

10.1 Issues in Urbanization: The Indian Debates

At the outset of the book, several questions were posed. Have Indian cities grown too rapidly in some sense? Is there a natural tendency for city growth to slow down? How important is the urban bias of government policy, and what role have external shocks played in the growth patterns of Indian cities? How does rural emigration interact with city growth?

The book's key findings are presented in the introductory chapter, and thus only a few are repeated here. Indian city growth has not been particularly rapid by the standards of most Third World countries, although in recent decades it has been rapid by its own historic standards. But the overurbanization debate has not been provoked simply by the pace of city growth: rather, the absence of critical city growth "engines" has mattered to the debate as well. These engines include employment growth in the entire urban formal sector and, in particular, in modern manufacturing employment.

That industrial employment growth has been at best a sputtering engine is confirmed in our simulations. But the thesis that increasing population pressure on agricultural land has been a critical force pushing the rural poor into urban squatter settlements is simply not borne out by our analysis. While population pressure *does* increase city growth modestly, it does *not* increase the share of the population living in urban areas. Instead, as the Rybczynski theorem from international trade leads us to expect, output and employment in labor-intensive rural sectors rise disproportionately fast with population growth. These findings, reported in chapters 4 and 6, are consistent with Pandey's (1977) analysis of urbanization across Indian states.

The engine of city growth is complicated. Rapid economic advance tends to be highly urbanizing, but the rate of city growth is conditioned by the circumstances that set these forces in motion. Productivity gains in the urban informal sector give rise to the largest short-run increase in urbanization, not manufacturing. But in either case, sectoral inter-actions are critical to the urbanization response since the engines of urban growth slow down if other sectors, especially agriculture, lag behind. Unbalanced growth forces certainly foster urbanization in small, open economies (SOE), but in India's semiclosed environment, lagging rural productivity causes much of the energy of urban engines to be dissipated by agricultural price increases, the latter induced by inelastic factor and intermediate input supplies.[1]

On the other hand, rural productivity gains have little impact on urbanization in the absence of coincident urban productivity or price shocks. Chapters 4 and 6 find that, in general, productivity gains in agriculture actually serve to retain rural labor in the short run. In the long run, agricultural prices decline in response to the productivity gains, but only small amounts of labor are released to the cities. But even these effects have changed over time as Indian agriculture has evolved. In particular, India's green revolutions have been associated with a dramatic rise in the share of intermediate inputs in gross agricultural output. Since these inputs are in part produced by urban sectors, and since the growth in intermediate input use has permitted supply to in-crease far more rapidly than value added, food price increases have been stifled.

Central to the overurbanization debate is the role of rural-urban migration and its underlying forces. The annual city immigration rate was more than 4.1 percent during the boom period of the early 1960s, accounting for nearly two-thirds of urban population growth. There-after, the immigration rate declined sharply to between 1.5 and 1.75 percent, and migrants accounted for only 38 to 45 percent of urban population growth. What explains these events? Were Indian migrants pushed off the land, or were they pulled by conditions in the cities? In general, rural push forces—including population growth, productivity stagnation, and drought—seem to have had only modest effects on urbanization.[2] These results are consistent with those of B. Banerjee

1. A similar point is made by Mellor (1976, p. 139).

2. This finding is consistent with that of Pandey (1977), who reports that measures of rural population pressure are not associated with urbanization across Indian states, while industrialization clearly is. On the other hand, the micro surveys discussed in Singh and de Souza (1980) do suggest that push forces matter, although their results are contaminated by an element of simultaneity.

(1986; see also Kannappan, 1987), who has found that recent migrants to Delhi did not have the substantial unemployment spells that would be expected if migration were provoked mainly by rural distress.[3]

Chapter 6 analyzes the sources of Indian city growth and finds that endogenous and exogenous forces were about equally important in determining urbanization. The endogenous forces included Engel effects, the growth of government, rising skill intensity of the labor force, and capital deepening. The exogenous forces included world price shocks, domestic productivity slowdown and speedup, changing incomes policies, and demographic events. When taken together, these endogenous and exogenous forces dispel any mystery about Indian city growth: the model simulates an urbanization pattern virtually identical to that observed (chap. 3).

City growth in the early 1960s represented a dramatic acceleration over earlier periods. This boom reflected in part unusually favorable external events, but it also stemmed from the determined industrialization efforts embedded in India's five-year plans (chap. 9). What, then explains the apparent city growth slowdown after the mid-1960s? To some degree, the subsequent change in these exogenous forces—adverse world price movements that raised the cost of urban production, deteriorating manufacturing productivity, a decline in foreign capital inflows and government savings, and an incomes policy that caused modern sector labor costs to accelerate in the late 1960s—all contributed significantly to the simulated urban labor force growth slowdown from 6.44 percent in 1960–64 to 3.82 percent in 1965–81.

Nonetheless, the city growth slowdown would have occurred even in the absence of these forces. The rapid growth of the 1960s would have generated labor bottlenecks that would, by themselves, have curtailed urban growth. As W. Arthur Lewis has taught us, urbanization can take place rapidly in an environment of elastic labor supplies and near-surplus labor. Eventually, however, urban factor supply curves become more steeply sloped, so that the engines of city growth slow down. These constraints are all the more critical in an economy confronted by slow export growth and dwindling foreign investment and aid, which restrict international trade options. Our simulations suggest (chap. 8) that future city growth rates will decline still further to a rate slightly less than 3 percent per annum by the middle of the twenty-first century, while the urban population share will slowly drift up toward 50 percent.

India's city growth performance is certainly unspectacular by the standards of most Third World nations. This fact leads chapter 7 to pose

---

3. B. Banerjee (1986) also found that the educated were more likely to migrate, a finding consistently generated in our simulations.

Table 10.1. Urban Skill Mix and Skilled and Unskilled Labor Force Growth Rates: India, 1960–1981 (Benchmark run)

Year	Skilled Labor (millions)	Annual Growth Rate (%)	Unskilled Labor (millions)	Annual Growth Rate (%)	Total Labor Force (millions)	Annual Growth Rate (%)	Skill Share (%)	Capital/Urban Labor ('000 of 1960 Rupees)	Annual Urban Capital Stock Growth Rate (%)
1960	2.874		23.226		26.100		12.4	3.79	
1964	3.508	5.1	29.996	6.6	33.504	6.4	10.5	3.89	7.2
1971	5.058	5.4	37.854	3.4	42.912	3.6	11.8	4.72	6.5
1977	6.560	4.4	47.703	3.9	54.263	4.0	12.1	5.12	5.4
1981	8.023	5.2	55.357	3.8	63.380	4.0	12.6	5.48	5.7

the following question: What makes India different from its neighbors? Indian cities have grown 0.7 to 1.0 percent per annum more slowly than the average Third World city. Slightly slower population growth, relatively modest capital inflows, less impressive productivity growth, and unfavorable world price movements together account for a third to a half of the growth gap. The rest stems from factors related to the structure of the Indian economy—its production and demand characteristics, its degree of openness, and the role of government. India's urban growth experience would have been considerably different had public policies and the economic environment been more favorable. But India is neither Taiwan nor Côte d'Ivoire, and it is unlikely ever to exhibit the spectacular urban growth rates found in these and other smaller and more open developing countries.

Has Indian public policy contained an "urban bias"? The answer hinges on the period and the policy being considered. In terms of investment allocation, we find evidence that rates of return on urban projects were higher than on rural projects in the early 1960s and that public investment allocation may, if anything, have been prorural. That bias appears to have reversed by the mid-1970s, although the deadweight losses attributable to the misallocation were probably small at any point over the past three decades. A significant prourban bias *did* consistently exist in the sense that a more activist public rural investment policy would have increased real incomes of the poor throughout the period. But there is no evidence from this study or others (Mellor, 1976; Gandhi, 1966) that the combined effects of taxation and government expenditures served to drain resources from the countryside.

Finally, what were the skill characteristics of urban growth? Did Indian growth pull in the skilled or unskilled most rapidly? From table 10.1, it is clear that the rapid growth of the early 1960s was accomplished by a decrease in urban skill intensity, as that period was fueled by growth in relatively unskilled labor-intensive manufacturing. Skill intensities rose thereafter, and by 1981 a modest amount of skill deepening had taken place.[4] The greatest urban skill deepening occurred during the late 1960s, a period of declining factor productivity in manufacturing but pronounced capital deepening. While urban manufacturing growth led the way in the early 1960s, the latter half of the decade was dominated by the growth of modern services, activities that are inherently skill intensive. Thus, growth of the modern service sector was largely re-

---

4. This skill deepening and the implied higher propensity to migrate by the educated appear to be general phenomena in the developing world. See Kannappan (1985). B. Banerjee (1986) has found that the rural educated are more likely to migrate in India as well, as we pointed out above.

sponsible for urban skill deepening—a pattern noted in the counterfactual simulations of chapter 9.

10.2 Connections between City Growth and Economic Development

Compared with Third World averages, India did not develop rapidly between 1960 and 1981. Much of the difference can be attributed to far lower total factor productivity growth rates (chap. 7). Indeed, while poor productivity growth can account for only a portion of India's slow city growth experience after 1964 (chap. 6), it can account for a great deal of the poor economic performance overall.

Underlying India's dismal productivity growth performance are structural and intrasectoral distortions. To some degree, these could be reduced by appropriate rural policies (notably, providing insurance incentives to encourage peasant farmers to switch to higher yield but riskier crop mixes: see Singh, 1979) and industry-oriented packages (in particular, by removing location and input pricing distortions created by current policies: see Sekhar, 1983). In the presence of such distortions, traditional policies that are oriented toward capital formation will have only a modest impact, mainly because returns are low. This was the key flaw of the Mahalanobis strategy (chap. 9). Policies that favored urban manufacturing at the expense of rural production ultimately resulted in increasing input and urban food costs, as well as in sharply declining returns to investment.

Many public sector policies needlessly reduce real incomes of the poor as well. Excessive modern sector investment is one such practice.[5] As chapter 9 shows, the Mahalanobis strategy channels investment to the most capital-intensive sectors, thereby minimizing the impact of new investment on labor demand, and hence on unskilled wages. The neglect of agriculture also results in food price hikes, again hurting the poor. Migration restrictions and incomes policies tend to diminish the earnings of most unskilled workers still further.

Furthermore, highly "prorural" development strategies reduce city growth rates only slightly, largely because urban-rural linkages have become so strong in India. Manufacturing has always been a major user of raw materials, so an augmented supply of those raw materials en-

5. As Mellor (1976, pp. 110–24) and Bardhan (1984) note, the inefficiency costs are exacerbated by the tendency of the Mahalanobis strategy to focus on the capital goods sector within manufacturing and, in particular, in public industrial enterprises. The result was the development of a very capital-intensive, inefficient capital goods industry along with the neglect of consumer manufactures.

courages urban-based manufacturing growth. Because city workers are heavy consumers of foodstuffs, any improvement in food production that lowers food prices also lowers urban wages, thus stimulating city growth. In addition, because Indian agriculture has become increasingly dependent on manufactured intermediates, agricultural output growth stimulates the demand for manufacturing output, creating urban employment. As the Indian economy is relatively closed to trade, all of these urban-rural linkages tend to be stronger than in the SOE in which such linkages spill over into changes in foreign trade volumes. India's poor export performance also implies that the major outlet for increased output must be the domestic market. Thus, if rural demands lag behind, urban output will suffer. Furthermore, the growth of Indian towns and cities appears to have spurred agricultural productivity in nearby areas by generating increased demand and improving the supply of critical intermediate inputs (Dasgupta and Basu, 1985).

In summary, while Indian economic growth may well be greater in the 1990s than it was in the 1960s and 1970s, strong forces limit the extent to which it can be carried by highly unbalanced sectoral productivity advance favoring urban sectors. Development is likely to be most dramatic in the coming decade if urban *and* rural productivity advance are both enhanced simultaneously.

10.3 Modeling India and Other Developing Countries

Let us turn to a third set of findings coming from the previous chapters and consider what we have learned about computable general equilibrium models. Our general assessment in chapter 3 was that BMW's simulation of a recent portion of Indian economic history provided a surprisingly close fit to reality (even though our vision of that reality was often blurred by imperfect data). In addition, counterfactual simulation with BMW has offered detailed insight into the determinants of city growth. Nevertheless, some of our tales about Indian city growth could have been told without the help of an elaborate CGE model. But this statement can only be made ex post facto: the analyst cannot start by assuming which urbanization and growth forces are most important, which interactions matter most, and which assumptions are most critical.

Although BMW is a complex computer program, it is *not* a black box. We were surprised at the number of times the model yielded results inconsistent with our economic intuition. But unanticipated results were never accepted (nor hidden) out of deference to the program's inscrutable omniscience. Instead, virtually all results were subjected to scrutiny that enabled us to determine exactly which forces were, and which were not, driving the results. In other words, BMW is not a black box; nor should other CGE models be viewed as black boxes. The model is a tool, not a Ouija board.

Like all models, a CGE can only provide plausible answers to the questions it was designed to address. And like all models, it makes assumptions. The BMW model of India assumes that prices and quantities are, for the most part, determined by the simultaneous clearing of all markets. As such, it is designed to explain medium-term and long-run phenomena. It was not designed to assess short-run responses to shocks, for here disequilibrium rather than equilibrium assumptions seem appropriate. Similarly, BMW has been developed so that we can address questions relating to spatial movements and sectoral growth. But it cannot be expected to provide great insights into policies and shocks impinging on only a very narrow part of the economy.

One of the most valuable contributions of BMW (and something that can in principle be obtained from other CGE models) is a clear understanding of the model's errors. Just as one would examine residuals in econometric work, we devote considerable attention to those episodes and those parts of the economy in which the model did not seem to fit Indian history well. By analyzing the errors, we have been able to identify periods and sectors for which a neoclassical model does poorly and to highlight the need for further research. It turns out that the main errors all have fairly obvious explanations.[6]

One also may ask what can be learned from BMW that could not be learned from a different framework. Relative to other CGEs, the BMW India model richly details government behavior and focuses on infrastructure, capital market fragmentation, and the rural-urban spatial division (as do Kelley and Williamson, 1984). But CGE models do not offer the only means by which to analyze urbanization. It would have been possible to develop a small econometric model of Indian city growth.[7] Such models are obviously useful. Furthermore, they avoid "one-point estimation" of many parameters, which is inherent in most CGE models. But such models are highly aggregative; they typically contain few explanatory variables and cannot be used to analyze ur-

6. We chose to let these errors stand rather than programming new statements that would have eliminated them. By keeping the errors exposed, we avoided the temptation of moving to a "black box" that fits perfectly but is much like a regression, with a dummy variable for each major outlier. BMW is a reasonably pure neoclassical statement of an economy with a large government sector, and the findings are valuable for highlighting where the model both does and does not fit history well.

7. The derivation of a small econometric model from a general equilibrium structure is presented in Becker and Morrison (1988).

banization with the richness offered here. Rather than designating one method as inferior to the other, it makes more sense to regard them as complementary, each with different strengths and weaknesses.

Demographic forecasting offers yet another way to analyze urbanization (see, for example, Rogers, 1984). These models typically have extensive detail with respect to demographic variables: in particular, they usually contain many regions, population groups, migration probabilities, fertility rates, and age- and sex-specific death rates. What they do not have are behavioral specifications or endogenous economic variables. But it is improper to assert smugly the superiority of economic models: ours, after all, aggregates highly over demographic variables and treats all of them, but not migration, as exogenous.

10.4 Can We Generalize from India?

BMW has been designed to capture critical features of the Indian economy. Our assessment is that it does so rather well, enabling us to draw a large set of conclusions concerning the country's urbanization and growth process. But to what extent can these conclusions be generalized to other countries? The answer hinges on the similarity between India's demo-economic structure and that of other developing countries. Naturally, authors like their findings to be as general as possible. Alas, there are some major obstacles in the way.

A leading obstacle is the greater openness of most developing countries relative to India. In India's semiclosed economy, a sectoral demand boom can fizzle if the costs of traded goods or nontraded inputs are bid up rapidly. In an SOE, traded goods' supply curves are flatter, since traded goods can be imported at a fixed price. Thus, a booming sector is not held back so much by the presence of a stagnant, low-productivity sector in an SOE; indeed, the more unbalanced the productivity advance, the more unbalanced the output growth. But India, with its small, moribund export sector and pervasive import controls, cannot accommodate truly dramatic unbalanced growth quite so easily. In consequence, unbalanced urban-rural sectoral productivity advance, a driving force behind rapid city growth, will have a much more pronounced impact in an SOE than in India.

Two other key features of India's economic structure are its relatively large and developed rural nonagricultural sector and urban manufacturing's dependence on domestically produced raw materials rather than on imported intermediates. The latter feature ensures that rural and urban areas are far more closely integrated than, say, in many African countries. This linkage makes "runaway city growth" difficult if not impossible and ensures reasonably balanced growth, but it also tends to put the brakes on the overall rate of economic progress.[8] The large rural service sector essentially competes with the urban sectors for released peasant labor, but it can also release labor to agriculture and to the cities, thus reducing competition between them. If Indian agriculture continues to modernize rapidly—and one should not be excessively optimistic here—then the presence of a large rural service sector will provide something of a surplus labor pool that will continue to permit rapid growth of output (but, less happily, continue to depress unskilled wages) both in farming and in the cities.

In short, India has many unique features. Thus, the question remains: Are there any generalizable findings? The most important ones probably center on the role of government. The inegalitarian nature of public sector employment (bidding up skill differentials) and demands (consuming urban goods) is unlikely to be unique to India. So is the need to follow proagricultural policies if large welfare gains for the poor are a target. As a whole, the inefficient government policies outlined above are unlikely to be dramatically different in most other Third World economies. This comment applies most strongly to urban incomes policies and migration restrictions. Furthermore, while IMF-style policies are likely to produce much more growth in SOEs, they are unlikely to be more egalitarian than in India. The distinction between policies that generate large real GDP gains and those that increase living standards of the poor is also generally valid.

The forces driving India's city growth slowdown are to some extent also general, although they operate most strongly in a semiclosed economy. The relative unimportance of rural push factors is probably widespread; it was certainly true of nineteenth-century industrial revolutions as well (Williamson, 1990). Similarly, the importance of *unbalanced* rates of productivity advance, rather than their average level, in driving urbanization is likely to be even stronger in the SOEs, as Kelley and Williamson (1984) have shown. The importance of urban nonmanufacturing sectors and rural nonagricultural sectors in understanding growth and urbanization in India is undoubtedly matched elsewhere as well.

One of the striking findings from our counterfactual simulations was that the misallocation of investment has never been terribly important in India. In a sense, economic inefficiencies are more likely to matter at the firm level: returns to investment are, after all, fairly low everywhere. Since SOEs have more rigidly determined spheres of comparative advantage, sectoral investment choices are probably more important than in India.

8. A similar point is made by Bardhan (1984, p. 21).

In extending the model to other countries—or to India of the 1990s—several modifications need to be considered. In particular, the choice of sectors and the degree of openness must vary from country to country. So, too, must the assumed degree of factor market integration and assumptions concerning domestic restrictions on the tradeability of goods across space. Public sector behavior is also largely country specific. Finally, countries such as India that have experienced significant modernization in portions of their agricultural economies probably should have more than one agricultural sector in a CGE model. In summary, much of the model's structure and many lessons from the model can be extended beyond India—but uncritical adaptation is ill advised.

10.5 Will Indian City Growth *Really* Decelerate?

Chapter 8 offered projections of urban growth in the coming decades. We reported in the Benchmark projections that, if India's demo-economic environment continued to be like that during 1977–81, urban labor force annual growth rates would be about 2.86 percent during the 1980s and 2.85 percent during the 1990s. In the Stable scenario, which examined what would happen if conditions of the early 1960s persisted for an extended period, predicted city growth rates were considerably higher, 3.40 and 3.26 percent, respectively. The Favorable scenario yielded similar results. When we made the Benchmark projection in chapter 8, we did not have much information available for the 1980s. Now we do. So, does the economic experience of the 1980s suggest any changes in those Benchmark forecasts?

The 1980s have turned out to look rather different from the late 1970s. In terms of production, agriculture's performance has improved a bit, and the service sectors have continued to exhibit strong growth (table 10.2). But the growth rate of industrial output has more than doubled, making the sectoral engine of growth effects closer to the Stable or Favorable patterns than those assumed in Benchmark.[9]

Even more striking than the rejuvenation of Indian industry has been the accompanying rise in capital inflows. By the mid-1980s, India's balance of payments figures were much more like those of the early 1960s than the late 1970s. As with the industrial spurt and the increase in real GDP growth (annual growth in output per worker rose from 1.2 percent in epoch IV to 2.9 percent in 1981–86), the capital inflows are a strongly urbanizing force.

Furthermore, government deficits have increased sharply during the

---

9. Annual manufacturing employment growth increased but not as rapidly, from 2.8 percent in 1977–81 to 3.2 percent in 1981–85.

Table 10.2. India's Economic Environment: 1981–1986 versus 1977–1981 (annual growth rates of values in 1980 rupees)

	Annual Real Growth Rates (%)					Secondary School Enrollment Ratio (%)	Capital Inflows/GDP (%)
	GDP	Industry	Manufacturing	Agriculture	Services		
1970						26.0	
1976						26.0	
1978	5.8	7.4	10.8	2.9	8.2	28.0	1.86
1979	−4.6	−2.2	−1.8	−12.8	2.9	30.0	1.00
1980	7.0	1.5	−0.3	12.1	6.0	31.0	1.50
1981	5.7	5.2	5.4	4.3	7.4	33.0	0.05
1977–81	3.4	2.9	3.4	1.2	6.1	—	1.10
1982	3.2	5.6	6.9	−3.1	7.9	35.0	0.81
1983	8.0	5.2	5.1	11.3	6.8	34.0	1.12
1984	4.0	5.5	5.5	−0.6	7.4	35.0	1.95
1985	5.2	6.5	6.8	1.4	7.7	—	3.47
1986	5.0	6.5	6.1	1.5	6.9	—	2.31
1981–86	5.1	5.9	6.1	2.0	7.4	—	1.93

Source: World Bank (1988a).

1980s. The effect on capital formation has been small, leading to a decline in gross domestic investment as a share of GDP from 26.8 percent in 1977–81 to 26.3 percent in 1982–86. But government expenditures as a share of GDP rose considerably: from 17.2 percent in 1977 to 19.4 percent in 1981, and to a peak of 24.4 percent in 1985 (World Bank, 1988a, p. 213). Since government mainly purchases urban goods, the rise in its expenditures should have caused city growth rates to quicken. Relative price movements also appear to be quite favorable for urbanization, as the relative prices of fuels and nonfuel primary products fell even more rapidly during the 1981–86 period than they did during the early 1960s.

Finally, the data suggest a dramatic rise in secondary education beginning in about 1976. For the preceding decade, the secondary school enrollment rate was virtually constant at 25 percent; it then rose steadily to 35 percent by 1985. This undoubtedly has lead to a considerable increase in the skilled labor growth rate during the present decade, creating urban growth by itself and contributing to the other events noted above.

In summary, the conditions of the early and mid-1980s seem to be far closer to the conditions assumed in the Favorable counterfactual simulations than to the Benchmark ones. If the conditions of the early and mid-1980s persist, then, it seems reasonable to anticipate a city growth rate of around 3.4 percent per annum in the 1980s and 3.2 percent per annum in the 1990s. These projections, implying an increase in India's urban population from 156 million in 1981 to 218 million in 1991 and 299 million by 2001, are probably overestimates, given the likely declines in aggregate population growth rates in the future.[10] Relying on the Planning Commission projections but adjusting slightly for the imperfect sensitivity of urbanization to population growth, it seems plausible that city growth rates will be around 3.3 percent in the 1980s and 2.9 percent in the following decade.

For those who fear rapid city growth, our forecasts contain only a slight city growth deceleration for the present and coming decades—but they also suggest that acceleration is most unlikely.

10. Premi (1981) surveys several demographic forecasts. On average, they suggest likely population declines from 2.2 percent in the 1970s to 1.5 to 1.9 percent in the 1980s and slightly less than that in the 1990s. The World Bank (1988b, p. 274) forecasts a decline from 2.2 to 1.8 percent for the period 1986–2000. The Planning Commission (1983, pp. 44–45) forecasts an annual growth rate between 1981 and 1991 of 2.0 to 2.1 percent and rates of 1.65 to 1.75 percent during the 1991–2001 period.

Appendix A • Mathematical Statement of the BMW Model of India

Equations

1. Production

(1) $\quad Q_i = A_i Q_{i,F}^{\alpha_{i,F}} Z_i^{\alpha_{i,z}} \prod_j Q_{i,j}^{\alpha_{i,j}}$

$\quad Q_{i,F} = \{\xi_i \phi_i^{(\sigma_i - 1)/\sigma_i} + (1 - \xi_i)[z_i L_i]^{(\sigma_i - 1)/\sigma_i}\}^{\sigma_i/(\sigma_i - 1)}$

$\quad \phi_i = \{\xi_i' [x_i K_i]^{(\sigma_i' - 1)/\sigma_i'} + (1 - \xi_i')[y_i S_i]^{(\sigma_i' - 1)/\sigma_i'}\}^{\sigma_i'/(\sigma_i' - 1)};$

$\quad \sum_j \alpha_{ij} + \alpha_{i,F} + \alpha_{i,z} = 1$

$\quad i = M, KS, US, PSU, PSR, RS$

$\quad j = A^*, M^*, KS, k,$

$\quad k = \begin{cases} PSU \text{ when } i = M, KS, US \\ PSR \text{ when } i = RS \end{cases}$

Note: Table A.1 depicts the set J ($j\epsilon\{J\}$) of intermediate inputs used by producing sector i.

Table A.1. The BMW Input–Output Matrix for India, 1960

Producing Sectors	Absorbing Sectors									
	M	KS	PSU	US	A	RS	PSR	H,KS	H,US	H,RS
M*	z	x	x	x	x	x	x			
KS	x	z	y	x	x	x	y			
PSU	x	x	z	x				x	x	
US				z						
A*	x	x	y	x	z	x	y			
RS						z				
PSR					x	x	z			x
Z	x	x	x	x	x	x	x			

Entries marked "x" have positive values: an "x" in the (i,j) entry indicates that producing sector i produces intermediate goods for absorbing sector j. Entries marked "y" are permitted by the model to be positive but are calculated in Nakajima et al. (1983) to be approximately zero. The nonhousing diagonal entries are marked "z." Empty cells are set at zero. Precision regarding gross output matters in the derivation of productivity growth parameters; it is also necessary since M* and M, and A* and A, are not identical.

(2) $\quad Q_A = A_A \cdot [x_A K_A]^{\alpha_{A,K}} \cdot [y_A S_A]^{\alpha_{A,S}} \cdot [z_A L_A]^{\alpha_{A,L}} \cdot R_A^{\alpha_{A,R}} \cdot Z_A^{\alpha_{A,Z}} \cdot \prod_j Q_{A,j}^{\alpha_{A,j}},$

$\quad j = M^*, KS, PSR, A^*$

$\quad$ defining $\alpha_{A,F} \equiv \alpha_{A,K} + \alpha_{A,S} + \alpha_{A,L};$

$\quad \sum_j \alpha_{A,j} + \alpha_{A,F} + \alpha_{A,R} + \alpha_{A,Z} = 1$

(3) $\quad Q_{H,j} = A_{H,j} \cdot H_j^{\alpha_{H,j}} \cdot R_{U,j}^{\alpha_{R,j}} \cdot Q_{k,H,j}^{\alpha_{k,H,j}}$

$$\sum_{i=H,R,(k,H)} \alpha_{ij} = 1$$

$\alpha_{R,RS} = 0$ (that is, no land term is present in rural housing)

$j = KS, US, RS$

$k = \begin{cases} PSU \text{ when } j = KS, US \\ PSR \text{ when } j = RS \end{cases}$

2. Value Added/Gross Price Relationships

(4) $\quad P_i' = P_i - \sum_j P_{ij}^{tax} \dfrac{Q_{i,j}}{Q_i} - \dfrac{\overline{P_Z} Z_i (1 + \tau_{IMP,Z})}{Q_i} \equiv \alpha_{i,F} \cdot P_i$

$i = M, A, KS, PSU, PSR, US, RS$

$j = A^*, M^*, KS, k$

$k = \begin{cases} PSU \text{ when } i = M, KS, US \\ PSR \text{ when } i = RS, A \end{cases}$

(5) $\quad P_{i,j}^{tax} = P_j$ for all (i,j) except $(i = A$ or RS and $j = M^*)$

where $P_{A,M^*}^{tax} = P_{RS,M^*}^{tax} = P_{M^*}(1 + \tau_{A,M})$

3. Composite Commodities

(6) $\quad Q_{i^*} = \left[\psi_i^* Q_{i,IMP}^{\left(\frac{\sigma_{i,COM}-1}{\sigma_{i,COM}}\right)} \right.$

$\left. + (1 - \psi_i^*)(Q_i - Q_{i,EXP})^{\left(\frac{\sigma_{i,COM}-1}{\sigma_{i,COM}}\right)} \right]^{\left(\frac{\sigma_{i,COM}}{\sigma_{i,COM}-1}\right)}$

4. Primary Factor Markets

A. Labor Markets

(7) $\quad \tilde{W}_{i,L} = P_i' \dfrac{Q_i}{Q_{i,F}} \cdot (1 - \xi_i) \left[\dfrac{Q_{i,F}}{z_i L_i} \right]^{1/\sigma_i} \equiv \dfrac{W_{i,L}}{z_i}$

for $i = M, KS, PSU, US, PSR, RS$

(8) $\quad \tilde{W}_{i.S} = P_i' \dfrac{Q_i}{Q_{i.F}} \xi_i (1 - \xi_i') \left[\dfrac{Q_{i.F}}{\phi_i} \right]^{1/\sigma_i} \cdot \left[\dfrac{\phi_i}{y_i S_i} \right]^{1/\sigma_i'} \equiv \dfrac{W_{i.S}}{y_i}$

$$\text{for } i = M, KS, PSU, US, PSR, RS$$

(9) $\quad \tilde{W}_{A.j} = P_A \cdot \alpha_{A.j} \left[\dfrac{Q_A}{b \cdot J_A} \right] = \dfrac{W_{A.j}}{b_A}$

$$\text{for } j, J = L, S$$

$$\text{and } b = \begin{cases} z \text{ for } j = L \\ y \text{ for } j = S \end{cases}$$

B. Labor Migration

(10) $\quad W_{A.j} = W_{RS.j} = W_{PSR.j}$

$$j = L, S$$

(11) $\quad (1 - \tau_{Y.FS}) \cdot W_{M.S} = (1 - \tau_{Y.FS}) \cdot W_{KS.S} = (1 - \tau_{Y.FS}) W_{PSU.S}$

$$= (1 - \tau_{Y.US}) \cdot W_{US.S}$$

(12) $\quad W_{M.L} = W_{KS.L} = W_{PSU.L} = W_{US.L}$

(13) $\quad \dfrac{W_{A.L}}{COL_{L_R}} = \dfrac{W_{M.L}}{COL_{L_U}} - C_{M.L},$

$$\text{given } COL_{L_U} = COL_{L_{US}}$$

(14) $\quad \dfrac{W_{A.S} \cdot (1 - \tau_{Y.A})}{COL_{S_R}} = \dfrac{W_{M.S} \cdot (1 - \tau_{Y.FS})}{COL_{S_U}} - C_{M.S},$

$$\text{given } COL_{S_U} = COL_{S_{US}}$$

C. Capital Markets

(15) $\quad \tilde{r}_i = P_i' \dfrac{Q_i}{Q_{i.F}} \cdot \xi_i' \cdot \xi_i \cdot \left[\dfrac{Q_{i.F}}{\phi_i} \right]^{1/\sigma_i} \cdot \left[\dfrac{\phi_i}{x_i K_i} \right]^{1/\sigma_i'} = \dfrac{r_i}{x_i}$

$$i = M, KS, PSU, PSR, US, RS$$

(16) $\quad \tilde{r}_A = P_A \cdot \alpha_{A.K} \left[\dfrac{Q_A}{x_A K_A} \right] = \dfrac{r_A}{x_A}$

D. Private Firm and Public Enterprise Investment Allocation

(17)   MINIMIZE {Return Differentials $= r_M^* \cdot (1 - \tau_{\pi,M}) -$
$\{I_{i,M,FS}\}$

$$r_{KS}^* \cdot (1 - \tau_{\pi,KS})\}$$

such that desired investment in the urban formal sector is completely allocated:

$$I_{M,FS} = \sum_i I_{i,M,FS}; \quad i = M, KS$$

and where r_i^* is the net rental rate expected to prevail in the following year:

$$r_i^* = \left\{ r_i + \left. \frac{\partial r_i}{\partial K_i} \right|_{K_i} \cdot [I_{i,M,FS} - \delta_i K_i] \right\} - \delta_i P_{M^*}; \quad i = M, KS$$

(18)   MINIMIZE {Return Differentials $= r_{RS}^* - r_A^*\}$
$\{I_{i,M,R}\}$

such that desired investment in rural production is completely allocated:

$$I_{M,R} = \sum_i I_{i,M,R},$$

$$i = RS, A$$

and where

$$r_i^* = \left\{ r_i + \left. \frac{\partial r_i}{\partial K_i} \right|_{K_i} \cdot [I_{i,M,R} - \delta_i K_i] \right\} - \delta_i P_{M^*}$$

$$i = RS, A$$

Funds available for capital accumulation in the urban informal sector can go only to one "industry," US. Investment in the US sector must thereby equal capital made available for investment by informal sector savers, after allowing for housing investment:

(19) $P_{M^*} I_{M,US} = s_{L_U} L_{US} - P_{US} I_{H,US,US} + s_{S_U} S_{US}$

$$- P_{KS} I_{H,KS,US} + \delta_{US} P_{M^*} K_{US}$$

Sectorwide discount rates are weighted averages of expected returns on private capital:

(20) $$i_{FS} = \frac{\sum_j (1 - \tau_{\pi,j}) K_j r_j^*}{P_{M^*} \sum_j K_j}$$

$$j = M, KS$$

(21) $$i_A = \frac{\sum_j K_j r_j^*}{P_{M^*} \sum_j K_j}$$

$$j = RS, A$$

(22) $$i_{IFS} = \frac{r_{US}}{P_{M^*}} - \delta_{US}$$

Total private and public enterprise investment, I_M, equals

(23) $$I_M = I_{M,US} + I_{M,R} + I_{M,FS}$$

E. Intermediate Input Markets

(24) $$Z_i = \frac{P_i \alpha_{i,z} Q_i}{\bar{P}_z},$$

$$i = RS, PSR, US, PSU, KS, A, M$$

(25) $$Q_{i,j} = \frac{P_i \alpha_{i,j} Q_i}{P_{i,j}^{tax}}$$

$$\text{where } j = KS, M^*, A^*, k$$

$$i = A, M, PSU, PSR, RS, US, KS$$

$$k = \begin{cases} PSU \text{ when } j = KS, US, M \\ PSR \text{ when } j = A, RS \end{cases}$$

(26) $$P_{k,H,j} = \frac{P_{H,j} \alpha_{k,H,j} Q_{H,j}}{Q_{k,H,j}}$$

$$j = KS, US, RS$$

$$k = \begin{cases} PSU \text{ for } j = US, KS \\ PSR \text{ for } j = RS \end{cases}$$

$$\text{where } P_{k,H,j} = \begin{cases} P_k \text{ for } j = KS, RS \\ P_{PSU}(1 + \tau_{PSU,H,US}) \text{ for } j = US \end{cases}$$

F. Land Markets

Let $r^*_{H,j}$ and $d^*_{U,j}$ be the structure and land rents perceived by urban consumers. Let $r_{H,j}$ and $d_{U,j}$ be the ("net") structure and land rents received by asset owners. Note that $\tau_{H,KS}$ is the only nonzero property tax rate.

Define P_{Hj} = nominal unit rental cost of housing of type j, including property taxes and user charges on public services;

$\quad\quad\quad P^S_{Hj}$ = nominal net unit rental cost of housing of type j, net of property taxes and public services user charges;

$\quad\quad\quad V_{H,j}$ = taxable value of urban residential property per housing service unit, $j = US, KS, RS$.

Then for KS housing

$$(27) \quad P^S_{H,KS} = i_{FS} \cdot V_{H,KS} = P_{H,KS} - \tau_{H,KS} V_{H,KS} - \frac{P_{PSU,H,KS} Q_{PSU,H,KS}}{Q_{H,KS}}$$

Therefore

$$P^S_{H,KS} = \frac{i_{FS}}{(i_{FS} + \tau_{H,KS})} \cdot (1 - \alpha_{PSU,H,KS}) \cdot P_{H,KS}$$

$$(28) \quad P^S_{H,j} = (1 - \alpha_{k,H,j}) P_{H,j}$$

$$\text{for } j = US, RS$$

$$k = \begin{cases} PSU \text{ for } j = US \\ PSR \text{ for } j = RS \end{cases}$$

To relate structure and land rents to the price of owner-occupied housing, it is first necessary to relate "gross" and "net" rents. Euler's theorem ensures product exhaustion:

$$(29a) \quad P_{H,KS} = \frac{r^*_{H,KS} \cdot H_{KS}}{Q_{H,KS}} + \frac{d^*_{U,KS} \cdot R_{U,KS}}{Q_{H,KS}} + \frac{P_{PSU,H,KS} \cdot Q_{PSU,H,KS}}{Q_{H,KS}}$$

Net factor payments must also add up:

(29b) $\quad P_{H,KS} = \dfrac{r_{H,KS} \cdot H_{KS}}{Q_{H,KS}} + \dfrac{d_{U,KS} \cdot R_{U,KS}}{Q_{H,KS}} + \tau_{H,KS} \cdot V_{H,KS}$

$\qquad\quad + \dfrac{P_{PSU,H,KS} Q_{PSU,H,KS}}{Q_{H,KS}}$

Substitute $V_{H,KS}$ from 27 into 29b:

(29c) $\quad P_{H,KS} = \dfrac{r_{H,KS} H_{KS}}{Q_{H,KS}} + \dfrac{d_{U,KS} R_{U,KS}}{Q_{H,KS}} + \dfrac{\tau_{H,KS}}{(\tau_{H,KS} + i_{FS})}$

$\qquad\quad \cdot \left[P_{H,KS} - \dfrac{P_{PSU,H,KS} Q_{PSU,H,KS}}{Q_{H,KS}} \right] + \dfrac{P_{PSU,H,KS} Q_{PSU,H,KS}}{Q_{H,KS}}$

so that

$$P_{H,KS} - \dfrac{P_{PSU,H,KS} Q_{PSU,H,KS}}{Q_{H,KS}}$$

$$= \left[\dfrac{\tau_{H,j} + i_{FS}}{i_{FS}} \right] \cdot \left[\dfrac{r_{H,KS} H_{KS}}{Q_{H,KS}} + \dfrac{d_{U,KS} R_{U,KS}}{Q_{H,KS}} \right]$$

Then bring the farthest term on the righthand side over to the left in 29a; note that the lefthand sides of 29a and 29c are now identical. Equating them gives us an expression for gross rents in terms of net rents.

(30) $\quad r^{*}_{H,KS} = \left[1 + \dfrac{\tau_{H,KS}}{i_{FS}} \right] r_{H,KS}$

$\qquad\qquad$ while $r^{*}_{H,j} = r_{H,j}$ for $j = US, RS$

(31) $\quad d^{*}_{U,KS} = \left[1 + \dfrac{\tau_{H,KS}}{i_{FS}} \right] d_{U,KS}$

$\qquad\qquad$ and $d^{*}_{U,US} = d_{U,US}$

Then from the first order conditions

(32) $\quad d^{*}_{U,KS} = \dfrac{P_{H,KS} \alpha_{R,KS} Q_{H,KS}}{R_{U,KS}} = \dfrac{(i_{FS} + \tau_{H,KS})}{i_{FS}(1 - \alpha_{PSU,H,KS})} \cdot \dfrac{P^{S}_{H,KS} \alpha_{R,KS} Q_{H,KS}}{R_{U,KS}}$

where the second term is derived from rearranging 27 to express $P_{H,KS}$ in terms of $P_{H,KS}^S$ and then substituting into 32. Finally, to express the rental rate equality in terms of net rents, substitute from 31 into 32:

$$(33) \quad d_{U,j} = \frac{P_{H,j}^S \alpha_{R,j} Q_{H,j}}{R_{U,j} \cdot (1 - \alpha_{PSU,H,j})}$$

$$j = KS,\ US$$

For land in agricultural use,

$$(34) \quad d_A = \frac{P_A \alpha_{A,R} Q_A}{R_A}$$

Finally, urban land rental market equilibrium requires:

$$(35) \quad d_{U,KS} = d_{U,US} \cdot \text{GRADIENT}$$

As noted, Euler's theorem applies to the housing services production equations. That is, total user rent equals site rent plus structure rent plus property taxes plus public service charges. The gross price relationships corresponding to equation 4 are thus

$$(36) \quad P_{H,j} = \frac{r_{H,j} \cdot H_j + P_{k,H,j} \cdot Q_{k,H,j} + d_{U,j} \cdot R_{U,j}}{Q_{H,j}}$$

$$j = US,\ RS$$

$$k = \begin{cases} PSU \text{ for } j = US \\ PSR \text{ for } j = RS \end{cases}$$

and $R_{U,RS} = 0$. Equation 36 is the untaxed housing sectors' analog to 29.

Rearranging 27 to solve for $V_{H,KS}$, substituting into 29b, and rearranging gives

$$(37) \quad P_{H,KS} = \frac{(i_{FS} + \tau_{H,KS})}{(i_{FS} + \alpha_{PSU,H,KS} \cdot \tau_{H,KS})} \cdot$$

$$\left[\frac{r_{H,KS} H_{KS} + P_{PSU} Q_{PSU,H,KS} + d_U R_{U,KS}}{Q_{H,KS}} \right]$$

G. Factor Employment

(38) $\quad J_{URB} = J_{US} + (J_{KS} + J_M + J_{PSU})$

$\qquad \equiv J_{US} + J_U$ $\left.\right\} J = L, S$

(39) $\quad J_R = J_{PSR} + J_{RS} + J_A$

$\qquad\qquad J = L, S$

(40) $\quad J = J_{URB} + J_R$

$\qquad\qquad J = L, S$

(41a) $\quad N_U = S_U + L_U + C$

(41b) $\quad N_R = S_R + L_R$

(42) $\quad N = N_U + N_R$

(43) $\quad R = (R_{U,US} + R_{U,KS}) + R_A = R_U + R_A$

5. Foreign Trade Sector and World/Domestic Price Relationships

(44) $\quad \displaystyle\sum_i P_i Q_{i,EXP} (1 + \tau_{i,EXP}) + \overline{F} - \sum_i \overline{P}_i^W Q_{i,IMP} - \overline{P}_Z \sum_j Z_j = 0$

$\qquad\qquad i = A, M$

$\qquad\qquad j = PSU, PSR, KS, US, A, M, RS.$

(45) $\quad Q_{i,EXP} = Q_{i,EXP}^O \left[\dfrac{P_i \cdot (1 + \tau_{i,EXP})}{\overline{P}_i^W} \right]^{-\eta_i}$

$\qquad\qquad i = A, M$

(46) $\quad P_i = P_{i^*}(1 - \psi_i^*) \left[\dfrac{Q_{i^*}}{Q_i - Q_{i,EXP}} \right]^{1/\sigma_{i,COM}}$

$\qquad\qquad i = A, M$

(47) $\quad \overline{P}_i^W (1 + \tau_{i,IMP}) = P_{i^*} \psi_i^* \left[\dfrac{Q_{i^*}}{Q_{i,IMP}} \right]^{1/\sigma_{i,COM}}$

$\qquad\qquad i = A, M$

6. Government Sector

A. Government Taxes

(48) $T = \tau_M P_{M^*} D_M + \tau_{H,KS} V_{H,KS} Q_{H,KS} + \tau_{A,M} P_{M^*} (Q_{A,M} + Q_{RS,M})$

$\qquad + \tau_{Y,A} Y_{R,S}^{**} S_R + \tau_{Y,US} Y_{US,S}^{**} S_{US} + \tau_{Y,FS} [Y_{FS,S}^{**} S_U + Y_C^{**} C]$

$\qquad + \sum_i \tau_{\pi,i} [r_i - \delta_i P_{M^*}] K_i + \sum_j \{\tau_{j,EXP} Q_{j,EXP} P_j + \tau_{j,IMP} Q_{j,IMP} \overline{P}_j^W\}$

$\qquad i = M, KS$

$\qquad j = A, M$

(49) $\text{GOVREV} = T + F + \sum_i K_i (r_i - \delta_i P_{M^*})$

$\qquad i = PSU, PSR$

B. Government Spending and Savings

(50) $G_S = \beta_G \cdot \text{GOVREV} \; ; \qquad G_S \leq \text{GOVREV}$

(51) $\text{GOV}_{KS} = \text{GOVREV} - G_S$

(52) $G_i = g_i G_S$

$\qquad i = A, M, KS, PSU, PSR, RS, US$

7. Household Demand, Savings, and Income

(53) $v_{ij} = P_{i,j} \cdot \gamma_{i,j} + \beta_{i,j} \cdot [Y_j^* - \sum_k (P_{k,j} \cdot \gamma_{k,j})],$

$\qquad i,k = A^*, M^*, T, S, H$

(54) $c_j = \sum_i v_{i,j}$

(55) $s_j = Y_j^* - c_j$

(56) $COL_j = \sum_i \dfrac{P_{i,j} v_{i,j}}{c_j}$

$\qquad j = L_R$, covering households supplying L_A, L_{RS}, L_{PSR}

$= S_R$, covering households supplying S_A, S_{RS}, S_{PSR}

$= L_U$, covering households supplying L_M, L_{KS}, L_{PSU}

$= L_{US}$, covering households supplying L_{US}

$= S_U$, covering households supplying S_M, S_{KS}, S_{PSU}

$= S_{US}$, covering households supplying S_{US}

$= C$, covering capitalists and landlords.

Households face the following prices:

(57) $\quad P_{A^*,j} = P_A^*$

$\qquad$ for all j

$P_{M^*,j} = P_M^*(1 + \tau_M)$

$\qquad$ for all j

$P_{T,j} = P_{KS}$

$\qquad$ for all j

$P_{S,j} = P_{RS}$

$\qquad$ for $j = L_R$, S_R

$P_{S,j} = P_{US}$

$\qquad$ for $j = L_U$, S_U, L_{US}, S_{US}, C

$P_{H,j} = P_{H,KS}$

$\qquad$ for $j = S_{US}$, S_U, C

$P_{H,j} = P_{H,US}$

$\qquad$ for $j = L_{US}$, L_U

$P_{H,j} = P_{H,RS}$

$\qquad$ for $j = L_R$, S_R

Household gross incomes, Y_j^{***}, are:

(58) $\quad Y_j^{***} = W_j + J^{-1}[P_{H,RS}^S Q_{H,RS,j} + d_A \hat{R}_j R_A$

$$+ \hat{KS} H_{R,j} \sum_i K_i(r_i - \delta_i P_{M^*})],$$

where $i = A, RS$

$j = L_R, S_R$

with J = number of households of type j

and $W_{L_R} = W_{A,L}$; $W_{S_R} = W_{A,S}$

(59) $\quad Y_j^{***} = W_j + J^{-1}[P^S_{H,k}Q_{H,k,j} + \widehat{KS}H_{US,j}K_{US}(r_{US} - \delta_{US}P_{M^*})$

$\qquad + \widehat{KS}H_{M,j} \sum_i \psi_i(1 - \tau_{\pi,i}) K_i(r_i - \delta_i P_{M^*})] + REB_j,$

$i = M, KS$

$j = L_U, L_{US}, S_U, S_{US}$

$k = \begin{cases} US \text{ for } j = L_U, L_{US} \\ KS \text{ for } j = S_U, S_{US}; \end{cases}$

$\widehat{KS}H_{US,j} = 0$ for $j = L_U, S_U$

$\widehat{KS}H_{M,j} = 0$ for $j = L_{US}, S_{US}$

and $W_{L_U} = W_{L_{US}} = W_{M,L}$; $W_{S_U} = W_{M,S}$; $W_{S_{US}} = W_{US,S}$

(60) $\quad REB_j = \begin{cases} \dfrac{\tau_{PSU,H,US}P_{PSU}Q_{PSU,H,US}Q_{H,US,j}}{J \cdot Q_{H,US}}, \text{ for } J_{ij} = L_U, L_{US} \\ 0 \qquad \text{otherwise} \end{cases}$

REB_j is the per household rebate on PSU taxes collected from type j households. These "shadow taxes" thus have price effects without reducing nominal incomes.

(61) $\quad \widehat{KS}H_{R,C} \cdot [(r_A - \delta_A P_{M^*})K_A + (r_{RS} - \delta_{RS}P_{M^*})K_{RS}] + d_A \hat{R}_C R_A$

$Y_C^{***} = \dfrac{\qquad + \widehat{KS}H_{M,C} \cdot [\psi_M(1 - \tau_{\pi,M})(r_M - \delta_M P_{M^*})K_M}{C}$
$\qquad\qquad\qquad + \psi_{KS}(1 - \tau_{\pi,KS})(r_{KS} - \delta_{KS}P_{M^*})K_{KS}] + P^S_{H,KS}Q_{H,KS,C}$

Four household groups, $J = S_R, S_U, S_{US},$ and C, face income taxes. Taxable income for these groups is given by Y_j^{**}.

$$(62) \quad Y_j^{**} = Y_j^{***} - \frac{P_{H,k}^s Q_{H,k,j}}{J},$$

$$j, J = S_R, S_U, S_{US}, C$$

$$k = \begin{cases} RS \text{ for } j = S_R \\ KS \text{ for } j = S_U, S_{US}, C \end{cases}$$

Disposable incomes:

$$(63) \quad Y_j^* = Y_j^{***} - \tau_{Y,k} Y_j^{**} + TRF_j,$$

$$j = L_R, S_R, L_U, L_{US}, S_U, S_{US}, C.$$

$$k = \begin{cases} A \text{ for } j = S_R \\ FS \text{ for } j = S_U, C \\ US \text{ for } j = S_{US} \\ L \text{ for } j = L_R, L_U, L_{US} \end{cases}$$

$$\text{and } \tau_{Y,L} = 0$$

$$(64) \quad \sum_j \hat{R}_j = 1,$$

$$j = L_R, S_R, C$$

$$(65) \quad \sum_j K\hat{S}H_{R,j} = 1,$$

$$j = L_R, S_R, C$$

$$\left(K\hat{S}H_{R,j} = \sum_i K_{i,j}(0) \Big/ \sum_i K_i(0); \ i = A, RS \right)$$

These capital ownership shares are assumed to remain constant at their base year (0) values.

$$(66) \quad \sum_j K\hat{S}H_{M,j} = 1,$$

$$j = L_U, S_U, C$$

$$\left(K\hat{S}H_{M,j} = \sum_j K_{i,j}(0) \Big/ \sum_i K_i(0) \right);$$

$$i = M, KS$$

(67) $\sum_j K\hat{S}H_{US,j} = 1$

$j = L_{US}, S_{US}$

$K\hat{S}H_{US,j} = K_{US,j}(0)/K_{US}(0))$

8. Private Consumption Demand

(68) $P_{i,j}D_i = \sum_j v_{h,j} \cdot J$

$h = A^*, M^*, T, S, H$

$j,J = L_R, S_R, L_U, L_{US}, S_{US}, S_U, C;$

$$i = \begin{cases} h \text{ for } h = A^*, M^* \\ KS \text{ for } h = T \\ RS \text{ for } h = S \text{ and } j = L_R, S_R \\ US \text{ for } h = S \text{ and } j = S_U, S_{US}, C, L_U, L_{US} \\ (H,US) \text{ for } h = H \text{ and } j = L_U, L_{US} \\ (H,KS) \text{ for } h = H \text{ and } j = S_U, S_{US}, C \\ (H,RS) \text{ for } h = H \text{ and } j = S_R, L_R \end{cases}$$

where J = number of households in group j

(69) $P_i D_{i,j} = v_{H,j} \cdot J$

$i = (H,US), (H,KS)$

$$j,J = \begin{cases} L_{US}, L_U \text{ for } i = (H,US) \\ S_{US}, s_U, C \text{ for } i = (H,KS) \end{cases}$$

where $D_{H,j} = Q_{H,j}$

9. Investment and Savings

A. Housing Investment

(70) $I^*_{H,RS} = \min\{[s_{L_R}L_R + s_{S_R} S_R]P^{-1}_{RS}, I^N_{H,RS} + \delta_{H,RS}H_{RS}\}$

$I_{H,RS} = \max\{0, I^*_{H,RS}\}$

$I^N_{H,RS} = \theta_{H,RS} \cdot [\hat{r}^{\epsilon_H}_{H,RS} - 1]$

(71) $I^*_{H,h,j} = \min\left\{\dfrac{s_j J}{P_h}, I^N_{H,h,j} + \delta_{H,h}H_{h,j}\right\}$

$$I_{H,h,j} = \max\{0, I^*_{H,h,j}\}$$

$$I^N_{H,h,j} = \theta_{H,h} \cdot [\hat{r}^{\epsilon_H}_{H,h,j} - 1]$$

$$j, J = L_{US}, L_U, S_{US}$$

$$h = \begin{cases} US \text{ for } j, J = L_{US}, L_U \\ KS \text{ for } j, J = S_{US} \end{cases}$$

(72) $\quad I^*_{H,KS,FSC} = \min\{[s_{S_U}S_U + s_C C]P^{-1}_{KS}, I^N_{H,KS,FSC}$

$$+ \ \delta_{H,KS}(H_{KS,C} + H_{KS,S_U})\}$$

$$I_{H,KS,FSC} = \max\{0, I^*_{H,KS,FSC}\}$$

$$I^N_{H,KS,FSC} = \theta_{H,KS}[\hat{r}^{\epsilon_H}_{H,KS,FSC} - 1]$$

(73) $\quad I_{H,KS,j} = \dfrac{s_j J}{\sum\limits_{i,I} s_i I} I_{H,KS,FSC}$

$$i, I, j, J = S_{U,} C$$

(74) $\quad I_{H,KS} = I_{H,KS,FSC} + I_{H,KS,S_{US}}$

(75) $\quad I_{H,US} = I_{H,US,L_U} + I_{H,US,L_{US}}$

(76) $\quad \hat{r}_{H,RS} = \dfrac{r_{H,RS} - \delta_{H,RS}P_{RS}}{i_A P_{RS}}$

(77) $\quad \hat{r}_{H,h,j} = \dfrac{r_{H,h} - \delta_{H,h} \cdot P_h}{i_k P_h}$

$$j = FSC, S_{US}, L_{US}, L_U$$

$$h = \begin{cases} KS \text{ for } j = FSC, S_{US} \\ US \text{ for } j = L_{US}, L_U \end{cases}$$

$$k = \begin{cases} FS \text{ for } j = FSC, L_U \\ IFS \text{ for } j = L_{US}, S_{US} \end{cases}$$

(78) $\quad r_{H,US} = \dfrac{\alpha_{H,US}Q_{H,US}P^s_{H,US}}{H_{US}(1 - \alpha_{PSU,H,US})}$

(79) $\quad r_{H,KS} = \dfrac{\alpha_{H,KS}Q_{H,KS}P^s_{H,KS}}{H_{KS}(1 - \alpha_{PSU,H,KS})}$

$$(80) \quad r_{H,RS} = \frac{\alpha_{H,RS} Q_{H,RS} P_{H,RS}}{H_{RS}}$$

$$(81) \quad \text{HOUSING} = P_{RS} I_{H,RS} + P_{US} I_{H,US} + P_{KS} I_{H,KS}$$

B. Aggregate and Sectoral Savings for Nonhousing Investment

$$(82) \quad \text{PRIVATE SAVINGS} = \sum_i (1 - \psi_i)(1 - \tau_{\pi,i})(r_i - \delta_i P_{M^*}) K_i$$
$$+ \sum_l \delta_l P_{M^*} K_l + \sum_j s_j J,$$

$$i = M, KS$$
$$l = M, KS, US, RS, A$$
$$j = L_{US}, L_U, L_R, S_{US}, S_U, S_R, C$$

Private savings is divided into informal sector investment, $I_{M,US}$, given in equation 19, formal sector investment, $I_{M,FS}$, and rural private investment, $I_{M,R}$.

$$(83) \quad I_{M,FS} = P_{M^*}^{-1} \cdot \left[\sum_i (1 - \psi_i)(1 - \tau_{\pi,i})(r_i - \delta_i P_{M^*}) K_i + \sum_i \delta_i P_{M^*} K_i \right.$$
$$\left. + \sum_j s_j J - \sum_h I_{H,h,j} P_h + \text{URBCAP}(s_C C - I_{H,KS,C} P_{KS}) \right],$$

$$i = M, KS$$
$$J, j = S_U, L_U$$
$$h = \begin{cases} US \text{ for } j = L_U \\ KS \text{ for } j = S_U \end{cases}$$

$$(84) \quad \text{URBCAP} = [C \cdot Y_C^*]^{-1} \left\{ \left[(1 - \tau_{Y,FS}) K \hat{S} H_{M,C} \cdot \right. \right.$$
$$\left. \sum_i \psi_i (1 - \tau_{\pi,i})(r_i - \delta_i P_{M^*}) K_i \right] + P_{H,KS}^s Q_{H,KS,C} \right\},$$

$$i = M, KS.$$

$$(85) \quad I_{M,R} = P_{M^*}^{-1} \left\{ \sum_i \delta_i P_{M^*} K_i + \sum_j s_j J - P_{RS} I_{H,RS} \right.$$

$$+ (1 - \text{URBCAP})(s_C C - I_{H,KS,C} P_{KS}) \Bigg\},$$

$$i = A, RS$$

$$j, J = S_R, L_R$$

Total investment:

(86) $\quad TI_{M,i} = I_{M,i} + \dfrac{G_i}{P_{M^*}}$

$$i = R, US$$

(87) $\quad TI_{M,i} = I_{i,M,R} + \dfrac{G_i}{P_{M^*}}$

$$i = A, RS$$

(88) $\quad TI_{M,i} = I_{i,M,FS} + \dfrac{G_i}{P_{M^*}}$

$$i = M, KS$$

(89) $\quad TI_{M,FS} = \sum_i TI_{M,i}$

$$i = M, KS$$

(90) $\quad TI_{M,i} = G_i P_{M^*}^{-1} + \delta_i K_i$

$$i = PSU, PSR$$

These definitions imply the following identities: Private investment in value terms is

(91) $\quad P_{M^*} I_M = \text{PRIVATE SAVINGS} - \text{HOUSING},$

and total investment in value terms is

(92) $\quad P_{M^*} TI_M = \text{PRIVATE SAVINGS} - \text{HOUSING} + G_S + \sum_i \delta_i P_{M^*} K_i$

$$= \sum_l P_{M^*} TI_{M,l},$$

$$i = PSU, PSR$$

$$l = R, US, FS, PSU, PSR$$

10. Market Clearing

(93) $\quad Q_{M^*} = D_{M^*} + TI_M + \sum_i Q_{i,M^*}$

$$i = A, PSU, PSR, KS, RS, US$$

(94) $\quad Q_{A^*} = D_{A^*} + \sum_i Q_{i,A^*}$

$$i = PSU, PSR, KS, RS, US, M$$

(46a) $\quad Q_i = Q_{i^*} \left[\dfrac{P_{i^*} (1 - \psi_i^*)}{P_i} \right]^{\sigma_{i,COM}} + Q_{i,EXP}$

$$i = A, M$$

(95) $\quad Q_{PSU} = \sum_i Q_{i,PSU}$

$$i = KS, M, US, (H, US)$$

(96) $\quad Q_{PSR} = \sum_i Q_{i,PSR}$

$$i = A, RS, (H, RS)$$

(97) $\quad Q_{KS} = D_{KS} + \text{GOV}_{KS}/P_{KS} + I_{H,KS} + \sum_i Q_{i,KS}$

$$i = PSR, PSR, A, M, US, KS$$

(98) $\quad Q_i = D_i + I_{H,i}$

$$i = US, RS$$

(99) $\quad Q_{H,i} = D_i$

$$i = (H, US), (H, RS), (H, KS)$$

A final identity:

(100) $\quad \text{GDP} = \sum_i P_i' Q_i + \sum_i P_{H,j}^s Q_{H,j}$

$$+ \ \tau_M P_{M^*} D_M + \tau_{H,KS} V_{H,KS} Q_{H,KS}$$

$$+ \sum_{l} \{P_l \tau_{l,EXP} Q_{l,EXP} + \bar{P}_l^w \tau_{l,IMP} Q_{l,IMP}\};$$

$$i = M, KS, PSU, PSR, US, RS, A$$
$$j = US, KS, RS$$
$$l = A, M$$

11. Dynamic Equations

A. Accumulation of Capital and Residential Structures

$$(101) \quad K_i = (1 - \delta_i) K_i(-1) + TI_{M,i}(-1)$$
$$i = M, KS, A, RS, US, PSU, PSR$$

$$(102) \quad H_j = (1 - \delta_{H,j}) \cdot H_j(-1) + I_{H,j}(-1)$$
$$j = US, RS, KS$$

B. Land Growth and Technological Progress

$$(103) \quad x_i = x_i(-1) \cdot e^{\lambda_{Ki}}$$
$$i = A, RS, M, KS, US, PSU, PSR$$

$$(104) \quad y_i = y_i(-1) \cdot e^{\lambda_{Si}}$$
$$i = A, RS, M, KS, US, PSU, PSR$$

$$(105) \quad z_i = z_i(-1) \cdot e^{\lambda_{Li}}$$
$$i = A, RS, M, KS, US, PSU, PSR$$

$$(106) \quad A_A = A_A(-1) \cdot e^{\lambda_A \cdot \text{RAIN}}$$

$$(107) \quad A_i = A_i(-1) \cdot e^{\lambda_i}$$
$$i = RS, M, KS, US, PSU, PSR, (H,KS), (H,US),$$
$$(H,RS)$$

$$(108) \quad R_i = (1 + \rho) R_i(-1),$$
$$i = A, U$$

C. Training and Skills Investment

Training and skills investment are exogenous. Define $J(0)$ as the number of households of type j prior to intraperiod equilibrium adjustments and $J(-1)$ as the number of households of type j at the end of the preceding period. Then,

$$(109) \quad S_j(0) = (1 + \hat{BR}_i)S_j(-1) + \hat{TR}_j L_j(-1)$$

$$j = R, US, U$$

$$i = \begin{cases} R \text{ for } j = R \\ U \text{ for } j = U, US \end{cases}$$

Consequently,

$$(110) \quad L_j(0) = (1 + \hat{BR}_i - \hat{TR}_j) \cdot L_j(-1)$$

$$j = R, US, U$$

$$i = \begin{cases} R \text{ for } j = R \\ U \text{ for } j = U, US \end{cases}$$

$$(111) \quad C = C(-1) + \phi_c \dot{N} = C(-1) + \frac{1}{1 - \phi_c} \cdot$$

$$\left[\sum_j (S_j(0) + L_j(0) - S_j(-1) - L_j(-1)) \right];$$

$$j = R, US, U$$

Glossary

A. Subscripts

i. Sector Subscripts (Production)

A	Agriculture
H,KS	urban "luxury" (pucca) housing; housing stock originally constructed in KS sector
H,US	urban nonluxury housing (katcha housing, squatter settlements); housing stock originally constructed in US sector
H,RS	rural housing; housing stock originally constructed in RS sector
KS	capital-intensive services (defense, education, administration, finance, commerce, construction of H,KS housing); urban based
PSU	urban public services (electricity, gas, water, transportation, and communications)
PSR	rural public services (public roads, irrigation projects, rural transport, rural government)
M	manufacturing (urban manufacturing and mining)
US	urban unskilled-labor–intensive services (domestics, personal services, construction of H,US housing, small-scale commercial and repair services, small-scale transport)
RS	rural labor-intensive services and manufacturing (domestics, personal services, rural housing construction, other rural construction; rural commerce, manufacturing and repair services)

ii. Factor Subscripts (Production; Including Goods Not Directly Produced but Used as Intermediates)

K	capital
L	unskilled labor
R	land
S	skilled labor
Z	imported raw materials, including fuel but not manufactures

M^* composite manufacturing good, containing both imports and domestic production

A^* composite agricultural good, containing both imports and domestic production

iii. Location Subscripts

FS formal sector (urban): KS, PSU, M sector

IFS informal sector (urban): US sector

FSC formal sector plus capitalists and landlords (urban residents other than informal sector workers, plus landlords)

R rural

U urban

iv. Commodity Subscripts (Demand)

A^* food, a composite of domestic A sector production and imports

M^* clothing and durables, a composite of domestic M sector production and imports

T transportation and communications (KS sector)

S labor-intensive personal services (RS or US sector)

H housing rent (H,KS; H,US; or H,RS sectors)

v. Household Subscripts (Demand)

C capitalists and landlords

L_R rural unskilled

S_R rural skilled

L_U formal sector unskilled workers (in M, KS, PSU sectors)

L_{US} informal sector unskilled (in US sector)

S_U formal sector skilled workers (in M, KS, PSU sectors)

S_{US} informal sector skilled workers (in US sector)

B. Parameters

A number in parentheses indicates the equation in which the parameter first appears.

$\alpha_{A,j}$ output elasticity (and cost share) of the jth (primary or intermediate) input in the A sector; $j = K,S,L,R,Z,M^*,$ KS,PSR,A^* (2)

$\alpha_{i,F}$ output elasticity (and cost share) of composite of primary inputs in ith sector (a value-added share in gross output); $i = M,KS,PSU,US,RS,PSR,A$ (1)

$\alpha_{H,j}$ output elasticity (and cost share) of housing stock input into housing services production of type j; $j = KS,US,$ RS (3)

$\alpha_{i,z}$ output elasticity (and cost share) of Z in the ith sector, $i = A,M,KS,PSU,US,RS,PSR$ (1)

$\alpha_{i,j}$ output elasticity (and cost share) of jth intermediate input in the ith sector for $i = M,KS,PSU,US,PSR,RS$; and $j = A^*,M^*,KS$, k where $k = PSU$ for $i = M,KS,US$; $k = PSU$ for $i = RS$, $k = 0$ otherwise (1)

$\alpha_{k,H,j}$ output elasticity (and cost share) of public services of type k in housing production of type j; $j = KS,US,RS$; $k = PSU$ for $j = KS,US$; $k = PSU$ for $j = RS$ (3)

$\alpha_{R,j}$ output elasticity (and cost share) of urban land in urban housing production, $j = US,KS$ (3)

β_G marginal propensity to save out of government revenue (taxes, foreign inflows and aid, and earnings on public service investment) (50)

$\beta_{i,j}$ marginal propensity to consume the ith commodity out of supernumary income; by the jth household type; $i = A^*,M^*,T,S,H$; $j = L_R,S_R,L_U,L_{US},S_U,S_{US},C$ (53)

γ_i marginal propensity by the government to spend on public services of type i; $i = PSU,PSR$ (52)

$\gamma_{i,j}$ or $\gamma_{k,j}$ subsistence bundle, ith (or kth) commodity, jth household type; i or $k = A^*,M^*,T,S,H$; $j = L_R,S_R,L_U,L_{US},$ S_U,S_{US},C (53)

$\delta_{H,j}$ depreciation rate on residential (housing) structures, $j = US,RS,KS$ (70)

δ_i depreciation rate for physical ("productive") capital in sector i; $i = A,RS,PSR,PSU,US,KS,M$ (17)

ϵ_H elasticity parameter in the net housing investment functions (70)

$\theta_{H,j}$ multiplicative parameter in the net housing investment function, $j = US,KS,RS$ (70)

λ_i rate of total-factor productivity growth in the ith sector attributable to neutral, disembodied, sector-specific technological change, $i = A, RS, PSR, PSU, US, KS, M, (H, US), (H, RS), (H, KS)$ (106)

η_i export demand price elasticity faced by Indian producers in sector i; $i = A, M$ (45)

λ_{Ki} sector-specific rate of augmentation of physical capital through technological change, $i = A, RS, PSR, PSU, US, KS, M$ (103)

λ_{Si} sector-specific rate of skilled labor augmentation through technological change, $i = A, RS, PSR, PSU, US, KS, M$ (104)

λ_{Li} sector-specific rate of unskilled labor augmentation through technological change, $i = A, RS, PSR, PSU, US, KS, M$ (105)

ξ_i distribution parameter in the ith sector value-added CES production function $(Q_{i,F})$, $i = M, KS, PSU, US, RS, PSR$ (1)

ξ_i' distribution parameter in the ith sector composite capital function (ϕ_i), $i = M, KS, PSU, US, RS, PSR$ (1)

ρ rate of augmentation of land stock through technological change   (108)

σ_i elasticity of substitution between "composite capital," ϕ, and unskilled labor in the ith sector value-added production function $(Q_{i,F})$, $i = M, KS, PSU, US, RS, PSR$ (1)

σ_i' elasticity of substitution between capital and skilled labor in the ith sector composite capital function (ϕ_i), $i = M, KS, PSU, US, PSR, RS$ (1)

$\sigma_{i,COM}$ elasticity of substitution between domestic and imported components of the ith composite good; $i = A, M$ (6)

$\tau_{A,M}$ tax (or subsidy) rate on agricultural intermediate inputs purchased from manufacturing   (5)

$\tau_{H,KS}$ property tax rate on the value of urban capital-intensive housing   (29b)

$\tau_{i,EXP}$ export tax/subsidy rate on goods exported from sector i; $i = A, M$ (44)

$\tau_{i,IMP}$ import tariff rate on imported goods of type i; $i = A, M$ (47)

$\tau_{IMP,Z}$ tax rate on imported Z goods   (4)

$\tau_{PSU,H,US}$ "shadow" tax rate for use of public services paid by consumers of US housing   (60)

$\tau_{Y,FS}$ income tax rate on personal income (excluding rental income from owner-occupied housing) for skilled workers in the formal sector, and for capitalists   (11)

$\tau_{Y,US}$ income tax rate on personal income (excluding rental income from owner-occupied housing) for skilled informal sector workers   (11)

$\tau_{Y,A}$ income tax rate for personal income (excluding rental income from owner-occupied housing) for skilled farmers and workers in rural areas   (14)

$\tau_{\pi,j}$ proportional "corporate" profit tax rate in sector j; $j = M,KS$ (17)

τ_M sales tax rate on consumption of M sector goods   (48)

ϕ_c share of capitalists and landlords in the total population   (111)

ψ_i after tax, "corporate" pay-out (dividend) rate; $i = M,KS$ (59)

ψ_i^* distribution parameter in the ith composite good function; $i = A,M$ (6)

GRADIENT   fixed ratio of land rental rate applicable at H,KS sites to the rate on H,US sites, reflecting the fact that KS housing is built on more valuable urban land   (35)

g_i proportion of the government physical capital investment fund spent on i sector projects; $i = A,M,KS,PSU,PSR, RS,US$ (52)

$\hat{R}_j$ proportion of rural private capital stock owned by households of type j; $j = L_R,S_R,C$ (61)

$\widehat{KSH}_{R,j}$ proportion of rural private capital stock (from RS,A sectors) owned by households of type j; $j = L_R,S_R,C$ (58)

$\widehat{KSH}_{US,j}$ share of urban informal sector private sector stock owned by households of type j; $j = L_{US},S_{US}$ (59)

$\widehat{KSH}_{M,j}$ share of urban formal sector private capital stock owned by households of type j; $j = L_U,S_U,C$ (59)

$\hat{BR}_i$ net "birth" rate (births $\cong$ labor force entrants less retirees, excluding transfers) in sector i; $i = R$ for $TR_j = TR_R$; $i = U$ for $TR_j = TR_{US}, TR_U$ (109)

$\hat{TR}_j$ rate of transfer of workers from unskilled to skilled category in sector j; $j = R$ (rural), US (urban informal sector), U (urban formal sector)   (109)

C. Exogenous Variables

$A_{H,j}$ intercept in the jth housing production function; $j = KS, US, RS$ (3)

A_i intercept in the ith sector's production function; $i = M, KS, PSU, US, A, PSR, RS$ (1)

C number of capitalists and landlords   (53)

$\bar{F}$ nominal value of foreign aid and private capital inflow   (49)

H_j jth type housing stock; $j = KS, US, RS$ (3)

$H_{h,j}$ hth type housing stock owned by workers in sector j; $j = L_U, L_{US}, S_{US}, S_U, C$; $h = US$ for $j = L_U, L_{US}$; $h = KS$ for $j = S_{US}, S_U, C$ (71)

$K_i(0)$ initial capital stock in production sector i; $i = A, RS, M, KS, US$ (65)

$K_{i,j}(0)$ initial capital stock in sector i owned by household type j; $j = L_R, S_R, C$ for $i = A, RS$; $j = L_U, S_U, C$ for $i = M, KS$; $j = L_{US}, S_{US}$ for $i = US$ (65)

L total unskilled labor stock   (40)

N total labor force   (42)

$\bar{P}_i^W$ c.i.f. price ("world price") of imports of type, i; $i = A, M$, used in making composite goods i^* (44)

$\bar{P}_Z$ price per unit of imported raw materials   (3)

$Q_{i,EXP}^O$ multiplicative parameter in export demand function faced by Indian producers in sector i; $i = A, M$ (45)

R total land stock   (43)

R_A rural land stock   (2)

R_U urban land stock   (43)

RAIN   index of aggregate rainfall in India (1960–61 $= 100$), entered as part of the intercept in the A sector's production function   (106)

S total skilled labor force stock   (40)

x_i augmentation level of physical capital through technological change in sector i; $i = M,KS,PSU,US,A,RS,PSR$ (1)

y_i augmentation level of skilled labor through technological change in sector i; $i = M,KS,PSU,US,A,RS,PSR$ (1)

z_i augmentation level of unskilled labor through technological change in sector i; $i = M,KS,PSU,US,A,RS,PSR$ (1)

$C_{M,L}$ cost of moving from rural to urban areas for unskilled workers   (13)

$C_{M,S}$ cost of moving from rural to urban areas for skilled workers   (14)

D. Endogenous Variables

C_j nominal consumption by jth type of household; $j = L_R,S_R,L_U,S_U,L_{US},S_{US},C$ (54)

COL_j cost of living index for the jth household; $j = L_R,S_R, L_U,S_U,L_{US},S_{US}$ (13)

C number of capitalists and landlords   (48)

d_A nominal rent per hectare of farmland   (34)

$d_{U,i}$ net nominal rent (the amount received by land owners) per hectare of urban land containing H,i type structures; $i = US,KS$ (29b)

$d^*_{U,KS}$ gross nominal rent per hectare of urban land containing KS type structures   (29a)

GDP   gross domestic product   (100)

D_i total private consumption demand for goods of type i; $i = M^*,{}^*,KS,RS,US,(H,US), (H,RS),(H,KS)$ (48; see also 68)

$D_{i,j}$ private consumption demand for good i by class j; $i = (H,US), (H,KS)$; $j = L_{US},L_U$ for $i = (H,US)$; $j = S_{US},S_U,C$ for $i = (H,KS)$ (69)

GOVREV   "total government revenue" for taxes, foreign aid, and remitted profits from public services, plus other capital transfers from abroad   (49)

G_i nominal government net investment in sector i; $i =$ PSU, PSR, KS, M (52)

G_S total government savings   (50)

GOV_{KS} nominal government expenditures on KS services   (51)

HOUSING   total gross investment in housing   (81)

i_A discount rate applicable in rural areas   (21)

i_{FS} discount rate applicable in the urban formal sector and in government evaluation of housing stock   (20)

i_{IFS} discount rate applicable in the urban informal sector   (22)

$I_{i,M,FS}$ investment of physical capital in sector i; $i = M, KS$ (17)

$I_{M,FS}$ nonhousing total private urban formal sector physical capital investment   (17)

$I_{i,M,R}$ private rural physical capital investment in sector i; $i = RS, A$ (18)

$I_{M,R}$ total private nonhousing rural physical capital investment   (18)

$I_{M,US}$ private physical capital investment in the urban US sector   (19)

I_M total private nonhousing physical capital investment demand   (23)

$I_{H,RS}^N$ "intended" net housing investment in rural areas   (73)

$I_{H,RS}^*$ "intended" gross rural housing investment, given savings constraints   (70)

$I_{H,j}$ total investment housing demand, for housing produced by sector j; $j = RS, KS, US$ (70)

$I_{H,h,j}^N$ "intended" net housing investment for housing produced in sector h by consumers of type j; $j = L_{US}, L_U, S_{US}, S_U, C, FSC$; $h = US$ for $j = L_{US}, L_U$; $h = KS$ for $j = S_{US}, S_U, C, FSC$ (71)

$I_{H,h,j}$ gross investment demand for housing of type h by consumers of type j; $j = L_{US}, L_U, S_{US}, S_U, C, FSC$; $h = US$ for $j = L_{US}, L_U$; $h = KS$ for $j = S_{US}, S_U, C, FSC$ (71)

$I_{H,h,j}^*$ "intended" gross demand for housing investment of type h by consumers of type j, given their savings constraints; $j = L_{US}, L_U, S_{US}, S_U, C, FSC$; $h = US$ for $j = L_U, L_{US}$; $h = KS$ for $j = S_{US}, S_U, C, FSC$ (71)

K_i physical (productive) capital in the ith sector, $i = M,KS,$ PSU,US,A,RS,PSR (1)

L_i unskilled labor in the ith sector; $i = M,KS,PSU,US,$ A,RS,PSR (1)

L_R unskilled labor in rural areas   (39)

L_U unskilled labor in the urban "formal" sectors ($KS,M,$ and PSU)   (38)

L_{URB} unskilled labor in urban employment   (38)

N_j total labor force in location j; $j = U,R$, including capitalists and landlords   (41)

$P_{H,j}$ nominal rental cost of jth type of housing; $j = KS,$ US,RS (26)

$P_{k,H,j}$ price per unit of public service inputs into housing of type j paid by consumers of type k; $j = US,RS,KS$; $k = PSU$ for $j = US,KS$; $k = PSR$ for $j = RS$ (26)

$P_{i,j}^{tax}$ user cost per unit of good j paid by sector i; $i = A,M,KS,$ PSU,PSR,US,RS; $j = A^*,M^*,KS,k$; $k = PSU$ for $i = M,KS,US$; $k = PSR$ for $i = RS,A$ (4)

P_i' per unit value-added price of output of sector i; $i = A,M,KS,PSU,PSR,US,RS$ (4)

P_i per unit price of sector i output; $i = A,M,KS,PSU,$ PSR,US,RS (4)

P_{j^*} per unit price of composite good j; $j = A,M$ (5)

$P_{H,j}^S$ nominal net unit rental cost of jth type of housing, *after* property taxes and public services user charges; $j = KS,US,RS$ (27)

$P_{i,j}$ price of jth commodity paid by ith household; $i = A^*,M^*,T,S,H$; $j = L_R,S_R,L_U,S_U,L_{US},S_{US},C$ (57)

PRIVATE SAVINGS   Total gross savings by households, private firms, and public enterprises in the M and KS sector   (82)

ϕ_i "composite capital" in the ith sector; $i = M,KS,PSU,US,$ RS,PSR (1)

Q_i output of the ith sector; $i = M,KS,PSU,US,A,RS,$ PSR (1)

Q_{i^*} output of the ith composite good; $i = A,M$ (6)

$Q_{H,j}$ "rental units" produced by the jth type housing stock; $j = KS,US,RS$ (3)

$Q_{i,IMP}$ quantity imported of good i; $i = A,M$ (6)

$Q_{i,EXP}$ exported quantity of good i; $i = A,M$ (6)

$Q_{H,k,j}$ "rental units" of type k housing stock consumed by household of type j; $j = L_R,L_U,S_R,S_U,L_{US},S_{US},C$; $k = KS$ for $j = S_U,S_{US},C$; $k = US$ for $j = L_U,L_{US}$; $k = RS$ for $j = S_R,L_R$ (58)

$Q_{i,F}$ composite of primary inputs in the ith sector; $i = M,KS, PSU,US,RS,PSR$ (1)

$Q_{i,j}$ intermediate input of the jth good into the ith sector; for $i = M,KS,PSU,US$, $j = M^*,KS,PSU,A^*$; for $i = A,RS,PSR$, $j = A^*,M^*,KS,PSR$ (1)

$Q_{k,H,j}$ public services inputs of type k as an intermediate good into housing of type j; $j = KS,US,RS$; $k = PSU$ for $j = KS,US$; $k = PSR$ for $j = RS$ (3)

REB_j "shadow rebate" returning income to L_U and L_{US} households paying a shadow tax on public services inputs into their housing (thus providing marginal price effects but no *nominal* income loss)   (59)

r_i pretax returns to physical capital in sector i; $i = M,KS, PSU,PSR,US,RS,A$ (15)

r_i^* expected pretax quasi rents, after accounting for depreciation on investment per unit of physical capital in sector i; $i = M,KS,RS,A$ (17)

$\bar{r}_i$ pretax returns to efficiency capital in sector i; $i = M,KS, PSU,PSR,US,RS,A$ (15)

$\hat{r}_{H,RS}$ profitability index of the RS type of housing   (70)

$\hat{r}_{H,h,j}$ relative profitability index of the hth type of housing for households of type j; $j = L_U,L_{US},S_{US},FSC$; $h = KS$ for $j = FSC,S_{US}$; $h = US$ for $j = L_{US},L_U$ (71)

$r_{H,j}$ net of tax rate of return to structures of type j (structure rents on type j housing); $j = KS,RS,US$ (29b)

$r_{H,KS}^*$ gross of tax rate of return to KS structures (structure rents on KS housing   (29a)

$R_{U,j}$ urban land stock used in production of housing services of type (H,j); $j = KS,US$ (3)

s_j nominal saving by households of type j; $j = L_R,S_R,L_U, S_U,L_{US},S_{US},C$ (19)

S_i	skilled labor in sector i; $i = M, KS, PSU, US, A, RS,$ PSR (1)
S_R	rural skilled labor force (39)
S_{URB}	skilled labor force in urban areas (38)
S_U	skilled labor in urban "formal" sectors (38)
T	government tax revenue (48)
$TI_{M,FS}$	total nonhousing investment, in physical capital units, in the urban formal sector, excluding public services (89)
$TI_{M,i}$	total nonhousing investment, in physical capital units, in sector i; $i = R, US, A, RS, M, KS, PSU, PSR$ (86)
TI_M	total nonhousing investment in physical capital (92)
URBCAP	proportion of income of capitalists and landlords from urban sources (83)
V_A	unit value of farmland (per hectare) (18)
$V_{H,j}$	taxable value of residential property per housing service unit; $j = US, KS, RS$ (27)
$v_{i,j}$	nominal expenditures by jth households on ith commodity; $i = A, M, T, S, H$; $j = L_R, S_R, L_U, S_U, L_{US}, S_{US}, C$ (53)
$\tilde{W}_{i,L}$	efficiency wage; unskilled labor in ith sector; $i = M, KS,$ PSU, US, PSR, RS, A (7)
$W_{i,L}$	annual earnings; unskilled labor in ith sector; $i = M, KS,$ PSU, US, PSR, RS, A (7)
$\tilde{W}_{I,S}$	efficiency wage; skilled labor in ith sector; $i = M, KS,$ PSU, US, PSR, RS, A (8)
$W_{I,S}$	annual earnings; skilled labor in ith sector; $i = M, KS,$ PSU, US, PSR, RS, A (8)
Y_j^{***}	gross, nontransfer incomes of a household of type j, including imputed rents to owner-occupied housing; $j = L_R, S_R, L_U, S_U, L_{US}, S_{US}, C$ (58)
Y_j^{**}	taxable income of household of type j; $j = S_R, S_U, S_{US}$ (48)
Y_j^{*}	disposable income, including net transfers, of a household of type j; $j = L_R, S_R, L_U, S_U, L_{US}, S_{US}, C$ (53)
Z_i	raw material (imported) inputs used in ith sector; $i = M,$ KS, PSU, US, A, RS, PSR (1)

Appendix B • The Indian Economy in 1960

This appendix summarizes both the raw data sources and the procedures used for deriving model parameters from those data. Truly thorough descriptions of the data set and calibration procedures are extremely long; they are detailed in Nakajima et al. (1983) and Beider et al. (1983), respectively.

B.1 The Choice of a Base Year

We chose 1960 as our static Benchmark year for three reasons.[1] First, the year is well enumerated. A flurry of informative National Sample Survey (NSS) studies occurred around 1960, and a national census was taken in 1961. Statistical time series often begin in 1960 as well, with values reported in 1960 prices. Second, 1960–61 was also a fairly "normal" year. Rainfall was just slightly above average. World price movements were limited in the early 1960s. Foreign capital inflows were reasonably typical in 1960, which took place in the middle of the second Five-Year Plan (2FYP) era and did not represent the onset of a new epoch. In summary, it is reasonably plausible to characterize the 1960 Indian economy as being in a state of equilibrium. This is not to say that steady-state growth existed: India was in the midst of a major industrialization push that saw impressive increases in savings and industrial capital formation. But these movements were long term in nature, and 1960 did not represent a dramatic break with the immediate past.

B.2 Determining Static Parameters for BMW

In addition to specifying functional forms for the relationships among key economic variables that comprise the BMW model, one of the major tasks in implementing a mathematical model is the determination of parameter values. Ideally, all parameters would be estimated directly from observations from the Indian economy. Unfortunately, direct estimation typically is impossible for economic general equilibrium models, and the BMW model of India is no exception.

The mathematical description of the model (appendix A) lists 227 parameters relevant to the static (single-period) model.[2] Only 87 of these—primarily intermediate goods value shares, capital depreciation rates, factor substitution elasticities, and parameters relating to govern-

1. Unless stated otherwise, "1960" always refers to the period July 1960–June 1961, corresponding to the crop year.

2. This list excludes demographic, skill accumulation, and technological progress parameters, which apply only to the dynamic (multiyear) model.

ment expenditure behavior—are specified directly. In the case of depreciation rates and substitution elasticities, static consistency restrictions do not permit us to determine parameter values. Of the remaining parameters, 22 are dependent on other parameters since value shares must sum to unity, and 45 are eliminated by a priori assumptions of equality with other parameters.

Thus, 58 parameter values must be obtained indirectly. Another 15 variables exogenous to the static model have initial values that cannot be specified directly. These include the 10 production and housing service function intercepts, which depend on the units chosen to measure inputs and outputs. The remaining 5 variables consist of 2 urban housing stocks for which reliable data do not exist, and 3 imported goods prices.

The BMW model's general purpose is to calculate values for endogenous variables in hypothetical situations (counterfactual experiments), including a simulation that hypothesizes that exogenous variables take the values observed historically. It is common practice to use these historical data to "validate" the model, and this procedure involves two components.

The first component involves solution of the unknown static parameters and exogenous variables. Our procedure is a standard one for CGE modelers; it involves accumulating an extensive data set for a particular year, including information on variables that would normally be endogenous to the model's solution. The information on these normally endogenous variables is then used to solve the model "backward" to obtain the missing parameter values. Once a static data set with these newly found parameter values has been determined, the data set can be used to run the model forward. The endogenous variable solutions obtained from this exercise then can be compared with observed historical time series for a given period. As is explained in appendix C, these comparisons can be used both to determine values for key dynamic parameters and to assess the model's ability to replicate Indian history.

In the BMW model, with 73 static unknowns to be determined indirectly, a "static initial conditions" (SIC) program must be supplied with 73 pieces of information endogenous to the main model and independent in terms of the BMW equations. For example, given value shares from an input-output matrix, it would be redundant to specify both output prices and value-added prices, since the two are related by production cost functions. Development of the data list and the associated initial conditions programming strategy involves a compromise using the most reliable and accessible data and making a solution for the parameters theoretically possible, and preferably not requiring extensive iteration through complex nonlinear programming algorithms.

Table B.1 shows the distribution by method of identification of the

Table B.1. Parameters and Unknown "Exogenous" Variables of the Static BMW Model

Description	Total	Residually Determined	Specified Exogenously	Specified Equal	Indirectly Determined
			Dependent		
1. Import prices	3				3
2. Production and housing function intercepts	10				10
3. Nested CES production function substitution and share parameters	24		12		12
4. Production intermediates value shares	33		33		
5. Nonagricultural value-added shares	6	6			
6. Primary input shares in agriculture	4	1	2		1
7. CES import function parameters	4		2		2
8. Export function elasticities	2		2		
9. Export function intercepts	2				2
10. Housing sector value shares	8	3	1		4
11. Depreciation rates	10		10		
12. Urban housing stocks	2				2
13. Housing investment function parameters	4		1	2	1
14. Government expenditure parameters	9	1	8		
15. Tax rates	13		1		12
16. PSU price differential	1		1		
17. Marginal savings propensities	7		7		
18. Marginal consumption propensities	35	7	3	24	1
19. Subsistence consumption levels	35			19	16
20. Corporate dividend rates	2				2
21. Urban land rent gradient	1		1		
22. Share of capitalists in population	1		1		
23. Land ownership shares	3	1	2		
24. Capital ownership shares	8	3			5
Total	227	22	87	45	73

227 parameters and unknown exogenous variables of the BMW model. Of the 73 requiring indirect identification, most are production or housing function parameters, consumer demand parameters or tax rates. Table B.2 gives the 73 variables and relations included in the SIC model as normally endogenous information to be used exogenously in the backward solution routine. These observations include data on production, prices, labor use, tax revenues, income, and savings. Note also

Table B.2. Additional Information* Specified for the Static Initial Conditions (SIC) Model

Description	Number
Domestic output levels	7
Export levels	2
Domestic output prices	10
Posttax Z goods price	1
Composite goods prices	2
Value share of capital in manufacturing	1
Sectoral employment	10
Tax revenues	10
Ratios of tax rates	3
Taxable incomes	3
Urban–rural cost-of-living ratios	2
Total housing investment	1
Savings by household sector	5
Total corporate savings	1
Ratio of corporate dividend rates	1
Urban property values	2
Ratio of urban–rural land rental rates	1
Share of luxury housing consumed by capitalists	1
Share of rural housing consumed by skilled workers	1
Share of urban land used in luxury housing	1
Net rental rate equalities	6
Disposable income equalities	2
Total	73

*Values endogenous to the main BMW program but used as exogenous information to determine static parameters in SIC.

that 8 of the 73 pieces of information are equations—6 rental rate equalities and 2 income equalities. The general rationale for adding conditions not part of the main model stems from our interest in trends over time toward or away from equilibrium. Consequently, it is desirable to start the model off in equilibrium, so that simulated model behavior in early years will not be dominated by transient responses to an initial disequilibrium.

The 12 domestic output and composite goods prices mentioned in table B.2 are chosen to be unity simply as a matter of definition. The innocuous result of this restriction is that the units of output are fixed. Since all the sectors are aggregates of many different commodities, familiar "physical" units cannot be applied and the arbitrary definition is chosen for convenience. However, since domestic output and composite goods prices are related by the CES aggregation function, this means that the initial prices of imported agricultural and manufacturing goods cannot be independently specified but rather must be solved endogenously in SIC.

The remainder of the appendix discusses and presents the static parameters and exogenous variables. While the 73 values obtained in the backward solution SIC routine are solved for in block recursive fashion, the discussion below addresses all 227 static parameters and exogenous variables and proceeds by topic, rather than closely following the SIC solution procedure.

B.3 The Indian Production Structure

B.3.1 1960 Output (Value Added) by Sector

All nonhousing outputs are calculated by aggregating national accounts data outside the SIC program described in section B.2. Raw data for 1960 are taken from Central Statistical Office (CSO) (1963), but must be adjusted to conform to the BMW model's sectors.[3]

The M sector (urban manufacturing) includes the urban portions of factory output (Rs. 10.560b)—small enterprise manufacturing and mining. These and other urban shares are taken from Srinivasan and Bardhan (1974, p. 28). Manufacturing is also credited with a small portion of "professional and liberal arts" under the assumption that some of these are ancillary services.

Rural services and manufacturing (RS) includes the rural components of factory and small-scale manufacturing and mining. It also includes "traditional" components of rural domestic services and "other commerce and transport," which also has a modern component.

Total value added in agriculture, animal husbandry, forestry, and fishing sums to Rs. 69.000b. Of this 96.41 percent took place in rural areas and comprises the A sector. Urban agricultural activities are allocated to the traditional urban services (US) sector. US also receives the urban components of domestic services and other commerce and transport, excluding trucking services and public bus services.

The modern services (KS) sector includes skill-intensive urban services and urban public administration. It receives all banking and insurance, and all urban public administration. It receives roughly half of urban professional and liberal arts services, which is distributed in proportion to labor force (Institute of Applied Manpower Research [IAMR], 1963, p. 74), and all trucking services. The public sector domination of KS (59 percent of output is generated by public administration) is an important factor in the counterfactual simulations, since the fates of government and KS are closely intertwined. This linkage also

---

3. A detailed description of the adjustments appears in Nakajima et al. (1983, chap. 3).

creates extreme skill intensity for *KS*, reflecting the bureaucracy's use of skilled labor.

Urban public services (*PSU*) includes all communication and railways' value added, and part of professional and liberal arts services. It also includes urban bus services, which are derived from "other transport" using Manne and Rudra's (MR's) (1965) input-output table. Rural public services and public administration (*PSR*) receives rural components of bus services, professional and liberal arts services, and public administration. Rural shares of public administration and professional services value added are determined by rural shares of skilled labor employment in these sectors.

B.3.2 Housing Value Added: 1960

One of the more vexing aspects of obtaining a consistent data set for India involves estimates of housing, both in terms of structure value and services provided. The 1960 national accounts value for housing services is Rs. 5.3b, less than Rs. 13 per capita. These figures are quite inconsistent with Dholakia's (1974) residential dwelling stock valuation of Rs. 93.01b or the Reserve Bank of India's (RBI) Rs. 71.13b that he cites. As structures provide over 88 percent of input values, gross rates of return to housing implied by national account and capital stock figures are at most 6.5 to 8.5 percent; net rates must be close to zero.

Since these returns are far lower than returns to capital in private sector activities, the national accounts values imply that 1960 India was experiencing asset market disequilibrium of a sort that could not be explained merely by capital market fragmentation. Rather than accepting this disequilibrium, we choose to infer housing output values, deriving them from the SIC program.

To obtain a rural housing services (*HRS*) value, we begin by taking assumed rural housing stock (section B.5) and depreciation values. We then require that after-tax and depreciation rates of return to investments in rural housing and *RS* be equal:

$$r_{HRS} - \delta_{HRS} P_{RS} = (r_{RS} - \delta_{RS} P_M)(1 - \tau_{YA}),$$

and solve for r_{HRS}. Cobb-Douglas technology is assumed, with structures and public services the only inputs. Once public service inputs ($Q_{PSR,HRS}$) are known, the first-order condition,

$$r_{HRS} H_{RS}/(P_{PSR} Q_{PSR,HRS}) = \alpha_{HRS}/(1 - \alpha_{HRS}),$$

can be solved for α_{HRS}, structures' share in *HRS*. P_{PSR} is set equal to unity in the base year, while $Q_{PSR,HRS}$ is determined residually to equal total *PSR* gross output, less inputs into *A* and *RS* sectors, where these inputs are determined by the input–output table. Then the input demand efficiency condition,

$$r_{HRS} H_{RS}/(P_{HRS} Q_{HRS}) = \alpha_{HRS},$$

can be solved for Q_{HRS}.

Determining urban housing values is somewhat more complex, as the housing sector includes both modern (*HKS*) and traditional and squatter (*HUS*) settlements. We assume public service value shares in both *HUS* and *HKS* housing are the same ($\alpha_{PSU,HKS} = \alpha_{PSU,HUS}$), but that low-quality housing inhabitants pay a higher (shadow) price for their public amenities. It is somewhat arbitrarily assumed that the cost of obtaining a unit of public services is 7.5 times greater for the poor than for the rich.

To derive urban housing service values, begin by noting that the value of a unit of an infinite life structure must be

(B.1a) $\quad V_{HKS} = \dfrac{P_{HKS}}{i_{FS} + \tau_{HKS}} [1 - \alpha_{PSU,HKS}]$

(B.1b) $\quad V_{HUS} = \dfrac{P_{HUS}}{i_{IFS}} [1 - \alpha_{PSU,HUS}],$

where τ_{HKS} is the property tax rate applied to high-quality housing. Then, with prices normalized to unity, it is approximately true that

$$V_{HUS}/V_{HKS} = (i_{FS} + \tau_{HKS})/i_{IFS}.$$

Assuming (as seems overwhelmingly likely) that the property values estimated by Dholakia and the RBI capture both structure and site values, we have information available on total property values (PROPVAL$_i$ ≡ $Q_i V_i$) of both housing types. Hence,

(B.2) $\quad \dfrac{Q_{HUS}}{Q_{HKS}} = \dfrac{\text{PROPVAL}_{US} \cdot V_{HKS}}{\text{PROPVAL}_{KS} \cdot V_{HUS}} = \dfrac{\text{PROPVAL}_{US} \cdot i_{IFS}}{\text{PROPVAL}_{KS} \cdot (i_{FS} + \tau_{HKS})}$

Now, equality of public amenity value shares and an assumption of Cobb-Douglas technology for both *HUS* and *HKS* housing implies

(B.3) $\dfrac{Q_{PSU,HUS} \cdot (7.5 \, P_{PSU})}{Q_{HUS} P_{HUS}} = \dfrac{(Q_{PSU,H} - Q_{PSU,HUS}) \, P_{PSU}}{Q_{HKS} P_{HKS}}$,

so that, collecting terms and substituting from equation B.2,

(B.4) $Q_{PSU,HUS} = \dfrac{Q_{PSU,H} \cdot \text{PROPVAL}_{US} \cdot i_{IFS}}{\text{PROPVAL}_{US} \cdot i_{IFS} + 7.5 \cdot \text{PROPVAL}_{KS} \, (i_{FS} + HKS)}$

Once $Q_{PSU,HUS}$ is known, given information on public amenities provided to households (i.e., $Q_{PSU,H}$), $Q_{PSU,HKS}$ can be determined residually. Since the return to HUS property must equal the value of housing services provided less the cost of public service inputs,

$$\text{PROPVAL}_{US} i_{IFS} = P_{HUS} \cdot Q_{HUS} - 7.5 \, P_{PSU} Q_{PSU,HUS}$$

then can be solved to yield a value of Q_{HUS}. Q_{HKS} can be solved for in a similar fashion.

B.3.3 Intermediate Input Use

BMW assumes that sectoral production can be described by a nested CES function over primary factor inputs, combined with a Cobb-Douglas relationship over intermediates and value added. This specification generates constant intermediate input value shares, enabling derivation of intermediate demands from sectoral value-added values and an input–output (IO) table. Intermediate demands then yield the gross output figures in table B.3.

Deriving an IO table consistent with BMW sectoral definitions is tedious and is detailed in Nakajima et al. (1983). The IO table consists of six producing sectors (*A, M, KS, PSU, PSR,* and *Z*) and ten absorbing sectors (*A, RS, M, KS, US, PSU, PSR, HKS, HUS,* and *HRS*). *RS* is not included as a producing sector, although it contains rural manufacturing. This exclusion is a practical one: no spatial division of manufactured intermediates is available, the rural share of large-scale factories' net output is only 20 percent, and most of these factories are likely to be plantations and food-processing industries.

We rely on MR's (1965) thirty-sector input–output table for 1960 India. In addition, the 1963 IO table of Venkatramaiah, Kulkani, and Argade (VKA) (1972) is also used.[4] MR's main limitations are an absence of spatial content and unsurprising aggregation of nonrail trans-

---

4. These particular IO tables are used because of their proximity to 1960 and because

Table B.3. Output by Sector: India, 1960

	Value Added (Rs. billion)	% of Nonhousing Total	Gross Output* (Rs. billion)	% of Nonhousing Total
Rural sectors:				
A	66.309	48.4	73.641	41.7
RS	14.535	10.6	16.913	9.6
PSR	5.460	4.0	5.775	3.3
Total rural	86.304	63.0	96.329	54.6
Urban sectors:				
M	18.533	13.5	37.066	21.0
KS	13.151	9.6	20.183	11.4
US	13.201	9.6	16.461	9.3
PSU	5.881	4.3	6.431	3.6
Total nonhousing	137.070	100.0	176.470	100.0
Housing:				
HRS	5.769			
HUS	1.988			
HKS	4.426			
Total housing	12.183			

*Excluding diagonal entries.

port, banking and insurance, communications, public administration, domestic services, trade and commerce, and housing services sectors into just two categories: "trade, transport, and indirect taxes," and "industries not included elsewhere." Restriction of BMW's IO matrix to off-diagonal elements undoubtedly reduces the errors generated by these aggregations, but does not eliminate them. Finally, the MR value-added figures differ substantially from those recorded in the national accounts. Consequently, it is necessary in most cases to convert their table to shares of gross output, rather than simply using flow values.

The purpose of including an imported Z goods input in BMW is to capture realistically those commodities not produced domestically (or those facing severe output constraints). Their presence is important to understanding how India's economy interacts with the rest of the world. Z goods include the imported components of chemical fertilizer, petroleum products, and crude oil. We assume that the noncompeting imported component of these goods' *intermediate* use is proportionate to the importance of imports in their total availability. Z goods shares of these products are: 34.08 percent (chemical fertilizer intermediates),

---

they cover most of the BMW model's sectors. Other input–output tables for India are available in Ghosh (1968, 1973) and Saluja (1980).

25.88 percent (petroleum products), and 92.77 percent (crude oil). While all nonhousing sectors use some Z goods inputs, 43 percent are consumed by the M sector; most of the rest go to the transport industry components of KS, PSU, and PSR. Table B.4 gives the 1960 commodity flows among industries and from Z inputs.[5]

The distribution of intermediates produced by PSR is not well documented. However, PSR output is consumed only by A, RS, and HRS, so that allocation problems are not severe. HRS consumption is limited mainly to electricity; estimates of the rural–urban (and HKS–HUS) division of household electricity consumption are derived from the NCAER (1972, pp. 71–72) and CSO (1978, table 239). A and RS consume public transport services and electricity, but estimates of consumption of irrigation, extension services, and other public services are unavailable. Nevertheless, since PSR produces only intermediates, these demands must sum to gross PSR output. Accordingly, we assume that the unknown component of intermediate demand for PSR goods is distributed in the same proportion as the components for which we have information and scale up known demands to sum to gross output.

A similar scaling procedure must be used for PSU. In this case, directly estimated intermediate input use exceeds 75 percent of gross output, reducing the degree of uncertainty surrounding IO values. Household electricity use is allocated by rules comparable to those used for HRS consumption estimates. PSU's transport services are not consumed directly by individuals in BMW, and they are allocated to urban producing sectors in proportion to unskilled labor employment.[6]

Manufactured intermediates are provided mainly to urban and rural construction, which are assumed to account for all uses of glass, wooden, and nonmetallic mineral products and which absorb 71 percent of off-diagonal M^* intermediates. Urban construction use of M^* products is restricted to modern sector (KS) construction, thereby undoubtedly understating M^* flows to the US sector. However, any alternative assumption would have been equally arbitrary, and it is likely that KS absorbed the vast majority of these intermediates. The allocation procedures for petroleum products and chemical fertilizers are the same as those for imported Z goods. Rubber products (mainly vehicle tires) are allocated in proportion to estimated transport industry use.

Finally, intermediates provided by the KS sector are limited to provision of motor transport. Financial services are thus assumed to be

5. US and RS uses of Z (and other) goods are combined in MR; thus their shares are assumed to equal rural and urban weights in the construction industry (the only industry for which MR provides a rural–urban breakdown).

6. However, *private* transport services are consumed directly; see B.8.2.

Table B.4. Interindustry Commodity Flows, 1960 (Rs. billion)

Consuming Sector	Producing Sector					
	Z	A*	PSR	M*	KS	PSU
A	Chemical fertilizers 0.103 Petroleum products 0.048 0.151		4.703	Chemical fertilizers 0.200 Petroleum products 0.138 Food industries 0.550 Jute textiles 0.039 Coal 0.010 Rubber products 0.033 1.029	Motor transport 1.157	—
RS	0.044	Forestry products 0.076 Other 0.649 0.725	0.665	Manufacturing for rural construction 0.694 Other 0.110	Motor transport 0.098	—
PSR	Petroleum products 0.069	0	—	Petroleum products 0.199 Rubber products 0.042 0.241	0	—
M	Petroleum products 0.084 Crude oil 0.404 0.488	Forestry products 1.021 Food grains 0.230 Plantations 0.712 Other agriculture 11.333 13.296	—		Motor transport 0.334	Railways 3.326 Electricity 0.955 Urban bus services 0.151 4.432

Continued on next page

Table B.4. Continued

KS	Petroleum products 0.170	Forestry products for construction 0.613	—	Petroleum products 0.486 Manufacturing for construction 5.610 Rubber products 0.084 6.180		Urban bus services 0.069
US	0.080	Forestry products for construction 1.188	—	Other 0.201	Motor transport 0.061	Rail transport 1.171 Bus services 0.200 Rail used in "other services" 0.367 1.738
PSU	Petroleum products 0.133	0	—	Petroleum products 0.380 Rubber products 0.042 0.422	0	
HRS			0.407	—	—	Electricity —
HUS			—	—	—	Electricity 0.076
HKS			—	—	—	Electricity 0.116
Totals	1.135	15.822	5.775	8.877	1.650	6.431

270

produced solely for final consumption. Perhaps surprisingly, VKA indicates that agriculture consumes over 70 percent of all road transport. In contrast, manufacturing uses more than twice as much railway transport. Presumably, these differences reflect the greater penetration of roads into agricultural areas.[7]

It is straightforward to go from table B.4 to table B.5, which presents the BMW model's IO coefficients. The entry in the ith row and jth column gives the fractional contribution of intermediates produced by sector i in the total output of sector j.[8] The IO coefficients document the dependence of urban manufacturing on other sectors, along with agriculture's autonomy. This asymmetry suggests that urban leakages will be far greater than rural ones on the production side—in contrast to and offset by the greater rural demand leakages associated with Engel effects.

Over time, Indian agriculture's structure has changed strikingly, necessitating changes in the agricultural production coefficients in column 1 of table B.5. Fortunately, detailed data on intermediate input use by agriculture is available in CSO (1975, table C.1). These changes reflect growing input use associated with adoption of "green revolution" packages and growing mechanization.

7. Note, too, our assumption that producing sectors sell goods CIF: that is, they are responsible for the delivery of products to the next using sector, or to the consumer. One would have different IO entries if the sales were assumed to be FOB, with larger gross outputs in the service sectors. Difficulties in making allocations among the nonhousing service sectors make this latter procedure more imprecise.

8. The urban housing coefficients derived here are not used. Instead, the two IO coefficients are assumed to be identical and acquire a value that exhausts available *PSU* output.

Table B.5. Input-Output Coefficients, 1960

Producing Sector	Consuming Sector									
	A	RS	PSR	M	KS	US	PSU	HRS	HUS	HKS
A*	d	0.042	0.000	0.358	0.030	0.072	0.000	—	—	—
PSR	0.064	0.039	d	—	—	—	—	0.179	—	—
M*	0.014	0.048	0.042	d	0.167	0.012	0.066	—	—	—
KS	0.016	0.006	0.000	0.000	d	0.004	0.000	—	—	—
PSU	—	—	—	0.120	0.002	0.105	d	—	0.083	0.043
Z	0.002	0.003	0.012	0.013	0.005	0.005	0.021	—	—	—
Value-added shares of gross output	0.904	0.862	0.946	0.500	0.797	0.802	0.914	0.821	0.917	0.957

d: "diagonal" entries excluded

B.3.4 Other Production Parameters

Recall from appendix A that all sectors other than agriculture and housing have nested CES production functions. Each contains a multiplicative constant A_i (or $A_{H,i}$) term. Once outputs, factor inputs, and all other technological parameters are known, these constants are given by the equalities imposed by equations 1 to 3. These base year A_i parameters thus act as scale factors, translating units of capital and labor into units of output.

For the outer and inner nest substitution elasticities (σ_i and σ_i', respectively), we take estimates provided by Fallon and Layard (FL) (1975). They estimate nested CES production function parameters using international cross-section data from 1961–63, with capital, skilled labor, and unskilled labor as the primary inputs. Their sample covers twenty-three nations at various stages of development and includes India. Their definition of skilled labor as that with eight or more years of schooling clearly is highly correlated with our definition of administrative and professional workers as skilled.

FL's sectoral allocation is limited to mining, manufacturing, construction, and electricity-gas-water (EGW). Their manufacturing conforms closely to our M sector. EGW obviously is similar to BMW's PSU, although it does not include the bureaucracy and transport components. Our KS and PSR sectors have components of EGW, while KS also contains some construction activity. Following Kelley and Williamson (KW) (1984), we take the KS sector's substitution elasticities to be an average of the EGW and construction elasticities. We then restrict substitution elasticities for the public service sectors to be less than or equal to those for KS, following a "stylized fact" that public sectors are less flexible than private sectors. Thus, the three heavily public sectors, PSU, PSR, and KS, all have substitution elasticities that are low relative to the main private sectors, M and A (for which σ and σ' are restricted to unity by the Cobb-Douglas formulation).

FL's sectors provide little guide for parameterizing US, though the construction sector comes closest. We choose the US elasticities to represent the stylized fact that substitution possibilities are considerable in the private service sectors, though relatively less so between skilled labor and capital.

Finally, BMW's RS sector includes substantial components from mining, as well as manufacturing and construction. Given the substantial uncertainty and aggregation involved, we took KS parameter values for RS, but adjusted them to ensure that SIC generated the observed A/RS investment ratio. This procedure is discussed in appendix C. The outcome of this solution is to yield RS substitution elasticities lower than all other sectors (see table B.6).

The SIC consistency program is needed to determine the ξ_i and ξ_i' production function share parameters. In the nested CES functions, ignoring sectoral subscripts, efficiency conditions imply

$$\xi' = \left[1 + \frac{W_S}{r} \left(\frac{S}{K} \right)^{1/\sigma'} \right] - 1$$

Table B.6. Production Parameter Values for the Static BMW Model

1. Unskilled Labor/Composite Capital Substitution Elasticity

		Unskilled Labor/Composite Capital Share Parameter	
σ_{RS}	0.800	ξ_{RS}	0.5455
σ_{PSR}	0.900	ξ_{PSR}	0.9758
σ_M	1.110	ξ_M	0.7029
σ_{KS}	0.930	ξ_{KS}	0.8630
σ_{US}	1.100	ξ_{US}	0.3703
σ_{PSU}	0.930	ξ_{PSU}	0.5980

2. Skilled Labor/Capital Substitution Elasticity

		Composite Capital Share Parameter	
σ_{RS}'	0.615	ξ_{RS}'	0.7651
σ_{PSR}'	0.700	ξ_{PSR}'	0.3610
σ_M'	0.850	ξ_M'	0.6320
σ_{KS}'	0.730	ξ_{KS}'	0.5116
σ_{US}'	0.700	ξ_{US}'	0.9495
σ_{PSU}'	0.600	ξ_{PSU}'	0.9798

3. Production Function Intercepts

A_A	1.0296	A_{US}	2.3155
A_{RS}	2.1025	A_{PSU}	1.0619
A_{PSR}	2.8431	A_{HRS}	0.1395
A_M	4.7243	A_{HUS}	0.3839
A_{KS}	5.3306	A_{HKS}	0.2869

4. Agriculture and Housing Share Parameters

$\alpha_{K,A}$	0.1485	$\alpha_{H,HRS}$	0.9875
$\alpha_{R,A}$	0.2700	$\alpha_{PSR,HRS}$	0.0125
$\alpha_{H,HUS}$	0.7365	$\alpha_{H,HKS}$	0.8375
$\alpha_{PSU,HUS}$	0.0442	$\alpha_{PSU,HKS}$	0.0442
$\alpha_{R,HUS}$	0.2193	$\alpha_{R,HKS}$	0.1183

5. Depreciation Rates

δ_A	0.0300	δ_{US}	0.0500
δ_{RS}	0.0800	δ_{PSU}	0.0193
δ_{PSR}	0.0204	δ_{HRS}	0.0490
δ_M	0.0457	δ_{HUS}	0.0490
δ_{KS}	0.0319	δ_{HKS}	0.0169

and

$$(B.5) \quad \xi = \left[1 + \frac{W_L}{P_\phi} \left(\frac{L}{\phi} \right)^{1/\sigma} \right] - 1.$$

Thus, given wages, P_ϕ, substitution elasticities, and factor inputs, share values can be determined. This solution itself requires equilibrium wage (section B.8.1) and rental rates. Rental rates for US, PSU, and PSR are determined residually, using Euler's theorem. That is, r_i equals value added less all factor payments other than capital, divided by K_i. Net rental rates in RS and KS are equated to those in A and M, respectively. Finally, capital share values for A and M and land's share in A are taken from Dholakia (1976) to derive r_A and r_M. Land's share in agriculture secularly declined over time; we adjust by reducing $\alpha_{R,A}$ from 0.27 in 1960 to 0.21 by 1979.

The initial source for depreciation rate estimates is Dholakia (1974, p. 190). δ_{RS} is taken to be an average rate for nonagricultural machinery and rural construction; δ_{PSR} is taken to be the depreciation rate of public irrigation facilities; δ_{KS} is taken as the rate for urban nonresidential construction; δ_M is set at the rate for the nonagricultural machinery; and δ_A is taken from rates for agricultural implements and machinery, plantation construction, plantation machinery, and farm structures. L. C. Gupta (1969) provides an estimate of δ_{PSU}. δ_{US} is assumed to be an average of δ_{KS} and δ_{RS}. We use Dholakia's (1974) urban housing estimate of 1.93 percent for δ_{HKS}, but his values for HRS and HUS seem implausibly low. We instead use 4.9 percent for these housing types, an intermediate value from Sinha (1976, pp. 117–19).

Obviously, considerable uncertainty surrounds true values for δ_A, δ_{RS}, and δ_{US}, and these values affect other variables endogenous to SIC. Consequently, these depreciation rates were adjusted when the resulting revised consistent data set generated by SIC had more plausible solution values elsewhere. In particular, sectoral labor distributions and factor shares were constrained to take plausible values.

The remaining production function parameters pertain to housing's factor shares (table B.6). Rates of return to structures in HRS, HUS, and HKS are equated to rates of return in RS, US, and KS, respectively. Factor shares can then be obtained, given efficiency conditions and estimates of rural housing stock and public services inputs. Urban land rental rates are linked to the rate of return to land in agriculture; this rate, plus information on land use in housing and housing services output is used to determine $\alpha_{R,HUS}$ and $\alpha_{R,HKS}$.

How plausible are these estimated housing and production parameter values? At the very least, they appear to be consistent with the limited

Table B.7. Factor Input Shares in Value-Added and Composite Capital, by Sector

Sector	Value-added Share				Composite Capital (ϕ) Share	
	L	ϕ	K	S	K	S
A	0.454	0.247	0.165	0.082	0.669	0.331
RS	0.331	0.669	0.260	0.409	0.388	0.612
PSR	0.027	0.973	0.161	0.812	0.165	0.835
M	0.315	0.685	0.334	0.349	0.490	0.510
KS	0.137	0.863	0.249	0.614	0.288	0.712
US	0.666	0.334	0.242	0.092	0.725	0.275
PSU	0.419	0.581	0.371	0.210	0.639	0.361

information available. KW (1984) draws on Muth (1971) to employ a land output elasticity in urban housing of 0.1; we use land stock estimates that yield output elasticities of 0.12 for *HKS* (modern) housing and 0.22 for *HUS* (traditional and squatter) housing. Land unit values are typically less for *HUS* housing, and *HUS*'s greater land share reflects this stylized fact.

The estimated production parameters, together with first-order efficiency conditions, can be used to derive factor shares (table B.7). Quite plausibly, unskilled labor has the largest shares in *A* and *US*. Capital shares in *PSU* and *M* are larger than elsewhere, and are lowest in rural nonmanufacturing activities. Skilled labor earns the majority of income in both sectors with large public administration components, *KS* and *PSR*. The only rather surprising outcome is skilled labor's high share in *RS*. This *RS* distribution reflects an aggregation cost, since *RS* skilled are concentrated in only a few professional services categories.

B.4 The Employment Distribution

Indian employment data are remarkably comprehensive. In fact, the skilled/unskilled labor division for urban sectors can be generated independently of SIC. However, we are unable to confidently distribute rural skilled workers by sector.

Skilled workers include professional and technical workers; administrators; some working proprietors; manufacturers' agents; aircraft pilots; navigators; some road transport drivers; railway supervisors; traffic controllers; telephone, telegraph, and related telecommunication operators; some fire fighters; some electricians and precision instrument makers; and some farmers and farm managers. The remaining labor force is defined as unskilled.[9]

9. The detailed description of these occupational groups is given in National Sample

Obviously, many skill levels exist among these skilled occupations, and determining the cutoff point between skilled and unskilled is somewhat arbitrary. Still, we avoid defining labor groups by educational achievement for several reasons. Educational achievement is but one element of a vector of skill determinants. Moreover, the fact that many unskilled or semiskilled urban jobs are filled by workers with many years of schooling (often of low quality) gives the misleading appearance of great need for educated workers in the cities. The occupation-based definition of skill also permits BMW to be consistent with labor market segmentation theories. If "skilled" jobs are allocated according to rules only tangentially related to labor quality, then it will be inappropriate to define skilled labor along education status lines.

Finally, if skill status is determined solely by education, it would be necessary to project dramatic skill deepening. The stock of "educated" (matriculate and above) Indian workers grew at an annual rate of 6.6 percent (Dholakia, 1974, p. 137).[10] Employment in professional and administrative occupations grew less than half as rapidly and began from a 1960 level (7.345m) that was only modestly greater than the stock of educated workers (5.162m). Therefore, barring an implausible rise in administrative and professional workers' skills, many newly educated workers did not find "skilled" positions. Furthermore, 6 to 7 percent growth in the skilled labor force along with capital stock growth rates of 5 to 6 percent provide forces that would work to dramatically raise unskilled wages (and probably factor shares). History records far less dramatic rises. Nor is India's slow growth easily associated with dramatic skill deepening.

Labor force estimates rely on NSS16 and IAMR (1963). Both present sectoral employment estimates by rural and urban location. Agricultural workers include rural agricultural cultivators and laborers, plantation workers, and forestry, fishing, livestock, and hunting workers. Some 36 percent of the A labor force (and 34 percent of all rural workers) are women; only 15 percent (of whom a large majority are in US) of urban workers are women, implying that urban women are in occupations omitted by national income statistics. This large rural–urban differential in female labor force participation, combined with far higher proportions of rural than urban workers belonging to "scheduled" castes or tribes,

Survey, (round 16, NSS16, 1960, table 4.12, pp. 29–30). See also Nakajima et al. (1983, chap. 2).

10. The educational flow statistics given in the *Statistical Abstract: India 1977* (SA1977: CSO, 1977, p. 501) suggest flows at least twice as great as Dholakia's, as well as larger stocks. See Nakajima et al. (1983, p. 29).

ensures that urban and rural productivity will differ, even correcting for skill type.

IAMR (1963, p. 74) provides an occupational classification of public sector employees used to determine *PSU*, *PSR*, and *KS* employment. There is no option but to make the strong assumption that all central and state government employees are urban (and hence in the *KS* and *PSU* sector), while all local government and quasi-government establishment employees are rural. *RS* employment is then determined as the residual rural labor force.

The *PSU* skilled labor force can be inferred from NSS16's (1960, table 4.12) detailed occupational classification; the remaining public sector skilled are assigned to *KS*. For unskilled workers, urban public clerical and sales workers are assigned to *KS*; the remainder are allocated to *PSU*.

NSS16 (table 3.7) also provides a total rural skilled labor force figure of 4.471 million. This number is reasonably consistent with CSO (1978, pp. 500–509) 1960–61 rural enrollment figures (10,825,714 secondary and middle school plus 361,583 university students) and Dholakia's (1974, p. 113) combined rural stock estimate of 2.5 million educated at these levels. However, the *PSR* skilled figure implied by IAMR is inconsistent with output and total employment figures, and so is determined in SIC.

M sector activities are readily separated in IAMR and NSS16; all remaining urban workers therefore must belong to *KS* or *US*. *US* skilled workers are defined as those in urban agriculture and (from NSS16, 1960, table 4.12) in wholesale and retail trade; the skilled residual accrues to *KS*. The *KS* unskilled consist of various clerical workers; *US* then receives the residual.

The remaining task is to determine rural skilled–unskilled ratios. In agriculture, gross output plus output shares of land, capital and intermediate inputs are known; thus the total wage bill is known residually. Equating *RS* and *A* net rates of return permit us to derive capital's share of *RS* value added; the *RS* wage bill then follows. Given wages rates, total labor shares, and total sectoral employment, Euler's theorem then makes calculation of *A* and *RS* skill categories straightforward. L_{PSR} and S_{PSR} are then determined residually from total rural stocks. A final residual in this semirecursive system is *PSR*'s capital rental share.

Strikingly, rural skilled labor exceeds urban skilled labor (table B.8). In contrast with KW's (1984) "representative developing country" (RDC), 1960 India is far more rural (Table B.9). Much of this difference lies in India's larger rural nonagricultural sector. As in BMW, KW's skilled labor ratios are vastly greater in the modern services sectors than elsewhere in the economy.

Table B.8. Sectoral Employment Distribution: India, 1960

	Skilled Labor	Unskilled Labor	% Skilled	Total Employment
	(millions)			(millions)
A	4.578	132.422	1.2	134.000
RS	1.601	24.440	6.1	26.041
PSR	1.292	0.667	66.0	1.959
Rural total	4.471	157.529	2.8	162.000
M	1.103	7.043	13.5	8.146
KS	1.336	2.371	36.0	3.707
US	0.234	10.577	2.2	10.811
PSU	0.201	3.235	5.8	3.436
Urban total	2.874	23.226	11.0	26.100
India total	7.345	180.755	3.9	188.100
% Urban	39.1	12.8		13.9

Table B.9. Labor Force Distribution (%) by Skill and Sector: India (BMW) and Kelley-Williamson's (KW) "Representative Developing Country"

Sector	Unskilled (L)		Skilled (S)		Total (L + S)	
	KW	BMW	KW	BMW	KW	BMW
A	60.1	70.4	0.0	0.8	60.0	71.2
Other rural	7.3	13.3	0.0	1.5	7.3	14.9
Total rural	67.4	83.7	0.0	2.4	67.4	86.1
M	9.7	3.7	2.5	0.6	12.2	4.3
US	10.0	5.6	0.0	0.1	10.0	5.7
KS + PSU	2.9	3.0	7.5	0.8	10.4	3.8
Total urban	22.6	12.3	10.0	1.5	32.6	13.9
Total	90.0	96.1	10.0	3.9	100.0	100.0

B.5 Sectoral Capital Stocks

The main sources available for determining capital stocks are Dholakia (1974), Mukherjee (1969), Wolf (1978) and V. K. R. V. Rao (1983). While these studies differ in some respects, they mostly complement each other. Dholakia establishes the most consistent estimates available, but excludes "government administration" (while including public enterprises), for which we use Mukherjee's estimates. Obviously, valuing public infrastructure is a highly speculative activity.

Urban and rural capital–output ratios in agriculture are assumed to be identical for the purpose of allocating agricultural capital. Similar equalities are assumed for both large- and small-scale manufacturing. Nevertheless, since M is dominated by large-scale manufacturing and

RS's manufacturing component is mainly small scale, *RS* manufacturing is much less capital-intensive than *M*'s.

Estimates of capital employed in trade are allocated to *US* and *RS* in proportion to urban and rural output shares, excluding structural capital, which is attributed to "modern" *KS* trading facilities. *KS* trade certainly includes some inventories and *US* and *RS* trade some structures, but a more sophisticated allocation is not possible. All capital in "other services" and "transport animals" also is divided between *RS* and *US* in proportion to their services' components outputs.

KS capital includes construction assets, banking industry capital, private vehicles, public administration infrastructure, and structures used in private trade. Location of all inventories in the *RS* and *US* sectors both adds substantially to their capital stocks and enhances the skilled labor-intensive nature of *KS*.

PSR capital consists largely of public irrigation facilities. Its electricity infrastructure is determined from CSO (1972, pp. 166–67), assuming *PSR* provides electricity used in agriculture and rural industry and commerce. A small portion of capital in "vehicles excluding bullock carts" is allocated to *PSR* to account for rural public buses. *PSU* contains the remaining electricity capital, as well as vehicles for urban public buses. It also receives all railway, shipping, communication, airways, and other transport companies' capital, less those buildings and structures used for public enterprise administration (included in *KS*).

Public administration capital is allocated to *KS*, *PSR*, and *PSU* in proportion to skilled employment levels (table B.9). Capital–output ratios (even after adjustments discussed below) in *PSU* and *PSR* are high, although by far the largest amount of India's 1960 capital stock is in agriculture.

The *PSU* and *PSR* stocks in table B.10 imply implausibly low rates of return. The fundamental problem is that much *PSU* and *PSR* output is not sold competitively and may face a subsidized or zero price. Thus, public service value added is calculated on a factor cost basis, but capital rents are typically undervalued or omitted altogether. We must therefore alter national accounts statistics or adjust capital stock figures to achieve a plausible rate of return. Both options require one to choose an essentially arbitrary rate of return to infrastructural capital. We chose to adjust capital stocks and altered them to yield net rates of return of about 5 percent.[11] The resulting capital estimates are *PSR*: Rs. 15.000 b; *PSU*: Rs. 28.834 b.

---

11. Alternatively, we could have paid out interest at the same rate on the additional capital to government (thus preserving private sector income and expenditure patterns), with government spending this unrecorded "income" on subsidies to the *PSU* and *PSR*

Table B.10. Nonhousing Capital Stock Estimates, by Sector

Sector	Components	Total	
		(Rs. billion)	
A	Agricultural implements and bullock carts	12.00	
	Farm houses, sheds, barns	11.00	
	Private land improvement and irrigation	36.25	
	Livestock	33.46	
	Working capital in agriculture	6.51	
	Plantations, forestry, fisheries	3.94	
	Rural share of agriculture (96.62%)	103.16	99.663
RS	Rural manufacturing and mining	11.279	
	Rural trade	10.560	21.843
PSR	Public irrigation	16.870	
	Rural electricity	2.894	
	Public bus services	0.800	
	Public administration	7.770	28.334
M	Urban manufacturing and mining	29.631	29.631
KS	Construction	1.800	
	Banks, other finance	1.380	
	Private vehicles	2.020	
	Structures and construction in administration of public enterprises	2.350	
	Private commerce	1.740	
	Public administration	8.230	17.520
US	Urban agriculture	3.497	
	Urban trade and commerce	19.346	22.843
PSU	Railways	27.460	
	Shipping, etc.	1.350	
	Communication, airways and other transport	3.040	
	Urban electricity	8.846	
	Urban public bus services	0.800	
	Less: structures used in administration of public enterprises attributed to KS	(2.350)	
	Public administration	2.100	41.246

Dholakia's (1974, p. 17) aggregate structure values are used in determining housing stocks. Assuming equal urban and rural housing stock–output ratios, H_{HRS} is determined. The urban housing breakdown is determined in SIC. Dholakia's urban housing values almost certainly incorporate site as well as structure values and are regarded as property values. As land is the only other primary input into housing services,

---

sectors (that now incur losses, as factor payments exceed revenues). The options would yield fairly similar outcomes; the main difference would be greater intermediate input use, particularly by the A, KS, and M sectors.

total structure values H_{KS} and H_{US} can be determined residually, given land rents and the rate of return on structures.

This return depends on i_{FS}, determined in SIC as a weighted average of the marginal productivities of M and KS capital, and on the land rental rate (d_{KS}^*), which is equated to the rate on agricultural land. Structure returns (r_{HKS}) are equated to a weighted average of net rates of return to assets that compete with structures for savers' funds. As noted, the site value R_{KS} and R_{US} terms are consistent with Muth's (1971) estimate of land output elasticities of about 0.1 for "modern" housing. As US housing is likely to be somewhat more land intensive, we use an HKS land elasticity of 0.1183 and a HUS land elasticity of 0.2193 determined in SIC iterations. The final housing values are thus:

	HRS	HUS	HKS
	(Rs. billion)		
Housing stocks (H_i)	45.390	8.805	24.467
Property values (PROPVAL$_i$)	—	14.830	32.790
Site values (R_i)	—	3.620	4.350
	(%)		
Gross structure rental rates	12.7	17.4	15.9
Gross land rental rates (d_i')	—	—	13.4

B.6 Government's Role in the Indian Economy

BMW has sixteen revenue sources and eight expenditure outlets for general government, which combines the union and state government accounts. Tax rates are determined in SIC (table B.11) by taking the ratio of tax yields to estimated tax base values.

The tax yield on rural intermediate use of manufactures $(\tau_{A,M})$ is taken from CSO (1966, pp. 385–90). It is separated from the general excise tax on M to stress the lightly taxed nature of the rural sector and to permit focused fiscal policy experiments. Personal income tax rates depend in part on effective rate differences facing different tax-paying classes. Along with tax yield and interclass tax "wedge" (TWDG) information, raw data on per worker earnings are provided exogenously (section B.8.1); tax rates are then easily determined. Raw data on personal income tax payments are given in CSO (1978). Matthew (1968) and Gandhi (1966) distinguish between personal taxes paid by agricultural and other workers, and this distinction serves as the basis for the TWDGs. Somewhat arbitrarily, we assume that informal sector workers face a wedge only about half that faced by skilled workers.

The statistical abstracts also serve as the basis for revenue figures for corporate income tax and other tax revenue. CSO (1962, pp. 485–87)

Table B.11. Government Parameter Values in BMW

Taxes	Rate (%)	1960 Yield (Rs. billion)
Personal income tax		
Rural skilled workers	2.02	0.442
Urban informal sector skilled	4.68	0.064
Urban formal sector skilled workers and capitalists	8.36	2.263
Corporate income tax		
M Sector	17.21	0.865
KS	8.60	0.232
Import duties		
A Sector	71.28	0.509
M	15.84	1.514
Z	3.91	0.043
Export tariffs		
A Sector	17.46	0.328
M	11.78	0.453
Sales tax on manufactures	50.00	6.639
Property tax on HKS housing	0.10	0.031
Tax on manufactured goods used as intermediates in RS and A	7.11	0.122
Total tax revenue		13.505
Nontax revenue (includes all foreign capital inflows)		
Foreign aid and capital inflows		4.856
PSR profits remitted to general government		0.569
PSU profits remitted		1.584
Total nontax revenue		7.009
Total government revenue		20.514
Ratio of urban informal sector skilled to rural skilled workers' income tax rate, TWDG$_1$	2.32	
Ratio of urban formal sector skilled to rural skilled workers' income tax rate, TWDG$_2$	4.15	
Ratio of KS to M sectors corporate income tax rate, TWDG$_3$	0.50	

Expenditures	% of total	
KS Goods		11.814
M: Investment		8.700
Investment allocation: sectoral breakdown		
A	0.00	0.000
RS	7.50	0.652
PSR	15.42	1.342
M	14.44	1.257
KS	27.58	2.399
US	0.00	0.000
PSU	35.06	3.050

Government savings rate: 42.41%

Figures refer to union and states' combined accounts.

is used to distinguish sectoral corporate tax revenue and rates. Property tax revenue data and resulting rates are from CSO (1970, p. 487). Disaggregated customs revenue figures are given in CSO (1966, table 146), while traded commodity values by type are obtained from RBI (1963, p. 22).

τ_M reflects excise taxes on the use of manufactures for consumption. This tax incorporates a myriad of actual taxes and serves as a residual. Hence, its yield is determined as the difference between recorded tax revenue and all other tax revenue. The rate chosen is then modified by iterating in SIC to derive a plausible τ_M value (0.50) that also yields plausible consumer demand parameters. This tax reflects the multiple imposition of fees on mobile items (the "octroi" system) as well as standard excise taxes, so that the high figure is not unexpected.

Expenditure and investment data can be determined from national accounts data. As government is assumed to control foreign capital inflows, government savings are determined as a residual that ensures equality of aggregate savings and investments. Public investment divided by the sum of tax revenue, nontax revenue, and foreign aid then gives the government's savings rate. As foreign capital inflows are counted as government savings, this rate will vary with inflows from abroad.

While figures do exist that could be used to estimate the sectoral allocation of government investment directly, such estimates would only capture *gross* effects. They would not capture the net impact of government investment policy on a sector, since we do not have estimates of the loss to particular savings pools (and hence sectoral investments) from government borrowing. Instead, BMW treats government debt increments as private savings activity that is invested in the pool from which the savings are drawn. Equivalently, government is forced to balance its budget in BMW, and recorded public investment is limited to that not made by borrowing from the public. Since the sectoral distribution of the borrowed fund component is unknown, so is the distribution of the nonborrowed component. Instead, these latter funds are allocated residually, ensuring that aggregate public and private sectoral investments equal observed values for those sectors with substantial public investments.

B.7 Housing and Physical Capital Investment

Data on combined M and KS corporate savings are given by Khatkhate and Deshpande (1971, p. 109). They report net savings; to this we add replacement investment. Outside the M and KS sectors, BMW assumes that all capital income is paid out to its owners. Estimates of housing investment are available from Sinha (1976, table 1.8) and CSO (1975), but the numbers reported are consistent only with implausibly low housing stock depreciation rates or a decline over time in the nation's housing stock. Instead, we infer an investment level that implies full replacement investment for depreciated assets and that permits housing stocks to grow at a rate equal to the labor force growth rate (table B.12).

SIC also requires information on the distribution of high-quality housing. In this case, the Committee on Distribution of Income and Levels of Living (1960) reports figures on the proportion of urban housing stock owned by the top decile in the income distribution (roughly the proportion of skilled workers and capitalists in the population). Sinha (1976, p. 104) reports values for various types of housing styles; we assume that the best of these were occupied by urban capitalists and rural landlords. These values are then taken as a proportion of the sum of high quality urban housing stock plus landlords' housing stocks; urban skilled workers' housing stocks are a residual.

Housing investment equations are restricted to have the same values for ϵ_H and θ_H. Thus, equation 71 becomes:

$$(B.6) \quad I^N_{H,h,j} = \theta_H \left[\hat{r}^{\epsilon_H}_{H,h,j} - 1 \right];$$

$$j = \text{consumer groups}$$
$$h = \text{housing types}$$

As $\hat{r}$ is an index of the return on housing investment relative to "productive" investments, ϵ_H can be interpreted as private investors' response elasticity to differentials in housing and nonhousing rates of return. We follow KW and choose a moderately high but hardly infinite value for ϵ_H, 3.0.

SIC raw data requirements include household (and unincorporated business) savings for five groups: rural and urban skilled and unskilled, and capitalists/landlords. Savings breakdowns by income class and rural or urban location are available in Khatkhate and Deshpande (1971, pp. 109–12) and NCAER (1972, table 21). Unfortunately, the resulting propensities imply an implausible deterioration in unskilled households' housing. Sufficient savings are instead allocated to each class to ensure that they are able to meet their 1960 housing depreciation requirements. The remaining private savings stock is allocated so that the ratios of their average propensities to save (*APS*) given in the 1972 NCAER survey are maintained. The resulting implied household savings estimates (Rs. 11.14b) are close to the national accounts Rs. 11.42b estimate of total household savings less unskilled housing replacement investment. But these latter values include unincorporated business savings treated as retained earnings in BMW and therefore must be removed

Table B.12. Housing and Nonhousing Investment and Savings Characteristics: India, 1960

A. Nonhousing investment, by sector

	Total	Total State and Union Government Investment	Private and Public Enterprise Nonreplacement Investment	Total Replacement Investment	Gross of Tax and Depreciation Rate of Return to Capital, %
			(Rs. billion)		
A	5.495	0.000	2.505	2.505	10.97
RS	3.037	0.652	1.013	1.747	15.97
PSR	2.657	1.342	1.164	0.306	5.84
M	2.822	1.256	0.815	1.354	21.54
KS	2.947	2.399	0.444	0.559	18.56
US	1.690	0.000	0.548	0.548	15.64
PSU	3.607	3.050	0.000	0.557	7.42
All nonhousing	22.255	8.699	6.489	8.655	

B. Housing Investment, by Sector

	Investment	Gross Rate of Return to Housing Stock, %
HRS	2.547	12.71
HUS	0.210	17.40
HKS	2.215	15.85
Total	4.972	

C. Per Worker Savings

	R,L	R,S	US,L	U,L	US,S	U,S	C
Total savings, Rs.	10.0	738.8	19.8	19.8	561.6	561.6	1682.2
Housing investment, Rs.	5.2	385.7	19.8	0.0	561.6	351.1	1051.7
Nonhousing investment, Rs.	4.8	353.1	0.0	19.8	0.0	210.5	630.5
Average propensity to save (%)*	2.87	14.55	1.80	1.80	8.80	8.80	15.24
Marginal propensity to save (%)	5.50	23.09	3.70	3.70	17.40	17.40	24.04

D. Asset Income Distribution to Households (%)

	R,L	R,S	US,L	U,L	US,S	U,S	C
Capital shares							
Rural	50.3	17.7	0.0	0.0	0.0	0.0	32.0
Urban informal	0.0	0.0	99.4	0.0	0.6	0.0	0.0
Urban formal	0.0	0.0	0.0	52.0	0.0	2.9	45.1
Land shares							
Rural	48.5	24.4	0.0	0.0	0.0	0.0	27.1
Housing shares							
HRS	78.6	21.4	0.0	0.0	0.0	0.0	0.0
HUS	0.0	0.0	45.5	54.5	0.0	0.0	0.0
HKS	0.0	0.0	0.0	0.0	4.3	48.7	46.9

Table B.12. *continued*

E. Aggregate Savings, by Source (Rs. billion)	
Corporate net savings	1.067
Unskilled rural labor's gross savings**	1.576
Skilled rural labor's gross savings	3.303
Unskilled urban labor's gross savings	0.461
Skilled urban labor's gross savings	1.614
Gross savings of capitalists and landlords	1.851

F. Miscellaneous Parameter Values	
ψ_m: M sector corporate payout (dividend rate)	0.835
ψ_{KS}: KS sector corporate payout rate	0.835
ϵ_H: Housing/nonhousing rate of return differential response elasticity by private savers	3.000
θ_H: Constant term in private savers' housing/nonhousing allocation function	0.113
α_{KM}: Capital's share in M sector gross output	0.1722

*Savings expressed relative to disposable income, but including imputed rents on housing.
**Figures *include* replacement investment for depreciated housing, but *exclude* replacement investment for private, noncorporate physical capital.

from estimates of pure "household" savings. Therefore, the household *APS*s are scaled down to yield the 1960 national accounts figures.

Our estimates of the housing investments reflect savings pool estimates. These restrictions immediately yield the rural skilled housing investment. To divide total *HKS* housing investment between skilled urban workers and capitalists/landlords, we assume that initial investments are proportionate to the share of the *HKS* housing stock each group owns.

Corporate savings by sector, housing investment by sector, private investment by sector, and θ_H remain to be determined. Furthermore, sectoral investment allocations are determined by rates of return to capital in each sector, which depend on the amount of savings used up in housing investment, which in turn depends on interest rates. This interdependency cannot be collapsed into a small-dimensional system of *N* equations and *N* unknowns because of discontinuities in functional forms. Consequently, the system of equations is determined in SIC by iterating until (in practice, readily) convergence is obtained.

Corporate savings depend heavily on factor incomes, which depend on capital's share in manufacturing (taken from Dholakia, 1976). Given $\alpha_{M.K}$, r_M can be inferred; assuming net rate of return equalization yields r_{KS}. Net *M* and *KS* profits are then found by accounting for corporate income taxes and depreciation. Assuming equal *M* and *KS* net capital income earnings retention rates yields corporate dividend rates, ψ_M and ψ_{KS} (table B.12, part F). Using these corporate dividend rates, rental rates, and capital stocks, capital ownership shares for the urban skilled are obtained by subtracting wages from total taxable income, assuming real incomes for each skill class are equated across sectors. To solve for housing investment shares, θ_H, and the proportion of capitalists' and landlords' incomes obtained from urban sources (URBCAP), SIC follows a long loop. Housing investment is first subtracted from the appropriate savings pools to obtain nonhousing investments. These are then distributed among the component sectors, and the resulting interest rates i_R and i_{FS} are calculated. Investment is allocated within savings pools to equalize expected sectoral net rates of returns. Then, given all other sources of capitalist income and i_{FS}, a new value for URBCAP is obtained. As interest rates determine the relative attractiveness of housing investment, θ_H can be solved for so as to attain the observed level of housing investment, thus allowing for recalculation of the investment shares and a return to the top of the loop. If an initial set of estimates does not yield a solution, SIC returns to the top of the loop and inputs the new value of URBCAP. In practice, convergence has not been a problem.

B.8 Workers' Incomes and Demands

B.8.1 Incomes

As values for employment, output, and nonhousehold consumption of goods and services are largely specified exogenously, most income and expenditure parameter values must be solved for in SIC. The first step involves calculating the number of capitalists and landlords, a class assumed not to engage in productive activity. Minhas (1974, p. 260) reports that there were 437,000 rural households with landholdings above fifty acres in 1960, while NCAER (1972, p. 63) reports some 461,000 rural and 402,000 urban households above the "middle-class" range in 1967. Converting 1967 households to 1960 workers gives a total of 587,000 rural landlords and 513,000 urban capitalists, for a combined total of 1.1 million. Income estimates for the groups are given by the NCAER studies; a weighted average is used in aggregation.

After capitalists, the next 10.8 urban percentiles comprise the skilled labor category, assuming that all professional and administrative (skilled) workers fit into the income distribution right below the capitalist class. NCAER surveys indicate that this group earned about 33 percent of urban disposable income, and hence a slightly greater fraction of taxable income. For skilled workers, we use an estimate from Nakajima et al. (1983, p. 107) that they earned 37.9 percent of urban taxable income, implying an income of Rs. 6082 (table B.13). These figures are above but close to estimates of per family income of those whose heads

Table B.13. Income per Worker and Related Parameters

Household Group	Per Worker Income (Rupees)			Wage Rate (Rs.)	% of Gross Income from	
	Gross	Taxable	Disposable		Labor Income	Rents on Capital, Land and Housing
R,L	348	319	348	227	65.2	34.8
R,S	5,176	4,900	5,077	3,432	66.3	33.7
US,L	1,100	1,011	1,100	782	71.1	28.9
U,L	1,100	1,011	1,100	782	71.1	28.9
US,S	6,658	5,847	6,385	5,789	87.0	13.0
U,S	6,894	6,082	6,385	6,022	87.4	12.6
C	11,875	10,000	11,038	—	0.0	100.0

Initial parameters and exogenous variables:
COL_L: urban–rural cost-of-living ratio for unskilled workers, 1.00.
COL_S: urban–rural cost-of-living ratio for skilled workers, 1.00.
CML: annualized psychological and monetary cost of moving from rural to urban areas, unskilled workers, Rs. 555.
CMS: annualized psychological and monetary cost of moving from rural to urban areas, skilled workers, Rs. 2155.
C: number of capitalists, 1.10 million.

are administrative or professional workers (see NCAER, 1967, pp. 111–12).[12]

The NCAER study also suggests that the rural skilled earned 14 to 21 percent of rural income. The wide range stems from uncertainty concerning the rural household-to-worker conversion. As rural female labor force participation rates are high, it is likely that the proportion of households with a skilled worker are substantially greater than the proportion of rural workers who are skilled. Calculations indicate a 1960 rural skilled worker's taxable income in the range of 2500 to 4000 rupees. The true figure probably lies around the upper end of this range. A 1962 NCAER survey (NCAER, 1972, p. 68) finds an average *household* income for the top rural decile of Rs. 4359. As skilled workers are only 2.75 percent and landlords only 0.36 percent of the rural labor force, it is clear that the rural skilled come from households with average incomes above the NCAER figure; we settle on an estimate of Rs. 4900.

The *CML* and *CMS* terms introduce a wedge between rural and urban earnings. They incorporate the flow value of financial and psychological migration costs and labor quality differences due to the far higher proportions in rural areas of secondary workers and "scheduled castes and tribes." Consequently, we choose *CML* and *CMS* values that are consistent with plausible income, capital share, and demand patterns, thereby effectively endogenizing the terms.

12. The 1967–68 NCAER survey (1967, p. 62) reports that salaries were the source of 51.6 percent of all urban income. If the urban skilled workers' share of taxable income was 35 percent, then the implied per worker income for that group would be Rs. 5613. To this must then be added rents on owner-occupied housing.

The other exogenous data on incomes and demand patterns are rural land and housing share distributions. Data on the distribution of rural land ownership are taken from Minhas (1974, p. 260). The urban housing stock distribution is discussed above (section B.7), while the rural distribution is based on the assumption that a rural skilled worker owns housing worth about 60 percent of his urban counterpart's.

To determine wage rates, we start with sectoral total value-added and capital shares, from which labor shares in M and KS can be determined. Since both employment levels are known for both sectors, one solves for unskilled and skilled wage rates. Urban informal and rural skilled and unskilled wages are then determined by equating them to the (net of tax and wedge) urban formal sector wages for their labor type.

Determining total incomes involves adding up income sources. For capitalists and landlords, given URBCAP and landlords' land ownership share, their ownership share of rural capital can be obtained residually from their nonurban income. The rural skilleds' capital income share is similarly determined; residual capital income then goes to the rural unskilled. This capital income, plus their land rents, wages, and shadow rents on owner-occupied housing gives peasant incomes. Similar restrictions on urban workers' incomes can be used to determine the distribution of urban formal and informal sector capital earnings, and hence total incomes.

B.8.2 Demand Parameters

Our objective here is to choose demand parameters consistent with the findings of Lluch, Powell, and Williams (LPW) (1977), with Indian consumer expenditure surveys and consumption demand estimates (particularly Ray, 1980), and with previously determined sectoral outputs. Most important are parameters consistent with the largest consumption expenditure: peasants' food demand. Rao (1983, p. 83) reports a food share in peasant expenditures of 61.96 percent, while Ray (1980, p. 601) gives a peasant income demand elasticity (ϵ) for food of 0.72. Then, since the ELES equations in appendix A (53–56) imply $\beta_{ij} = \delta v_{ij}/\delta Y_j^*$, it follows that $\beta_{11} = 0.446$ as

$$(B.7) \quad \epsilon_{ij} = 0.72 = \beta_{ij} \cdot \frac{Y^*}{v_{ij}} = \frac{\beta_{ij}}{.6196}$$

LPW's estimates (1974, pp. 46–47) for the poorer countries in their sample suggest that food expenditures will comprise about 60 to 65 percent of total required expenses, which are about 55 to 65 percent of total expenditures. Peasants' γ_A/Y^* is then found to equal 52 percent after solving the restriction

$$(\gamma_A/Y^*) + 0.446 \, (Y_{desc}/Y^*) = 0.6196.$$

Once the discretionary income (Y_{desc}) share is known, we can solve backward for γ_A and the peasant worker's marginal propensity to save (MPS).

To obtain a marginal propensity to save for urban workers, note that for any class, savings equals $MPS \cdot Y_{desc}$; therefore, $MPS/APS = Y^*/Y_{desc}$. Now certainly Y_{desc}/Y^* is no smaller for urban unskilled than for rural unskilled workers. We further restrict all households to have the same ratio of one β to another, with differences in actual β values resulting only because workers have different MPS values. This restriction and Rao's (1983, p. 83) finding of urban unskilled workers' food shares in total consumption of about 0.6 together yield an equation in which the urban unskilled γ_A is an implicit function of Y_{desc}/Y^*.

Y_{desc} and hence MPS values for the skilled and capitalists/landlords are chosen to replicate observed savings patterns. Actual increments in household income and savings between 1960 and 1967 are calculated, generating a national household net savings marginal propensity of 14 percent. We then restrict these groups' MPS's to achieve an aggregate 14 percent MPS, given 1960–61 observed group employment growth rates and income shares, and assuming that the three high income groups' MPS maintained a ratio to one another consistent with that found by Bhalla (1980, p. 740).

Economywide averages for the remaining β terms are taken to be the unweighted average of LPW's estimates for Korea, Thailand, the Philippines, and Panama. Economy-wide βs must sum to $1 - 0.14 = 0.86$; for any given class of workers the βs are scaled up or down to equal that group's marginal propensity to consume. These estimates also appear to be consistent with Ray's estimates for India.

The remaining γ parameters include those for housing. These are found by solving for each group j the demand equation

$$\gamma_{H,j} = P_{H,j}\gamma_{H,j} + \beta_{H,j}Y_{desc_j},$$

since we have already determined housing consumption patterns. The $\gamma_{T,j}$ are determined by substituting consumption share estimates from Rao (1983, p. 77). We further restrict all workers to have the same required T good expenditure and for total expenditures on KS (including T) goods to sum to total production. The resulting γ is Rs. -8.2, but there is no obvious problem in accepting a slightly negative consumption intercept. The $\gamma_{S,j}$ (traditional services) are found in a manner analogous to that for T goods. The γ_M values are not restricted by equality of demand and supply, as manufacturers are traded internationally. However, SIC has to choose γ_M values that replicate sales tax revenues and that yield urban–rural cost-of-living ratios of unity.[13] These restrictions, along with expenditure shares taken from Rao, yield M consumption intercepts. The remaining γs are for A; they are given residually by the household budget constraints. The full set of consumption parameters is given in table B.14. Note that the decline across income classes in the proportion of disposable income devoted to unprocessed, unprepared food overstates the decline on all food products, since processed food is recorded as a manufacture, and prepared food is part of services output.

B.9 The Foreign Trade Sector

BMW replicates observed trade patterns (table B.15). Figures on imports and exports by sector are derived from the World Bank (1981, tables 3.2 and 3.3); the sources for customs tax revenues are mentioned in section B.6. The η_i export price elasticity terms (45) are taken from Dervis, de Melo, and Robinson (DDR) (1982, pp. 224–30). Finally, SIC requires input data on the substitution elasticity between domestic and imported goods in "composite" agriculture, A^*, and urban manufacturing, M^*, as given by $\sigma_{i,COM}$ in the CES aggregation functions (6).

As noted, our treatment of international trade closely follows Armington (1969) and DDR (1982). While DDR's trade elasticities fit the Indian historical experience well, their substitution parameters do not. Actual and predicted exports and sectoral shares were compared for the period 1960–65; the differences were then used to adjust the σ_{COM} estimates. Since India is a partially closed economy, with trade policies containing many bureaucratic obstacles to rapid adjustment to price changes, it is unsurprising that these iterative procedures yield σ_{COM} values considerably lower than DDR's values for Turkey.

The iterative procedure used in deriving σ_{COM} values consistent with historical import trends follows our procedure for estimating rates of technological change (appendix C). However, it is important to note

13. Actual cost-of-living ratios are a matter of dispute. However, they do not appear to be great, and we start off the model by assuming that they are nonexistent (i.e., COL_j = 1). The estimate made by Chatterjee and Bhattacharya (1974, p. 195) is that the 1963 living costs for poor urban households were about 12 percent higher than for poor rural households, and about 20 percent higher for top income classes. As accommodating these differences would force us to choose a dual price structure and to explain those differences in a manner consistent with our model, these modest initial differences are ignored.

Table B.14. Consumption Parameters and Patterns: India, 1960

			Worker/Household Group			
Good	R,L Rural Unskilled	R,S Rural Skilled	U,L and US,L Urban Unskilled	U,S and US,S Urban Skilled	C Capitalists/ Landlords	Economywide Average
			I. β Parameters: Shares of Marginal Expenditure			
A*	0.446	0.363	0.455	0.390	0.359	0.406
T	0.090	0.073	0.092	0.079	0.072	0.082
M*	0.129	0.105	0.131	0.112	0.103	0.117
S	0.186	0.151	0.189	0.162	0.149	0.169
H	0.094	0.077	0.096	0.083	0.076	0.086
Marginal propensity to save	0.055	0.231	0.037	0.174	0.240	0.140
			II. γ Parameters: Required Consumption Expenditures (Rs.)			
A*	123.3	270.5	371.7	−190.3	−1438.1	
T	−8.2	−8.2	−8.2	−8.2	−8.2	
M*	15.1	415.3	51.1	615.3	292.1	
S	16.5	958.5	84.7	1884.7	3604.7	
H	12.0	33.6	37.8	588.7	1443.7	
			III. Per Worker Consumption Expenditures, by items (Rs.)			
A*	204.4	1432.5	625.9	1068.1	1071.6	
T	8.1	226.4	41.1	245.9	498.6	
M*	30.7	638.6	98.0	857.1	774.2	
S	50.3	1442.2	186.3	2368.5	4649.4	
H	29.2	279.6	89.5	855.2	1975.2	
Disposable income spent on unprocessed food, %	58.7	28.2	56.0	16.7	9.7	

Table B.15. Foreign Trade Parameters and Values

	Sector		
	A	M	Z
Parameters and exogenous variables			
η: export price demand elasticity	2.5	2.5	
σ_{COM}: elasticity of substitution	3.0	2.25	
ψ_i^*: import share parameter in			
Armington commodity aggregate	0.0056	0.1200	
$\bar{P}_i^W$	0.0019	0.0576	0.9624
$\bar{Q}_{i,EXP}^O$	17,837,839.0	6,386.5698	
Trade flows and shares			
		(Rs. billion)	
Imports, actual	2.9843	7.2852	1.0919
Imports, SIC	0.7142	9.5553	1.0919
Exports	1.8770	3.8470	
Q_i	72.9873	44.2880	

that in this case, every time we change $\sigma_{A,COM}$ or $\sigma_{M,COM}$, it is necessary to adjust both the other initial conditions *and* the other dynamic parameters estimated by forcing the model to track an observed set of variables for a period of time.[14]

Determining the remaining parameters in SIC is straightforward. The first step is to calculate domestic demand Q_i^* for each imported good by summing over intermediate use, investment demand, and final consumption demand. For A and M, since both domestic output and composite goods prices in 1960 are unity, the first-order condition for the CES aggregation becomes, from (46):

$$(B.8) \quad 1 - \psi_i^* = \left[\frac{Q_i - Q_{i,EXP}}{Q_i} \right]^{1/\sigma_{COM.i}},$$

$$i = A, M$$

where ψ_i^* is the share of imports in the "production" of the composite good, and $Q_i - Q_{i,EXP}$ equals total domestic production of good i for use in domestic consumption. As all righthand terms in B.8 are known, the aggregation import shares are determined.

14. This parameterization method could have been (but was not) extended to the η_i terms. In tracking total trade and its distribution we have essentially three independent variables (Z imports are determined separately; knowing values of both other imported goods plus capital inflows and the value of one exported commodity implies the remaining exported good's value). As we currently use only two controls to adjust three targets, further assistance could have been used. In practice, however, DDR's values for η_i performed well.

From B.8, one can return to equation 6 and solve for import quantities. Thus, information on demand, production and exports yields imports residually. In practice, the overidentification here provides a useful check on the plausibility of several variables determined previously in SIC or in the raw data adjustments. The estimated import quantities were sufficiently close to the actual ones that no further data modifications were made.

The absence of a scaling parameter in equation 6 makes it impossible to define all initial prices related to traded goods as unity, since the units would be inconsistent. World prices of these goods must be solved for using first-order efficiency conditions. CIF prices can be derived readily, and once the import tariff rates are determined (section B.6), world prices follow immediately. The final parameter to be determined in SIC is $Q_{i,EXP}^{O}$; once P_i^{W} is known it can be determined from equation 45.

Appendix C • Dynamic Parameters

This appendix briefly describes the methods used in deriving dynamic parameters, the data sources used in determining these parameters, and time series used to assess the BMW model's performance. The notes are necessarily brief, but they should enable the reader to understand our methodology and main data sources.

Once static parameters have been estimated, static counterfactual simulations of the 1960 Indian economy can be run. To simulate an annual time series, the static data set must be updated to conform to the conditions of successive years. Part of the alterations to the data set are generated by the static solution itself: an endogenously determined investment vector adds to sectoral capital stocks in the following period. In addition, we must document and incorporate those exogenous variables that help drive the economy over time. These variables include world price trends for internationally tradable goods, skilled and unskilled labor force growth, productivity advance by sector, and growth in urban sites and rural arable land stocks.

C.1 Exogenous Variables Series

C.1.1 Population and Employment

Because BMW is a model of labor force behavior, we do not distinguish between labor force and population growth: only the former matters. Employment data from three decennial series of India, in 1961, 1971, and 1981, serve as the cornerstone for the construction of key labor force time series. In addition, these data are critical in constructing time series for sectoral real output, sectoral investment, and sectoral relative price indices.

The primary labor force data sources are the national censuses (CSO, 1961, 1971, 1974, 1981a). Section 3.3 discusses the comparability problems and provides growth estimates. Because of shifts in definitions that appear to limit the counting of secondary workers in 1971 and 1981, recorded aggregate labor force growth is far below the recorded 1961–81 population growth rate of 2.21 percent. There are no obvious reasons to anticipate the dramatic decline in national labor force participation rates (LFPRs). Indeed, Premi (1982) records the prime age male population growing at roughly 2.5 percent, while 1971 and 1961 age pyramids (United Nations, 1981, p. 83) do not show an obvious pattern of change. Nor, to our knowledge, has there been independent confirmation of cohort-specific LFPR declines in India. We therefore assume that participation rates were constant over the period and that the aggregate employment growth rate equalled the national population growth rate.

Skilled labor growth rates are based on estimates of professional and administrative employment growth based on the National Sample Surveys (calculated from *Sarvekshana,* various issues); unskilled employment growth is therefore taken as a residual. Skilled labor force is thus assumed to grow at 3.8 percent during the period 1960–81; unskilled labor grows at 2.1 percent.

C.1.2 Land Expansion

Land stock expansion is difficult to estimate. Physical expansion of virgin land probably was quite limited during the 1960s and 1970s. Effective land expansion was not, though, as irrigated areas grew. BMW uses an estimate of 1 percent annual agricultural land stock growth, a figure based on Sanderson and Roy's (1979, p. 158) estimate of gross cropped area growth between 1960–61 and 1975–76. As no estimates of effective urban land growth are available, we assume that total land available for urban housing grew at the same rate as rural agricultural land. These numbers are also identical to those employed by Kelley and Williamson (1984, p. 244), except that KW assume R_A growth declines to 0.5 percent after 1973. As India's second green revolution appeared to maintain its momentum through the late 1970s, BMW did not incorporate a similar slowdown.

C.1.3 World Prices

As mentioned in the text, the world price of manufactures serves as the model's numeraire and is thus set equal to unity in all periods. Imported A and Z goods are thus defined relative to manufacturing. Time series on these prices are taken from the World Bank (1981, table 3.6); trends are shown in table 6.1.

C.1.4 Foreign Capital Inflows and Government Savings

Capital inflows are determined residually as the difference between gross domestic investment and recorded gross domestic savings, using the gross domestic capital formation deflator to put both series into real terms. Government savings are taken directly from the *National Accounts Statistics* (NAS) (CSO, 1975, 1979, 1981b, 1984). As noted, the model assumes that all capital inflows are received by government, so that the public sector savings pool includes both government savings and capital inflows.

C.1.5 Government Investment Allocation

As is discussed in appendix B, the public sector investment allocation is properly a residual to the extent that total investment in each savings pool must be greater than or equal to that generated by private savings. We periodically alter government savings parameters to meet this consistency requirement, which is determined once sectoral investments are determined (C.2.4). Government investment shares are given in table C.1. While these patterns tell little about intrapool capital allocation (and also exclude public enterprise replacement investment), the lack of support for private rural and urban informal sector activities is apparent.

C.1.6 Rainfall Patterns

The series is taken from Sanderson and Roy (1976, pp. 24–25) for the period 1960–76. Thereafter, the index is set to unity. The monsoon quality index they offer is based on an aggregate of thirty-one geographical regions. The index is necessary, given the striking variability of

Table C.1. Trends in Government Investment Shares (% of Total Investment Allocated to Each Sector)

				Sector			
Year	A	RS	PSR	M	KS	US	PSU
1960	0.0	11.7	27.0	0.0	19.9	6.3	35.1
1965	0.0	12.5	20.2	14.0	17.6	1.5	34.2
1972	0.0	12.5	14.2	14.0	23.6	1.5	34.2

rainfall in India and given that agriculture is by far the most important sector throughout the period of analysis.

C.1.7 Tax Rates

Tax rates are altered periodically in the model in order to capture secular shifts in government fiscal activity. Data on real government tax revenue and its distribution according to tax type are taken from the NAS and *Statistical Yearbooks*. For the most part, government revenue expands naturally as the economy grows; we are reluctant as well to alter public sector parameters. Nonetheless, several striking changes in fiscal patterns did occur during the early 1960s (table C.2), and we incorporate them. No changes in tax parameters are made for years beyond 1965. Obviously, the main changes to occur were the increased protection of manufactured imports, coinciding with the development of India's own industrial sector, and the increased reliance on corporate income taxes.

C.1.8 Agricultural Use of Intermediate Inputs

Changes in agricultural use of intermediate inputs are described in appendix B. The NAS serves as the data source for these changes (table C.3). The remarkable time series generated by the NAS documents the

Table C.2. Changes in Tax Parameters (%)

Year	$\tau_{IMP,M}$	$\tau_{\pi,M}$	$\tau_{\pi,KS}$	$\tau_{IMP,Z}$	$\tau_{EXP,A}$	$\tau_{S,M}$
1960	15.8	17.2	8.6	3.9	17.5	50.0
1961	22.8	19.8	9.9	5.9	16.5	52.0
1962	29.8	22.8	11.4	7.9	15.5	54.1
1963	36.8	26.2	13.1	9.9	14.4	56.2
1964	43.8	30.1	15.0	11.9	13.5	58.5
1965	50.8	34.6	17.3	13.9	12.5	60.8

Table C.3. Adjustment to the Agricultural Sector's Intermediate Share Coefficients

Producing Sector	Year								
	1960	1964	1965	1972	1976	1978	1979	1980	1981
PSR	0.064	0.074	0.074	0.085	0.088	0.091	0.096	0.096	0.096
M	0.014	0.014	0.030	0.047	0.053	0.056	0.069	0.063	0.065
KS	0.016	0.016	0.016	0.016	0.016	0.016	0.016	0.016	0.016
PSU	0.000	0.000	0.000	0.000	0.000	0.000	0.000	0.000	0.000
Z	0.002	0.002	0.010	0.020	0.022	0.024	0.031	0.031	0.033
Value-added share	0.904	0.894	0.870	0.833	0.821	0.813	0.788	0.794	0.790

rise of manufactures and petroleum products as intermediate inputs in agriculture; it also documents the marked decline in value-added share.

C.2 Time Series for Assessing the Historical Counterfactual

C.2.1 Sectoral Employment and Urbanization

Sectoral employment data are needed for deriving output and other series, and so are discussed first. Raw census data come from CSO (1961, 1971, 1981a). As discussed in chapter 3, imperfect comparability of definitions adds considerable uncertainty to both our aggregates and sectoral divisions.

The first issue involves aggregating census employment data into the four urban and three rural sectors that employ labor directly in our model. We are extremely fortunate in that the censuses do provide urban and rural employment by industrial classification. However, these classifications do not match exactly across censuses. The 1961 census uses the ISIC (International Standard Industrial Classification) delineations, while those for 1971 and 1981 depend on the Indian Census Economic

Table C.4. Employment Allocation to BMW Sectors from ISIC/ICEC Categories

Rural Employment

Agriculture (A)
  Agriculture: cultivators and agricultural laborers
  Fishing
  Forestry

Rural services and manufacturing (RS)
  Mining
  Manufacturing
  Hotels and restaurants
  Land and water transportation
  Storage services
  Banking, insurance, real estate, and business services
  Recreation and personal services
  Construction, excluding road, telegraph, waterway, and hydroelectric projects
  Wholesale and retail trade

Rural public services and public administration (PSR)
  Electricity, gas, and water
  Railroads
  Pipelines and bridges
  Air transportation
  Communication
  Public administration
  Sanitary and medical services
  Construction of roads, telegraph, waterway, and hydroelectric projects

Table C.4. *Continued*

Urban Employment

Urban manufacturing (M)
 Mining
 Manufacturing and repair services
 Construction of industrial plants

Modern/capital-intensive urban services (KS)
 Motor freight, water, and pipeline transportation
 Storage
 Banking, insurance, real estate, and business services
 Public administration
 Legal and educational services
 Recreation services
 International services
 Electrical installation
 Wholesale trade in textiles, chemicals, petroleum, stationery, machinery, rubber,
   clocks, and medical supplies
 Welfare services and trade organizations

Informal urban services (US)
 Urban agriculture
 Urban fishing
 All nonmechanized transportation
 Personal services
 All urban services not elsewhere classified
 Activities related to construction (e.g., plumbing and tile setting)
 Wholesale trade in wood, skins, furniture
 Religious and community services

Urban public services (PSU)
 Electricity, gas, and water
 Railroads and tramways
 Air transportation
 Communication
 Sanitary and medical services
 Public construction, including telephone lines, waterways, dams, and hydroelectric
   projects

Classification (ICEC) distinctions. Fortuitously, an obscure section of the 1961 census (CSO, 1961, vol. 1, pt. II-A(ii), p. xlviii) provides the necessary information to match the classifications. Armed with this information, we then distribute workers to the seven employing sectors. As all censuses distinguish urban from rural employment, the critical decisions involve (1) determining total urban and rural labor force growth, and (2) allocating urban workers to the *M, KS, US,* and *PSU* sectors, and rural workers to the *A, RS,* and *PSR* sectors. Table C.4 describes this allocation; further detail is provided in appendix B, and numbers are provided in table 3.9.

As mentioned, Indian employment data across the censuses are not strictly comparable. This is due primarily to differences in the effective definition of when an individual is in the labor force. Briefly, people qualified as belonging to the 1961 labor force if they responded that their "gainful occupation" was "working" in the *two weeks* prior to enumeration. In 1971, people were included in the labor force if their "main activity" was "working" in the *one week* prior to enumeration. Finally, people qualified for inclusion in the 1981 labor force by responding that they worked for 50 percent or more of their waking hours during the *preceding year*. These definitional distinctions produced startling results when the 1971 data were released: LFPRs appeared to have decreased during the 1960s for both males and females in both urban and rural areas. Most strikingly (and implausibly), the rural female labor force was reported to have fallen from 56 to 28 million workers.

There has been no consensus in India as to how to treat the noncomparability problem. From December 1971 to June 1972 the census resurveyed a sample of its original enumeration.[1] Unfortunately, the resurvey did not settle the issue. The adjusted LFPRs still declined from 1961 to 1971–72. Although the declines were smaller than those implied by the original 1971 census, they were still implausibly great, especially for rural women.

As noted above, our response was to assume constant aggregate LFPRs during the period 1960–81. But what of the urban–rural and sectoral allocations? First, it is apparent from table 3.9 that the regular census at least did not produce any dramatic discontinuities in trends across the three census dates.[2] Still, this is not to imply that sectoral labor force shares were unaffected by the definitional changes. On the contrary, it is most likely that the *A, RS,* and *US* sectoral employment growth and hence growth rates were underestimated by the enumeration changes that removed many part-time workers in 1971 and, to a lesser degree, in 1981.

For lack of a viable alternative, we nonetheless use the unadjusted census numbers to determine urban and rural labor force *shares* as the basis of comparison with our historical counterfactual simulation, although the total labor force is constrained to grow at the population growth rate. The census breakdowns are also used to allocate workers to specific sectors. The resulting bias is quite clearly to overstate the

---

1. The results are discussed in CSO (1974).

2. Nor did it produce any great aberrations with regard to the patterns of the labor force distribution based on the 1973 (round 27) and 1977 (round 32) NSS surveys. These are detailed in *Sarvekshana* (various issues) and Seal (1981).

"observed" growth of the *PSR*, *M*, *KS*, and *PSU* sectors and conceivably to overstate the rate of growth of urban employment.

C.2.2 Sectoral Output

Once employment distribution series and labor force growth rates have been determined, the next step in building a data set to compare the model's historical counterfactual simulation with is to construct a real output series. The NAS (CSO, 1975, 1979, 1984) reports two series on gross value added: a series in constant 1961 prices running from 1960 through 1970, and a series in constant 1970 prices running from 1970 through 1982. Both series are disaggregated into thirty-one industrial groupings. It is a simple matter to convert these output series into a single 1961 price series, since the two series overlap in 1970.

It is not as straightforward to distribute the NAS output figures to BMW's ten sectors. In particular the NAS figures do not provide the needed rural–urban breakdown. To bridge this gap, we rely on census employment figures. A detailed discussion of this procedure for 1960 is given in appendix B; similar allocations are made for 1961, 1971, and 1981.

Clearly, if labor productivity by industry did not vary across urban and rural areas, output within each disaggregated sector simply could be distributed, in proportion to the rural–urban employment distribution, to its urban or rural sector in our model. But the assumption of equal rural and urban productivity within an industry is obviously inappropriate, even at a thirty-one–sector level of disaggregation.

Fortunately, urban–rural productivity ratios by industrial classification were given in the 1981 issue of the NAS (CSO, 1981b, p. 150). As these data were provided for just one year, 1970, we were forced to use 1970 ratios for both 1971 and 1981. As appendix B discusses briefly, estimates from labor force and other surveys enabled us to determine 1960 sectoral outputs and productivity gaps; these gaps were assumed to be the same in 1961. Given these estimates of productivity (strictly, average gross product) differentials, then, for any industrial category, the share of urban output was estimated as

(C.1) $\quad s_u = PG \cdot L_u / (PG \cdot L_u + L_r)$

> where s_u = urban share of total output
> L_u = urban employment
> L_r = rural employment
> PG = "productivity gap": ratio of urban to rural *APL*.

This procedure gives sectoral output shares for the three census years. Linear interpolation over PG, L_u, and L_r can then be used to obtain an annual time series on urban-rural output shares by each disaggregated industrial category. The final step is to apply these output shares to gross value-added numbers in the NAS. Then aggregation from industrial categories to our model's sectors yields a full time series on sectoral gross value added at 1960 prices.

C.2.3 Domestic Product and Factor Prices

Computation of an annual product price series by sector is straightforward: we simply calculate nominal and constant price sectoral output series and divide. The nominal output series was constructed in the same manner as the real output series, again from NAS data.

Estimates of sectoral returns to capital and land are not generally available, although one can get some idea as to what they might be like from incremental capital–output ratio (ICOR) data (discussed in Rao, 1983, and Wolf, 1978). Wage data for agricultural laborers are available, as are those for unskilled urban workers (table 3.8); these are taken from Rao (1983). A broader indication of earnings trends is given by examining the income distribution figures from the NCAER surveys and the consumption distributions from the NSS surveys. Both of these research organizations distinguish households or workers by urban and rural location. A discussion of the time series from these surveys appears in Mills and Becker (1986, chap. 8). In general, these estimates are reasonably consistent with the wage indices, although they do suggest that the recorded industrial wage growth between 1964 and 1975 may be overstated. For the entire nation, the NCAER figures imply the real income growth rates, by quintile (Mills and Becker, 1986, p. 162), shown in table C.5.

In BMW, of course, wages are linked by equilibrium conditions, and the growth of urban industrial wages in the late 1960s implied by the wage data and captured by the NCAER (assuming most urban industrial workers are in the second highest quintile in the national income distribution) is not replicated. As labor shares rise during the period 1960–81 and capital and land shares decline in our model, the tendency for the top quintile's real earnings to grow more slowly than average is replicated in our historical counterfactual.

Finally, the reported urban–rural cost-of-living ratios (table 3.7) also are taken from Rao (1983, p. 27).

Table C.5. Average Real per Household Income Growth Rates (%) by Quintile

Quintile	1960–61 to 1964–65	1964–65 to 1967–68	1967–68 to 1975–76
Bottom	13.2	−11.8	4.2
Second	4.6	−8.9	3.6
Third	2.3	−4.6	2.7
Fourth	0.2	1.6	1.5
Top	0.7	1.3	0.6
per capita NNP (1970–71 Rs.)	1.9	−1.3	1.5

Note: comparison is inexact, as interquintile household movements are ignored.

C.2.4 Sectoral Capital Formation

The investment series was generated in a manner similar to that for output. The NAS reports a current price time series on gross domestic capital formation (GDCF), by industry of use, but does not disaggegate the using sectors by urban or rural location. Productivity-adjusted employment shares are used to distribute investment to rural and urban locations; standard sectoral aggregation rules are then used to allocate the investments to each of the model's seven nonhousing sectors. These are then deflated by a GDCF deflator, also provided by the NAS. NAS figures were also used to create domestic savings series, as the national accounts separately report household, corporate, and public sector savings.

C.3 Technological Progress

Most exogenous variables can be determined from prior research estimates. One set that cannot be adequately documented for India across the 1960s and 1970s is sectoral productivity advance. Instead, we estimate these rates.

To do so, we first assume that total factor productivity (TFP) growth was completely absent in each of the ten sectors and simulate the Indian economy from 1960 onward. In this zero TFP growth simulation, the economy is driven by endogenous accumulation forces, endogenous labor allocations, and those exogenous forces that can be documented externally. We then compare the actual historical behavior of sectoral output growth with that predicted by the model when productivity growth is absent. The gap between actual and simulated sectoral output growth is then treated as an initial estimate of TFP advance for each sector. Next, these "first pass" rates are incorporated into the model, and a new counterfactual simulation then yields another set of predicted outputs and hence productivity gaps. In practice, iteration on the sectoral productivity advance rates results in the rapid convergence of simulated output figures with historic ones; the final iteration provides our estimates of sectoral TFP growth. These rates for the nonhousing sectors appear in table 6.1.

Unsurprisingly, it was not possible to derive sectoral TFP growth rates that were constant over the twenty-one year period and that tracked the output series closely for each year (or even most years). The explanation for this failure is that Indian public policies and, to a degree, economic structure, changed strikingly over the period. These changes, and the basis for determining four epochs within the era 1960–81, are discussed in chapter 3.

It is important to reiterate that because we derive productivity growth rates as a residual, these rates incorporate the effects of policy changes and structural shocks not captured elsewhere in the model. Consequently, they cannot be expected to remain constant over an extended period. We therefore chose to determine TFP growth rates that pertained to particular epochs and that yielded observed sectoral output levels for the terminal year of each epoch.

This procedure effectively makes exogenous seven nonhousing output values that would otherwise be endogenous. Obviously, as is discussed in chapter 3, these values can no longer be used to assess model performance. Furthermore, with seven unknowns and the need to determine twenty-one nonhousing productivity growth rates, the system is still underidentified.[3] Rather than forcing the model to track more variables that are normally endogenous, thus further restricting our ability to evaluate model performance, we assume that there is no factor-specific productivity augmentation (excluding the agricultural productivity change assumptions discussed in section C.1.8).

There are two sets of exceptions to the TFP growth (T^*) estimation procedure just outlined. First, housing sector numbers from the NAS are not credible, as is explained in appendix B. We therefore chose to accept the relative price figures for housing implied by comparing the current and constant price national accounts series and instead chose housing T^* values that (roughly) replicate these trends. In practice, the consequences of replicating housing prices rather than quantities are not major. The T^* values derived for the three housing sectors are given in table C.6.

The second exception involves the estimation of T^*_{US}, the US sector's rate of factor productivity growth. This is a particularly difficult sector

---

3. There are seven productivity growth rates for each primary factor, plus seven Hicks-neutral multiplicative constants. Of these, seven are residually determined, given the other twenty-one in the nested CES framework.

Table C.6. Housing Productivity Growth Rates (%)

	1960–64	1965–71	1972–77	1978–81
$T_{H,R}^*$	0.0	3.7	1.0	1.0
$T_{H,US}^*$	0.0	2.0	2.0	2.0
$T_{H,KS}^*$	0.0	−2.0	−2.0	−2.0

to document accurately, and the output and price series derived from the national accounts are indeed perplexing: output growth is extremely rapid, and the sector's relative price rises erratically over time as well. Yet no extraordinary demand shifts occurred that can be readily documented, while the sector's unskilled labor-intensive supply curve should have been quite flat and stable over time.

In any event, the national accounts pattern cannot be sensibly replicated in a neoclassical general equilibrium model. When the simulated output series is forced to replicate "observed" outputs, relative P_{US} falls dramatically. This stems from a very low uncompensated price elasticity of demand for US goods, reflecting their status as an inferior good for the economy as a whole. Coupled with an elastic supply schedule, then, shifting the supply curve by raising the value of the intercept yields precipitous price declines.

Unfortunately, the "observed" historical price rises are as suspicious as the US output trends. Along with rising food prices, they should have caused a much greater increase in the historical urban–rural cost-of-living ratios than were in fact recorded. Still more striking, our model replicates the historical cost-of-living indices closely (table 3.7.)! Given this uncertainty over both US price and output trends, along with their apparent mutual inconsistency, we chose to give them equal weight in our T^* estimation procedure. The implicit assumption here is that the NAS adequately captures US production values but does not accurately divide them into price and output components. We therefore estimated T_{US}^* values that replicated both the output and price series, and then took an unweighted average of the two as our final estimate. Given the general equilibrium supply-and-demand conditions described above, the resulting output series does not in fact differ greatly from the national accounts values.

A final note on T^* estimation: for all sectors except agriculture, the TFP growth rate is equal to the production function intercept augmentation term, $e^{\lambda i}$. In agriculture's case, however, the share of value added in gross output diminishes over time, and the impact of these shrinking factor output elasticities also must be calculated in estimating T_A^*.

C.4 Other Parameters Based on Time Series

Three other sets of parameters were derived in a manner similar to the rates of technical progress. In determining savings rates, trade parameters, and some factor substitution elasticities, we assumed that the period 1960–67 was a Benchmark equilibrium era.

As is explained in appendix B, household savings rates generate private savings levels that, together with other sources of savings, ensure that the static Benchmark solution replicates observed 1960 gross domestic savings. In addition, household savings rates are scaled to ensure that the rate of growth of savings equals the observed rate for the Benchmark era. The possibility of determining both base year savings levels and increments over a period is given by the dependency of savings both on the ELES intercepts and on the sums of the marginal propensities to consume.

Determination of the σ_A^{COM} and σ_M^{COM} import–domestic composite good substitution elasticities also depends on tracking import time series through the Benchmark era. The resulting estimate of σ_M^{COM}, 2.25, is near the lower end of the likely range for such values suggested by Dervis, de Melo, and Robinson (1982, p. 263); the σ_A^{COM} value, 3.00, lies closer to their upper bound.

Finally, appendix B also discusses our determination of the σ_{RS} and σ'_{RS} terms. As is discussed above, government investment parameters ensure that 1960 investment in each savings pool is equal to that generated by the pool's household savings, retained earnings, and public investment. One such pool is that comprised by rural savers; their savings are allocated to the A, RS, and HRS sectors. Allocation within the pool, however, depends on relative rates of return, which in turn depend in part on σ and σ' values. Factor substitution elasticities within the rural pool are restricted to equal unity for agriculture, a stylized fact generally consistent with the econometric literature on Third World agriculture (Kelley and Williamson, 1984).

We therefore began by using KS sector substitution elasticity values, and then further restricted σ_{RS}/σ'_{RS} to equal 1.3, approximately the ratio (based on Fallon and Layard, 1975) estimated for both the M and KS sectors. Both σ_{RS} and σ'_{RS} are then adjusted until the simulated investment distribution between A and RS becomes consistent with that observed during the early 1960s.

In principle, the factor substitution elasticity, composite commodity substitution elasticity, and savings propensity adjustments must be determined simultaneously with the estimates of factor productivity advance. They were in fact estimated semi-iteratively: initial guesses at the σ and savings values were employed, and the T^* terms were then estimated. The substitution and savings parameters were then estimated precisely and assigned final values; we then iterated through the T^* terms once more. While the interdependency did not generate exact convergence after two iterations, the remaining errors were trivial.

References

Abbie, L., J. Harrison, and J. Wall. 1982. "Economic Returns to Investment in Irrigation in India." *World Bank Staff Working Paper* No. 536. Washington, D.C.: World Bank.

Adelman, I., and S. Robinson. 1978. *Income Distribution Policy in Developing Countries: A Case Study of Korea.* Stanford: Stanford University Press.

Ahluwalia, I. J. 1983. *Industrial Performance in India: An Analysis of Deceleration in Growth 1956–57 to 1979–80.* Unpublished manuscript (May).

Ahluwalia, M. S. 1978. "Rural Poverty and Agricultural Performance in India." *Journal of Development Studies* 14: 298–323.

Armington, P. 1969. "A Theory of Demand for Products Distinguished by Place of Production." *IMF Staff Papers* 16: 159–78.

Arnold, M. 1988. "Cessation of Famine: India since 1975." Department of Economics, University of Colorado. Processed (April).

Banerjee, A. 1971. "Productivity Growth and Factor Substitution in Indian Manufacturing." *Indian Economic Review* 6: 1–23.

———. 1975. *Capital Intensity and Productivity in Indian Industry.* Delhi: Macmillan Company of India.

Banerjee, B. 1984. "Information Flow, Expectations, and Job Search: Rural-to-Urban Migration Process in India." *Journal of Development Economics* 15: 239–57.

———. 1986. *Rural to Urban Migration and the Urban Labour Market.* Bombay: Himalaya (for the Institute of Economic Growth).

Bardhan, P. K. 1974. "The Pattern of Income Distribution in India: A Review." In *Poverty and Income Distribution in India,* eds., T. N. Srinivasan and P. K. Bardhan. Calcutta: Statistical Publishing Society.

———. 1984. *The Political Economy of Development in India.* Oxford: Basil Blackwell.

Bawa, U. 1969. "Agricultural Production and Capital Formation in India, 1951–52 to 1964–65." Cornell University, Department of Agricultural Economics, *Occasional Paper* No. 25 (October).

Becker, C. M. 1987. "Investment and Divestment Policies in South Africa and

Its Periphery." Unpublished manuscript. Paper presented at the AEA annual meetings, Chicago IL (December).

Becker, C. M., E. S. Mills, and J. G. Williamson. 1983. "Public Policy, Urbanization and Development: A Computable General Equilibrium Model of the Indian Economy." Vanderbilt University, Department of Economics, *Working Paper* No. 83-W14 (July).

―――. 1986. "Dynamics of Rural-Urban Migration in India." *Indian Journal of Quantitative Economics* 1: 1–43.

Becker, C. M., and A. R. Morrison. 1988. "The Determinants of Urban Population Growth in Sub-Saharan Africa." *Economic Development and Cultural Change* 36: 259–78.

Beider, P., C. M. Becker, E. S. Mills, and J. G. Williamson. 1983. "Determining Initial Conditions for the BMW General Equilibrium Simulation Model of India." Vanderbilt University, Department of Economics, *Working Paper* No. 83-W15 (July).

Beier, G. J., A. Churchill, M. Cohen, and B. Renaud. 1976. "The Task Ahead for the Cities of the Developing Countries." *World Development* 4: 363–409.

Bhagwati, J., and S. Chakravarty. 1969. "Contributions to Indian Economic Analysis." *American Economic Review* 59: 2–73.

Bhagwati, J., and P. Desai. 1970. *India: Planning for Industrialization.* London: Oxford University Press.

Bhagwati, J., and T. N. Srinivasan. 1975. *Foreign Trade Regimes and Economic Development: India.* New York: Columbia University Press.

Bhalla, S. J. 1980. "The Measurement of Permanent Income and Its Application to Savings Behavior." *Journal of Political Economy* 88: 722–44.

Bose, A. 1978. *Studies in India's Urbanization: 1901–2001*, 2nd ed. New Delhi: Tata McGraw-Hill.

Central Statistical Office (CSO). 1961. *Census of India 1961*, vol. 1, parts I-C(i) and II-A(ii). New Delhi: Government of India Press.

―――. 1962. *Census of India, 1961.* New Delhi: Government of India Press.

―――. 1962. *Statistical Abstract: India 1961.* New Delhi: Government of India Press.

―――. 1963. *Estimates of National Income: 1948–49 to 1961–62.* New Delhi: Government of India Press.

―――. 1966. *Statistical Abstract of the Indian Union 1965.* New Delhi: Government of India Press.

―――. 1971. *Census of India, 1971*, part II-B(iii). New Delhi: Government of India Press.

―――. 1972. *Statistical Abstract: India 1970.* New Delhi: Government of India Press.

―――. 1972. *Census of India, 1971.* New Delhi: Government of India Press.

―――. 1974. *Census of India, 1971.* Series-I-India, Paper 1 of 1974: *Report on Resurvey of Economic Questions—Some Results.* New Delhi: Government of India Press.

―――. 1975. *National Accounts Statistics 1960–61 to 1972–73: Disaggregated Tables.* New Delhi: Government of India Press.

———. 1978. *Statistical Abstract: India 1977*. New Delhi: Government of India Press.

———. 1979. *National Accounts Statistics, 1970–71 to 1976–77*. New Delhi: Government of India Press.

———. 1981a. *Census of India, 1981*. Series 1, part II, "Special Report and Tables Based on 5% Sample Data." New Delhi: Government of India Press.

———. 1981b. *National Accounts Statistics, 1970–71 to 1978–79*. New Delhi: Government of India Press.

———. 1984a. *Census of India, 1981*. Series 1, India, part II, "Special Report and Tables based on 5 Percent Sample Data." New Delhi: Government of India Press.

———. 1984b. *National Accounts Statistics, 1970–71 to 1981–82*. New Delhi: Government of India Press.

Chatterjee, G. S., and N. Bhattacharya. 1974. "On Disparities in Per Capita Household Consumption in India." In *Property and Income Distribution in India*, eds., T. N. Srinivasan and P. K. Bardhan. Calcutta: Statistical Publishing Company.

Chenery, H. B., and W. J. Raduchel. 1971. "Substitution in Planning Models." In *Studies in Development Planning*, ed. H. B. Chenery. Cambridge, MA: Harvard University Press.

Chuta, E., and S. V. Sethuraman (eds.). 1984. *Rural Small-Scale Industries and Employment in Africa and Asia*. Geneva: ILO.

Coale, A. J., and E. M. Hoover. 1958. *Population Growth and Economic Development in Low Income Countries*. Princeton, NJ: Princeton University Press.

Cole, W. E., and R. D. Sanders. 1985. "Internal Migration and Urban Employment in the Third World." *American Economic Review* 75: 481–94.

Committee on Distribution of Income and Levels of Living, 1960 (P. C. Mahalanobis, Chair). 1977. "Report." In *Committees and Commissions in India: 1947–73, Vol. IV: 1960–61*, ed. V. Kumar. Delhi: Concept Publishing Company.

Corden, W., and R. Findlay. 1975. "Urban Unemployment, Intersectoral Capital Mobility and Development Policy." *Economica* 42: 59–78.

Cutt, J. 1969. *Taxation and Economic Development in India*. New York.

Dandekar, K., and M. Sathe. 1980. "Employment Guarantee Scheme and Food for Work Program." *Economic and Political Weekly* (April 12).

Dasgupta, M., and S. Basu. 1985. "Urbanisation and Agricultural Yields: A Case Study of West Bengal." *Indian Journal of Regional Science* 17: 25–32.

Datt, R. 1981. "IMF Loan—A Boon or a Bane." *Indian Economic Almanac* (December): 11–23.

de Janvry, A., and K. Subbarao. 1984. "Agricultural Price Policy and Income Distribution in India." *Economic and Political Weekly* (December 22).

Dervis, K., J. de Melo, and S. Robinson. 1982. *General Equilibrium Models for Development Policy*. Cambridge: Cambridge University Press.

Dholakia, B. 1974. *The Sources of Economic Growth in India*. Baroda: Good Companions.

———. 1976. "Behavior of Income Shares in a Developing Economy—The Indian Experience." *Indian Economic Journal* 23: 295–310.

Dixit, A. K. 1969. "Marketable Surplus and Dual Development." *Journal of Economic Theory* 1: 203–19.

Domar, E. 1957. "A Soviet Model of Growth." In *Essays in the Theory of Economic Growth*. New York: Oxford University Press.

Engels, F. 1845. *The Condition of the Working Class in England*, 2nd ed. Ed. and trans. W. O. Henderson and W. H. Chaloner. Oxford: Basil Blackwell.

Evenson, R. E. 1976. "Productivity Measurement in the Developing Countries: The Indian Case." In *On the Measurement of Factor Productivities*, ed. F. L. Altmann. Gottingen: Vandenhoeckel Ruprecht.

Evenson, R. E., and D. Jha. 1973. "The Contribution of Agricultural Research System to Agricultural Production in India." *Indian Journal of Agricultural Economics* 28: 212–30.

Fallon, P. R., and P. R. G. Layard. 1975. "Capital-Skill Complementarity, Income Distribution, and Output Accounting." *Journal of Political Economy* 83: 279–301.

Frisch, R. 1959. "A Complete Scheme for Computing All Direct and Cross Price Elasticities in a Model with Many Sectors." *Econometrica* 27: 177–96.

George, P. S. 1984. "Some Aspects of Public Distributions of Foodgrains in India." *Economic and Political Weekly* (September 29).

Gandhi, V. 1966. *Tax Burden on Indian Agriculture*. Cambridge, MA: Harvard Law School.

Ghosh, A. 1968. *Planning, Programming and Input-Output Models: Selected Papers on Indian Planning*. Cambridge: Cambridge University Press.

———. 1973. *Programming and Interregional Input-Output Analysis: An Application to the Problem of Industrial Location in India*. Cambridge: Cambridge University Press.

Griliches, Z. 1969. "Capital-Skill Complementarity." *Review of Economics and Statistics* 51: 456–68.

Gupta, D. B. 1985. "Urban Housing in India." *World Bank Staff Working Paper* No. 730. Washington, D.C.: World Bank.

Gupta, L. C. 1969. *The Changing Structure of Industrial Finance in India*. Oxford: Clarendon Press.

Hamermesh, D., and J. Grant. 1979. "Econometric Studies of Labor–Labor Substitution and Their Implications for Policy." *Journal of Human Resources* 14: 518–42.

Harris, J. R., and M. Todaro. 1970. "Migration, Unemployment and Development: A Two-Sector Analysis." *American Economic Review* 60: 126–42.

Healey, J. M. 1965. *The Development of Social Overhead Capital in India: 1950–60*. Oxford: Basil Blackwell.

Henderson, J. V. 1977. *Economic Theory and the Cities*. New York: Academic Press.

———. 1988. *Urban Development: Theory, Fact and Illusion*. New York: Oxford University Press.

Henderson, P. D. 1975. *India: The Energy Sector*. London: Oxford University Press.

Hoselitz, B. F. 1955. "Generative and Parasitic Cities." *Economic Development and Cultural Change* 3: 278–93.

———. 1957. "Urbanization and Economic Growth in Asia." *Economic Development and Cultural Change* 5: 42–54.

Houthakker, H. S. 1957. "An International Comparison of Household Expenditure Patterns, Commemorating the Centenary of Engel's Law." *Econometrica* 25: 532–51.

Hymer, S., and S. Resnik. 1969. "A Model of an Agrarian Economy with Non-Agricultural Activities." *American Economic Review* 59: 493–501.

Institute of Applied Manpower Research. 1963. *Fact Book on Manpower*. New Delhi: Institute of Applied Manpower Research.

International Labour Office (ILO). 1977. *Labour Force Estimates and Projections, 1950–2000*, 2nd ed. Geneva: ILO.

ILO-ARTEP. 1981. *Women in the Indian Labour Force*. Bangkok: International Labour Organisation.

James, J. A. 1984. "The Use of General Equilibrium Analysis in Economic History." *Explorations in Economic History* 21: 231–53.

Jorgenson, D. W. 1984. "Econometric Methods for Applied General Equilibrium Analysis." In *Applied General Equilibrium Analysis*, eds. H. E. Scarf and J. B. Shoven. Cambridge: Cambridge University Press.

Joshi, V., and I. M. D. Little. 1987. "Indian Macro-Economic Policies." *Economic and Political Weekly* (February 28): 374.

Kamerschen, D. R. 1969. "Further Analysis of Over-Urbanization." *Economic Development and Cultural Change* 17: 235–53.

Kannappan, S. 1983. *Employment Problems and the Urban Labor Market in Developing Nations*. Ann Arbor, MI: University of Michigan Graduate School of Business Administration, Division of Research.

———. 1985. "Urban Employment and the Labor Market in Developing Nations." *Economic Development and Cultural Change* 33: 699–730.

———. 1987. "Review of Biswajit Banerjee, *Rural to Urban Migration and the Urban Labour Market*." *Economic and Political Weekly* (April 11).

Kelley, A. C., and J. G. Williamson. 1984. *What Drives Third World City Growth? A Dynamic General Equilibrium Approach*. Princeton, NJ: Princeton University Press.

Kelley, A. C., J. G. Williamson, and R. J. Cheetham. 1972. *Dualistic Economic Development: Theory and History*. Chicago: University of Chicago Press.

Kesselman, J. R., S. H. Williamson, and E. R. Berndt. 1977. "Tax Credits for Employment Rather than Investment." *American Economic Review* 67: 330–49.

Keyfitz, N. 1980. "Do Cities Grow By Natural Increase or By Migration?" *Geographic Analysis* 12: 142–56.

———. 1982. "Development and the Elimination of Poverty." *Economic Development and Cultural Change* 30: 649–70.

Khatkhate, D. R., and K. L. Deshpande. 1971. "Estimates of Saving and Investment in the Indian Economy: 1950–51 to 1962–63." In *Studies in Capital Formation, Savings and Investment in a Developing Economy*, eds., P. C. Malhotra and A. C. Minocha. Bombay: Somaiya Publications.

Kripalani, G. K., G. S. Tolley, and M. R. Payne. 1982. "Agricultural Development Strategy and Urbanization in India: A Simulation Analysis of Expected Future Trends." Paper presented at the Conference on Urbanization Processes and Policies in Developing Countries. University of Chicago (May).

Krishna, R., and G. S. Raychaudhuri. 1980. "Trends in Rural Savings and Private Capital Formation in India." *World Bank Staff Working Paper* No. 382. Washington, D.C.: World Bank.

Kuchal, S. C. 1965. *The Industrial Economy of India*. Allahabad: Chaitanya Publishing House.

Ledent, J. 1980. *Comparative Dynamics of Three Demographic Models of Urbanization*. Laxenburg, Austria: International Institute of Applied Systems Analysis (RR-80-1).

———. 1982. "Rural-Urban Migration, Urbanization, and Economic Development." *Economic Development and Cultural Change* 30: 507–538.

Leibenstein, H. 1957. "The Theory of Underemployment in Backward Economies." *Journal of Political Economy* 65: 91–103.

Lewis, W. A. 1954. "Development with Unlimited Supplies of Labor." *Manchester School of Economics and Social Studies* 20: 139–92.

———. 1978. *The Evolution of the International Economic Order*. Princeton, N.J.: Princeton University Press.

Linn, J. 1979. "Policies for Efficient and Equitable Growth in Cities in Developing Countries." *World Bank Staff Working Paper* No. 342. Washington, D.C.: World Bank.

Lipton, M. 1976. *Why Poor People Stay Poor: Urban Bias in World Development*. Cambridge, MA: Harvard University Press.

Lluch, C. 1973. "The Extended Linear Expenditure System." *European Economic Review* 4: 21–32.

Lluch, C., A. A. Powell, and R. A. Williams. 1977. *Patterns in Household Demand and Saving*. New York: Oxford University Press.

Mahalanobis, P. C. 1953. "Some Observations on the Process of Growth in National Income." *Sankhya* 12: 307–12.

———. 1955. "The Approach of Operational Research to Planning in India". *Sankhya* 16: 3–130.

Malhotra, P. C., and A. C. Minocha (eds.). 1971. *Studies in Capital Formation, Savings, and Investment in a Developing Economy*. Bombay: Somaiya Publications.

Manne, A. S., and A. Rudra. 1965. "A Consistency Model of India's Fourth Plan." *Sankhya* Series B, 27: 57–144.

Mansur, A., and J. E. Whalley. 1984. "Numerical Specification of Applied General Equilibrium Models." In *Applied General Equilibrium Analysis*, eds. H. E. Scarf and J. B. Shoven. Cambridge: Cambridge University Press.

Matthew, E. T. 1968. *Agricultural Taxation and Economic Development in India*. New York: Asia Publishing House.

Mayhew, H. 1861. *London Labour and the London Poor*, vols. I–IV. London: Griffin Bohn.

Mazumdar, H. 1959. *Business Saving in India*. Groningen: J. B. Wolters.

McAlpin, M. 1983. *Subject to Famine: Food Crises and Economic Change in Western India.* Princeton, NJ: Princeton University Press.

Mehra, S. 1976. "Some Aspects of Labour Use in Indian Agriculture." Department of Agriculture, Cornell University, *Occasional Paper* No. 88 (June).

Mehta, S. S. 1980. *Productivity, Production Functions and Technical Change.* New Delhi: Concept Publishing.

Mellor, J. W. 1976. *The New Economics of Growth: A Strategy for India and the Developing World.* Ithaca, NY: Cornell University Press.

Mills, E. S. 1972. *Studies in the Structure of the Urban Economy.* Baltimore: Johns Hopkins University Press.

Mills, E. S., and C. M. Becker, 1986. *Studies in Indian Urban Development.* New York: Oxford University Press.

Mills, E. S., and B. Hamilton. 1988. *Urban Economics.* Glenview, Il: Scott, Foresman, and Co.

Mills, E. S., and B. N. Song. 1977. "Korea's Urbanization and Urban Problems, 1945–1975." *Working Paper* No. 7701. Seoul: Korea Development Institute.

Minhas, B. S. 1974. "Rural Poverty, Land Redistribution and Development Strategy." In *Poverty and Income Distribution in India*, eds. T. N. Srinivasan and P. K. Bardhan. Calcutta: Statistical Publishing Company.

Mohammed, S. 1981. "Trade, Growth and Income Distribution: A Case Study of India." *Journal of Development Economics* 9: 131–47.

Mohan, R. 1977. "Development, Structural Change and Urbanization: Explorations with a Dynamic Three Sector General Equilibrium Model Applied to India, 1951–1984." Ph.D. dissertation. Princeton University.

———. 1979. *Urban Economic and Planning Models.* Baltimore: Johns Hopkins University Press.

———. 1985. "Urbanization in India's Future." *Population and Development Review* 11: 619–45.

Mukherjee, M. 1969. *National Income of India: Trend and Structure.* Calcutta: Statistical Publishing Society.

Muth, R. F. 1969. *Cities and Housing.* Chicago: University of Chicago Press.

———. 1971. "The Derived Demand for Urban Land." *Urban Studies* 8: 243–54.

Nakajima, K., C. M. Becker, E. S. Mills, and J. G. Williamson. 1983. "A Data Set for the BMW Computable General Equilibrium Model of India." Vanderbilt University, Department of Economics, *Working Paper* No. 83-W18 (August).

National Buildings Organisation. 1981. *Handbook of Housing Statistics.* Delhi: Government of India.

National Council of Applied Economic Research (NCAER). 1961. *Saving in India.* New Delhi: NCAER.

———. 1967. *All India Consumer Expenditure Survey*, vol. II. New Delhi: NCAER.

———. 1972. *All India Household Survey of Income, Saving, and Consumer Expenditure.* New Delhi: NCAER.

National Sample Survey, 16th Round. 1960. *Percentage Distribution of Em-*

ployed Persons by Sex and Occupation. New Delhi: Government of India Press (December).

Nigam, R. 1971. "The Growth and Performance of the Corporate Sector in India." In *Studies in Capital Formation, Savings, and Investment in a Developing Economy*, eds. P. C. Malhotra and A. C. Minocha. Bombay: Somaiya Publications.

Oughton, E. 1982. "The Maharashtra Droughts of 1970–73." *Oxford Bulletin of Economics and Statistics* 44: 169–97.

Padmanabha, P. 1983. *Census of India, 1981.* Series 1, papers 2 and 3. New Delhi: Government of India Press.

Panda, M. K., and S. K. Chakrabarti. 1982. "Economic Growth in India—Comparison of GNP and BNG (Basic Needs Goods) Index Numbers." *Indian Economic Review* 17: 207–22.

Pandey, S. M. 1977. "Nature and Determinants of Urbanization in a Developing Economy: The Case of India." *Economic Development and Cultural Change* 25: 265–78.

Planning Commission, Government of India, Task Forces on Housing and Urban Development. 1983. *Planning of Urban Development.* New Delhi: Government of India Press.

Premi, M. K. 1982. *The Demographic Situation in India.* Honolulu: East-West Center, *East-West Center Discussion Paper* No. 80 (February).

Preston, S. H. 1979. "Urban Growth in Developing Countries: A Demographic Reappraisal." *Population and Development Review* 5: 195–215.

Rao, H. 1977. "Urban versus Rural or Rich versus Poor?" *Economic and Political Weekly* 12: 40.

Rao, V. K. R. V. 1983. *India's National Income 1950–1980.* New Delhi: Sage Publications, India.

Rattso, J., H. Sarkas, and L. Taylor. 1981. "A Five-Sector Macro Policy Model for India." Processed. Paper presented at a World Bank research seminar.

Ravenstein, E. G. 1885. "The Laws of Migration." *Journal of the Statistical Society* 48: 167–227.

———. 1889. "The Laws of Migration." *Journal of the Statistical Society* 52: 214–301.

Ray, R. 1980. "Analysis of a Time Series of Household Expenditure Surveys for India." *Review of Economics and Statistics* 57: 595–602.

Ray, S. K., R. W. Cummings, Jr., and R. Herdt. 1979. "Agricultural Prices, Production, and Growth." *Economic and Political Weekly* (September 23).

Redford, A. 1926. *Labour Migration in England, 1800–1850.* Manchester: Manchester University Press.

Reserve Bank of India. 1961. *Report on Currency and Finance for the Year 1960–61.* Bombay: Reserve Bank of India.

———. 1963. *India's Balance of Payments: 1948–49 to 1961–62.* Bombay: Reserve Bank of India.

Reserve Bank of India Bulletin. Various issues.

Robinson, S. 1988. "Multisectoral Models." In *Handbook of Development Economics*, vol. II, eds. H. Chenery and T. N. Srinivasan. Amsterdam: North Holland.

Rogers, A. 1977. *Migration, Urbanization, Resources, and Development.* Laxenburg, Austria: International Institute for Applied Systems Analysis (RR-77-14).

————. 1984. *Migration, Urbanization and Spatial Population Dynamics.* Boulder, CO: Waterview Press.

Sahni, B. 1967. *Saving and Economic Development with Special Reference to India.* Calcutta: Scientific Book Agency.

Sakong, I., and G. Narasimham. 1974. "Interindustry Resource Allocation and Technological Change: The Situation in Indian Manufacturing." *The Developing Economies* 12: 123–32.

Saluja, M. R. 1980. *Input-Output Tables for India.* New Delhi: Wiley Eastern.

Sanderson, F., and S. Roy. 1979. *Food Trends and Prospects in India.* Washington, D.C.: Brookings Institution.

Sarma, J. S., and S. Roy. 1979. "Foodgrain Production and Consumption Behavior in India, 1960–77." In *Two Analyses of Indian Foodgrain Production and Consumption Data.* International Food Policy Research Institute, *Research Report* No. 12 (November).

Sarvekshana. Various issues. Journal of the National Sample Survey.

Sato, K. 1972. "Additive Utility Function with Double-Log Consumer Demand Functions." *Journal of Political Economy* 80: 102–24.

Seal, K. C. 1981. "Women in the Labour Force in India: A Macro Level Statistical Profile." In *Women in the Indian Labour Force.* Bangkok: International Labour Organization.

Seers, D. 1977. "Indian Bias? A Review Article of Why Poor People Stay Poor." *Social and Economic Studies* 26: 3.

Sekhar, U. 1983. "Industrial Location Policy: The Indian Experience." *World Bank Staff Working Paper* No. 620. Washington, D.C.: World Bank.

Sen, A. K. 1982. *Poverty and Famines.* London: Oxford University Press.

Shoven, J. B., and J. Whalley. 1984. "Applied General Equilibrium Models of Taxation and International Trade." *Journal of Economic Literature* 22: 1007–51.

Shukla, T. 1965. *Capital Formation in Indian Agriculture.* Bombay: Vora and Co.

Sinclair, S. W. 1978. *Urbanisation and Labor Markets in Developing Countries.* London: Croom Helm.

Singh, A. M., and A. de Souza. 1980. *The Urban Poor.* New Delhi: Manohar Publications.

Singh, I. J. 1979. *Small Farmers and the Landless in South Asia.* Washington, D.C.: World Bank.

Sinha, B. 1976. *Housing Growth in India.* New Delhi: Arnold-Heinemann.

Song, B. N., and R. J. Struyk. 1976. "Korean Housing: Economic Appraisal and Policy Alternatives." *Working Paper* No. 7603. Seoul: Korea Development Institute.

Sovani, N. V. 1962. "The Analysis of Overurbanization." *Economic Development and Cultural Change* 12: 216–22.

Srinivasan, T. N., and P. K. Bardhan (eds.). 1974. *Poverty and Income Distribution in India.* Calcutta: Statistical Publishing Society.

Srivastava, D. K. 1981. "Policy Simulations with a Macroeconometric Model of the Indian Economy." *Journal of Policy Modeling* 3: 337–59.

Taylor, L. 1976. *Macro Models for Developing Countries*. New York: McGraw-Hill.

Todaro, M. 1969. "A Model of Labor, Migration, and Urban Unemployment in Less Developed Countries." *American Economic Review* 59: 138–48.

United Nations. 1976. *Global Review of Human Settlements: A Support for Habitat*, 2 vols. Oxford: Pergamon Press.

———. 1979. *Concise Report on Monitoring of Population Policies*. Economic and Social Council, Population Commission, 20th Session, E/CN.9/338. New York: United Nations.

———. 1980. *Patterns of Urban and Rural Population Growth*. New York: United Nations, Department of International and Social Affairs.

———. 1982. *Population of India*. Economic and Social Commission for Asia and the Pacific. *Country Monograph Series* No. 10. New York: United Nations.

———. 1987. *The Prospects of World Urbanization Revised as of 1984–85*. New York: United Nations.

United States Bureau of the Census. 1975. *Historical Statistics of the United States, Colonial Times to 1970*, part I. Washington, DC.: Government Printing Office.

Venkatramaiah, P., A. R. Kulkani, and L. Argade. 1972. "Input–Output Table for India 1963." *Artha Vijnana* 14: 1–107.

Vyas, V. S. 1983. "Regional Unbalances in Foodgrains Production in the Last Decade." *Economic and Political Weekly, Review of Agriculture* (December): A-151–56.

Williamson, J. G. 1985. *Did British Capitalism Breed Inequality?* London: Allen and Unwin.

———. 1988. "Migration and Urbanization." In *Handbook of Development Economics*, vol. 1, eds. H. Chenery and T. N. Srinivasan. Amsterdam: North-Holland.

———. 1990. *Coping with City Growth during the British Industrial Revolution*. Cambridge: Cambridge University Press.

Williamson, J. G., and P. H. Lindert. 1980. *American Inequality: A Macroeconomic History*. New York: Academic Press.

Wolf, M. 1978. "Capital and Growth in India, 1950–71." *World Bank Staff Working Paper* No. 279. Washington D.C.: World Bank (November).

World Bank. 1981. *Economic Situation and Prospects of India*. Washington, D.C.: South Asia Region, Report No. 3401-IN (April).

———. 1983. *World Tables, 3rd ed.* Baltimore: Johns Hopkins University Press.

———. 1984. *World Development Report 1984*. New York: Oxford University Press.

———. 1988a. *World Tables 1987, 4th ed.* Washington, D.C.: World Bank.

———. 1988b. *World Development Report 1988*. New York: Oxford University Press.

Yotopoulos, P. A., and J. Nugent. 1976. *Economics of Development: Empirical Investigations*. New York: Harper and Row.
Zelinsky, W. 1971. "The Hypothesis of the Mobility Transition." *Geographic Review* 61: 219–49.

Index